French Feminism Reader

French Feminism Reader

edited by
Kelly Oliver

ROWMAN & LITTLEFIELD PUBLISHERS, INC.
Lanham • Boulder • New York • Oxford

ROWMAN & LITTLEFIELD PUBLISHERS, INC.

Published in the United States of America
by Rowman & Littlefield Publishers, Inc.
4720 Boston Way, Lanham, Maryland 20706
http://www.rowmanlittlefield.com

12 Hid's Copse Road
Cumnor Hill, Oxford OX2 9JJ, England

British Library Cataloguing in Publication Information Available

Library of Congress Cataloging-in-Publication Data

French feminism reader / [edited by] Kelly Oliver.
    p.   cm.
    Includes bibliographical references and index.
    ISBN 0-8476-9766-5 (cloth : alk. paper)—ISBN 0-8476-9767-3 (pbk. : alk. paper)
    1. Feminism—France.   2. Feminist theory—France.   I. Oliver, Kelly, 1958– .
HQ1617.F747   2000
305-42'0946—dc21   99-086127

Printed in the United States of America

♾ ™ The paper used in this publication meets the minimum requirements of
American National Standard for Information Sciences—Permanence of Paper for
Printed Library Materials, ANSI/NISO Z39.48-1992.

CONTENTS

PREFACE

FRENCH FEMINISM IN AN AMERICAN CONTEXT

Kelly Oliver

It is important for the reader of this volume to know feminism in France is as varied as it is any place else in the world. This collection focuses on the issues and figures that have been the most influential to feminist theory in the English-speaking world. It is also important to note that the women's movement in France is as much about political and social activism as it is about theory. Like the women's movements in the United States, England, Australia, and elsewhere, activism is central to the women's movement in France. This volume represents the work of feminist theorists, many of whom also engage in political and social activism. Here, however, the focus will be on feminist theory rather than on activism per se.

Even once we narrow our focus to feminist theory, there is still more to feminism in France than the table of contents of this collection might suggest. This is not only because the amount of feminist theory in France is vast and could not be included in one volume but also because the aim of this collection is to provide one volume of essays that represents the issues and figures that have become the most central in an English-speaking context. Even further narrowing our focus to that context, there is far too much material that has had a significant impact on Anglo-American feminism to include in one volume. Still, *French Feminism Reader* provides a representative sample of French feminism in an Anglo-American context.

This collection represents two main trends in French feminist theory that have had a significant influence on, and are in dialogue with, Anglo-American feminist theory: social theory and psychoanalytic theory. While some feminists in France are more concerned with patriarchal social institutions and material and economic conditions, others are more concerned with psychic structures and patriarchal colonization of the imaginary and culture. Both of these trends move away from traditional discussions of Nature toward discussions of socially constructed notions of sex, sexuality, and gender roles. While feminists interested in social theory focus on the ways in which social institutions shape our notions of sex, sexuality, and gender roles, feminists interested in psychoanalytic theory focus on cultural representations of sex, sexuality, and gender roles and the ways that they affect the psyche. These two trends come together in productive ways in some of the most exciting work represented in this collection. This negotiation between social theory and psychoanalytic theory speaks to one of the most promising tensions in recent feminist theory in the English-speaking world.

Whether they identify themselves as materialists, Marxists, psychoanalysts, feminists, or postfeminists, many of the writers in this collection are concerned with the connection between the social and the psyche. What is the relationship between social transformation and individual transformation and vice versa? Does social change necessitate changes in individual attitudes, behaviors, and psychic identities? Does individual change necessitate change in social institutions and political systems? Or, does change implicate both the social and psychic realms at the same time? Anglo-American theorists such as Judith Butler, Teresa de Lauretis, and Teresa Brennan who have recently been struggling with these questions have been influenced by the thinking of French feminists represented in this volume.

Feminism in twentieth-century France is defined by a history of controversies and antagonisms, especially those between materialist feminists and psychoanalytic feminists. In the early 1970s the women's movement in France coalesced, if briefly, into the *Mouvement de Libération des Femmes*, or the Women's Liberation Movement, called the MLF. In May of 1968 there were monumental protests, riots, and strikes on college campuses and elsewhere in France. Like the student movements in the United States prompted by the Vietnam War at the same time, the student movements in France produced a sense of optimism about the possibility and necessity of change. Along with students, many intellectuals, faculty, and workers took part in the protests against the government. Although the political situation changed very little as a result of the protests of May 1968, the attitudes and politics of intellectuals changed. There was hope that populist movements could affect transformation. Although much of the writing after May 1968 reflects disillusion with this optimism, it was in this spirit that the MLF was born.

The name *Mouvement de Libération des Femmes* was first used by the media reporting on a group of women who were arrested for putting a wreath on the Tomb of the Unknown Soldier at the Arc de Triomphe and dedicating it to a person more unknown than him, his wife.[1] The right to legal abortions was the mobilizing issue of the MLF in the 1970s. On April 5, 1971, the weekly magazine *Le Nouvel Observateur* published a Manifesto signed by 343 women who claimed to have had illegal abortions. Simone de Beauvoir was at the top of the list followed by some of the most famous women in France.

As more women and groups of women became part of the feminist movement in France, more disagreements and factions arose within the movement. Affiliation with the MLF became problematic when in 1979 Antoinette Fouque registered the name *Mouvement de Libération des Femmes* as the trademark, and MLF as the logo, of the organization she led, *Psych et Po* (short for *Psychoanalyse et Politique*, or psychoanalysis and politics). Psych et Po, a group interested in Lacanian psychoanalysis, also started a press called *des femmes* and opened several des femmes bookstores in Paris. Psych et Po's take-over of the name of the women's liberation movement was a source of great controversy among feminists in France. The controversy over Psych et Po didn't stop there. Claire Duchen reports that "Hélène Cixous who has been closely associated with the group [Psych et Po] even asserted at a conference in New York that French women did not use the words lesbian or feminist and was angrily contradicted by other French women present."[2]

Like their Anglo-American counterparts, feminists in France disagree on questions of equality versus difference, relations to men, the status and nature of femininity and masculinity, and the role of feminism and feminist theory. Some of the writers in this collection (Cixous, Kristeva) whose ideas about women, language, and marginalization have been very influential on feminism in the Anglo-American context have disassociated themselves from the feminist movement in France. Others criticize the feminist movement for its heterosexism (Wittig). Still others criticize what has been called "French feminism" by the English-speaking world (Delphy). In spite of their problematic relationship to "feminism," the work of these theorists has been useful for feminist theory in the Anglo-American context.

Starting with Simone de Beauvoir's distinction between sex and gender, which points to the social construction of gender stereotypes, to Monique Wittig and Colette Guillaumin's more radical claims that sex and race are themselves socially constructed, the denaturalization of sex, gender, and race have been important to Anglo-American feminism. French feminists and American feminists alike have had varied reactions to Beauvoir's attempts to make women equal to men by denying marriage and motherhood, criticizing love relations, and rejecting stereotypical gender roles. Even among the theorists in this volume who favor difference over equality there is much disagreement about what difference is and what difference it makes. While Luce Irigaray argues that so-

cial change can only take place when our laws reflect sexual difference between
men and women, Colette Guillaumin and Christine Delphy argue that historically the concept of difference, especially natural difference, has been used to
keep women oppressed. In dialogue with the French debates over equality and
difference, Anglo-American feminist theory continues to struggle with these
same issues.

The introductory material before each selection is designed to orient the
reader to the context in which the author is writing. The introductions include
biographical information, a brief summary of the influences and intellectual context of the author's work, the major themes in the author's corpus of writing, the
main concerns in the selection included in this collection, and a selected bibliography of primary and secondary texts by and about the author. This introductory material along with the selections in this volume should give the reader a
good sense of some of the debates in feminist theory in France that have been
of most interest in an Anglo-American context.

NOTES

1. For a history of the MLF see Claire Duchen's *Feminism in France* (London: Routledge, 1986). For more information about the feminist movement in France and its
importation to the English-speaking world, see also Claire Duchen, ed., *French Con-
nections* (Amherst: University of Massachusetts Press, 1987); Sherry Turkle, *Psychoanalytic Politics* (New York: Basic Books, 1978); Dorothy Kaufmann-McCall, "Politics of Difference: The Women's Movement in France from May 1968 to Mitterrand,"
Signs 9, no. 2 (Winter 1983); Elaine Marks and Isabelle de Courtivron's introduction
to *New French Feminisms* (New York: Schocken Books, 1981); Gayatri Spivak,
"French Feminism in an International Frame," *Yale French Studies* 62 (1981); Alice
Jardine, *Gynesis: Configurations of Woman and Modernity* (Ithaca: Cornell University Press, 1981); Toril Moi, *Sexual/Textual Politics* (London: Methuen, 1985); Toril
Moi, "Feminist Readings: French Text/American Contexts," *Yale French Studies* 62
(1981); Eva Martin Sartori and Dorothy Wynne Zimmerman, eds., *French Women
Writers* (Lincoln: University of Nebraska Press, 1991); Christine Delphy, "The Invention of French Feminism: An Essential Move," *Yale French Studies* 87 (1995).
2. Duchen, *Feminism in France,* 24.

ACKNOWLEDGMENTS

I would like to thank Doris Rita Alphonso and Jennifer Hansen for writing helpful introductory sections to most of the chapters. Thanks also to all of my friends and colleagues who not only answered my question "What would you most like to see in a collection of French feminism?" but also encouraged me to put this collection together, including Natalie Alexander, Alison Brown, Tina Chanter, Jennifer Hansen, Tamsin Lorraine, Elissa Marder, Gail Wiess, Cynthia Willett, Emily Zakin, and Ewa Ziarek.

Thanks to the following presses and journals for copyright permission to reprint selections included in this volume:

Alfred A. Knopf, a division of Random House, for permission to reprint parts of Simone de Beauvoir's *The Second Sex*, trans. H. M. Parshley (New York: Random House, 1989), copyright 1952 and renewed 1980 by Alfred A. Knopf, Inc.

Editions du Seuil for permission to reprint parts of Michèle Le Doeuff's *Hipparchia's Choice*, trans. T. Selous (Blackwell, 1989), pp. 56–57, 100–106, 220–30. [L'Étude et le rouet—Des femmes de la philosophie etc., by Michèle Le Doeuff, © 1989 Editions du Seuil.]

Elsevier Science for permission to reprint Christine Delphy's "Rethinking Sex and Gender," *Women's Studies International* 16, no. 2 (1993): 1–9.

Transaction Publishers for permission to reprint the following articles from *Feminist Issues*: Colette Guillaumin's "The Question of Difference" 2, no. 1 (1982): pp. 33–52, and "Race and Nature: The System of Marks" 8, no. 2 (1988): pp. 25–43; and Monique Wittig's "The Straight Mind" 1, no. 1 (1980):

pp. 103–12, "One Is Not Born a Woman" 1, no. 4 (1981): pp. 47–54, "The Category of Sex" 2, no. 2 (1982): p. 63–68, and "Homo Sum" 10, no. 1 (1990): pp. 3–11.

The University of Chicago Press for permission to reprint Hélène Cixous' "The Laugh of the Medusa," *Signs* 1, no. 4 (1976): pp. 249–64, and "Castration or Decapitation," *Signs* 7, no. 1 (1981): pp. 41–55.

Columbia University Press for permission to reprint parts of Julia Kristeva's "From Filth to Defilement" from *Powers of Horror*, trans. Leon Roudiez (New York: Columbia University Press, 1982), pp. 56–59, 65–72, and 77–79, "Women's Time" from *New Maladies of the Soul*, trans. Ross Guberman (New York: Columbia University Press, 1995), pp. 201–24, and "From One Identity to an Other" and "Motherhood [according to Giovanni Bellini]" from *Desire in Language*, ed. Leon Roudiez (New York: Columbia University Press, 1980), pp. 133–40, 145–47, and 237–43; and Luce Irigaray's "Each Sex Must Have Its Own Rights" and "Body to Body against the Mother" from *Sexes and Genealogies*, trans. Gillian Gill (New York: Columbia University Press, 1993), pp. 1–5, 9–21.

Cornell University Press for permission to reprint parts of Luce Irigaray's "Women on the Market" and "Questions I" from *This Sex Which Is Not One*, trans. Catherine Porter (Ithaca, N.Y.: Cornell University Press, 1985), pp. 170–91, 148–55, and "Sexual Difference" from *An Ethics of Sexual Difference*, trans. Carolyn Burke and Gillian Gill (Ithaca, N.Y.: Cornell University Press, 1993), pp. 5–19.

Routledge Press for permission to reprint parts of Hélène Cixous' *Rootprints: Memory and Life Writing*, with Mirelle Calle-Gruber, trans. Eric Prenowitz (New York: Routlege, 1997), pp. 31, 48–49, 50–56.

1

ONE IS NOT BORN A WOMAN

Simone de Beauvoir

INTRODUCTION

by Jennifer Hansen

Simone (Lucie Ernestine Marie Bertrande) de Beauvoir was born in Paris on January 9, 1908, and died in Paris on April 14, 1986, spending her entire life in the neighborhood of Montparnasse. Beauvoir's philosophical and feminist contributions are some of the most profound of the twentieth century, and many of the other women in this collection labor in her debt. Beauvoir grew up in a bourgeoisie family of a devout Catholic mother, Françoise de Beauvoir, and an agnostic father, Georges de Beauvoir, a lawyer and amateur actor who introduced her to literature at an early age. After World War I, the Beauvoir family lost some of its wealth and the young Simone watched her mother toil to maintain their household in what seemed to be tedious and repetitive work. Such perceptions about the role of mothers left her quite delighted to pursue a teaching career once her parents informed her that they would not be able to supply her with a dowry for a good marriage.

Beauvoir received two baccalaureate degrees and then went on to pursue a doctorate in philosophy at the Sorbonne. Léon Brunschvicg supervised her thesis on Leibniz. She passed the competitive state examination, the *agrégation de philosophie*, in 1929 and was ranked second in her class—second to Jean-Paul Sartre. She was the youngest student ever to pass the agrégation. In 1929 Beauvoir made the acquaintance of Jean-Paul Sartre at a study session for the agrégation—the beginning of what would become a companionship of more than fifty years.

Early on Beauvoir taught at the lycée (high school) level until she was able to support herself solely on the earnings of her writings. She taught from 1929 to 1943 in lycées in Paris, Rouen, and Marseilles. In 1943, when the mother of her student Nathalie Sorokine accused her of corrupting a minor, Beauvoir left teaching and pursued a brief career in radio. When Sartre was released from a World War II prison camp in 1941, Beauvoir joined him in participating in the Parisian Resistance network. In 1945, Beauvoir, Maurice Merleau-Ponty, and Sartre founded the journal *Les temps modernes* as a forum for working out the new political vision of left-wing French intellectuals after World War II. She was a lifelong opponent of colonialism, supporting the Algerian revolution, and she subscribed to Marxist principles, which moved her to support the communist revolutions in the U.S.S.R., Cuba, and China.

Beauvoir claims that the biggest success of her life was her relationship with Sartre, which was based on a pact of mutual intellectual and emotional support. They forged their relationship as "essential," while leaving open the possibility for each to develop other "contingent" relationships with others. Beauvoir strongly believed that marriage was a bourgeois arrangement that trapped and stunted women's intellectual growth and freedom. She and Sartre never had children; however, Beauvoir did adopt a lycée philosophy teacher, Sylvie le Bon, to carry on her legacy and oversee her archive. Le Bon became her closest companion after Sartre's death in 1980.

In addition to the international success and influence of Beauvoir's most famous work, *The Second Sex*, she received the Prix Goncourt for one of her several novels, *The Mandarins*. The Catholic Church banned both of these books because of their "radical" stances on marriage and motherhood. Though she published *The Second Sex* in 1949, Beauvoir did not come to see herself as a feminist until the late 1960s and announced this "conversion" to the whole world in a famous interview in 1972 with Alice Schwartzer. She became extremely active in the MLF, marching on November 11, 1971, for the right to abortion, and she signed the famous *Manifeste des 343* in *Le Nouvel Observateur* in 1971, confessing to having had an abortion. In 1972 she became the president of *Choisir* and the president of the League for the Rights of Women in 1974. In 1979, she cofounded with Christine Delphy and Monique Wittig *Questions féministes*, a journal dedicated to pursuing feminist studies from a materialist framework.

Both Sartre and Beauvoir attended Kojève's famous lectures on Hegel, whose influence is apparent in her analysis of 'Woman as Other' in *Second Sex*. Beauvoir applied a master-slave dialectic analysis of the relationship of men to women, in which men become the essential, transcendent subjects of the world and women are relegated to the purely immanent and contingent realms of experience. From Heidegger, Beauvoir takes both the belief that human beings are *thrown* into social conditions that indelibly shape their existence and that beings are not things, or essences, but projects that in their activities reveal the world and bestow meaning upon it. And from Kierkegaard, she develops her ethics of ambiguity in which humans must act in the world without prior knowledge of the outcome of their actions. Finally, Beauvoir saw herself as committed to the philosophical insights of Sartre's existentialist philosophy, and she employed many of his concepts in both *The Ethics of Ambiguity* and *The Second Sex*. She claimed that she was contributing an ethics to Sartre's phenomenological contributions on existence.

In the introduction to *The Second Sex*, Beauvoir asks the important question: "Are there women, really?" Might not "women" or "femininity" be the creations of men, molded and shaped to satisfy their sexual, nutritional, and emotional needs? Beauvoir is among the first feminist thinkers to develop what has now become widely known as a social constructionist portrait of gender, believing that women are not born as women but are made into women by the pressures and expectations of a patriarchal world. Beauvoir explains that the relationship between the two sexes may be necessary for the continuation of both but it is not a reciprocal relationship. Men are the norm—the essential beings of Western culture—and also represent all that is positive about human endowments and creations.

According to Beauvoir, women, on the contrary, represent merely what men are not. Women are defined wholly in terms of their deficiency to men and therefore represent what is base, frivolous, and contingent to human experience. For Beauvoir, the concept of 'Woman' is synonymous with the concept of the 'Other.' 'Woman' cannot be defined concretely or positively, but only as the dark, nebulous side of 'Man'. Women, claims Beauvoir, have no shared history of oppression, no shared cultural traditions, no shared religions like other oppressed groups such as racial minorities or Jews. Beauvoir also claims that within patriarchal culture, men are those creatures capable of transcendence—they are capable of acting upon the world and bestowing meaning upon it—while women are immanent beings who derive their meaning from their relationship to men.

In her chapters of *The Second Sex* "The Mother" and "The Woman in Love" Beauvoir demonstrates the ways in which women are not destined to be the second sex or merely immanent beings. Women, though they align themselves with men, do so only in order to escape their freedom. For Beauvoir, all human beings, regardless of biological differences, are born free and must struggle to engender their liberty; all human beings must rebel against traps and lures, as well as oppressive social conditions, to become all that they have potential to be in this world. Women, however, evade their freedom; they are in *bad faith*—to use Sartre's term—because they content themselves with finding the meaning of their existence in the successes of the men they marry or of their sons.

Sartre's "bad faith" paradigm

Beauvoir argues that women are not born with a maternal instinct. Through diaries and literary examples, she argues that many women are fearful, anxious, and distressed about the prospect of bearing and rearing a child. Most often, women undertake motherhood to fulfill an obligation to the marriage contract or as a means to feel superior in one area of their lives. If she feels herself always dependent upon her husband, then by having a child a woman establishes herself, for a time, as the essential and necessary being in relation to the dependent child. However in either case—fulfillment of an obligation or establishment of her own superiority—women endanger the well-being of their children. If a free and independent woman does not choose motherhood, then the mother runs the risk of infantilizing or abusing her children. If they are boys, she might take her revenge upon them, knowing that one day they will benefit from privileges that the mother does not enjoy. Little girls will be overprotected, for the mother might feel guilt and shame for bringing a girl into a world in which she will become a victim, like her mother, of male domination.

Likewise, women who are not free and independent and enter into romantic relationships with men jeopardize their own health and well-being. When women fall in love with men, quite often they are seeking in men their own necessity or importance. If an essential being, a man, loves a merely contingent being, a woman, then she becomes essential as long as she is seen as his other half. Because, however, men do not need women as much as women need men, men soon lose interest in women who live to serve them. Once a man has won the heart of a woman, she holds little interest for him. He may withdraw all affection, which places the woman in a precarious position. If her entire self-worth is tied up with the man's esteem for her, then she will feel worthless and debased when he withdraws that esteem, and she may go mad.

Only when women transcend their roles as the ones who tend to men's needs will they finally be capable of securing fulfilling relationships. If a woman engages in projects in the world, outside of the home, then she will be capable of bringing something to a relationship rather than merely escaping the burden of her freedom by associating herself with a man who does act in the world. Beauvoir does not overlook the fact that various legal and economic changes must take place in tandem with the resolve of women to struggle against patriarchy. For example, she exposes the paradoxical attitudes that men have toward abortion: they denounce it while individually seeking it as a remedy to unwanted pregnancies with their lovers. Furthermore, men will both support war and the killing of others, while fervently opposing abortion, even going so far, Beauvoir shows, as to believe that the life of the fetus is more important than that of the mother if the pregnancy causes complications to her health.

BIBLIOGRAPHY

Selected Primary Sources

1948. *The Ethics of Ambiguity*. Translated by Bernard Frechtman. New York: Philosophical Library. [*Pour une morale de l'ambiguïté*. Paris: Gallimard, 1947.]
1952. *The Second Sex*. Translated by H. M. Parshley. New York: Knopf. [*Le Deuxième Sexe*. 2 vols. Paris: Gallimard, 1949.]
1954. *She Came to Stay*. Translated by Yvonne Moyse and Roger Senhouse. Cleveland: World Publishing. [*L'Invitée*. Paris: Gallimard, 1943.]
1956. *The Mandarins*. Translated by Leonard M. Friedman. Cleveland: World Publishing. [*Les Mandarins*. Paris: Gallimard, 1954.]
1959. *Memoirs of a Dutiful Daughter*. Translated by James Kirkup. Cleveland: World Publishing. [*Mémoires d'une jeune fille rangée*. Paris: Gallimard, 1958.]
1965. *Force of Circumstance*. Translated by Richard Howard. New York: Putnam. [*La Force des Choses*. Paris: Gallimard, 1963.]
1966. *A Very Easy Death*. Translated by Patrick O'Brian. New York: Putnam. [*Une mort très douce*. Paris: Gallimard, 1964.]
1968. *Les Belles Images*. Translated by Patrick O'Brian. New York: Putnam. [*Les Belles Images*. Paris: Gallimard, 1966.]
1969. *The Woman Destroyed*. Translated by Patrick O'Brian. New York: Putnam. [*La Femme rompue*. Paris: Gallimard, 1968.]
1972. *Coming of Age*. Translated by Patrick O'Brian. New York: Putnam. [*La Vieillesse*. Paris: Gallimard, 1970.]
1974. *All Said and Done*. Translated by Patrick O'Brian. New York: Putnam. [*Tout compte fait*. Paris: Gallimard, 1972.]
1984. *Adieux: A Farewell to Sartre*. Translated by Patrick O'Brian. New York: Pantheon. [*La Cérémonie des adieux suivi des Entretiens avec Jean-Paul Sartre. Août–Septembre 1974*. Paris: Gallimard, 1981.]

Selected Secondary Sources

Bair, Deirdre. 1990. *Simone de Beauvoir: A Biography*. London: Cape.
Bergoffen, Debra B. 1997. *The Philosophy of Simone de Beauvoir: Gendered Phenomenologies, Erotic Generosities*. Albany: State University of New York Press.
Fulbrook, Edward, and Kate Fulbrook. 1998. *Simone de Beauvoir: A Critical Introduction*. Cambridge: Polity Press.
Moi, Toril. 1994. *Simone de Beauvoir: The Making of an Intellectual Woman*. Cambridge: Blackwell Publishers.
Schwartzer, Alice. 1984. *After the Second Sex: Conversations with Simone de Beauvoir*. New York: Pantheon.

Simons, Margaret A., ed. 1995. *Feminist Interpretations of Simone de Beauvoir*. University Park: Pennsylvania State University Press.

————. 1999. *Beauvoir and the Second Sex*. Lanham, Md.: Rowman & Littlefield.

Vintges, Karen. 1996. *Philosophy as Passion: The Thinking of Simone de Beauvoir*. Translated by Anne Lavelle. Bloomington: Indiana University Press.

INTRODUCTION TO *THE SECOND SEX*

For a long time I have hesitated to write a book on woman. The subject is irritating, especially to women; and it is not new. Enough ink has been spilled in the quarreling over feminism, now practically over, and perhaps we should say no more about it. It is still talked about, however, for the voluminous nonsense uttered during the last century seems to have done little to illuminate the problem. After all, is there a problem? And if so, what is it? Are there women, really? Most assuredly the theory of the eternal feminine still has its adherents who will whisper in your ear: "Even in Russia women still are *women*"; and other erudite persons—sometimes the very same—say with a sigh: "Woman is losing her way, woman is lost." One wonders if women still exist, if they will always exist, whether or not it is desirable that they should, what place they occupy in this world, what their place should be. "What has become of women?" was asked recently in an ephemeral magazine.[1]

But first we must ask: what is a woman? "*Tota mulier in utero*," says one, "woman is a womb." But in speaking of certain women, connoisseurs declare that they are not women, although they are equipped with a uterus like the rest. All agree in recognizing the fact that females exist in the human species; today as always they make up about one half of humanity. And yet we are told that femininity is in danger; we are exhorted to be women, remain women, become women. It would appear, then, that every female human being is not necessarily a woman; to be so considered she must share in that mysterious and threatened reality known as femininity. Is this attribute something secreted by the ovaries? Or is it a Platonic essence, a product of the philosophic imagination? Is a rustling petticoat enough to bring it down to earth? Although some women try zealously to incarnate this essence, it is hardly patentable. It is frequently described in vague and dazzling terms that seem to have been borrowed from the vocabulary of the seers, and indeed in the time of St. Thomas it was considered an essence as certainly defined as the somniferous virtue of the poppy.

But conceptualism has lost ground. The biological and social sciences no longer admit the existence of unchangeably fixed entities that determine given characteristics, such as those ascribed to woman, the Jew, or the Negro. Science regards any characteristic as a reaction dependent in part upon a *situation*. If today femininity no longer exists, then it never existed. But does the word *woman*, then, have no specific content? This is stoutly affirmed by those who hold to the philosophy of the enlightenment, of rationalism, of nominalism: women, to them, are merely the human beings arbitrarily designated by the word *woman*. Many American women particularly are prepared to think that there is no longer any place for women as such; if a backward individual still takes herself for a woman, her friends advise her to be psychoanalyzed and thus get rid of this obsession. In regard to a work, *Modern Woman: The Lost Sex*, which in other respects has its irritating features, Dorothy Parker has written: "I cannot be just to books which treat of woman as woman. . . . My idea is that all of us, men as well as women, should be regarded as human beings." But nominalism is a rather inadequate doctrine, and the antifemininists have had no trouble in showing that women simply *are not* men. Surely woman is, like man, a human being; but such a declaration is abstract. The fact is that every concrete human being is always a singular, separate individual. To decline to accept such notions as the eternal feminine, the black soul, the Jewish character, is not to deny that Jews, Negroes, women exist today—this denial does not represent a liberation for those concerned, but rather a flight from reality. Some years ago a well-known woman writer refused to permit her portrait to appear in a series of photographs especially devoted to women writers; she wished to be counted among the men. But in order to gain this privilege she made use of her husband's influence! Women who assert that they are men lay claim none the less to masculine consideration and respect. I recall also a young Trotskyite standing on a platform at a boisterous meeting and getting ready to use her fists, in spite of her evident fragility. She was denying her feminine weakness; but it was for love of a militant male whose equal she wished to be. The attitude of defiance of many American women proves that they are haunted by a sense of their femininity. In truth, to go for a walk with one's eyes open is enough to demonstrate that humanity is divided into two classes of individuals whose clothes, faces, bodies, smiles, gaits, interests, and occupations are manifestly different. Perhaps these differences are superficial, perhaps they are destined to disappear. What is certain is that right now they do most obviously exist.

If her functioning as a female is not enough to define woman, if we decline also to explain her through "the eternal feminine," and if nevertheless we admit, provisionally, that women do exist, then we must face the question: what is a woman?

To state the question is, to me, to suggest, at once, a preliminary answer. The fact that I ask it is in itself significant. A man would never get the notion of writ-

ing a book on the peculiar situation of the human male.[2] But if I wish to define
myself, I must first of all say: "I am a woman"; on this truth must be based all
further discussion. A man never begins by presenting himself as an individual of
a certain sex; it goes without saying that he is a man. The terms *masculine* and
feminine are used symmetrically only as a matter of form, as on legal papers. In
actuality the relation of the two sexes is not quite like that of two electrical poles,
for man represents both the positive and the neutral, as is indicated by the common use of *man* to designate human beings in general; whereas woman represents only the negative, defined by limiting criteria, without reciprocity. In the
midst of an abstract discussion it is vexing to hear a man say: "You think thus and
so because you are a woman"; but I know that my only defense is to reply: "I
think thus and so because it is true," thereby removing my subjective self from
the argument. It would be out of the question to reply: "And you think the contrary because you are a man," for it is understood that the fact of being a man is
no peculiarity. A man is in the right in being a man; it is the woman who is in the
wrong. It amounts to this: just as for the ancients there was an absolute vertical
with reference to which the oblique was defined, so there is an absolute human
type, the masculine. Woman has ovaries, a uterus; these peculiarities imprison
her in her subjectivity, circumscribe her within the limits of her own nature. It
is often said that she thinks with her glands. Man superbly ignores the fact that
his anatomy also includes glands, such as the testicles, and that they secrete hor-
mones. He thinks of his body as a direct and normal connection with the world,
which he believes he apprehends objectively, whereas he regards the body of
woman as a hindrance, a prison, weighed down by everything peculiar to it. "The
female is a female by virtue of a certain *lack* of qualities," said Aristotle; "we
should regard the female nature as afflicted with a natural defectiveness." And
St. Thomas for his part pronounced woman to be an "imperfect man," an "incidental" being. This is symbolized in Genesis where Eve is depicted as made from
what Bossuet called "a supernumerary bone" of Adam.

Thus humanity is male and man defines woman not in herself but as relative
to him; she is not regarded as an autonomous being. Michelet writes: "Woman,
the relative being. . . ." And Benda is most positive in his *Rapport d'Uriel*: "The
body of man makes sense in itself quite apart from that of woman, whereas the
latter seems wanting in significance by itself. . . . Man can think of himself without woman. She cannot think of herself without man." And she is simply what
man decrees; thus she is called "the sex," by which is meant that she appears essentially to the male as a sexual being. For him she is sex—absolute sex, no less.
She is defined and differentiated with reference to man and not he with reference to her; she is the incidental, the inessential as opposed to the essential. He
is the Subject, he is the Absolute—she is the Other.[3]

I think the Platonic other gets wrongly interpreted

The category of the *Other* is as primordial as consciousness itself. In the most primitive societies, in the most ancient mythologies, one finds the expression of a duality—that of the Self and the Other. This duality was not originally attached to the division of the sexes; it was not dependent upon any empirical facts. It is revealed in such works as that of Granet on Chinese thought and those of Dumézil on the East Indies and Rome. The feminine element was at first no more involved in such pairs as Varuna-Mitra, Uranus-Zeus, Sun-Moon, and Day-Night than it was in the contrasts between Good and Evil, lucky and unlucky auspices, right and left, God and Lucifer. Otherness is a fundamental category of human thought.

Thus it is that no group ever sets itself up as the One without at once setting up the Other over against itself. If three travelers chance to occupy the same compartment, that is enough to make vaguely hostile "others" out of all the rest of the passengers on the train. In small-town eyes all persons not belonging to the village are "strangers" and suspect; to the native of a country all who inhabit other countries are "foreigners"; Jews are "different" for the anti-Semite, Negroes are "inferior" for American racists, aborigines are "natives" for colonists, proletarians are the "lower class" for the privileged. — *Marxy*

Lévi-Strauss, at the end of a profound work on the various forms of primitive societies, reaches the following conclusion: "Passage from the state of Nature to the state of Culture is marked by man's ability to view biological relations as a series of contrasts; duality, alternation, opposition, and symmetry, whether under definite or vague forms, constitute not so much phenomena to be explained as fundamental and immediately given data of social reality."[4] These phenomena would be incomprehensible if in fact human society were simply a *Mitsein* or fellowship based on solidarity and friendliness. Things become clear, on the contrary, if, following Hegel, we find in consciousness itself a fundamental hostility toward every other consciousness; the subject can be posed only in being opposed—he sets himself up as the essential, as opposed to the other, the inessential, the object.

But the other consciousness, the other ego, sets up a reciprocal claim. The native traveling abroad is shocked to find himself in turn regarded as a "stranger" by the natives of neighboring countries. As a matter of fact, wars, festivals, trading, treaties, and contests among tribes, nations, and classes tend to deprive the concept *Other* of its absolute sense and to make manifest its relativity; willy-nilly, individuals and groups are forced to realize the reciprocity of their relations. How is it, then, that this reciprocity has not been recognized between the sexes, that one of the contrasting terms is set up as the sole essential, denying any relativity in regard to its correlative and defining the latter as pure otherness? Why is it that women do not dispute male sovereignty? No subject will readily volun-

Why does there have to be an inessential? But it can be! [handwritten marginalia]

teer to become the object, the inessential; it is not the Other who, in defining himself as the Other, establishes the One. The Other is posed as such by the One in defining himself as the One. But if the Other is not to regain the status of being the One, he must be submissive enough to accept this alien point of view. Whence comes this submission in the case of woman?

There are, to be sure, other cases in which a certain category has been able to dominate another completely for a time. Very often this privilege depends upon inequality of numbers—the majority imposes its rule upon the minority or persecutes it. But women are not a minority, like the American Negroes or the Jews; there are as many women as men on earth. Again, the two groups concerned have often been originally independent; they may have been formerly unaware of each other's existence, or perhaps they recognized each other's autonomy. But a historical event has resulted in the subjugation of the weaker by the stronger. The scattering of the Jews, the introduction of slavery into America, the conquests of imperialism are examples in point. In these cases the oppressed retained at least the memory of former days; they possessed in common a past, a tradition, sometimes a religion or a culture.

The parallel drawn by Bebel between women and the proletariat is valid in that neither ever formed a minority or a separate collective unit of mankind. And instead of a single historical event it is in both cases a historical development that explains their status as a class and accounts for the membership of *particular individuals* in that class. But proletarians have not always existed, whereas there have always been women. They are women in virtue of their anatomy and physiology. Throughout history they have always been subordinated to man,[5] and hence their dependency is not the result of a historical event or a social change— it was not something that *occurred.* The reason why otherness in this case seems to be an absolute is in part that it lacks the contingent or incidental nature of historical facts. A condition brought about at a certain time can be abolished at some other time, as the Negroes of Haiti and others have proved; but it might seem that a natural condition is beyond the possibility of change. In truth, however, the nature of things is no more immutably given, once for all, than is historical reality. If woman seems to be the inessential which never becomes the essential, it is because she herself fails to bring about this change. Proletarians say "We"; Negroes also. Regarding themselves as subjects, they transform the bourgeois, the whites, into "others." But women do not say "We," except at some congress of feminists or similar formal demonstration; men say "women," and women use the same word in referring to themselves. They do not authentically assume a subjective attitude. The proletarians have accomplished the revolution in Russia, the Negroes in Haiti, the Indo-Chinese are battling for it in Indo-China; but the women's effort has never been anything more than a symbolic

So should there be a new name for (women)?

agitation. They have gained only what men have been willing to grant; they have taken nothing, but have only received.[6] *sex, too*
The reason for this is that women lack concrete means for organizing themselves into a unit which can stand face to face with the correlative unit. They have no past, no history, no religion of their own; and they have no such solidarity of work and interest as that of the proletariat. They are not even promiscuously herded together in the way that creates community feeling among the American Negroes, the ghetto Jews, the workers of Saint-Denis, or the factory hands of Renault. They live dispersed among the males, attached through residence, housework, economic condition, and social standing to certain men—fathers or husbands—more firmly than they are to other women. If they belong to the bourgeoisie, they feel solidarity with men of that class, not with proletarian women; if they are white, their allegiance is to white men, not to Negro women. The proletariat can propose to massacre the ruling class, and a sufficiently fanatical Jew or Negro might dream of getting sole possession of the atomic bomb and making humanity wholly Jewish or black; but woman cannot even dream of exterminating the males. The bond that unites her to her oppressors is not comparable to any other. The division of the sexes is a biological fact, not an event in human history. Male and female stand opposed within a primordial *Mitsein*, and woman has not broken it. The couple is a fundamental unity with its two halves riveted together, and the cleavage of society along the line of sex is impossible. Here is to be found the basic trait of woman: she is the Other in a totality of which the two components are necessary to one another.

One could suppose that this reciprocity might have facilitated the liberation of woman. When Hercules sat at the feet of Omphale and helped with her spinning, his desire for her held him captive; but why did she fail to gain a lasting power? To revenge herself on Jason, Medea killed their children; and this grim legend would seem to suggest that she might have obtained a formidable influence over him through his love for his offspring. In *Lysistrata* Aristophanes gaily depicts a band of women who joined forces to gain social ends through the sexual needs of their men; but this is only a play. In the legend of the Sabine women, the latter soon abandoned their plan of remaining sterile to punish their ravishers. In truth woman has not been socially emancipated through man's need—sexual desire and the desire for offspring—which makes the male dependent for satisfaction upon the female.

Master and slave, also, are united by a reciprocal need, in this case economic, which does not liberate the slave. In the relation of master to slave the master does not make a point of the need that he has for the other; he has in his grasp the power of satisfying this need through his own action; whereas the slave, in his dependent condition, his hope and fear, is quite conscious of the need he has

What are the unified the unified platforms of being woman

independent need of slave

for his master. Even if the need is at bottom equally urgent for both, it always
works in favor of the oppressor and against the oppressed. That is why the liberation of the working class, for example, has been slow.

Now, woman has always been man's dependent, if not his slave; the two sexes
have never shared the world in equality. And even today woman is heavily hand-
icapped, though her situation is beginning to change. Almost nowhere is her legal status the same as man's,[7] and frequently it is much to her disadvantage.
Even when her rights are legally recognized in the abstract, long-standing custom prevents their full expression in the mores. In the economic sphere men
and women can almost be said to make up two castes; other things being equal,
the former hold the better jobs, get higher wages, and have more opportunity
for success than their new competitors. In industry and politics men have a great
many more positions and they monopolize the most important posts. In addition
to all this, they enjoy a traditional prestige that the education of children tends
in every way to support, for the present enshrines the past—and in the past all
history has been made by men. At the present time, when women are beginning
to take part in the affairs of the world, it is still a world that belongs to men—
they have no doubt of it at all and women have scarcely any. To decline to be the
Other, to refuse to be a party to the deal—this would be for women to renounce
all the advantages conferred upon them by their alliance with the superior caste.
Man-the-sovereign will provide women-the-liege with material protection and
will undertake the moral justification of her existence; thus she can evade at once
both economic risk and the metaphysical risk of a liberty in which ends and aims
must be contrived without assistance. Indeed, along with the ethical urge of each
individual to affirm his subjective existence, there is also the temptation to forgo
liberty and become a thing. This is an inauspicious road, for he who takes it—
passive, lost, ruined—becomes henceforth the creature of another's will, frustrated in his transcendence and deprived of every value. But it is an easy road;
on it one avoids the strain involved in undertaking an authentic existence. When
man makes of woman the *Other*, he may, then, expect her to manifest deep-
seated tendencies toward complicity. Thus, woman may fail to lay claim to the
status of subject because she lacks definite resources, because she feels the necessary bond that ties her to man regardless of reciprocity, and because she is often very well pleased with her role as the *Other*.

But it will be asked at once: how did all this begin? It is easy to see that the
duality of the sexes, like any duality, gives rise to conflict. And doubtless the winner will assume the status of absolute. But why should man have won from the
start? It seems possible that women could have won the victory; or that the outcome of the conflict might never have been decided. How is it that this world
has always belonged to the men and that things have begun to change only re-

cently? Is this change a good thing? Will it bring about an equal sharing of the world between men and women?

These questions are not new, and they have often been answered. But the very fact that woman is the *Other* tends to cast suspicion upon all the justifications that men have ever been able to provide for it. These have all too evidently been dictated by men's interest. A little-known feminist of the seventeenth century, Poulain de la Barre, put it this way: "All that has been written about women by men should be suspect, for the men are at once judge and party to the lawsuit." Everywhere, at all times, the males have displayed their satisfaction in feeling that they are the lords of creation. "Blessed be God . . . that He did not make me a woman," say the Jews in their morning prayers, while their wives pray on a note of resignation: "Blessed be the Lord, who created me according to His will." The first among the blessings for which Plato thanked the gods was that he had been created free, not enslaved; the second, a man, not a woman. But the males could not enjoy this privilege fully unless they believed it to be founded on the absolute and the eternal; they sought to make the fact of their supremacy into a right. "Being men, those who have made and compiled the laws have favored their own sex, and jurists have elevated these laws into principles," to quote Poulain de la Barre once more.

Legislators, priests, philosophers, writers, and scientists have striven to show that the subordinate position of woman is willed in heaven and advantageous on earth. The religions invented by men reflect this wish for domination. In the legends of Eve and Pandora men have taken up arms against women. They have made use of philosophy and theology, as the quotations from Aristotle and St. Thomas have shown. Since ancient times satirists and moralists have delighted in showing up the weaknesses of women. We are familiar with the savage indictments hurled against women throughout French literature. Montherlant, for example, follows the tradition of Jean de Meung, though with less gusto. This hostility may at times be well founded, often it is gratuitous; but in truth it more or less successfully conceals a desire for self-justification. As Montaigne says, "It is easier to accuse one sex than to excuse the other." Sometimes what is going on is clear enough. For instance, the Roman law limiting the rights of woman cited "the imbecility, the instability of the sex" just when the weakening of family ties seemed to threaten the interests of male heirs. And in the effort to keep the married woman under guardianship, appeal was made in the sixteenth century to the authority of St. Augustine, who declared that "woman is a creature neither decisive nor constant," at a time when the single woman was thought capable of managing her property. Montaigne understood clearly how arbitrary and unjust was woman's appointed lot: "Women are not in the wrong when they decline to accept the rules laid down for them, since the men make these rules without consulting them. No wonder intrigue and strife abound." But he did not go so far as to champion their cause.

It was only later, in the eighteenth century, that genuinely democratic men began to view the matter objectively. Diderot, among others, strove to show that woman is, like man, a human being. Later John Stuart Mill came fervently to her defense. But these philosophers displayed unusual impartiality. In the nineteenth century the feminist quarrel became again a quarrel of partisans. One of the consequences of the industrial revolution was the entrance of women into productive labor, and it was just here that the claims of the feminists emerged from the realm of theory and acquired an economic basis, while their opponents became the more aggressive. Although landed property lost power to some extent, the bourgeoisie clung to the old morality that found the guarantee of private property in the solidity of the family. Woman was ordered back into the home the more harshly as her emancipation became a real menace. Even within the working class the men endeavored to restrain woman's liberation, because they began to see the women as dangerous competitors—the more so because they were accustomed to work for lower wages.[8]

In proving woman's inferiority, the antifeminists then began to draw not only upon religion, philosophy, and theology, as before, but also upon science—biology, experimental psychology, etc. At most they were willing to grant "equality in difference" to the *other* sex. That profitable formula is most significant; it is precisely like the "equal but separate" formula of the Jim Crow laws aimed at the North American Negroes. As is well known, this so-called equalitarian segregation has resulted only in the most extreme discrimination. The similarity just noted is in no way due to chance, for whether it is a race, a caste, a class, or a sex that is reduced to a position of inferiority, the methods of justification are the same. "The eternal feminine" corresponds to "the black soul" and to "the Jewish character." True, the Jewish problem is on the whole very different from the other two—to the anti-Semite the Jew is not so much an inferior as he is an enemy for whom there is to be granted no place on earth, for whom annihilation is the fate desired. But there are deep similarities between the situation of woman and that of the Negro. Both are being emancipated today from a like paternalism, and the former master class wishes to "keep them in their place"— that is, the place chosen for them. In both cases the former masters lavish more or less sincere eulogies, either on the virtue of "the good Negro" with his dormant, childish, merry soul—the submissive Negro—or on the merits of the woman who is "truly feminine"—that is, frivolous, infantile, irresponsible—the submissive woman. In both cases the dominant class bases its argument on a state of affairs that it has itself created. As George Bernard Shaw puts it, in substance, "The American white relegates the black to the rank of shoeshine boy;

and he concludes from this that the black is good for nothing but shining shoes."
This vicious circle is met with in all analogous circumstances; when an individual (or a group of individuals) is kept in a situation of inferiority, the fact is that he *is* inferior. But the significance of the verb *to be* must be rightly understood here; it is in bad faith to give it a static value when it really has the dynamic Hegelian sense of "to have become." Yes, women on the whole *are* today inferior to men; that is, their situation affords them fewer possibilities. The question is: should that state of affairs continue?

Many men hope that it will continue; not all have given up the battle. The conservative bourgeoisie still see in the emancipation of women a menace to their morality and their interests. Some men dread feminine competition. Recently a male student wrote in the *Hebdo-Latin*: "Every woman student who goes into medicine or law robs us of a job." He never questioned his rights in this world. And economic interests are not the only ones concerned. One of the benefits that oppression confers upon the oppressors is that the most humble among them is made to *feel* superior; thus, a "poor white" in the South can console himself with the thought that he is not a "dirty nigger"—and the more prosperous whites cleverly exploit this pride.

Similarly, the most mediocre of males feels himself a demigod as compared with women. It was much easier for M. de Montherlant to think himself a hero when he faced women (and women chosen for his purpose) than when he was obliged to act the man among men—something many women have done better than he, for that matter. And in September 1948, in one of his articles in the *Figaro littéraire*, Claude Mauriac—whose great originality is admired by all—could[9] write regarding women: "*We* listen on a tone [*sic!*] of polite indifference . . . to the most brilliant among them, well knowing that her wit reflects more or less luminously ideas that come from *us*." Evidently the speaker referred to is not reflecting the ideas of Mauriac himself, for no one knows of his having any. It may be that she reflects ideas originating with men, but then, even among men there are those who have been known to appropriate ideas not their own; and one can well ask whether Claude Mauriac might not find more interesting a conversation reflecting Descartes, Marx, or Gide rather than himself. What is really remarkable is that by using the questionable *we* he identifies himself with St. Paul, Hegel, Lenin, and Nietzsche, and from the lofty eminence of their grandeur looks down disdainfully upon the bevy of women who make bold to converse with him on a footing of equality. In truth, I know of more than one woman who would refuse to suffer with patience Mauriac's "tone of polite indifference."

I have lingered on this example because the masculine attitude is here displayed with disarming ingenuousness. But men profit in many more subtle ways

from the otherness, the alterity of woman. Here is miraculous balm for those afflicted with an inferiority complex, and indeed no one is more arrogant toward
women, more aggressive or scornful, than the man who is anxious about his virility. Those who are not fear-ridden in the presence of their fellow men are much
more disposed to recognize a fellow creature in woman; but even to these the
myth of Woman, the Other, is precious for many reasons.[10] They cannot be
blamed for not cheerfully relinquishing all the benefits they derive from the
myth, for they realize what they would lose in relinquishing woman as they fancy
her to be, while they fail to realize what they have to gain from the woman of tomorrow. Refusal to pose oneself as the Subject, unique and absolute, requires
great self-denial. Furthermore, the vast majority of men make no such claim explicitly. They do not *postulate* woman as inferior, for today they are too thoroughly imbued with the ideal of democracy not to recognize all human beings
as equals.

In the bosom of the family, woman seems in the eyes of childhood and youth
to be clothed in the same social dignity as the adult males. Later on, the young
man, desiring and loving, experiences the resistance, the independence of the
woman desired and loved; in marriage, he respects woman as wife and mother,
and in the concrete events of conjugal life she stands there before him as a free
being. He can therefore feel that social subordination as between the sexes no
longer exists and that on the whole, in spite of differences, woman is an equal.
As, however, he observes some points of inferiority—the most important being
unfitness for the professions—he attributes these to natural causes. When he is
in a co-operative and benevolent relation with woman, his theme is the principle of abstract equality, and he does not base his attitude upon such inequality
as may exist. But when he is in conflict with her, the situation is reversed: his
theme will be the existing inequality, and he will even take it as justification for
denying abstract equality.[11]

So it is that many men will affirm as if in good faith that women *are* the equals
of man and that they have nothing to clamor for, while *at the same time* they will
say that women can never be the equals of man and that their demands are in
vain. It is, in point of fact, a difficult matter for man to realize the extreme importance of social discriminations which seem outwardly insignificant but which
produce in woman moral and intellectual effects so profound that they appear
to spring from her original nature.[12] The most sympathetic of men never fully
comprehend woman's concrete situation. And there is no reason to put much
trust in the men when they rush to the defense of privileges whose full extent
they can hardly measure. We shall not, then, permit ourselves to be intimidated
by the number and violence of the attacks launched against women, nor to be
entrapped by the self-seeking eulogies bestowed on the "true woman," nor to

profit by the enthusiasm for woman's destiny manifested by men who would not for the world have any part of it.

We should consider the arguments of the feminists with no less suspicion, however, for very often their controversial aim deprives them of all real value. If the "woman question" seems trivial, it is because masculine arrogance has made of it a "quarrel"; and when quarreling one no longer reasons well. People have tirelessly sought to prove that woman is superior, inferior, or equal to man. Some say that, having been created after Adam, she is evidently a secondary being; others say on the contrary that Adam was only a rough draft and that God succeeded in producing the human being in perfection when He created Eve. Woman's brain is smaller; yes, but it is relatively larger. Christ was made a man; yes, but perhaps for his greater humility. Each argument at once suggests its opposite, and both are often fallacious. If we are to gain understanding, we must get out of these ruts; we must discard the vague notions of superiority, inferiority, equality which have hitherto corrupted every discussion of the subject and start afresh.

Very well, but just how shall we pose the question? And, to begin with, who are we to propound it at all? Man is at once judge and party to the case; but so is woman. What we need is an angel—neither man nor woman—but where shall we find one? Still, the angel would be poorly qualified to speak; for an angel is ignorant of all the basic facts involved in the problem. With a hermaphrodite we should be no better off, for here the situation is most peculiar; the hermaphrodite is not really the combination of a whole man and a whole woman, but consists of parts of each and thus is neither. It looks to me as if there are, after all, certain women who are best qualified to elucidate the situation of woman. Let us not be misled by the sophism that because Epimenides was a Cretan he was necessarily a liar; it is not a mysterious essence that compels men and women to act in good or in bad faith, it is their situation that inclines them more or less toward the search for truth. Many of today's women, fortunate in the restoration of all the privileges pertaining to the estate of the human being, can afford the luxury of impartiality—we even recognize its necessity. We are no longer like our partisan elders; by and large we have won the game. In recent debates on the status of women the United Nations has persistently maintained that the quality of the sexes is now becoming a reality, and already some of us have never had to sense in our femininity an inconvenience or an obstacle. Many problems appear to us to be more pressing than those which concern us in particular, and this detachment even allows us to hope that our attitude will be objective. Still, we know the feminine world more intimately than do the men because we have our roots in it, we grasp more immediately than do men what it means to a human being to be feminine; and we are more concerned with such knowledge. I have said that there are more pressing problems, but this does not prevent us from seeing some importance in asking how the fact of being women will affect our lives. What opportunities precisely have been given us and what withheld? What fate awaits our younger sisters, and what directions should they take? It is significant that books by women on women are in general animated in our day less by a wish to demand our rights than by an effort toward clarity and understanding. As we emerge from an era of excessive controversy, this book is offered as one attempt among others to confirm that statement.

But it is doubtless impossible to approach any human problem with a mind free from bias. The way in which questions are put, the points of view assumed, presuppose a relativity of interest; all characteristics imply values, and every objective description, so called, implies an ethical background. Rather than attempt to conceal principles more or less definitely implied, it is better to state them openly at the beginning. This will make it unnecessary to specify on every page in just what sense one uses such words as *superior, inferior, better, worse, progress, reaction*, and the like. If we survey some of the works on woman, we note that one of the points of view most frequently adopted is that of the public good, the general interest; and one always means by this the benefit of society as one wishes it to be maintained or established. For our part, we hold that the only public good is that which assures the private good of the citizens; we shall pass judgment on institutions according to their effectiveness in giving concrete opportunities to individuals. But we do not confuse the idea of private interest with that of happiness, although that is another common point of view. Are not women of the harem more happy than women voters? Is not the housekeeper happier than the working-woman? It is not too clear just what the word *happy* really means and still less what true values it may mask. There is no possibility of measuring the happiness of others; and it is always easy to describe as happy the situation in which one wishes to place them.

In particular those who are condemned to stagnation are often pronounced happy on the pretext that happiness consists in being at rest. This notion we reject, for our perspective is that of existentialist ethics. Every subject plays his part as such specifically through exploits or projects that serve as a mode of transcendence; he achieves liberty only through a continual reaching out toward other liberties. There is no justification for present existence other than its expansion into an indefinitely open future. Every time transcendence falls back into immanence, stagnation, there is a degradation of existence into the "*en-soi*"—the brutish life of subjection to given conditions—and of liberty into constraint and contingence. This downfall represents a moral fault if the subject consents to it; if it is inflicted upon him, it spells frustration and oppression. In both cases it is an absolute evil. Every individual concerned to justify his existence feels that his existence involves an undefined need to transcend himself, to engage in freely chosen projects.

Now, what peculiarly signalizes the situation of woman is that she—a free and autonomous being like all human creatures—nevertheless finds herself living in a world where men compel her to assume the status of the Other. They propose to stabilize her as object and to doom her to immanence since her transcendence is to be overshadowed and forever transcended by another ego (*conscience*) which is essential and sovereign. The drama of woman lies in this conflict between the fundamental aspirations of every subject (ego)—who always regards the self as the essential—and the compulsions of a situation in which she is the inessential. How can a human being in woman's situation attain fulfillment? What roads are open to her? Which are blocked? How can independence be recovered in a state of dependency? What circumstances limit woman's liberty and how can they be overcome? These are the fundamental questions on which I would fain throw some light. This means that I am interested in the fortunes of the individual as defined not in terms of happiness but in terms of liberty.

Quite evidently this problem would be without significance if we were to believe that woman's destiny is inevitably determined by physiological, psychological, or economic forces. Hence I shall discuss first of all the light in which woman is viewed by biology, psychoanalysis, and historical materialism. Next I shall try to show exactly how the concept of the "truly feminine" has been fashioned—why woman has been defined as the Other—and what have been the consequences from man's point of view. Then from woman's point of view I shall describe the world in which women must live; and thus we shall be able to envisage the difficulties in their way as, endeavoring to make their escape from the sphere hitherto assigned them, they aspire to full membership in the human race.

NOTES

1. *Franchise*, dead today.
2. The Kinsey Report [Alfred C. Kinsey and others: *Sexual Behavior in the Human Male* (W. B. Saunders Co., 1948)] is no exception, for it is limited to describing the sexual characteristics of American men, which is quite a different matter.
3. E. Levinas expresses this idea most explicitly in his essay *Temps et l'Autre*. "Is there not a case in which otherness, alterity [*altérité*], unquestionably marks the nature of a being, as its essence, an instance of otherness not consisting purely and simply in the opposition of two species of the same genus? I think that the feminine represents the contrary in its absolute sense, this contrariness being in no wise affected by any relation between it and its correlative and thus remaining absolutely other. Sex is not a certain specific difference . . . no more is the sexual difference a mere contradic-

tion. . . . Nor does this difference lie in the duality of two complementary terms, for two complementary terms imply a pre-existing whole. . . . Otherness reaches its full flowering in the feminine, a term of the same rank as consciousness but of opposite meaning."

I suppose that Levinas does not forget that woman, too, is aware of her own consciousness, or ego. But it is striking that he deliberately takes a man's point of view, disregarding the reciprocity of subject and object. When he writes that woman is mystery, he implies that she is mystery for man. Thus his description, which is intended to be objective, is in fact an assertion of masculine privilege.

4. See C. Lévi-Strauss: *Les Structures élémentaires de la parenté*. My thanks are due to C. Lévi-Strauss for his kindness in furnishing me with the proofs of his work, which, among others, I have used liberally in Part II.

5. With rare exceptions, perhaps, like certain matriarchal rulers, queens, and the like.—Tr.

6. See Part II, ch. viii.

7. At the moment an "equal rights" amendment to the Constitution of the United States is before Congress.—Tr.

8. See Part II, pp. 115–17.

9. Or at least he thought he could.

10. A significant article on this theme by Michel Carrouges appeared in No. 292 of the *Cahiers du Sud*. He writes indignantly: "Would that there were no woman-myth at all but only a cohort of cooks, matrons, prostitutes, and bluestockings serving functions of pleasure or usefulness!" That is to say, in his view woman has no existence in and for herself; he thinks only of her *function* in the male world. Her reason for existence lies in man. But then, in fact, her poetic "function" as a myth might be more valued than any other. The real problem is precisely to find out why woman should be defined with relation to man.

11. For example, a man will say that he considers his wife in no wise degraded because she has no gainful occupation. The profession of housewife is just as lofty, and so on. But when the first quarrel comes, he will exclaim: "Why, you couldn't make your living without me!"

12. The specific purpose of Book II of this study is to describe this process.

THE MOTHER

It is in maternity that woman fulfills her physiological destiny; it is her natural "calling," since her whole organic structure is adapted for the perpetuation of the species. But we have seen already that human society is never abandoned wholly to nature. And for about a century the reproductive function in particular has no longer been at the mercy solely of biological chance; it has come under the voluntary control of human beings.[1] . . .

. . . [P]regnancy is above all a drama that is acted out within the woman herself. She feels it as at once an enrichment and an injury; the fetus is a part of her

[handwritten at top: may have to take into account Beauvoir's lack of experience as a mother]

body, and it is a parasite that feeds on it; she possesses it, and she is possessed
by it, ~~~~ents the future and, carrying it, she feels herself vast as the world;
but this v~~~~lence annihilates her, she feels that she herself is no longer anything. A ne~~~~s going to manifest itself and justify its own separate existence,
she is proud ~~~~ut she also feels herself tossed and driven, the play-thing of
obscure forc~~~~ specially noteworthy that the pregnant woman feels the immanence of l~~~~t just the time when it is in transcendence: it turns upon
itself in nausea a ~~~~mfort; it has ceased to exist for itself and thereupon becomes more sizabl~~~~ ever before. The transcendence of the artisan, of the
man of action, contain~~~~ e element of subjectivity; but in the mother-to-be the
antithesis of subject and ~~~~ject ceases to exist; she and the child with which she
is swollen make up togeth~~~~ an equivocal pair overwhelmed by life. Ensnared
by nature, the pregnant wom in is plant and animal, a stock-pile of colloids, an
incubator, an egg; she scares children proud of their young, straight bodies and
makes young people titter contemptuously because she is a human being, a conscious and free individual, who has become life's passive instrument.

Ordinarily life is but a condition of existence; in gestation it appears as creative; but that is a strange kind of creation which is accomplished in a contingent
and passive manner. There are women who enjoy the pleasures of pregnancy
and suckling so much that they desire their indefinite repetitions; as soon as a
baby is weaned these mothers feel frustrated. Such women are not so much
mothers as fertile organisms, like fowls with high egg-production. And they seek
eagerly to sacrifice their liberty of action to the functioning of their flesh: it
seems to them that their existence is tranquilly justified in the passive fecundity
of their bodies. If the flesh is purely passive and inert, it cannot embody transcendence, even in a degraded form; it is sluggish and tiresome; but when the
reproductive process begins, the flesh becomes root-stock, source, and blossom,
it assumes transcendence, a stirring toward the future, the while it remains a
gross and present reality. The disjunction previously suffered by the woman in
the weaning of an earlier child is compensated for; she is plunged anew into the
mainstream of life, reunited with the wholeness of things, a link in the endless
chain of generations, flesh that exists by and for another fleshly being. The fusion sought in masculine arms—and no sooner granted than withdrawn—is realized by the mother when she feels her child heavy within her or when she
clasps it to her swelling breasts. She is no longer an object subservient to a subject; she is no longer a subject afflicted with the anxiety that accompanies liberty, she is one with that equivocal reality: life. Her body is at last her own, since
it exists for the child who belongs to her. Society recognizes her right of possession and invests it, moreover, with a sacred character. Her bosom, which was
previously an erotic feature, can now be freely shown, for it is a source of life;

[handwritten right margin: but that own is]

[handwritten bottom: still predicated on belonging to another]

even religious pictures show us the Virgin Mother exposing her breast as she be-
seeches her Son to save mankind. With her ego surrendered, alienated in her
body and in her social dignity, the mother enjoys the comforting illusion of feeling that she is a human being *in herself, a value.*

But this is only an illusion. For she does not really make the baby, it makes itself within her; her flesh engenders flesh only, and she is quite incapable of establishing an existence that will have to establish itself. Creative acts originating
in liberty establish the object as value and give it the quality of the essential;
whereas the child in the maternal body is not thus justified; it is still only a gratuitous cellular growth, a brute fact of nature as contingent on circumstances as
death and corresponding philosophically with it. A mother can have *her* reasons
for wanting *a* child, but she cannot give to *this* independent person, who is to exist tomorrow, his own reasons, just justification, for existence; she engenders him
as a product of her generalized body, not of her individualized existence. . . .

. . . The dangerous falsity of two currently accepted preconceptions is clearly
evident. . . .

The first of these preconceptions is that maternity is enough in all cases to
crown a woman's life. It is nothing of the kind. There are a great many mothers
who are unhappy, embittered, unsatisfied. Tolstoy's wife is a significant example; she was brought to childbed more than twelve times and yet writes constantly in her journal about the emptiness and uselessness of everything, including herself. She tells of calm and happy moments, when she enjoyed being
indispensable to her children, and she speaks of them as her sole weapon against
the superiority of her husband; but all this was absolutely insufficient to give
meaning to her boresome existence. At times she felt capable of anything, but
there was nothing for her beyond caring for the children, eating, drinking, sleeping; what should have brought happiness made her sad. She wished ardently to
bring her children up well, but the eternal struggle with them made her impa-
tient and angry.

The mother's relation with her children takes form within the totality of her
life; it depends upon her relations with her husband, her past, her occupation,
herself; it is an error as harmful as it is absurd to regard the child as a universal
panacea. This is also Helene Deutsch's conclusion in the work, often quoted
above, in which she examines the phenomena of maternity in the light of her
psychiatric experience. She gives this function a high importance, believing that
through it woman finds complete self-realization—but on condition that it is
freely assumed and *sincerely* wanted; the young woman must be in a psychological, moral, and material situation that allows her to bear the effort involved;
otherwise the consequences will be disastrous. In particular, it is criminal to rec-
ommend having a child as a remedy for melancholia or neurosis; that means the

So true!

unhappiness of both mother and child. Only the woman who is well balanced, healthy, and aware of her responsibilities is capable of being a "good" mother. As we have seen, the curse which lies upon marriage is that too often the individuals are joined in their weakness rather than in their strength—each asking from the other instead of finding pleasure in giving. It is even more deceptive to dream of gaining through the child a plenitude, a warmth, a value, which one is unable to create for oneself; the child brings joy only to the woman who is capable of disinterestedly desiring the happiness of another, to one who without being wrapped up in self seeks to transcend her own existence. To be sure, the child is an enterprise to which one can validly devote oneself; but it represents a ready-made justification no more than any other enterprise does; and it must be desired for its own sake, not for hypothetical benefits. As Stekel well says:[2]

Children are not substitutes for one's disappointed love, they are not substitutes for one's thwarted ideal in life, children are not mere material to fill out an empty existence. Children are a responsibility and an opportunity. Children are the loftiest blossoms upon the tree of untrammeled love. . . . They are neither playthings, nor tools for the fulfillment of parental needs or ungratified ambitions. Children are obligations; they should be brought up so as to become happy human beings.

I don't know about that

Obligation is a moral choice

There is nothing *natural* in such an obligation: nature can never dictate a moral choice; this implies an engagement, a promise to be carried out. To have a child is to undertake a solemn obligation; if the mother shirks this duty subsequently, she commits an offense against an existent, an independent human being; but no one can impose the engagement upon her. The relation between parent and offspring, like that between husband and wife, ought to be freely willed. And it is not true, even, that having a child is a privileged accomplishment for woman, primary in relation to all others; it is often said of a woman that she is coquettish, or amorous, or lesbian, or ambitious, "for lack of a child"; her sexual life, the aims, the values she pursues, would in this view be substituted for a child. In fact, the matter is originally uncertain, indeterminate: one can say as well that a woman wants a child for lack of love, for lack of occupation, for lack of opportunity to satisfy homosexual tendencies. A social and artificial morality is hidden beneath this pseudo-naturalism. That the child is the supreme aim of woman is a statement having precisely the value of an advertising slogan.

What about the daddy?

The second false preconception, directly implied by the first, is that the child is sure of being happy in its mother's arms. There is no such thing as an "unnatural mother," to be sure, since there is nothing natural about maternal love; but, precisely for that reason, there are bad mothers. And one of the major truths proclaimed by psychoanalysis is the danger to the child that may lie in parents who are themselves "normal." The complexes, obsessions, and neuroses of adults have their roots in the early family life of those adults; parents who are themselves in conflict, with their quarrels and their tragic scenes, are bad company for the child. Deeply scarred by their early home life, their approach to their own children is through complexes and frustrations; and this chain of misery lengthens indefinitely. In particular, maternal sado-masochism creates in the daughter guilt feelings that will be expressed in sado-masochistic behavior toward her children, and so on without end.

There is an extravagant fraudulence in the easy reconciliation made between the common attitude of contempt for women and the respect shown for mothers. It is outrageously paradoxical to deny woman all activity in public affairs, to shut her out of masculine careers, to assert her incapacity in all fields of effort, and then to entrust to her the most delicate and the most serious undertaking of all: the molding of a human being. There are many women whom custom and tradition still deny the education, the culture, the responsibilities and activities that are the privilege of men, and in whose arms, nevertheless, babies are put without scruple, as earlier in life dolls were given them to compensate for their inferiority to little boys. They are permitted to play with toys of flesh and blood. Woman would have to be either perfectly happy or a saint to resist the temptation to abuse her privileges. Montesquieu was perhaps right when he said that it would be better to turn over to women the government of the State rather than that of her family; for if she is given opportunity, woman is as rational, as efficient, as a man; it is in abstract thought, in planned action, that she rises most easily above her sex. It is much more difficult, *as things are*, for her to escape from her woman's past, to attain an emotional balance that nothing in her situation favors. Man, also, is much more balanced and rational at work than at home; he makes his business calculations with mathematical precision, but he becomes illogical, lying, capricious, at home with his wife, where he "lets down." In the same way she "lets down" with her child. And her letting down is more dangerous because she can better defend herself against her husband than can the child against her. It would clearly be desirable for the good of the child if the mother were a complete, unmutilated person, a woman finding in her work and in her relation to society a self-realization that she would not seek to attain tyrannically through her offspring; and it would also be desirable for the child to be left to his parents infinitely less than at present, and for his studies and his diversions to be carried on among other children, under the direction of adults whose bonds with him would be impersonal and pure.

Even when the child seems a treasure in the midst of a happy or at least a balanced life, he cannot represent the limits of his mother's horizon. He does not take her out of her immanence; she shapes his flesh, she nourishes him, she takes care of him. But she can never do more than create a situation that only the child himself as an independent being can transcend; when she lays a stake on his future, her transcendence through the universe and time is still by proxy, which is to say that once more she is doomed to dependency. Not only her son's ingratitude, but also his failure will give the lie to all her hopes: as in marriage or love, she leaves it to another to justify her life, when the only authentic course is freely to assume the duty herself.

We have seen that woman's inferiority originated in her being at first limited to repeating life, whereas man invented reasons for living more essential, in his eyes, than the not-willed routine of mere existence; to restrict woman to maternity would be to perpetuate this situation. She demands today to have a part in that mode of activity in which humanity tries continually to find justification through transcendence, through movement toward new goals and accomplishments; she cannot consent to bring forth life unless life has meaning; she cannot be a mother without endeavoring to play a role in the economic, political, and social life of the times. It is not the same thing to produce cannon fodder, slaves, victims, or, on the other hand, free men. In a properly organized society, where children would be largely taken in charge by the community and the mother cared for and helped, maternity would not be wholly incompatible with careers for women. On the contrary, the woman who works—farmer, chemist, or writer—is the one who undergoes pregnancy most easily because she is not absorbed in her own person; the woman who enjoys the richest individual life will have the most to give her children and will demand the least from them; she who acquires in effort and struggle a sense of true human values will be best able to bring them up properly. If too often, today, woman can hardly reconcile with the best interests of her children an occupation that keeps her away from home for hours and takes all her strength, it is, on the one hand, because feminine employment is still too often a kind of slavery, and, on the other, because no effort has been made to provide for the care, protection, and education of children outside the home. This is a matter of negligence on the part of society; but it is false to justify it on the pretense that some law of nature, God, or man requires that mother and child belong exclusively to one another; this restriction constitutes in fact only a double and baneful oppression.

It is fraudulent to maintain that through maternity woman becomes concretely man's equal. The psychoanalysts have been at great pains to show that the child provides woman with an equivalent of the penis; but enviable as this *sev?asi*n manly attribute may be, no one pretends that its mere possession can justify or be the supreme end of existence. There has also been no dearth of talk about the sacred rights of the mother; but it is not as mothers that women have gained the right to vote, and the unwed mother is still in disrepute; it is only in marriage

oh yes, people *do* pretend this!

that the mother is glorified—that is, only when she is subordinated to a husband. As long as the latter remains the economic head of the family, the children are much more dependent on him than on her, though she is much more occupied with them than he is. That is the reason, as we have seen, why the relation of the mother to her children is intimately affected by that which she maintains with her husband.

Thus the relations between husband and wife, the tasks of housekeeping, and maternity, form a whole in which all the factors affect each other. Affectionately united with her husband, the wife can cheerfully carry the housekeeping load; happy in her children, she will be forbearing with her husband. But such harmony is not easy to attain, for the various functions assigned to woman are out of tune with one another. The women's magazines are full of advice to the housekeeper on the art of preserving her sexual attractiveness while washing dishes, of continuing to be well dressed during pregnancy, of reconciling coquetry, maternity, and economy. But even the wife who follows such counsel unswervingly will soon be distracted and disfigured by her cares; it is very difficult to remain desirable with dishpan hands and a body deformed by maternities. This is why the amorous type of woman feels resentment toward the children who ruin her seductiveness and deprive her of her husband's attentions. If, on the other hand, she is of the deeply maternal type, she is made jealous by her husband's claim to own the children along with everything else.

Then again, the "good" housekeeper is in opposition to the activities of life, as we have seen: the child is the foe of waxed floors. Maternal love often loses itself in the angry scolding that goes with the care of a well-kept home. It is not surprising that the woman who struggles among these contradictions very often passes her days in a state of nervousness and acrimony; she always loses in one way or another, and her gains are precarious, they are not registered in any surely successful outcome. She can never find salvation in her work itself; it keeps her busy but it does not justify her existence, for her justification rests with free personalities other than her own. Shut up in the home, woman cannot herself establish her existence; she lacks the means requisite for self-affirmation as an individual; and in consequence her individuality is not given recognition. Among the Arabs and the Indians and in many rural populations a woman is only a female domesticated animal, esteemed according to the work she does and replaced without regret if she disappears. In modern civilization she is more or less individualized in her husband's eyes; but unless she completely renounces her ego, engulfing herself like the Natasha of *War and Peace* in a passionate and tyrannical devotion to her family, she suffers from being reduced to pure generality. She is *the* housekeeper, *the* wife, *the* mother, unique and undiscriminated: Natasha delights in this supreme self-abasement and, by rejecting all comparisons, denies the existence of *others*. But modern Western woman wants, on the contrary, to feel that people distinguish her as *this* housekeeper, *this* wife, *this* mother, *this* woman. That is the satisfaction she will seek in social life.

NOTES

1. See Book I, pp. 118 ff., where the reader will find a historical account of birth control and abortion.
2. *Frigidity in Woman,* Vol. II, pp. 305, 306.

THE WOMAN IN LOVE

The word *love* has by no means the same sense for both sexes, and this is one cause of the serious misunderstandings that divide them. Byron well said: "Man's love is of man's life a thing apart; 'Tis woman's whole existence." . . .

Men have found it possible to be passionate lovers at certain times in their lives, but there is not one of them who could be called "a great lover[1]; in their most violent transports, they never abdicate completely; even on their knees before a mistress, what they still want is to take possession of her; at the very heart of their lives they remain sovereign subjects; the beloved woman is only one value among others; they wish to integrate her into their existence and not to squander it entirely on her. For woman, on the contrary, to love is to relinquish everything for the benefit of a master. As Cécile Sauvage puts it: "Woman must forget her own personality when she is in love. It is a law of nature. A woman is nonexistent without a master. Without a master, she is a scattered bouquet." The fact is that we have nothing to do here with laws of nature. It is the difference in their situations that is reflected in the difference men and women show in their conceptions of love. The individual who is a subject, who is himself, if he has the courageous inclination toward transcendence, endeavors to extend his grasp on the world: he is ambitious, he acts. But an inessential creature is incapable of sensing the absolute at the heart of her subjectivity; a being doomed to immanence cannot find self-realization in acts. Shut up in the sphere of the relative, destined to the male from childhood, habituated to seeing in him a superb being whom she cannot possibly equal, the woman who has not repressed her claim to humanity will dream of transcending her being toward one of these superior beings, of amalgamating herself with the sovereign subject. There is no other way out for her than to lose herself, body and soul, in him who is represented to her as the absolute, as the essential. Since she is anyway

doomed to dependence, she will prefer to serve a god rather than obey tyrants—
parents, husband, or protector. She chooses to desire her enslavement so ardently that it will seem to her the expression of her liberty; she will try to rise
above her situation as inessential object by fully accepting it; through her flesh,
her feelings, her behavior, she will enthrone him as supreme value and reality:
she will humble herself to nothingness before him. Love becomes for her a religion. . . .

. . . Now, the woman in love . . . feels . . . a passionate desire to transcend the
limitations of self and become infinite, thanks to the intervention of another who
has access to infinite reality. She abandons herself to love first of all to *save herself*; but the paradox of idolatrous love is that in trying to save herself she *denies
herself* utterly in the end. Her feeling gains a mystical dimension; she requires
her God no longer to admire her and approve of her; she wants to merge with
him, to forget herself in his arms. "I would wish to be a saint of love," writes Mme
d'Agoult.[2] "I would long for martyrdom in such moments of exaltation and as-
cetic frenzy." What comes to light in these words is a desire for a complete destruction of the self, abolishing the boundaries that separate her from the
beloved. There is no question here of masochism, but of a dream of ecstatic
union.

In order to realize this dream, what woman wants in the first place is to serve;
for in responding to her lover's demands, a woman will feel that she is necessary;
she will be integrated with his existence, she will share his worth, she will be justified. Even mystics like to believe, according to Angelus Silesius, that God
needs man; otherwise they would be giving themselves in vain. The more demands the man makes, the more gratified the woman feels. Although the seclu-
sion imposed by Victor Hugo on Juliette Drouet weighed heavily on the young
woman, one feels that she is happy in obeying him: to stay by the fireside is to
do something for the master's pleasure. She tries also to be useful to him in a
positive way. She cooks choice dishes for him and arranges a little nest where he
can be at home; she looks after his clothes. "I want you to tear your clothes as
much as possible," she writes to him, "and I want to mend and clean them all
myself." She reads the paper, clips out articles, classifies letters and notes, copies
manuscripts, for him. She is grieved when the poet entrusts a part of the work
to his daughter Léopoldine.

Such traits are found in every woman in love. If need be, she herself tyran-
nizes over herself in her lover's name; all she is, all she has, every moment of her
life, must be devoted to him and thus gain their *raison d'être*; she wishes to possess nothing save in him; what makes her unhappy is for him to require nothing
of her, so much so that a sensitive love will invent demands. She at first sought
in love a confirmation of what she was, of her past, of her personality; but she

also involves her future in it, and to justify her future she puts it in the hands of one who possesses all values. Thus she gives up her transcendence, subordinating it to that of the essential other, to whom she makes herself vassal and slave. It was to find herself, to save herself, that she lost herself in him in the first place; and the fact is that little by little she does lose herself in him wholly; for her the whole of reality is in the other. The love that at the start seemed a narcissistic apotheosis is fulfilled in the bitter joys of a devotion that often leads to self-mutilation. . . .

Yet the descent from generous warmth of feeling to masochistic madness is an easy one. The woman in love who before her lover is in the position of the child before its parents is also liable to that sense of guilt she felt with them; she chooses not to revolt against him as long as she loves him, but she revolts against herself. If he loves her less than she wants him to, if she fails to engross him, to make him happy, to satisfy him, all her narcissism is transformed into self-disgust, into humiliation, into hatred of herself, which drive her to self-punishment. During a more or less lengthy crisis, sometimes for life, she will make herself a voluntary victim, she will struggle furiously to hurt her ego that has been unable to gratify him to the full. At this point her attitude is genuinely masochistic.

But we must not confuse this case, in which the woman in love seeks her own suffering in order to take vengeance upon herself, with those cases in which her aim is the affirmation of her man's liberty and power. It is a commonplace—and seemingly a truth—that the prostitute is proud to be beaten by her man; but what exalts her is not the idea of her beaten and enslaved person, it is rather the strength and authority, the supremacy of the male upon whom she is dependent: she also likes to see him maltreat another male; indeed, she often incites him to engage in dangerous fighting, for she wants her master to possess and display the values recognized in the environment to which she belongs. . . .

. . . On the level of love, as on that of eroticism, it seems evident that masochism is one of the bypaths taken by the unsatisfied woman, disappointed in both the other and herself; but it is not the natural tendency of a happy resignation. Masochism perpetuates the presence of the ego in a bruised and degraded condition; love brings forgetfulness of self in favor of the essential subject.

. . . The man in love is tyrannical, but when he has obtained what he wants he is satisfied; whereas there are no limits to woman's exigent devotion. A lover who has confidence in his mistress feels no displeasure if she absents herself, if occupied at a distance from him; sure that she is his, he prefers to possess a free being than to own a thing. For the woman, on the contrary, the absence of her lover is always torture; he is an eye, a judge, and as soon as he looks at anything other than herself, he frustrates her; whatever he sees, he robs her of; away from him, she is dispossessed, at once of herself and of the world; even when seated at her side reading or writing or whatever, he is abandoning her, betraying her. She hates his sleep. But Baudelaire grew tender over woman in sleep: "Your beautiful eyes are weary, my poor loved one"; and Proust is enchanted in watching Albertine[3] sleep. The point is that male jealousy is simply the will to exclusive possession; the loved woman, when sleep restores the disarmed candor of childhood, belongs to no one: that certitude is enough. But the god, the master, should not give himself up to the repose of immanence; the woman views this blasted transcendence with a hostile eye; she detests the animal inertia of his body which exists no longer *for her* but *in itself*, abandoned to a contingence of which her contingence is the price.[4]

At the least the woman will be able to find her joy in this enrichment which she brings to her beloved; she is not Everything to him, to be sure, but she will try to believe herself indispensable; there are no degrees in necessity. If he "cannot get along without her," she considers herself the foundation of his precious existence, and she derives her own value from that. Her joy is to serve him—but he must gratefully recognize this service; the gift becomes a demand in accordance with the usual dialectic of devotion.[5] And a woman with a scrupulous mind is bound to ask herself: does he really need *me*? The man is fond of her, desires her, with a personal tenderness and desire; but would he not have an equally personal feeling for someone else in her place? Many women in love permit themselves to be deluded; they would like to ignore the fact that the general is involved in the particular, and man furthers the illusion because he shares it at first; his desire often has a fire that seems to defy time; at the moment when he wants that woman, he wants her passionately, he wants her only. And, to be sure, that moment is an absolute—but a momentary absolute. Not realizing this, duped, the woman goes on to the eternal. Deified by the master's embrace, she believes she has always been divine and destined for the god—she and nobody else. But male desire is as ephemeral as it is imperious; once allayed, it dies rather quickly; whereas it is most often afterward that woman becomes love's captive. This is the burden of a whole fluent literature and of many facile songs. "A young man passed her way, a girl sang. . . . A young man sang, a girl wept."

And if the man is lastingly attached to the woman, that is still no sign that she is necessary to him. What she claims, however, is this: her abdication of self saves her only on condition that it restores her empire; reciprocity cannot be evaded. So she must either suffer or lie to herself. Most often she clutches at the straw of falsehood. She fancies that the man's love is the exact counterpart of the love she brings to him; in bad faith she takes desire for love, erection for desire, love for a religion. She compels the man to lie to her: "Do you love me? As much as yesterday? Will you always love me?" and so on. She cleverly poses her questions at a moment when there is not time enough to give properly qualified and sincere answers, or more especially when circumstances prevent any response; she asks her insistent questions in the course of a sexual embrace, at the verge of a convalescence, in the midst of sobs, or on a railroad platform. She makes trophies of the extorted replies; and if there are no replies, she takes silence to mean what she wishes; every woman in love is more or less a paranoiac. I recall a friend who said in reference to a long silence on the part of her distant lover: "When one wants to break off, one writes to announce the break"; then, having finally received a quite unambiguous letter: "When one really wants to break off, one doesn't write."

In considering such confidences, it is often difficult to determine just where pathological delirium beings. As described by the frantic woman in love, the behavior of the man always seems to be fantastic: he is a neurotic, a sadist, a repressed personality, a masochist, a devil, an unstable type, a coward, or all of these put together. He defies the most searching psychological explanations. "X. adores me, he is madly jealous, he would like to have me wear a mask on the street; but he is so strange a creature and is so much on his guard against love that when I ring his doorbell, he meets me on the landing and won't even let me in." Or, again, "Z. used to adore me. But he was too proud to ask me to go and live with him in Lyon. I went there and made myself at home with him. After eight days, without any argument, he put me out. I saw him again twice. When I telephoned him for the third time, he hung up in the middle of the conversation. He is a neurotic." These mysterious stories are cleared up when the man states in explanation: "I absolutely was not in love with her," or "I was on friendly terms with her, but I wouldn't be able to live with her a month." When bad faith becomes too obstinate, it leads to the insane asylum, for one of the constant characteristics of erotomania is that the behavior of the lover seems enigmatic and paradoxical; on account of this quirk, the patient's mania always succeeds in breaking through the resistance of reality. A normal woman sometimes yields in the end to the truth and finally recognizes the fact that she is no longer loved. But so long as she has not lost all hope and made this admission, she always cheats a little.

Even in mutual love there is fundamental difference in the feelings of the lovers, which the woman tries to hide. The man must certainly be capable of justifying himself without her, since she hopes to be justified through him. If he is necessary to her, it means that she is evading her liberty; but if he accepts his liberty, without which he would be neither a hero nor even a man, no person or thing can be necessary to him. The dependence accepted by woman comes from her weakness: how, therefore, could she find a reciprocal dependence in the man she loves in his strength?

A passionately demanding soul cannot find repose in love, because the end she has in view is inherently contradictory. Torn and tortured, she risks becoming a burden to the man instead of his slave, as she had dreamed; unable to feel indispensable, she becomes importunate, a nuisance. This is, indeed, a common tragedy. If she is wiser and less intransigent, the woman in love becomes resigned. She is not all, she is not necessary: it is enough to be useful; another might easily fill her place: she is content to be the one who is there. She accepts her servitude without demanding the same in return. Thus she can enjoy a modest happiness; but even within these limits it will not be unclouded. . . .

She regards love as a free sentiment and at the same time a magic spell; and she supposes that "her" male continues, of course, to love her as a free agent while he is being "bewitched," "ensnared," by a clever schemer. A man thinks of a woman as united with him, in her immanence; that is why he readily plays the Boubouroche[6]; it is difficult for him to imagine that she is also another person who may be getting away from him. Jealousy with him is ordinarily no more than a passing crisis, like love itself; the crisis may be violent and even murderous, but it is rare for him to acquire a lasting uneasiness. His jealousy is usually derivative: when his business is going badly, when he feels that life is hurting him, then he feels his woman is flouting him.[7]

Woman, on the other hand, loving her man in his alterity and in his transcendence, feels in danger at every moment. There is no great distance between the treason of absence and infidelity. From the moment when she feels less than perfectly loved, she becomes jealous, and in view of her demands, this is always pretty much her case; her reproaches and complaints, whatever the pretexts, come to the surface in jealous scenes; she will express in this way the impatience and ennui of waiting, the bitter taste of her dependence, her regret at having only a mutilated existence. Her entire destiny is involved in each glance her lover casts at another woman, since she has identified her whole being with him. Thus she is annoyed if his eyes are turned for an instant toward a stranger; but if he reminds her that she has just been contemplating some stranger, she firmly replies: "That is not the same thing at all." She is right. A man who is looked at by a woman receives nothing; no gift is given until the feminine flesh becomes prey. Whereas the coveted woman is at once metamorphosed into a desirable and desired object; and the woman in love, thus slighted, is reduced to the status of ordinary clay. And so she is always on the watch. What is he doing? At whom is he looking? With whom is he talking? What a desire has given her, a smile can take away from her; it needs only an instant to cast her down from "the pearly light of immortality" to the dim light of the everyday. She has received all from love, she can lose all in losing it. Vague or definite, ill-founded or justified, jealousy is maddening torture for the woman, because it is radically at variance with love: if the treason is unquestionable, she must either give up making love a religion or give up loving. This is a radical catastrophe and no wonder the woman in love, suspicious and mistaken in turn, is obsessed by the desire to discover the fatal truth and the fear that she will. . . .

Genuine love ought to be founded on the mutual recognition of two liberties; the lovers would then experience themselves both as self and as other: neither would give up transcendence, neither would be mutilated; together they would manifest values and aims in the world. For the one and the other, love would be revelation of self by the gift of self and enrichment of the world. In his work on self-knowledge[8] George Gusdorf sums up very exactly what *man* demands of love.

Love reveals us to ourselves by making us come out of ourselves. We affirm ourselves by contact with what is foreign and complementary to us. . . . Love as a form of perception brings to light new skies and a new earth even in the landscape where we have always lived. Here is the great secret: the world is different, I myself *am different*. And I am no longer alone in knowing it. Even better: someone has apprised me of the fact. Woman therefore plays an indispensable and leading role in man's gaining knowledge of himself.

This accounts for the importance to the young man of his apprenticeship in love[9]; we have seen how astonished Stendhal, Malraux, were at the miracle expressed in the phrase: "I myself, I am different." But Gusdorf is wrong when he writes: "And *similarly* man represents for woman an indispensable intermediary between herself and herself," for today her situation is not *similar*; man is revealed in a different aspect but he remains himself, and his new aspect is integrated with the sum total of his personality. It would be the same with woman only if she existed no less essentially than man as *pour-soi:* this would imply that she had economic independence, that she moved toward ends of her own and transcended herself, without using man as an agent, toward the social whole. Under these circumstances, love in equality is possible, as Malraux depicts it between Kyo and May in *Man's Fate*. Woman may even play the virile and dominating role, as did Mme de Warens with Rousseau, and, in Colette's *Chéri*, Léa with Chéri.

But most often woman knows herself only as different, relative; her *pour-autrui*, relation to others, is confused with her very being; for her, love is not an intermediary "between herself and herself" because she does not attain her subjective existence; she remains engulfed in this loving woman whom man has not only revealed, but created. Her salvation depends on this despotic free being that has made her and can instantly destroy her. She lives in fear and trembling before this man who holds her destiny in his hands without quite knowing it, without quite wishing to. She is in danger through an other, an anguished and powerless onlooker at her own fate. Involuntary tyrant, involuntary executioner, this other wears a hostile visage in spite of her and of himself. And so instead of the union sought for, the woman in love knows the most bitter solitude there is; instead of cooperation, she knows struggle and not seldom hate. For woman, love is a supreme effort to survive by accepting the dependence to which she is condemned; but even with consent a life of dependency can be lived only in fear and servility.

Men have vied with one another in proclaiming that love is woman's supreme accomplishment. "A woman who loves as a woman becomes only the more feminine," says Nietzsche; and Balzac: "Among the first-rate, man's life is fame, woman's life is love. Woman is man's equal only when she makes her life a perpetual offering, as that of man is perpetual action." But therein, again, is a cruel deception, since what she offers, men are in no wise anxious to accept. Man has no need of the unconditional devotion he claims, nor of the idolatrous love that flatters his vanity; he accepts them only on condition that he need not satisfy the reciprocal demands these attitudes imply. He preaches to woman that she should give—and her gifts bore him to distraction; she is left in embarrassment with her useless offerings, her empty life. On the day when it will be possible for woman to love not in her weakness but in her strength, not to escape herself but to find herself, not to abase herself but to assert herself—on that day love will become for her, as for man, a source of life and not of mortal danger. In the meantime, love represents in its most touching form the curse that lies heavily upon woman confined in the feminine universe, woman mutilated, insufficient unto herself. The innumerable martyrs to love bear witness against the injustice of a fate that offers a sterile hell as ultimate salvation.

NOTES

1. In the sense that a woman may sometimes be called "*une grande amoureuse.*"—TR.
2. She eloped with Franz Liszt and became the mother of Cosima Wagner. Under the name of Daniel Stern she wrote historical and philosophical books.—TR.
3. If Albertine were Albert it would be the same; Proust's attitude here is masculine in either case.
4. That is, when he loses his independent powers, his transcendence, even in sleep, it costs her hers, because she lives in and by him.—TR.
5. Which I have attempted to set forth in my essay *Pyrrhus et Cinéas*.
6. A naïve, easygoing character in a novel and a play by Courteline, deceived by his mistress and exploited by his friends.—TR.
7. This is brought out, for example, in Lagache's work: *Nature et formes de la jalousie.*
8. *La Découverte de soi* (Paris, 1948), pp. 421, 425.—TR.
9. See Book I, pp. 183, 247.

2

BEAUVOIR AND FEMINISM

Michèle Le Doeuff

INTRODUCTION

by Jennifer Hansen

Michèle Le Doeuff was born in France in 1948. She is politically of the generation of 1968 and the feminist movement in France, though her philosophical influences are more classical than postmodern. She received her Ph.D. in philosophy and has subsequently held positions in philosophy at the Ecole Normale Supérieure at Fontenay and the University of Geneva. She also is a researcher at the Centre National de la Recherche Scientifique (CNRS). Le Doeuff is an outspoken critic of the French government and its education policies.

Le Doeuff's work reflects a broad range of interests, notably literature, classical philosophy, and feminist theory. She published a translation of Francis Bacon's *New Atlantis* in 1983, as well as a translation and stage adaptation of Shakespeare's *Venus and Adonis* in 1986. She has also worked with the Théâtre de l'Aquarium on the play *Le Soeur de Shakespeare* (Shakespeare's sister). Le Doeuff published her first book, *The Philosophical Imaginary*, in 1981, and her second book, *Hipparchia's Choice: An Essay Concerning Women, Philosophy, Etc.*, in 1991.

True to her belief that philosophers or thinkers should not be constrained by dogmatic principles of writing, Le Doeuff writes in an innovative and refreshing voice. Her chapter headings, for example in *Hipparchia's Choice*, imitate medieval texts, while her essays intertwine subjective experiences, autobiographical moments, wit, literary allusion, and argumentation.

In *Hipparchia's Choice*, Le Doeuff tells us of her early passion for literature, identifying with the fools of Shakespeare. This identification proved to be quite prescient, because the fool's cynical attitude toward convention eventually led Le Doeuff to the study of philosophy. Once she settled into the profession of philosophy, however, two disappointments befell her that she divined were inextricably linked to one another: professional philosophy was not practiced by nonconformists and radicals such as Socrates, and she discovered the irrational fear that male philosophers had of women who dare philosophize. The strict dogmatism of professional philosophers—the prescribing of acceptable writing, the dismissal of subjective experience, the adherence to systems or models, and the need to keep philosophy pure as a discipline—appeared to be linked with its exclusion and derision of women.

Le Doeuff demonstrates that because philosophy constructs itself as a closed system, it projects all threats to the system onto 'others'. These others, such as women, savages, or children, represent all that is chaotic and irrational about the world and therefore must be barred from doing philosophy, lest they sully its findings. However, in this exclusionary move, the professional philosophers, mostly men, also created the very things they repress. They create images of women as irrational and chaotic, and then use this image to justify their exclusion.

The Philosophical Imaginary is a collection of essays that examines the role that images play in philosophers' arguments, that is the imaginary that runs through philosophical arguments. She argues that often the images that philosophers utilize to build their 'abstract' arguments violate the rules of evidence in their system, allowing them to make leaps in logic with metaphors rather than justify through logic their first principles. Furthermore these philosophers often draw their images from a stock of recognizable cultural images, originating in literature, folk tales, myths, other disciplines such as science or psychology, burgeoning technological inventions, and so on. The images that circulate within a culture, the cultural imaginary, also circulate between cultures, overrunning artificially erected boundaries between disciplines and countries. Though philosophers labor to keep the proper objects of investigation distinct from other disciplines, their use of metaphors and images from this larger context creeps through the back door, demonstrating to Le Doeuff the foolishness of creating boundaries between disciplines and peoples to begin with.

We could say that Le Doeuff is the champion of philosophy without borders, eschewing the exclusivity that traditional philosophers have practiced in regard to who is deemed fit to philosophize and what is an acceptable object of study. Le Doeuff sees feminist critique as a truly philosophical practice, for it roots out the contradictions and paradoxes in sexist philosophical thinking in a manner reminiscent of Socrates. Furthermore, feminist critique draws upon the resources of other disciplines such as literature, sociology, economics, history, and science to enrich its search for the truth of women's oppression. It brings philosophical pursuit back to earthly concerns, just as Socrates redirected the cosmologist's philosophical concerns to practical matters of virtue and politics.

Feminist critique also draws from various methods and models, freeing it from the constriction that a particular philosophical system tends to create.

Le Doeuff is an antifoundationalist, arguing that neither philosophy nor feminist theory should limit themselves to one system or one model. Philosophy also should shy away from any pretension to have settled all questions in advance by a systematic approach. Instead, philosophical investigations should always leave questions half answered or explored, awaiting contributions and debate from other thinkers. Though she does not subscribe to any one system as foundational to knowledge, she does believe that objects of philosophical pursuit are indeed universal. For example, studying the condition of women in society is not the fancy of a particular group of thinkers—an object of study created by purely subjective concerns—but an object of study that extends through history and across cultures. The truth of women's oppression, however, cannot be summed up in an abstract, general claim, but pours out of a plurality of voices that cannot be unified into a coherent *logos*.

In the following selections taken from *Hipparchia's Choice*, Le Doeuff explores the relationship that women have to philosophy, through the examples of Simone de Beauvoir and the theoretical debates that feminist thinkers engaged in during the women's movement in France. Le Doeuff's fascination with Beauvoir reflects both her admiration for her and her consternation over many of her statements and choices. Beauvoir's *The Second Sex* allowed women to begin theorizing about why they feel general malaise, or disorientation, in the universe. *The Second Sex* supplied its readers with a vocabulary and detailed explanations of the insidious ways in which women are made to feel inferior and inessential in society. Beauvoir chose a particular framework for her investigation, namely Sartre's existentialist ontology. Le Doeuff asks the question of whether using an existentialist ontology was at all necessary for Beauvoir to succeed in the task of exposing how patriarchy works and whether using such a framework might have hampered her insight into women's oppression. For example, Sartre only understood oppression as an instance of *bad faith*, of an agent fleeing from his/her responsibility to act in the world, of an agent allowing him/herself to be subjected by another. Beauvoir, likewise, tended to explore those oppressions that women face that could also be understood as moral failings in Sartre's system.

This critique of Beauvoir follows from a more general critique that a feminist's or a philosopher's goal ought not to be to align him/herself with a particular school of thought or particular thinker in order to uncover truths. When a feminist takes up a particular method, either explicitly or implicitly, she runs the risk of importing sexist assumptions into her conclusions. Le Doeuff considers that many of the conclusions of difference feminists, such as Luce Irigaray, tend to reinforce philosophical assumptions that ultimately work against supporting difference. Irigaray, she argues, searches for a language of the female sex, repressed or censored by the hegemony of powerful men in culture. Yet, if Irigaray's intention is to find a language for the female sex, then she herself is subjecting the plurality of female voices and experiences to the hegemony of powerful women in culture. Le Doeuff argues that, by subscribing to the insights of Lacan and other masculinist writers, thinkers such as Irigaray fail to snuff out many of the malignant effects of patriarchal thought. For Le Doeuff, if opening up discourse to allow for a plurality of viewpoints is the goal, then characterizing this as "allowing the repressed female voice to speak" is not the answer, for then we will only hear the speaking of a female voice that men created in the first place.

Le Doeuff accepts Beauvoir's belief that women belong to a 'group' that cannot call itself a 'we', for it has no shared traditions, history, or even experiences of oppression. If women cannot speak as a 'we', then how do we begin to theorize who women are, in their plurality? Le Doeuff responds that through collective work, collective projects, women might establish a community in which they support each other's different needs and experiences. All that is required of this group, forged through a shared desire to articulate and specify what women are outside of their relationship to men, is a 'minimal consensus'.

Le Doeuff envisions feminists moving beyond either the ideological commitments of equality feminism or difference feminism, for both camps subscribe to the writings of one great philosophical Subject or another. Both difference and equality feminists subscribe to a particular model of politics. Le Doeuff suggests those feminists and women philosophers (two identities that Le Doeuff sees as necessary to each other) move away from subscribing to *one* kind of model. Perhaps women philosophers might revision philosophy not as synonymous with famous male philosophers, but rather as an ongoing endeavor that requires the input of persons with radically different perspectives on the world and informed from different models. Philosophy should not be a discipline committed to preserving the systems of male philosophers but, rather, an open dialogue.

BIBLIOGRAPHY

Selected Primary Sources

1977. "Women and Philosophy." *Radical Philosophy* 17. Also in *French Feminist Thought*. Edited by Toril Moi. Oxford: Blackwell, 1987.
1979. "Operative Philosophy: Simone de Beauvoir and Existentialism." *Ideology & Consciousness* 6: 47–54.

1984. "The Public Employer." *m/f* 9: 3–18.
1987. "Ants and Women, or Philosophy without Borders."In *Contemporary French Philosophy*. Edited by A. Phillips Griffiths. Cambridge: Cambridge University Press.
1989. *The Philosophical Imaginary*. Translated by C. Gordon. London: Athlone. [*Recherches sur l'imaginaire philosophique*. Paris: Payot, 1980.]
1990. "Women, Reason, etc." *Differences* 2, no. 3: 1–13.
1991. *Hipparchia's Choice: An Essay Concerning Women, Philosophy, Etc.* Translated by T. Selous. Oxford: Blackwell; *L 'Étude et le rouet*. Paris: Éditions du Seuil, 1989.

Selected Secondary Sources

Deutscher, Max. 1987. "Stories, Pictures, Arguments." *Philosophy* 62, no. 240: 159–70.
———. 2000. *Michele Le Doeuff: Operative Philosophy and Imaginary Practice*. Amherst: Humanities Books.
Gatens, Moria. 1986. "Feminism, Philosophy and Riddles without Answers." In *Feminist Challenges*. Edited by Carole Pateman and Elizabeth Grosz. Boston: Northeastern University Press.
Grimshaw, Jean. 1996. "Philosophy, Feminism and Universalism." *Radical Philosophy* 76: 19–28.
Grosz, Elizabeth. 1987. "Feminist Theory and the Challenge to Knowledges." *Women's Studies International Forum* 10, no. 5: 475–80.
———. 1989. *Sexual Subversions*. Sydney: Allen & Unwin.
Morris, Michael. 1981–82. "Operative Reasoning: Michèle le Doueff, Philosophy and Feminism." *Ideology & Consciousness* 9: 71–101.
Mortley, Raoul. 1991. "Interview with Michèle Le Doeuff." *French Philosophers in Conversation*. London: Routledge, 80–91.

HIPPARCHIA'S CHOICE

which is analytical

which deals in particular with the case of Sartre and Simone de Beauvoir; which shows that the latter had a genius for the inappropriate, and wonders whether she might not have stretched existentialism beyond and above its means.

What a strange mixture *The Second Sex* is for a feminist reader of today, or for anyone whose main motive for reading is to find elements of thought which could be used to support a practice or a language which could become that of present or future debates. Such a reader would feel tempted to approach it selectively. Of course, there are countless observations, descriptions and analyses in the text which, for my part, I can only endorse. For example, when Simone de Beauvoir describes the repetitive nature of housework, when she analyzes the censorious treatment of aggressiveness in little girls, when she cites and criticizes Stekel's conceptions of frigidity or when she examines the prevailing conception of women's wages as *salaire d'appoint* or 'supplementary income' and the sorrows of conjugal life, she provides essential elements for a minutely detailed consciousness of the oppression of women. And certainly the book's detailed nature makes it very useful, because oppression always also exists where you would not expect to find it, where it might go unnoticed.

Yet side by side with these valuable analyses exploring women's condition, and indeed preceding them, we find a whole conceptual apparatus which is now somewhat outdated and which makes the book less accessible to more recent readers. What, for example, are we to make of this:

> Every individual concerned to justify his existence experiences this existence as an indefinite need for self-transcendence. Now what marks the specificity of woman's situation is that while she, like any other human being, is an autonomous freedom, she discovers and chooses herself in a world where men force her to assume herself as the Other: they claim to fix her as an object and to doom her to immanence, since her transcendence is to be perpetually transcended by another essential and sovereign consciousness.[1]

But is the problem really one of 'justifying one's existence'? Is it really necessary to use the concept of transcendence to bring the oppression of women in light? What happens if one refuses to give meaning to these categories? Is it not rash to hang a study of oppression on ideas like these?

What we chiefly sense in these lines is the aging of a philosophy which was in fashion in 1949. It must have been a factor in making the book more readable at the time, but it has since become a hindrance, now that we no longer speak fluent existentialist. This, and my vague perception that use of this language may have disadvantages, are the two reasons for the temptation I sometimes feel (and I do not think I am alone) to read this feminist *Summa* in a selective way. If many readers today skip those pages most imbued with existentialist doctrine and focus on the analyses of the 'world where men force her to', slipping over the transcended transcendences, they are giving *The Second Sex* an ordinary fate: *habent sua fata libri*, books have their own destiny and the most usual of these is to be fragmented—we'll take this and not that, says posterity.

However, it is fairer, and far more instructive, to read Simone de Beauvoir's essay as it is and to try to connect its two aspects, which seem heterogeneous, if only so that we can use it to ask one question that matters to us: in what respect, if any, is the choice of this or that philosophical frame of reference a crucial one for feminist studies? In the 1970s philosophist inflation also affected feminist theoretical productions, or 'women's books', by women who wanted to change things, but who rejected the label 'feminist'. The works of Luce Irigaray, for example, propound the idea that since philosophical discourse lays down the law to all other forms of discourse, it is the first that must be overthrown and disrupted, with the result that the 'main enemy' becomes 'idealist logic' or the 'metaphysical logos'. I do not know myself whether philosophical discourse lays down the law to anything at all. At any rate, Simone de Beauvoir's book gives a very different impression: although her posing of the problems in no way seeks to overthrow a 'metaphysical logos', she still manages to highlight issues and put forward thoughts of which the least one can say is that they galvanized women's movements pretty well everywhere and helped them get going.

Or rather we should say that, for twenty years, *The Second Sex* was the movement before the movement. In the one-on-one dialogue of reading, thousands of women found what later they got from meeting in groups: reference points for understanding the situation given to all of them, a language to express feelings of unease and the sharing of this unease. In the 1960s, when I discovered this book, it helped me greatly in at least two ways. At the time, officially, women no longer had any problems. Even the extraordinary scandal of the difficulty of obtaining contraception was hidden. This meant that all the existential difficulties we experienced had become secret, and each of us thought them her own personal problem; each of us, surprised at feeling so bad in those heady days of expansion and the Beatles, could only wonder what was odd about herself. Reading *The Second Sex* taught us to objectify the question, to look at the social world with a critical eye, instead of looking within ourselves for some hidden cause of an existential incapacity. It taught us simply to situate some of our difficulties and thus to free ourselves from their internalization. It also helped each to discover that she was not a special case and that her situation was more or less that of all women.

In an interview with an American journalist in 1976, Simone de Beauvoir said that her book influenced only women who wanted to be influenced and helped the development of only those women who had already started to develop by themselves. In talking about influence and looking at her work only from the point of view of a possible 'radicalization' of her women readers, she is not doing herself justice. A book which puts an end to loneliness, which teaches people to see, has greater and more immediate importance than all the manifestos in the world. Manifestos can be judged against the stand of 'influence', if indeed this is something that can be measured. A real book offers something else: the possibility of meeting a voice, an intelligence and a particular kind of generosity. Simone de Beauvoir taught the young women that we were to trust ourselves and to send the ball back—we who were too often surrounded by cruel words and glances quick to censure. . . .

THE EXTINGUISHED SUBJECT, AND HOW, NONETHELESS, THE IMPROBABLE LATER OCCURRED

A close reading of the first pages of *The Second Sex* shows us that Beauvoir is not proposing a single theory of the 'subject'; this term is used in at least three ways. There is the 'subject' who constitutes the other as inessential and as an object; this mode corresponds to 'male sovereignty'. There is the 'subject' of oppressed minorities, American or Haitian blacks, workers from the poor areas of Paris or the Jews of the ghettos, whom the white-christian-bourgeois-man regards as 'the other', but who can answer back and retain independence in relation to the dominator's viewpoint because a community exists which makes it possible to say 'we'. These minorities can organize 'themselves into an entity which can understand and place itself in confrontation.' Lastly, there is the subject who is completely extinguished as such, lost in submission to other people and in other people's point of view: women who, when they speak of women, say 'women' as men do and not 'we'; women who are scattered and whom no form of solidarity unites. These three modes are thus situated in a schema of objectifiable power relations and the text relates each of them to concrete parameters, which are seen as existing outside the account which seeks to reveal and understand them. A given mode is not chosen by a particular 'I'. It is the particular mode which decides whether the 'I' can be the despotic subject, the minority subject in struggle and resistance, or the extinguished subject, in other words woman.

Woman is extinguished because the traditional position deprives her of an external world to act in and subjects her to the other's point of view; 'these things may go together.' 'The restrictions that education and custom impose on woman now limit her grasp on the universe':[2] if our author lays so much stress throughout the book on feminine narcissism, it is in line with this idea. The only field of action left to 'woman' is herself, and herself through the look of the other. Of course Beauvoir does not forget that there are women workers, nor that any wife-mother has to bear a heavy burden of domestic work. However the last chapter is concerned to show that this 'daily labour' is 'thankless' in the strict

sense of the word, insofar as women do not receive 'the moral and social benefits they might rightfully count on'.[3] So is a person 'someone' only when the work
she or he does is validated and remunerated? We could look more deeply into
Beauvoir's thinking on this point. But let us see how the question of the community that she raises has been pursued dialectically by her women heirs.

The American Women's Liberation Movement, the French MLF of the
1970s and their equivalents in the other developed countries have not necessarily regarded *The Second Sex* as their *What Is To Be Done*? Besides, Simone
de Beauvoir would not have liked it if they had. And even though most of the
women involved in these movements have been very grateful to 'Simone', the
movements themselves started around issues which she considered more or less
settled (contraception, abortion[4]) and something she did not regard as possible:
the creation of, if not a community then at least a movement, whose founding
principle would be that solutions can only be collective. Through this, the awareness of belonging to a social group emerged, with at least the effect of enabling
each woman to discover that she was a woman among other women, indeed that
each woman is a woman to the extent that she is one woman among others. For
once, consciousness of womanhood was drawn from the sense of belonging to a
group.

Women were particularly seeking this consciousness because of upheavals in
the culture, which had long been unobtrusive or piecemeal and which became
more widespread after the war. The writing of *The Second Sex* and the hunger
with which women readers devoured the book can be seen as signs of the times.
Our great-grandmothers seldom had the opportunity to think about themselves
as women—this is the paradox—because their lives could not accommodate a
notion which would have gathered together categories which had to be kept separate: those of virgin, wife, prostitute, mother, widow, nun and, in some cases,
'lady'. They had first to be virgins, which was the opposite of being women, and
when they later became wives, and thus women, this was as 'someone's-woman',
which implies that they were never simply and absolutely women. To be only
when one belongs to someone is not to be, but to have the status of a perceptible quality, like sweetness according to Plato: 'To be sweet, but sweet to no one,
is impossible.'[5]

The beginnings of emancipation in relation to family structures created a new
being in the social reality: it became possible to be just a woman, without belonging to someone, or being an old maid or a 'fallen woman'. This category still
meets with fierce resistance in daily life: there are people who, knowing that I
am unmarried, still insist on calling me 'Mademoiselle', despite my age of more
than forty and my protestations. In French as in English, this is the symmetrical
counterpart of the custom of calling a married woman by the surname and first

name of her husband: one is either a Mrs John Smith—'Mrs' followed by a man's name—or a 'Miss'.

Just a woman, yes, but what is that? Where were we to find the new consciousness of self which social upheavals had made necessary? Women have sought to gain a consciousness of womanhood from very different sources. Some have felt themselves to be women through partial identification with a tradition—of jam-making and seduction by frills (grandmother's life without the heavy constraints of fidelity, multiple pregnancies and obedience with which grandmother was burdened); my generation has been greatly tempted by this tendency, which is by definition nostalgic and retrograde, since it offers a return to identification with tradition. Other women (of whom I am one) have thought it possible to feel ourselves to be women through a better understanding and awareness of our bodies—'our bodies, ourselves'—which is the opposite of retrogression, since women's traditional position forbade them to know even the most necessary things about themselves. Still other women, manifestly drawing their inspiration from some male authors, made it their aim to feel themselves to be women through a systematic project of differentiation: since men are this, I shall be that. In my opinion, this can at best lead only to wallowing in the mire of ideology. It is very difficult to establish that 'men are this', because they differ greatly from each other; wanting to differentiate oneself from a highly diverse reality is a sad and hollow plan of action which soon leads nowhere, for is there any place that no man has ever occupied? In looking for specificity, one condemns oneself to not-much and it moreover means accepting a derivative position, since seeking to define oneself by contrast means that one has accepted that the other has the power to determine things.

The collective Movement has not supplied a unanimous answer to the question, 'How does a woman of the second half of the twentieth century feel herself to be a woman?' This question is apparently in many people's heads, otherwise the glossy women's magazines would not have so many women readers. My suggestion that the Movement and women's magazines might have something in common should and must make my readers scream, since these magazines deal with our unease in such a perverse way: they begin by making their readers feel guilty about their failure-to-be-entirely-a-woman, then suggest ways in which the consumer society can help them improve themselves by pointing to an art, not of being a woman (there is no art which can make one be what one already unfailingly is), nor of becoming aware of oneself and clearly perceiving one's experience of oneself in the world (which would be a positive thing, but which would work towards the disappearance of the need which makes women read these magazines), but the art of being very-woman, remarkably-woman, more-woman than one's neighbour, more-woman than before one read and applied the recipes. This type of game assumes the existence of a womanly essence, which, depending on her efforts, is more or less developed in every woman, a world of competition between women and a panel who make the final judgement. It suggests that every woman should throw herself into the conquest of her own femininity, into the construction, which may well become a masquerade, of a self entirely marked by sexualization, which presupposes that one started off as a zombie or as ectoplasm in need of substance.[6]

Nevertheless the unease on which this flourishing trade feeds is real. It at least relates to the fact that women were long deprived of any way of acting in the world and of any chance of initiating anything, with the result that until recently it has scarcely been possible for them to say 'I', affirming themselves as the subjects of projects. But 'I' is not as independent as one might think from the consideration of what one is at the actual moment when one decides. A concrete self-awareness is involved in the consciousness of an intention to do something. An image of 'I am' is mixed into the definition of what one is going to do. Women's oppression is characterized by, among other things, the fact that they breathe an atmosphere saturated with 'you are', 'you are not' or 'you should be', which more or less prevents them from determining what they want and what they want to be.

'Men simply are, and that's it. Whereas women are something: whores, virgins, martyrs, beautiful, ugly, modest, experienced, tall, fat, small, thin . . . but they are something' writes Cathy Bernheim.[7] This is true, and yet we must at the same time say the opposite. Some men have a well determined 'self-awareness', and Sartre could not have written what he wrote without his. Whereas, when women separate themselves from the various somethings Cathy lists, they are left with a big nothing. Or they were left with a big nothing, not so long ago. Hence, moreover, this famous counter-questionnaire made up by women from the Movement in answer to one published by *Elle* in 1970:

Do you think that women are women:

- down to the tips of their fingernails;
- down to the point of collapse;
- down to their hate for their sisters;
- down to the limits of men's imagination?

The Movement has always been concerned with the question of concrete self-awareness, but fortunately has not replied with any dogma adopted by all. Beyond the various answerPs we have mentioned, one simply finds a kind of minimal consensus: one can know oneself as a woman by being among women and

through concern about what happens to other or to all women. Thus we saw lesbians joining in the struggle for contraception and abortion on demand, women
who had the means to 'get by' anyway calling for their legalization and reim-
bursement by social security, women without children setting up organizations
for building crèches, single women showing their concern for the daily problems
of housewives and Western women being appalled by clitoridectomy or the
forced wearing of the chador. This is what replaced nail varnish and the ac-
knowledgement of the lord and master in women's consciousness of self: a sense
of being women because they wanted more freedom, a better life and greater
dignity for all women. All those who got involved in the Movement, even tem-
porarily, thus gained a degree of autonomy and an awareness of collective belonging. Autonomy in the first instance in relation to the divisions established
and imposed by the culture; for ideology always has clear ideas about gender: a
man is a man and a woman must be feminine, in other words she must correspond to standards which are endlessly listed and honed, to the point where they
contradict each other. Autonomy too in relation to the men we love, if there are
men we love. I seem to remember that they tended (yesterday of course) to be
used to telling us who to be and how to behave. Whether or not they have preserved this annoying habit, we have at least learned to avoid its effects, inasmuch
as we no longer require their recognition of our being to be able to assume it.

This means we have also needed to find out about our own desires, a concern
our mothers were spared. The usual course of women's lives used to be reduced
to a sequence of events in which they did not have to ask themselves exactly what
it was they wanted: accepting an offer of marriage, fulfilling the conditions of a
role and then, for most, somehow or other confronting many contradictory demands. Those of more recent generations who have won material and personal
autonomy now need to know that, if there is a man in their lives, he is not there
to meet a practical or social need, nor because they have simply agreed to an offer, but because they wanted and still want him there. The less a woman needs
a man for something, including in order to feel herself to be a woman, the more
it must be recognized that she (I, you, they) is a desiring subject, who is not side-
stepping the life of a lover.

All this may shed some light on collective resistances to feminism. In the first
place these surely relate dully to the fact that feminism wants autonomy for all
women, while the dominant ideology seeks to maintain their dependency. But
they also relate to the fact that a free woman clearly acknowledges her feelings
as personal feelings, instead of displaying a simple 'probity', in other words an
attitude which arises from a given situation and is entirely shaped according to
what that situation demands. Indeed feminism is a kind of immodesty, which explains why it so often arouses derision. The traditional order requires women's

desire to be put out by the best possible extinguisher[8] and on no account to be the necessary condition of the relationship that a woman has with a particular man.

Honey is still sweet only if there is someone for whom it is sweet, but being a woman and belonging to no one has now become possible: we have moved from the status of 'qualities perceptible to the senses' to that of beings. Who are 'we'? Some women, who want all women to share this position? Or just a potential 'we', who will come into existence when all women share this position? Whatever the case, it is no easy thing to plan to live this way without evasions, particularly when there is no tradition to support our way of thinking. Many feminists have explored the past in an attempt to find positive role models for women, and they are there to be found. This is lacking in *The Second Sex*, as is the idea of a collective women's movement and no doubt for the same reason. Simone de Beauvoir did not try retrospectively to construct a portrait gallery of individual women who were clearly living their own lives, even in the limited field of literature. She is even qualified in her praise of Emily Brontë, Virginia Woolf and Katherine Mansfield.[9] No woman wrote *Moby Dick* or *The Trial*, she says, which in itself is not to display the best possible literary taste. Her failure to feel the strength of freedom which enabled the writing of *The Waves* or *Orlando* is linked to a prejudice which is not strictly literary: no one was an emancipated woman before me. According to the existentialist view, to create is 'to found the world anew', to do which one must 'unequivocally assume the status of a being who has freedom'. It is thus essential to tell oneself, 'I am the first and only one to do this.' The great difference between Simone de Beauvoir and the feminists of my generation, including those who paid tribute to her, is that each of us took the view that 'fortunately, I am not the only one, nor the first here; but I am certainly here, all the same'. . . .

THE GREAT DISORIENTATION

. . . For women theorists involved in the women's movement the feminist experience has been a true experience, in other words an encounter with an unexpected reality, in which a truly different and manifestly non-theoretical 'appeal' was created. With hindsight we can see that in the women's movement of the 1970s women had extreme difficulty in identifying who they were in what they were doing, and indeed in precisely describing the theoretical or practical basis of the action they were taking. Of course in the abstract it is not incorrect to say that feminism tried to bring to light a discontent, or unacknowledged sufferings and hardships:[10] a difficulty of being which the collective consciousness

refused and still refuses to see. It was research, 'in groups which formed, became deformed and then undone', into ills that were hidden even from the consciousness of the woman who suffered them, ills that she had always learned to
hide and ignore. This research could only be carried out in small, informal
groups and it often began with a kind of 'exchange of impressions'. Things that
the available conceptual frameworks do not enable one to understand, nor current language to articulate, can still manifest themselves in the form of vague impressions, often first regarded as strictly personal, until others confirm them and
add their own thoughts, remarks, tales and so on. By means of this mirroring relationship (which sometimes gave rise to panic and was at any rate hard to accept) gradually a collective awareness could emerge of what had been repressed
by each woman.[11] This is my most vivid and most precious memory from those
years: having gradually learned, with other women, to put a name to what was
hurting me, through the discovery that I was not the only one being hurt. This
enabled the rather lost woman I still was to face up to things; but for me as a
woman philosopher it was also a positive experience of disorientation. When one
thinks one has been trained in 'rigour', which, in principle, forbids one from ad-
vancing something which has not yet been entirely thought through and well-
founded, the discovery that whispered, impressionistic stories and openly subjective viewpoints can lead the way to an understanding of the most vital things
is a real lesson, which I have not yet fully integrated, but which teaches the following: it is better to allow yourself to start speaking before being completely
sure that you can justify what you say; otherwise, you will never speak at all.

I digested this lesson philosophically by avoiding the easy rationalization
which was an offer of thinking that women are destined to be impressionistic,
while men have access to rigorous thought. The value of impressionism lies in a
particular situation: when everything conspires to stop people from becoming
aware of what they are experiencing, it is essential that they give voice together
to little perceptions and intuitions, no matter how faltering. As for 'rigour', I have
come to realize that the idea I had of it came from an impoverished tradition of
philosophy, which can be contrasted with another. In the works of some Greeks,
some seventeenth-century authors or in *Capital* [Marx], one finds a demand for
exploratory rigour: when one investigates and tries to proceed with as tight an
argument as possible, it seems necessary to go beyond what is commonly said in
the hope of finding a coherent understanding. In the training we received,
'rigour' only ever meant a way of pruning everything that is not acceptable to all
at the outset. It only suppresses that which risks appearing whimsical or freak-
ish. This companion of the wisest conformism (as though wisdom was conformist!) produces both boredom and illusion at the same time: no one succeeds
in pruning as much as is necessary.

So, from my experience of the methodological subjectivism of the Women's Movement, I learned to draw on a more adventurous idea of rigour which tears the fabric of acquired ideas and moves towards lands whose very existence is not guaranteed in advance. *Capital* is made of bits and pieces, Descartes recounts his life story and his dreams, Bacon weaves his project with biblical memories, Greco-Roman myths and quotations from Virgil and Socrates often calls on strange bursts of imagination to help him in posing problems. Everything must be brought in to undo a world of commonplaces and at the forefront of the project is the demand for rigour: a tonic rigour, full of juice and very different from the safe rigorism, the self-censored (and always ready to censor) puritanism that we have learned. The imprecise and hesitant words proffered in women's groups took me back beyond my training to a rediscovery of the groping and stuttering contained in the project to produce philosophy: many clumsy attempts and much improvisation are needed before a clear and distinct idea is formed.

Disorientation then. Even if the Women's Movement can be characterized by its effort to bring to light aspects of the difficulty of being, it must be acknowledged that this is not a definition. Many women before me have said that the Movement was characterized by various rejections but that it did not articulate what the women involved collectively wanted. Two tendencies could broadly be identified: a feminism of equality and a feminism of difference, which often, moreover, declined the name 'feminism' and sought to separate itself from earlier struggles such as that of the suffragettes. However, these two currents (and anyway, were there only two of them?) coexisted and formed what was all things considered a single reality, whose type had never been seen before simply by reason of its lack of definition: the Movement never delineated its edges in any way. It did not form a party, with cards, membership and a manifesto, so that the issue of whether one was part of it or not remained deliberately vague. A woman from the 'Women's Movement' could be more or less anybody: a regular participant at meetings, a trade unionist who realized one day that her role in union delegations was purely decorative, or the wife of a revolutionary activist who discovered that her husband thought it absolutely right that she should be busy with the pots and pans while he debated the liberation of the masses with his comrades.[12] If the Movement had any particular effects it was due to its diffuse nature: it spread the idea that whatever the 'woman question' might be, it is not something strictly for specialists. Any woman who begins to rebel, to think it unreasonable that she should do all the housework and for this to be regarded as her responsibility, was and is 'in the Movement' and the Movement would have no meaning if it had not led women and men who never went near a meeting to rethink some aspects of their relationships.

Of course there were some women who carried the Movement and others who were more carried by it, but this is a distinction we can make now. When we speak of the Movement in the past, we refer to the former, who, without exception, have stopped meeting to explore issues together; but I do not think that the diffuse diffusion of the Movement is over. People still talk about it and, most importantly, they do so in their everyday private conversations: the fact that a neighbour is beaten by her husband is regarded, not as a subject of derision, but as a problem which needs tackling somehow or other. The very small number of women elected to the French National Assembly in 1988 was noted as an embarrassing fact by many journalists. And those of my friends who have daughters, whether children or adolescents, are very concerned about the lives these girls will be offered. It seems that my generation alerted at least a section of public opinion and sowed ideas which are still causing questions to be asked, even though we almost never meet these days.

This is truly something to marvel at, since, without any very clear definition of who was or was not a member, the Movement also lacked any precise boundaries in relation to its objects and projects. It was not based on a clear definition of what was wrong with the position of women; it was always polymorphous and scattered in groups that differed greatly from each other. Moreover, at the best moments, it began to speak a language which did not respect the usual rhetoric of political demands: many banners and slogans were judged incomprehensible by people who were otherwise well disposed. When confronted with these slogans, many men and women laughed heartily, finding them full of meaning and spice, while others really could not see what they meant and wondered if such phrases were worth the cloth and paint used to make the banner. 'Amnesiacs of the world, forget us' was one for the First of May; another, mocking leftist comrades, was 'One solution, something else'. Many were unhappy about 'A woman without a man is like a fish without a bicycle',[13] 'Democracy for men means demography for women'[14] and the wonderful, 'I'm a woman, why aren't you?', which is worth twenty years of surrealism, to my way of thinking. A British Christmas card which said 'The birth of a man who thinks he's God isn't such a rare event'[15] was fairly successful among my friends, while the one I particularly liked, *Nous mourrons de n'être pas assez ridicules*; which means something like: 'we are not ridiculous enough and it may kill us', was judged opaque by almost everyone.[16]

This was, from all points of view, an experience of strangeness: to our way of thinking, all these phrases were equally meaningful, but some people thought they were all weird while others adopted one but left the rest. You could never tell in advance which would be understood and by whom. Hence what I have just suggested: to our way of thinking, they were meaningful, all of them equally so, but without our ever being able to tell whether or not their meanings would be grasped. One of the great things about the Movement of the time was that it did not concern itself with the public plausibility of what it said. The possibility of incomprehension was accepted as a pendant to speaking freely despite the acknowledged impossibility of entirely justifying what one says. This is far from being the preserve of feminism: underlying every utterance are decisions which cannot be totally justified to everybody, but which make it possible to speak. No discourse can build its own foundations and thus anything that is said may seem 'strange' or 'weird' or devoid of meaning, at least to somebody. Even if it is said by Nabert, Sartre or Hamelin, when they are stripped of the connivance which makes what they say digestible. We can start with Socrates: 'strange' (*atopos* in Greek) says Glaucon of the description of the cave in *The Republic*. Like the disorientation we have described, strangeness has a status in philosophy: that of an indispensable opening. That which is *atopos* is bizarre, but it is also 'without a place' (a-topos): the term marks the unlocatable nature of what is said in the accepted frame of reference. This does not mean that its meaning need not then be made as clear as possible. We have managed to sow a little disorientation. If we did not make clear what project was bearing us along in the Movement, this was due to some underlying reasons, which should now be presented.

TWO INAPPROPRIATE WAYS OF THINKING IN ONE MOVEMENT

The feminism of difference is based on the idea that women's true femininity is suppressed, has been so for centuries as a result of our sex's submission to the other or to patriarchal structures and is now even more so because of a modern social life which erases differences and makes everyone the same. From the 'Psychanalyse et politique' group to the journal *Sorcières*, via the work of Luce Irigaray, women have tried to uncover a womanhood which is neither the distorted femininity of the slave-woman of yesterday, nor the afemininity of the modern woman (if she really exists). Moreover this tendency thought that in this it was doing a service to the whole of society: by bringing authentic difference into existence, women would accomplish an important historical task, for they would remind the uniform society that difference exists.

To borrow an expression from Hélène Védrine, many feminists, including herself and myself, stated their 'hesitations' at embarking on such a project.[17] But to hesitate is not to produce a polemic and this fact should be noted. It seems that we felt we should let these things be said, basically 'just in case'—just in case something important arose from this current of thought which did not appear likely to have any worrying negative consequences whatever the case. Anyway, when a group collectively analysed the ills women suffer, it recognized a sad difference. If, in a symmetrical way, some women were trying to uncover a difference which it would be pleasurable to think about, perhaps this was a necessary counterpoint. Of course there were sometimes debates between feminists of equality and partisans of neo-femininity, in particular because the latter were rather free with their (Lacanian) insults. One could easily find oneself being called a 'phallic woman': I remember a day when Catherine Deudon, one of the Movement's photographers, was very violently reproved because of a camera. The debates between the two tendencies never proved productive, a common problem in internal debates and one which scarcely encourages people to pursue them. Moreover, there was also certainly a common base of agreement, in relation to which these debates were trivial.

The feminism of difference and the feminism of equality have remained precariously adapted to the situation and the confused feeling that they are inappropriate may have done much to ensure that they coexist more or less peacefully (less rather than more, all the same). The former has not managed to prove itself, it has remained at the stage of programmatic utterances because it has run up against intrinsic problems. The most important relates to the problem of the sign, which is no small thing. For this neo-femininity wanted to be a language, a language in which 'women can speak their sex'.[18] Certainly sexual difference has always been largely a business of signs, regarded by some as not arbitrary (which means that their nature as signs is forgotten) and by others as revocable, though with difficulty. It is important to realize that they truly are difficult to revoke. It is an illusion to think that one can be an absolutely free spirit, soaring high above convention and paying no attention to the 'rest of humanity', a rest who feel uneasy when little girls are not dressed in pink slippers and little boys in blue. Like everyone else, I need to recognize that the absurd strength of convention is within me. After all, for thirty years I could not bear to part with my very long hair and it took the life or death question of chemotherapy to make me sacrifice this distinctive sign which I had chosen as such in childhood. Of course we can find philosophers, both men and women, who have not felt tied to the marks of sexual identity: Hipparchia left her loom behind and Descartes nicely writes: 'I am not one of those who think that tears and sadness belong only to women and that, in order to appear as a man of courage, one must force oneself always to wear a calm expression'. And ultimately the idea that we should be able to ask that freedom of philosophy must be defended. But in that case I need to know ('I' being anyone here) that I cannot identify with 'philosophy', in other words I cannot claim that it naturally speaks through my lips. For there are no known examples of people who have tried in a completely unbiased way to explore the entire system of signs governing the manifestation of 'femininity' and 'virility' in a different society or, a fortiori, in their own. It would take an angel or a perfectly balanced mixed group set on a libertarian project to do it. We might as well acknowledge the gap between radical freedom of thought, which philosophy promises, and the narrower freedom of which 'I' am (anyone is) capable. In relation to the question of sexual difference, no one is the Great Subject of philosophy or theory and this is why work can and does take place, started by one, continued by another, disputed by many.

The basic criticism to address to the neo-femininity current consists in noting that it represents an extreme form of voluntarism: it supposes that one can purely and simply repudiate an old system of signs—when it is hard even to be aware of fragments of it—and invent a new language which, far from being conventional, would be invented by nature and secreted by 'womanhood' (for why should one substitute one convention for another?), a language which would at once bring what it said into existence since, still according to the same current, one is located in relation to the gender split only when that difference is expressed. For if one were ipso facto differentiated in that way, all discussions of the question would be a waste of time. Such a doctrine seems contradictory in its principle, like a sort of cratylean dream applied to oneself.

Moreover, how can one hope to bring to light an authentic femininity, whose difference from what has gone before and from all former identities is certain? Identification with our foremothers was an integral part of the discovery we made in childhood of our place within sexual difference. With a bit of luck, we then found models for identification which were less restricted to the family circle, a few breaths of fresh air: we travelled, through space, through the social classes and, by reading, through history, thus realizing that, even within 'alienated femininity', different forms exist and wondering therefore if some might not be more pleasing than others. Above all, aside from these problems of specularity, we were drawn to things and activities, according to our tastes. When we reached adulthood, the state that Simone de Beauvoir calls that of a 'finished woman', the chance elements of our different journeys meant that there were perceptible differences between women; so much the better and there could be more still. In such a situation, to look for a language in which 'women can speak their sex' is, in fact, to reduce this diversity to a sameness, to speak in terms of a single femininity and thus to bring in a problem of models. For, once one accepts such a perspective, the old models come rushing forward, following the logic of the archetype according to which the older the model, the more of a model it is. Unsurprisingly, the neo-femininity current led to a return to pre-1940s fashions, crocheting, jam-making and motherhood considered as a fine art. One may like jam and knitting and think that motherhood is indeed only justifiable if it can become one of the fine arts, but it is a big step from there to accepting even for a moment that every women should conform to this model. And then many men have started to enjoy devoting part of their lives to jam or children: to want this type of 'difference' would mean forbidding them these choices.

Moreover, there is no way that this idea can support a collective democratic movement. If every woman cobbles together some idea of what a woman is, depending on her personal fantasies and chance experiences, not all of which are very pleasant, there is no reason why any group of women should agree, unless it is structured around a guru who can impose her speech as the speech of women. When there is freedom of speech and everyone tells her own story, we discover a kind of liberating differentiation. Even those physical events assumed to be most similar in all women, biologically speaking, can be experienced in extremely different ways. When Beauvoir talks rather sadly about puberty, she is speaking for herself alone and the chapter on this issue in *The Second Sex* should be read in the light of the *Memoirs of a Dutiful Daughter*. She recounts her experience twice: once in the mode of the universal and once in that of an autobiographical narrative. Obviously for her it was a sad fate. In women's groups, we discovered together that we cannot be certain that there is something that can be called puberty. It is the same thing with periods: some women from the preceding generation, including Annie Leclerc, thought that a woman should feel discomfort, women who felt no pain were suspected of having lost touch with the dark zone of femininity. However, others brought up their daughters in the strict belief that any woman who complained of headaches or other ills merely proved by this that she had fallen for obscurantist mythology. In the end, my generation understood that everyone is different. But as long as we stick to one model or another, there will be no serious medical research to try and find the painkilling drug which is needed by some women, but not all.

Trying to produce and impose a model of woman, however 'new', prevents one from getting to know and understand the plurality of the womanhood of real women. It quite simply prevents people from wanting to know about this plurality. For this reason we can link it to religious or political doctrines which have for centuries aimed to define the new man, inviting everyone to strip themselves of the old man to take on this new character. The idea goes back at least as far as St. Paul; stalinism and fascism brought it up again this century. Such a project is no doubt appropriate to the foundation of a religion or a tightly controlled political ideology, or to a form of association in which any variation appears as heresy or dissidence.

It matters little that the 'feminism of difference' has never had the practical means to be that much of a threat: it concerns us here only as an illustration of a permanent impasse, that of the ideology of difference, which arises from a contradiction. It starts by assuming that the existence of difference is valued, but then, by concentrating on one particular difference, it turns against its original programme, suppressing all differences which might exist on either side of the great dividing line which it has drawn. The only consistent way to give value to the fact of difference is to uncover differences by their thousands, or better, as Albert Jacquard suggests, countless differences which defy all lists. I believe, with him, that the quality of our existence depends on these differences, from all points of view. This being so, a binary system is of no use: it is the closest thing there is to pure identity.

However, this ideology could just about be justified on the grounds that any historical movement produces its own myths and ideology, which must be coped with somehow. Yet this myth was never appropriate to the Movement as it was. It might have suited an inactive movement: it had nothing to do with the various battles which women were starting and some of which are still going on. Groups which took up the issue of rape had primarily to deal with the police and medical and legal institutions which, instead of taking the charge seriously, tended and still tend to blame the victim. These groups also had to give psychological support to most of the rape victims when those around them failed to do so, to put it mildly. How could the praise of difference in any form have been an appropriate ideology for such a battle? A battle which taught many that there is no such thing as homogeneity when it comes to crime (an act of arson is imputed to its perpetrator, a rape to its victim) and that some individuals are less protected by the law than others (or than was thought), certainly less protected than property. The women fighting around this issue seem to me to be driven by not an ideology but a morality which acknowledges a de facto solidarity with and a duty to help those women whom society does not protect as it should. This morality deserves to be conceptualized and taught. If I have the strength, I shall try to do this.

All·the same, the feminism of difference has coexisted with another, more classic current in the history of feminism, which is the one we can call the 'feminism of equality' and which, in my opinion, was also precariously adapted to the precise situation. It was no more appropriate than the other for understanding the discoveries of the social movement of the 1970s. Equality is only a simple notion to the extent that it refers to the field of isonomy, in other words the sphere of rights defined by the law and the state. The principle of isonomy is respected when everyone is equal before the law and when the law includes this principle in its very formulation. At the beginning of this century feminism could easily understand itself and find its bearings in relation to the discrimination enshrined in the law. At the time French law did not respect the principle of isonomy. All women were excluded from citizens' rights; married women were excluded from taking a large number of legal actions, a situation the Napoleonic Code graciously called 'the incapacity of the married woman'. But reform followed reform and more or less erased that particular aspect of inequality: women now do as they choose with their earnings, vote and can be elected to public office; married women no longer need their husband's permission to do paid work, open a bank account or take someone to court. One might think that the issue of isonomy is now settled. And yet there are still all kinds of disparities, which lead to power relations being established in relationships between men and women. So where do these disparities stem from?

Here we are reaching the nub of the matter, both philosophically and historically speaking. The usual approach to this question, using received concepts and the maps available, prevents us from understanding the issues and produces a set of false problems or a loss of intellectual direction—not in the Women's Movement, but in everyday discussion. As disparities are seen to persist, despite the fact that isonomy is apparently an established principle, the phenomenon is explained by constructing a different arena from that of the law and the state. These disparities are then imputed to 'attitudes' and 'mentalities', to the well-known complexity and particular inertia of the world of customs, to civil society (which, in the liberal Western world, would object to too much state regulation), or else to the education given in families, in which the state would be embarrassed to intervene too directly. In arguing in this way, one begins to believe in the existence of entities which are then seen as responsible for the persistence of inequalities, as though the education given by families existed in itself and for itself, distinct from what happens in the political arena; as though the relationship between parents and children was in no way mediated by historical realities. All these considerations lead people to throw in the sponge.

But do we really have to give up or should we try to realize that these explanations are based on categories which we urgently need to challenge? The Movement was a school for disorientation. In it one could gain the feeling that neither frameworks for understanding nor ordinary language were suited to what needed saying. We need to push this disorientation to its limits, to try to realize that the very categories in terms of which we ordinarily see politics must be transformed. If, for example, Tocqueville's thought, that great source of today's commonplace ideas, blocks the necessary analysis of politics, or simply does not help us to undertake that analysis, then, although it is more interesting to read than twopenny catechisms, it must go the way of the Athens courgettes. It will henceforth be my concern (and I should be pleased if others would become involved too) to give at least some samples of the intellectual reorientation required by the historical existence of a movement which was able to convince a great many people of the fact that there is a problem. . . .

NOTES

1. *Le Deuxième sexe* (1949). The quotations used in the present work have been re-translated and references given are to the most recent French paperback edition: Paris, Gallimard, 'Folio-Essais' series, 1986 vol. I, pp. 1–31.
2. *Le Deuxième sexe*, vol. II, p. 637.
3. Ibid., pp. 589–90.
4. She says the law banning abortion is ineffective: abortion has become part of people's way of life and only 'bourgeois hypocrisy' stops this from being said. She adds that the arguments used against legalization of the procedure are 'absurd'. She never imagined that it would take another quarter of a century before that legalization was obtained, and not without difficulty. Basically, she minimizes the importance of non-legalization and of the repressive legislation by saying abortion has become widespread. She has the same attitude towards contraception (which continued to be banned in France until 1967); furthermore a kind of repugnance at treating one's body 'as a thing' shows through when she discusses this latter question. But, because the techniques exist, she regards the problem as settled.
5. *Theaetetus*, H. N. Fowler trans., London, Heinemann, and New York, G. P. Putnam's Sons, 1928, 160b.
6. 'You, a woman? Surely not!' said an editor from *Elle* looking our friend Cathy Bernheim up and down during a memorable press conference organized by the magazine in 1970 (see *Perturbation, ma soeur* by Cathy Bernheim, Paris, Le Seuil, 1983, p. 101). These words which were once explicitly addressed to Cathy are, in practice, said implicitly to all women every week: 'You, a woman? Surely not, as long as . . .'
7. Ibid., p. 82.
8. On the question of feminine desire and its prohibition, I should like to refer to 'Genèse d'une catastrophe', the postface to my translation of *Venus and Adonis* by Shakespeare, Paris, Alidades, 1986.
9. *Le Deuxième sexe*, vol. II, p. 636.
10. Cf. Claude Habib, 'Souvenirs du féminisme', Third Notebook, note 57.
11. However, the most active women in the Movement split into 'tendencies' along theoretical lines. The 'radical' tendency concerned itself with the issues of 'invisible work'—the unpaid work that the housewife does in the family—and men's appropriation of women's bodies. The journal *Questions féministes* reflected this tendency. Another was made up of women who had come from Trotskyist groups; this was particularly concerned with the additional problems of being a woman when one belongs to a group for whom life is already hard. *Les Cahiers du féminisme* continue this type of work. But, in every case, more was discussed than just theory. Observation of daily life, puns and biting or dazzling wit produced as much awareness of the position imposed on women as theories did.
12. Evelyne Le Garrec, *Les Messagères*, Paris, Des Femmes, 1976.
13. Attributed to Flo Kennedy, the first black American woman to become a lawyer.
14. Made up by Catherine Deudon.
15. Taken from Zöe Fairbairn's novel *Benefits*, London, Virago, 1980.
16. Made up by Liliane Kandel
17. Hélène Védrine, *Les Ruses*, p. 234.
18. Luce Irigaray, 'Misère de la psychanalyse' in *Critique*, October 1977.

3

SEX AND GENDER

Christine Delphy

INTRODUCTION

by Doris Rita Alphonso

Christine Delphy was born in France in 1941. She studied sociology at the University of Paris IV, Sorbonne, where she received her *Etudes des Supériores* in 1962. Subsequently, she attended the University of California at Berkeley and received the Eleanor Roosevelt Foundation for Human Relations Fellowship in 1964 for her work in the civil rights movement. Returning to Paris in 1966, Delphy took up the position of research assistant at the National Center for Scientific Research (CNRS). In 1970, the *Mouvement de Libération des Femmes* (MLF) was formed from several groups, including the *Féministes Révolutionnaires* in which Delphy was active; throughout the 1970s, Delphy devoted her energies to the MLF campaign for the rights to abortion and contraception. Also in 1970, Delphy transferred to University of Paris X, Nanterre, gaining tenure there in 1977. A founding member of the *Questions féministes* collective from 1977–1980, Delphy went on to found *Nouvelle Questions féministes*. In 1983, she returned to the CNRS to join the "Gender and Society" research group that selected and funded eighty research projects in women's studies between 1983 and 1989. The first full-length exposition of her materialist feminism, *Familiar Exploitation: A New Analysis of Marriage in Contemporary Western Societies* (with Diana Leonard), was published in 1992.

Christine Delphy coined the phrase "materialist feminism" to describe a feminist analysis of women's oppression that derives from the Marxist analysis of capitalism. She began to develop this theory in the early 1970s—along with other feminist activists, including Colette Guillaumin and Monique Wittig—in response to the radical left's subordination of women's issues to the class struggle. (Marxists believed that all other forms of oppression, including women's oppression, would disappear under the new socialist state). In seeking to account for the economic subordination of women within families, Delphy discovered that traditional Marxist analyses could not begin to account for women's exploitation. Consequently, she began to theorize two interlocking but independent class systems: capitalism and patriarchy. (Delphy is careful to say that women may, in fact, fall at different points along the axis of patriarchy and capitalism, so that some women may benefit from capitalist and some from patriarchal exploitation). Instead of trying to fit the family into a preexisting analysis of capitalist production, which tends to reduce women's labor to the reproduction of the labor force, Delphy's analysis starts from the assumption of the family unit as an economic system.

Distinguishing the general economy from a domestic economy, she further theorizes two independent modes of production: the capitalist mode of production and the domestic mode of production. In the capitalist mode of production, those who own the means of production appropriate the surplus product of wage labor. In the domestic mode, women's labor is appropriated by the patriarch (or the oldest male) of the family. The systematic appropriation of women's unpaid reproductive and productive labor, from which men primarily benefit, is called patriarchy. While patriarchy is subject to historical and cultural variations, it is both common and specific to women as a class, and it is their main enemy.

Delphy is best known for her analysis (begun in *The Main Enemy* and continued in *Familiar Exploitation*) of the exploitation of women's unpaid labor in families, which establishes the basis for her analysis of women as a class. Women's unpaid labor in the family is distinctive because it has no direct 'exchange value'. This is in part due to the fact that these services are highly personalized to the individual family members' needs. Domestic labor does not have discrete boundaries, since it is neverending and repetitive. Finally, any remuneration that women receive is not tied to the work performed but, rather, depends on the husband's standing in society. The wife of a professional performs the same tasks as the wife of a laborer, yet their resources are radically different. Moreover, how well a domestic laborer performs her job is not reflected in the resources that are available to her. What Delphy discovered in her studies of consumption within families is that it is quantitatively and qualitatively differentiated according to gender and generational differences. Women consumed less of 'shared' family resources, and often their consumption was limited to goods of lesser quality than those consumed by the men of the family. Delphy found that such discrepancies were justified by an appeal to the type of work performed and to the stereotype that men performed more physically demanding work.

Materialist feminism is antithetical to any theory that takes women's difference as a starting point for understanding women's oppression. It rejects the idea that there are natural or essential categories of sex, or any direct relation to the body from which a woman's writing can be expressed.

In several essays, including "The Invention of French Feminism: An Essential Move," Delphy argues that what is called "French feminism" in the Anglo-American feminist context is not representative of the feminist movement in France but, rather, imposes an outsider's view of French feminist thought. Far from innocent, the construction favors "a certain overly antifeminist political trend called *Psych et Po*" while it overlooks all other self-defined feminist theory and activism. The figures represented under this rubric, Delphy points out, are at best marginal to the women's movement in France, and at worst their theories are antithetical to feminist theories, political activism, and women's studies. Moreover, they are incompatible with other feminists' analyses because they rely on an essentialist definition of "sexual difference," or take women to have an existence that transcends social relations and historical contexts. The mistaken assertion of "sexual difference" not only conceals other differences like race and class but also conflates other categories that feminists have worked to distinguish in the last two decades—such as sex, gender, sex roles, and sexual preference.

Delphy argues that "French feminism" does not consist of the works of these theorists at all, but of the secondary literature that has been produced by Anglo-American feminists *about* these figures. French feminism is an invention of Anglo-American feminists that serves to mask an attraction to essentialist (not to mention classist and racist) theories for which they do not want to take responsibility. (In particular, French feminism represents the attempt to revive discredited psychoanalytic theories that rely on essentialist premises of "sexual difference.") In what amounts to an imperialistic gesture, these theories are made exotic and attractive by being attributed to another culture. By constituting French feminism from without, American feminists have both reduced all feminists in France to a single tendency and set apart from other feminisms worldwide this new homogenized object, French feminism. Finally, Delphy argues that this construction of French feminism has had a negative impact on the feminist movement at large, weakening it in crucial ways. It establishes the bad precedent of allowing nonfeminists and antifeminists to be passed off as feminists, gives them equal weight as self-defined feminists where feminist debates are concerned, and makes being a feminist practically irrelevant. While she does not argue that nonfeminist and antifeminist positions have *no* place in feminism, Delphy does argues that they should not have the *same* place.

In the selection included here, "Rethinking Sex and Gender," Delphy challenges the sex/gender distinction that originated with anthropologist Margaret Mead and was developed by Simone de Beauvoir. Delphy argues that the sex/gender distinction, no matter how it is construed, perpetuates a hierarchical relationship between men and women. She insists that we question the primacy given to sex in the sex/gender distinction: Why is sex taken as natural and gender taken as cultural? Why is sex taken as primary and gender taken as secondary? Delphy proposes that gender is primary to sex in the sense that biology itself is developed within the cultural context of the hierarchy between men and women.

Delphy argues that we cannot keep any version of the distinction between masculine and feminine and hope to overcome the hierarchy between men and women. She criticizes feminists and others who challenge sex as a natural category and yet maintain the distinction between masculine and feminine as a necessary cultural construct. Delphy insists that we must imagine a society without gender, without the distinction between masculine and feminine, in order to imagine a society that does not privilege men over women.

BIBLIOGRAPHY

Selected Primary Sources

1977. *The Main Enemy*. London: Women's Research and Resources Center. [L'Ennemi principal." *Partisans*, no. 54–55, July–Oct. 1970.]

1980."A Materialist Feminism Is Possible." Translated by Diana Leonard. *Feminist Review* 4: 79–104.

1981. "For a Materialist Feminism." *Feminist Issues* 1, no. 2: 69–76.

1981. "Women's Liberation in France: The Tenth Year." *Feminist Issues* 1, no. 2: 103–12.

1984. *Close to Home: A Materialist Analysis of Women's Oppression*. Amherst: University of Massachusetts Press.

1987. "Proto-Feminism and Anti-Feminism." In *French Feminist Thought*. Edited by Toril Moi. Oxford: Blackwell. ["Protofeminisme et antifeminisme." In *Les Temps Modernes*, no. 346 (1976): 1469–1500.]

1988. "Patriarchy, Domestic Mode of Production, Gender, and Class." In *Marxism and the Interpretation of Culture*. Edited by C. Nelson and L. Grossberg. London: Macmillan.

1991. "Is There Marriage after Divorce?" In *Sexual Divisions Revisited*. Edited by Diana Leonard and Sheila Allen. London: Macmillan.

1992. *Familiar Exploitation: A New Analysis of Marriage in Contemporary Western Societies* (with Diana Leonard). Oxford: Polity.

1992. "Mother's Union?" *Trouble and Strife* 24: 12–19.

1994. "Changing Women in a Changing Europe: Is Difference the Future for Feminism?" *Women's Studies International Forum* 27, no. 2: 187–201.

1995. "The Invention of French Feminism: An Essential Move." *Yale French Studies* 87: 190–221.

Selected Secondary Sources

Adkins, Lisa, and Diana Leonard. 1996. *Sex in Question: French Materialist Feminism.* Philadelphia: Taylor and Francis.
Barrett, Michele, and Mary McIntosh. 1979. "Christine Delphy: Towards a Materialist Feminism?" *Feminist Review* 1: 95–106.
Jackson, Stevi. 1996. *Christine Delphy.* Thousand Oaks, Calif.: Sage Publications.

RETHINKING SEX AND GENDER[1]

Up till now, most work on gender, including most feminist work on gender, has been based on an unexamined presupposition: that sex precedes gender. However, although this presupposition is historically explicable, it is theoretically unjustifiable, and its continued existence is holding back our thinking on gender. It is preventing us from rethinking gender in an open and unbiased way. Further, this lack of intellectual clarity is inextricably bound up with, on the one hand, the political contradictions produced by our desire as women to escape domination, and, on the other, our fear that we might lose what seem to be fundamental social categories.

What is common to these intellectual impasses and political contradictions is an inability (or a refusal) to think rigorously about the relationship between *division* and *hierarchy*, since the question of the relationship between sex and gender not only parallels this question, but is, in fact, the self-same issue.

What I want to do here is argue that in order to understand reality, and hence eventually to have the power to change it, we must be prepared to abandon our certainties and to accept the (temporary) pain of an increased uncertainty about the world. Having the courage to confront the unknown is a pre-condition for imagination, and the capacity to imagine another world is an essential element in scientific progress. It is certainly indispensable to my analysis.

FROM SEX ROLES TO GENDER

The notion of gender developed from that of sex roles, and, rightly or wrongly, the person who is credited with being the founding mother of this line of thought is Margaret Mead. Put very briefly, it is her thesis (Mead, 1935) that most societies divide the universe of human characteristics into two, and attribute one half to men and the other to women. For Mead, this division is quite arbitrary, but she does not condemn it unreservedly. She sees it as having many advantages for society, culture and civilisation.

Mead herself does not deal with either the sexual division of labour or differences in the status of men and women. As far as she is concerned, the division of labour is natural, and the few comments she does make about it show that she attributes it to the different reproductive roles of males and females, and to differences in physical strength between the sexes. These are, of course, the 'classic' reasons used within both anthropological and 'commonsense' (including feminist) thinking. Mead also does not question the hierarchy between the sexes. She either ignores it, or considers it legitimate. Nor does she discuss the prescribed differences between the sexes, except within the very limited domain of 'temperament' (under which heading she groups abilities, aptitudes, and emotional personality).

For a long time, Mead's analysis of prescribed differences was the major theme in the critique of sex roles—a critique that arose from a concern to defend the rights of individuals to express their individualities freely. In the process it was implied that 'masculine' and 'feminine' traits together constitute and exhaust the whole of human possibilities (see below).

Although the term is frequently accredited to her, Mead herself rarely uses the term 'sex roles' because she was not in fact concerned about these roles, still less critiquing them. Her concern was rather the analysis and critique of feminine and masculine 'temperaments'. In fact, the idea of sex roles was critically developed from the 1940s to the 1960s, that is, in the decades commonly considered to be a period when feminism was 'latent'—through the work of Mirra Komarovsky (1950), Viola Klein and Alva Myrdal (Myrdal and Klein, 1956), and Andrée Michel (1959, 1960). All these authors worked within a Parsonian sociological perspective, and saw a *role* as the active aspect of a *status*. Broadly speaking, 'status' was the equivalent of the level of prestige within society, and each status had roles which the individuals who held that status had to fulfil. This perspective is clearly sociological in the true sense of the word: people's situations and activities are held to derive from the social structure, rather than from either nature or their particular capacities.

Thus, when these authors spoke of the 'roles' of women and men, they were already taking a large step towards denaturalising the respective occupations and situations of the sexes. Their approach was not actually opposed to Mead's anthropological approach, but rather developed it in two ways:

1. They confirmed the arbitrary aspect of the division of qualities between the sexes, this time by an epistemological diktat: that is, by their postulate that everyone plays roles.

2. More importantly, they considered a social 'role' to be not simply the 'psychological' characteristics Mead had spoken about, but also (and principally) the work associated with a rung on the social ladder (a status), and hence a position in the division of labour.

The division of labour and the hierarchy between men and women therefore began to be accorded a cultural character, whereas Mead had considered them to be natural; and since they were cultural rather than natural, the authors stressed they were arbitrary. In addition, since the concept of sex roles also emerged within the framework of a feminist critique (even when the term feminist was not explicitly used), these authors all stressed that as the position of women was socially determined, it was changeable. Even though the concepts they used were Parsonian in origin, they questioned Parsons's theory and its premise of harmony between the sexes; and Andrée Michel, in particular, strongly criticised the containment of women within traditional roles, and also Parsons's idea that this was good for women and for society.

The term 'sex roles' then remained in use for a long time, until the concept of gender, which derived directly from it, appeared in the early 1970s. If we take one of the first works directly on 'gender', Ann Oakley's *Sex, Gender and Society*, published in 1972, we find the following definition:

'Sex' is a word that refers to the biological differences between male and female: the visible difference in genitalia, the related difference in procreative function. 'Gender', however, is a matter of culture: it refers to the social classification into 'masculine' and 'feminine'. (Oakley, 1985, p. 16)

Oakley's book is devoted partly to a critical account of recent research on the differential psychology of the sexes: to innate and acquired elements of aptitude ('talents' in Mead's terminology) and attitude ('temperamental') differences between women and men, and partly to an account of what anthropological research can teach us about the division of labour between the sexes. According to Oakley, psychological differences between the sexes are due to social conditioning, and there is no research that allows us to infer any biological determinism whatsoever. She also says that while a division of labour by sex is universal, the content of the tasks considered to be feminine or masculine varies considerably according to the society.

Oakley's use of the concept of gender thus covers all the established differences between men and women, whether they are individual differences (studied by psychologists), or social roles, or cultural representations (studied by sociologists and anthropologists). In addition, in her work the concept of gender covers everything that is variable and socially determined—variability being the proof that it is social in origin. She says: 'The constancy of sex must be admitted, but so too must the variability of gender' (op. cit., 1985, p. 16).

However, the facets that are missing from Oakley's definition, although they were already present in the work on sex roles, and which have become central to feminist positions and been developed subsequently, are the fundamental *asymmetry* (Hurtig and Pichevin, 1986) and *hierarchy* (Delphy, 1980; Varikas, 1987) between the two groups, or roles, or sexes, or genders.

SEX AND GENDER

With the arrival of the concept of gender, three things became possible (which does not mean they have happened):

1. All the differences between the sexes which appeared to be social and arbitrary, whether they actually varied from one society to another or were merely held to be susceptible to change, were gathered together in one concept.
2. The use of the singular ('gender' as opposed to 'genders') allowed the accent to be moved from the two divided parts to the principle of partition itself.
3. The idea of hierarchy was firmly anchored in the concept. This should, at least in theory, have allowed the relationship between the divided parts to be considered from another angle.

As studies have accumulated showing the arbitrariness of sex roles and the lack of foundation for stereotypes in one area after another, the idea that gender is independent of sex has progressed. Or rather, since it is a question of the content, the idea that both genders are independent of both sexes has progressed, and the aspects of 'sex roles' and sexual situations that are recognised to be socially constructed rather than biologically determined, have grown. Everyone working in the field has certainly now drawn the dividing line between what is social and cultural and what is natural in the same place—but then it would have been astonishing if they had. It is right that the question should remain open.

What is problematic, however, is that the on-going discussions around this question have presumed epistemological and methodological paradigms that should actually have been questioned. We have continued to think of gender in terms of sex: to see it as a social dichotomy determined by a natural dichotomy. We now see gender as the *content* with sex as the *container*. The content may vary, and some consider it *must* vary, but the container is considered to be invariable because it is part of nature, and nature 'does not change'. Moreover, part of the nature of sex itself is seen to be its *tendency to have a social content*/to vary culturally.

What should have happened, however, is that the recognition of the independence of the genders from the sexes should have led us to question whether gender is, in fact, independent of sex. But this question has not been asked. For most authors, the issue of the relationship between sex and gender is simply 'what sort of social classification does sex give rise to? Is it strong or weak, equal or unequal?' What they never ask is why sex should give rise to any sort of social classification. Even the neutral question 'we have here two variables, two distributions, which coincide totally. How can we explain this co-variance?' does not get considered. The response is always: sex comes first, chronologically and hence logically—although it is never explained why this should be so.

Actually, whether or not the precedence gets explained does not make much difference. The very fact of suggesting or admitting the precedence of sex, even implicitly, leads to one being located, objectively, in a theory where sex causes or explains gender. And the theory that sex causes gender, even if it does not determine the exact forms gender divisions take, can derive from only two logical lines of argument.

In the first line of argument, biological sex, and particularly the different functions in procreation of males and females that it provokes, necessarily gives rise to a minimal division of labour. I would include in this line of argument, with its naturalist premises, most contemporary anthropological accounts, feminist as well as patriarchal, from George Murdock (1949) to Martha Moia (1981) by way of Gayle Rubin (1975) [with just a few notable exceptions, such as Mathieu (1991) and Tabet (1982) . . .]. It fails to explain satisfactorily: first, the nature and the natural reason for this first division of labour; and second, the reasons it is extended into all fields of activity; that is, why it is not limited to the domain of procreation. It therefore fails to explain gender other than by suppositions that reintroduce upstream one or more of the elements it is supposed to explain downstream.

The second line of argument sees biological sex as a physical trait which is not only suitable, but destined by its intrinsic 'salience' (in psycho-cognitive terms) to be a receptacle for classifications. Here it is postulated that human beings have a universal need to establish classifications independently of, and prior to, any social practice.[2] But these two human needs are neither justified nor proven. They are simply asserted. We are not shown *why* sex is more prominent than other physical traits that are equally distinguishable, but which do not give birth to classifications that are (1) dichotomous and (2) imply social roles which are not just distinct but hierarchical.

I call this latter line of argument 'cognitivist', not because it is particularly held by the 'Cognitivists', but because it presumes certain 'prerequisites' of human cognition. The best known academic version of such theories is that of Lévi-Strauss, who, while not a psychologist, bases all his analyses of kinship, and (by extension) human societies, on an irrepressible and pre-social (hence psycho-logical) need of human beings to divide everything in two (and then into multi-ples of two). Lévi-Strauss (1969) was very much influenced by linguistics, in par-ticular by Saussure's phonology (Saussure, 1959), and he devised by analogous construction what the social sciences call 'structuralism'.

A rather more recent version of this thesis has been presented by Derrida (1976) and his followers, who say that things can only be distinguished by opposition to other things. However, while Saussure is concerned purely with linguistic struc-tures, Derrida and his clones want to draw philosophical conclusions about the im-portance of 'différance'. These conclusions themselves incorporate presupposi-tions about the conditions for the possibility of human knowledge, hence about the human spirit, which are very similar to those of Lévi-Strauss. Saussure's theory had no such ambitions, and its validity in its own field of reference—linguistics—should not be taken as a guarantee of its applicability elsewhere. We may agree things are only known by distinction and hence by differentiation, but these differentiations can be, and often are, multiple. Alongside cabbages and carrots, which are not 'op-posites' of each other, there are courgettes, melons, and potatoes. Moreover, dis-tinctions are not necessarily hierarchical: vegetables are not placed on a scale of value. Indeed, they are often used as a warning against any attempt at hierarchisa-tion: we are told not to compare (or to try to add) cabbages and carrots. They are incommensurable. They do not have a common measure. Therefore, they cannot be evaluated in terms of being more or less, or better or worse than one another.

Those who adhere to Derrida's thesis thus fail to distinguish between the dif-ferences on which language is based, and differences in social structures. The characteristics of cognition, in so far as they can be reduced to the characteris-tics of language, cannot account for social hierarchy. This is external to them. They therefore cannot account for gender—or they can do so only at the expense of dropping hierarchy as a constitutive element of gender.

Hence, neither of the two lines of argument that might justify a causal link from sex to gender is satisfactory. The presupposition that there *is* such a causal link thus remains just that: a presupposition.

But if we are to think about gender, or to think about anything at all, we must leave the domain of presuppositions. To think about gender we must rethink the question of its relationship to sex, and to think about this we must first actually ask the question. We must abandon the notion that we already know the answer. We must not only admit, but also explore, two other hypotheses: first, that the statistical coincidence between sex and gender is just that, a coincidence. The correlation is due to chance. This hypothesis is, however, untenable, because the distribution is such that the co-incidence between so-called biological sex and gender *is* 'statistically significant'. It is stronger than any correlation could be which is due to chance.

Second, that *gender* precedes sex: that sex itself simply marks a social division; that it serves to allow social recognition and identification of those who are dominants and those who are dominated. That is, that sex is a sign, but that since it does not distinguish just any old thing from anything else, and does not distinguish equivalent things but rather important and unequal things, it has historically acquired a symbolic value.

The symbolic value of sex has certainly not escaped the theoreticians of psychoanalysis. But what has entirely escaped them is that this should be one of the final *conclusions* of a long progression: the point of arrival and not of departure. Unfortunately, this blind spot is one that many feminists share with psychoanalysts.

As society locates the sign that marks out the dominants from the dominated within the zone of physical traits, two further remarks need to be made.

First, the marker is not found in a pure state, all ready for use. As Hurtig and Pichevin (1986) have shown, biologists see sex as made up of several indicators which are more or less correlated one with another, and the majority are continuous variables (occurring in varying degrees). So in order for sex to be used as a dichotomous classification, the indicators have to be reduced to just one. And, as Hurtig and Pichevin (1985) also say, this reduction 'is a social act'.

Second, the presence or absence of a penis[3] is a strong predictor of gender (by definition one might say). However, having or not having a penis correlates only weakly with procreative functional differences between individuals. It does not distinguish tidily between people who can bear children and those who cannot. It distinguishes, in fact, just some of those who cannot. Lots of those who do not have penises also cannot bear children, either because of constitutional sterility or due to age.

It is worth pausing here, because the 'cognitivists' think sex is a 'prominent trait' because they think physical sex is strongly correlated with functional differences, and because they assume that the rest of humanity shares this 'knowledge'. But they only think biological sex is a 'spontaneous perception' of humanity because they themselves are convinced that it is a natural trait that no one could ignore. To them it is self-evident that there are two, and only two, sexes, and that this dichotomy exactly cross-checks with the division between potential bearers and non-bearers of children.

To try to question these 'facts' is indeed to crack one of the toughest nuts in our perception of the world. We must, therefore, add to the hypothesis that gender precedes sex, the following questions: when we connect gender and sex, are we comparing something social with something which is *also* social (in this case, the way a given society represents 'biology' to itself)?

One would think that this would logically have been one of the first questions to be asked, and it is doubtless the reason why some feminists in France (for example, Guillaumin, 1982, 1985; Mathieu, 1980; and Wittig, 1992) have been opposed to using the term 'gender'. They believe it reinforces the idea that 'sex' itself is purely natural. However, not using the concept of gender does not mean one thereby directly questions the natural character of sex. So economising on the concept of gender does not seem to me the best way to progress.

'Sex' denotes and connotes something natural. It was, therefore, not possible to question 'sex' head on, all at one, since to do so involves a contradiction in terms. ('Naturalness' is an integral part of the definition of the term.) We had first to demonstrate that 'sex' is applied to divisions and distinctions which are social. Then we had not only to *separate* the social from the original term, which remains defined by naturalness, but to make the social *emerge*. That is what the notions of first 'sex roles' and 'gender' did. Only when the 'social part' is clearly established as social, when it has a *name* of its own (whether it be 'sex roles' or 'gender'), then and only then could we come back to the idea we started with. We had first to design and lay claim to a territory for the social, having a different conceptual location from that of sex, but tied to the traditional sense of the word 'sex', in order to be able, from this strategic location, to challenge the traditional meaning of 'sex'.

To end this section, I would say that we can only make advances in our knowledge if we initially increase the unknown: if we extend the areas that are cloudy and indeterminate. To advance, we must first renounce some truths. These 'truths' make us feel comfortable, as do all certainties, but they stop us asking questions—and asking questions is the surest, if not the only way of getting answers.

DIVISION, DIFFERENCES AND CLASSIFICATIONS

The debate on gender and its relationship to sex covers much the same ground as the debate on the priority of the two elements—division and hierarchy—which constitute gender. These are empirically indissolubly united, but they need to be distinguished analytically. If it is accepted that there is a line of demarcation between 'natural' and socially constructed differences, and that at least some differences are socially constructed, then there is a framework for conceptualising gender. This means, or should mean, recognising that hierarchy forms the foundation for differences—for all differences, not just gender.

However, even when this is accepted as an explanation, it is not accepted as a politics, nor as a vision of the future, by feminists. It is not their Utopia. All feminists reject the sex/gender hierarchy, but very few are ready to admit that the logical consequence of this rejection is a refusal of sex roles, and the disappearance of gender. Feminists seem to want to abolish hierarchy and even sex roles, but not difference itself. They want to abolish the contents but not the container. They all want to keep some elements of gender. Some want to keep more, others less, but at the very least they want to maintain the classification. Very few indeed are happy to contemplate there being simply anatomical sexual differences which are not given any social significance or symbolic value. Suddenly, the categories they use for analysis, which elsewhere clearly distinguish those who think difference comes *first* and hierarchy *afterwards* from those who think the contents of the divided groups are the *product* of the hierarchical division, become muzzy, and the divergence between the two schools fades away.

This is especially clear in the debates on values. Feminist (and many other!) theorists generally accept that values are socially constructed and historically acquired, but they seem to think they must nonetheless be preserved. There are two typical variants on this position. One says we must distribute masculine and feminine values throughout the whole of humanity; the other says that masculine and feminine values must each be maintained in their original group. The latter is currently especially common among women who do not want to share feminine values with men. I am not sure whether this is because they believe men are unworthy or incapable of sustaining these values, or because they know men do not want them anyway. But we might well ask how women who are 'nurturing' and proud of it are going to become the equals of unchanged men—who are going to continue to drain these women's time? This is not a minor contradiction. It shows, rather, that if intellectual confusion produces political confusion, it is also possible to wonder, in a mood of despair, if there is not, behind the intellectual haze, a deep and unacknowledged desire *not* to change.

In any case, both variants of the debate show an implicit interpretation of the present situation, which contradicts the problematic of gender. On the one hand, there is a desire to retain a system of classification, even though (it is said) it has outlived its function of *establishing* a hierarchy between individuals—which would seem to indicate that people do not *really* think that gender is a social classification. On the other hand, there is a vision of values which is very similar to Margaret Mead's, which can be summarised as: all human potentialities are already actually represented, but they are divided up between men and women. 'Masculine' plus 'feminine' subcultures, in fact culture itself, is not the product of a hierarchical society. It is independent of the social structure. The latter is simply superimposed upon it.

HIERARCHY AS NECESSARILY PRIOR TO DIVISION

This last view is contrary to everything we know about the relationship between social structure and culture. In the marxist tradition, and more generally in contemporary sociology whether marxist or not, it is held that the social structure is primary. This implies, as far as values are concerned, that they are, and cannot but be, appropriate to the structure of the society in question. Our society is hierarchical, and consequently its values are also hierarchically arranged. But this is not the only consequence, since Mead's model also allows for this.

Rather, if we accept that values are appropriate to social structures, then we must accept that values are *hierarchical* in general, and that those of the dominated are no less hierarchical than those of the dominants. According to this hypothesis, we must also accept that masculinity and femininity are not just, or rather not at all, what they were in Mead's model—a division of the traits which are (1) present in a potential form in both sexes, or (2) present in all forms of possible and imaginable societies. According to the 'appropriateness' paradigm (i.e. the social construction of values), masculinity and femininity are the cultural creations of a society based on a gender hierarchy (as well as, of course, on other hierarchies). This means not only that they are linked to one another in a relationship of complementarity and opposition, but also that this structure determines the *content of each of these categories* and not just their relationship. It may be that together they cover the totality of human traits *which exist today*, but we cannot presume that even together they cover the whole spectrum of human potentialities. If we follow the 'appropriateness' paradigm, changing the respective statuses of the groups would lead to neither an alignment of all individuals on a single model, nor a happy hybrid of the two models.

Both the other sorts of conjecture presuppose, however, that these 'models' (i.e. the 'feminine' and the 'masculine') exist *sui generis*, and both imply a projection into a changed future of traits and values that exist now, prior to the change in the social structure.

To entrust oneself to this sort of guesswork, which moreover is totally implicit, requires a quite untenable, static view of culture. Even if it was progressive when Margaret Mead was writing just to admit that cultures varied and that values were arbitrarily divided between groups, this view is no longer tenable. It assumes the invariability of a universal human subject, and this has been invalidated by historians' studies of 'mentalities', and by the social constructionist ap-

proaches inspired (even if generally unwittingly) by the marxist principles discussed above.

This vision of culture as static is, however, fundamental to all the variants of
the notion of positive complementarity between men and women (even if those
who hold such views do not recognise it).[4] They all presuppose that values precede their hierarchical organisation (as in Mead's model), and this stasis can only
lead us back to 'nature': in this case, to human nature.

Such a point of view, and only such a point of view, can explain why Mead was
afraid that everyone would become the same, which was counter to nature. The
fear that a generalised sameness, or absence of differentiation, would be provoked
by the disappearance of what is apparently the only kind of difference that we
know (for this viewpoint ignores all other sorts of variance)[5] is, of course, not new;
though currently the fear that the world will align on a single model often takes
the more specific form that the single model will be the current masculine model.
This (it is said) will be the price we shall have to pay for equality; and (it is said) it
is (perhaps) too high a price. However, this fear is groundless, since it is based on
a static, hence essentialist, vision of women and men, which is a corollary to the
belief that hierarchy was in some way added on to an essential dichotomy.

Within a gender framework such fears are simply incomprehensible. If
women were the equals of men, men would no longer equal themselves. Why
then should women resemble what men would have ceased to be? If we define
men within a gender framework, they are first and foremost dominants with
characteristics that enable them to remain dominants. To be like them would
also be to be dominants; but this is a contradiction in terms. If, in a collective
couple constituted of dominants and dominated, either of the categories is suppressed, then the domination is *ipso facto* suppressed. Hence, the other category of the couple is also suppressed. Or to put it another way, to be dominant
one must have someone to dominate. One can no more conceive of a society
where everyone is 'dominant' than of one where everyone is 'richest'.

It is also not possible to imagine the values of a future egalitarian society as
being the sum, or a combination, of existing masculine and feminine values, for
these values were created in, and by, hierarchy. So how could they survive the
end of hierarchy?

The vision of a society where values existed as 'entities', prior to their being
organised into a hierarchy, is, as I have said, static and ultimately naturalist. But
it is also not an isolated idea. It is part of a whole ensemble of ideas which includes: first, commonsense and academic theories of sexuality that involve a
double confusion: a confusion of anatomical sex with sexuality, and of sexuality
with procreation; and second, a deep cultural theme to which these theories
themselves refer back: namely that each individual is essentially incomplete in

so far as he or she is sexed. Emotional resistance and intellectual obstacles to thinking about gender both originate from this: from the individual and collective consciousness.

This is what I previously called 'a set of confused representations turning around a belief in the necessity of close and permanent relations between most males and most females' (Delphy, 1980). I wanted to call this set (of representations) 'heterosexuality', but it has been suggested that it would be better called 'complementarity'. Its emblem is the image of heterosexual intercourse, and this gives it a social meaning and an emotional charge which is explicable only by its symbolic value. It could, therefore, equally be called a *set* of representations of 'fitting together'.

It would be interesting to develop this reflection further in relation to two main sets of questions: first, how this whole set of ideas forms a view of the world as a whole which is more than the sum of its parts—which possesses a mystical and non-rational character (a cosmogony): and second, how this cosmogony informs and determines the explicit and implicit premises of much scientific research—including feminist research and lesbian research.

IMAGINATION AND KNOWLEDGE

We do not know what the values, individual personality traits, and culture of a non-hierarchical society would be like, and we have great difficulty in imagining it. But to imagine it we must think that it is possible. And it *is* possible. Practices produce values: other practices produce other values.

Perhaps it is our difficulty in getting beyond the present, tied to our fear of the unknown, which curbs us in our Utopian flights, as also in our progress at the level of knowledge—since the two are necessary to one another. To construct another future we obviously need an analysis of the present, but what is less recognised is that having a Utopian vision is one of the indispensable staging-posts in the scientific process—in *all* scientific work. We can only analyse what *does* exist by imagining what does *not* exist, because to understand what is, we must ask how it came about. And asking how it came to exist must involve two operations. The first I described earlier when I said that we must admit we do not know the answers when we think we do (Descartes's famous 'suspension of judgment'). The second operation is admitting, even if it is contrary to the evidence of our senses, that something which exists, need not exist.

In conclusion, I would say that perhaps we shall only really be able to think about gender on the day when we can imagine non-gender. But if Newton could do it for falling apples, we should be able to do it for ourselves as women.

NOTES

1. An earlier version of this article, 'Penser le genre: Quels problemes?', appeared in Marie-Claude Hurtig *et al*). (Eds) *Sexe et genre: de la hiérarchie entre les sexes*, 1991. Paris, Éditions du Centre National de la Recherche Scientifique.
   The present version was translated (by Diana Leonard) and appeared first in 1993 in *Women's Studies International Forum*, 16(1), pp. 1–9.
2. See, for example, Archer and Lloyd (1985), who say gender will continue because it is a 'practical way of classifying people'.
3. This is 'the final arbiter' of the dichotomous sex classification for the state according to Money and Ehrhardt (1972, quoted by Hurtig and Pichevin, 1985).
4. There is, however, no single meaning to complementarity. The paradigm of hierarchy as the basis of division *also* implies complementarity, although in a negative sense.
5. This would mean that I would only talk to a male baker since I would no longer be able to distinguish a female baker from myself.

REFERENCES

Archer, J. and Lloyd, B. (1985 revised edn.) *Sex and Gender*, Cambridge, Cambridge University Press.

Delphy, C. (1980) 'A Materialist Feminism *is* Possible', *Feminist Review*, no. 4, pp. 79–104.

Derrida, J. (1976) *Of Grammatology* (translated Gayatri Spivak), Baltimore, Johns Hopkins University Press.

Guillaumin, C. (1982) 'The Question of Difference', *Feminist Issues*, vol. 2, no. 1, pp. 33–52). Reprinted in Guillaumin (1995), chapter 11.

Guillaumin, C. (1982) 'The Question of Difference', *Feminist Issues*, vol. 2, no. 1, pp. 33–52.

Guillaumin, C. (1985) 'The Masculine: Denotations/Connotations'. *Feminist Issues*, vol. 5, no. 1.

Hurtig, M.-C. and Pichevin, M.-F. (1985) 'La variable sexe en psychologie: Donne ou construct?', *Cahiers de Psychologie Cognitive*, vol. 5, no. 2, pp. 187–228.

Hurtig, M.-C. and Pichevin, M.-F. (1986) *La différence des sexes*, Paris, Tierce.

Komarovsky, M. (1950) 'Functional Analysis of Sex Roles', *American Sociological Review*, vol. 15, no. 4.

Lévi-Strauss, C. (1969) *The Elementary Structures of Kinship*, London, Eyre and Spottiswoode.

Mathieu, N.-C. (1980) 'Masculinity/femininity', *Feminist Issues*, vol. 1, no. 1, pp. 51–69.

Mathieu, N.-C. (1991) *L'Anatomie politique. Catégorisations et idéologies du sexe*, Paris, Côté-femmes.

Mead, M. (1935) *Sex and Temperament in Three Primitive Societies*, New York: William Morrow.

Michel, A. (1959) *Famille, industrialisation, logement*, Paris, Centre National de Recherche Scientifique.

Michel, A. (1960) 'La femme dans la famille française', *Cahiers Internationaux de Sociologie*, 111.

Moia, M. (1981) *La Saumone*, Paris, Mercure de France.

Money, J. and Ehrhardt, A. (1972) *Man and Woman, Boy and Girl*, Baltimore, Johns Hopkins University Press.

Murdock, G. (1949) *Social Structure*, New York, Macmillan.

Myrdal, A. and Klein, V. (1956) *Women's Two Roles: Home and Work*, London, Routledge and Kegan Paul.

Oakley, A. (1972/1985) *Sex, Gender and Society*, London, Temple Smith (revised edition, 1985, Gower).

Oakley, A. (1976) 'Wisewoman and Medicine Man: changes in the management of childbirth', in Mitchell, J. and Oakley, A. (Eds) *The Rights and Wrongs of Women*, Harmondsworth, Penguin.

Rubin, G. (1975) 'The Traffic in Women: notes on the "political economy" of sex', in Reiter, R.R. (Ed.) *Toward an Anthropology of Women*, London and New York, Monthly Review Press, pp. 157–210.

Saussure, F. de (1959) *Course in General Linguistics* (trans. W. Baskin), London, The Philosophical Library.

Tabet, P. (1982) 'Hands, Tools, Weapons', *Feminist Issues*, vol. 2, no. 2, pp. 3–62.

Varikas, E. (1987) 'Droit naturel, nature féminine et égalité de sexes', *L'Homme et la Société*, vol. 21, nos 85–86, pp. 98–112.

Wittig, M. (1992) *The Straight Mind and Other Essays*, Boston, Beacon Press/Hemel Hempstead, Harvester Wheatsheaf.

4

SEX AND RACE ARE NOT NATURAL

Colette Guillaumin

INTRODUCTION

by Doris Rita Alphonso

Colette Guillaumin was born in France in 1934. She received her doctorate in sociology from the University of Paris, IV, Sorbonne, in 1969. One of the original founders (with Simone de Beauvoir and Christine Delphy, among others) of the feminist collective that produced the journal *Questions féministes* in 1977, she served on its editorial board until the collective disbanded in 1980. She now serves on the editorial board for another leading feminist journal, *Le Genre Humain*. Guillaumin is an active member in the International Association for the Study of Racism (The Netherlands), and the *Association Nationale des Etudes Féministes* (ANEF). Currently, she is director of research at the National Center for Scientific Research (CNRS) in Paris, where she heads a team on "Migration and Society." Her most recent work focuses on how the appropriation of women's labor (*sexage*) relates to the formation of national, religious, and cultural identities. In addition, she is a lecturer in feminist social theory at the University of Paris VII, Denis Diderot, participates in colloquia throughout France, and has been invited to give seminars in Germany, Belgium, Switzerland, and Canada. The recent publication, in English, of her collected essays, *Racism, Sexism, Power and Ideology*, has sparked new interest in her work.

Guillaumin's work arises in the context of debates in the social sciences that oppose essentialist and constructivist analyses. The first takes "race" to be a natural or biological category, while the latter takes "race" to refer to social or cultural groups. Guillaumin finds that both views share a belief in the existence of the category of race, a view that she contests. Instead of taking "race" as a given and then explaining racism as the product of race hierarchization (the received view), Guillaumin inverts the relations between race and racism. She argues that it is racist ideologies that produce the very idea of 'natural' races. Therefore, any

racism a precursor to race

appeal to 'natural' races in explaining the existence of racism is tautological. This
rather daring deconstructive move is rigorously substantiated by an account of
the sociohistorical process by which the belief in 'natural' categories, such as
race, are produced.

Guillaumin's work is also situated in the context of the burgeoning feminist
movement of the late 1960s from which two tendencies emerged: radical feminism and Marxist feminism. In the 1960s, radical feminists argued that women's
oppression and exploitation by men is the basis for capitalism and, therefore, the
primary form of oppression. Marxist feminists believed that women's oppression
does not precede the exploitation of the working class and held out hope for a
new socialist state in which all oppression is abolished, including sexism. Guillaumin's work is part of a third tendency, between radical and Marxist feminism,
called materialist feminism. This tendency provides an alternative because it
fashions a nonessentialist category of "woman" for political struggle. Feminist
materialism takes women to be a class in the Marxist sense while socially opposing them to men in patriarchy. In particular, Guillaumin's analysis provides
an analysis of women's oppression as a class while engaging in a critique of all
'natural' categories, including the category of "woman."

Over the past twenty-five years, Guillaumin has become one of France's leading social scientists on questions of sex and race ideologies, although her work is
less widely known than that of some other feminists in this volume. Her groundbreaking work *L'Idéologie raciste: Genèse et language actuel* (1972) offers a genealogy of the idea of race that establishes the basis for her original analysis of
racist, sexist, and right-wing ideologies. Because this work has not been translated, Guillaumin is known to English-speaking sociologists mainly through her
early essay "The Idea of Race and Its Elevation to Autonomous Scientific and
Legal Status" published in translation by UNESCO. Her work on sexist ideologies was published throughout the 1980s in *Feminist Issues*, where especially the
two-part essay "The Practice of Power and Belief in Nature" became known to
a feminist audience. Until the 1995 publication of her collected essays, *Racism,
Sexism, Power and Ideology*, Guillaumin's English-speaking audience was split
between the social scientists familiar with her analysis of racist ideologies and
feminists familiar with her analysis of sexist ideologies. However, the strength of
her analysis lies in its ability to see racism and sexism as parallel ideologies, both
relying on a shared belief in innate 'natural' differences.

Guillaumin offers a feminist materialist critique of social relations that is
grounded in the appropriation of human bodies. She shares with other feminist
materialists the idea that women as a class are appropriated for their labor. Unlike other Marxist materialists, Guillaumin's analysis does not delimit labor to
capitalist production; instead she maintains that the power of labor lies within
bodies and cannot be extricated from social and material realities. The appro-

priation of labor is accomplished through the appropriation of bodies, bodies that are marked by 'natural' race or sex differences. To parallel slavery (*esclavage*), the process by which women are appropriated is termed *sexage* by Guillaumin. Her analysis shows that just as slavery relies upon racist ideologies that are based on the idea of 'natural' races, *sexage* relies upon sexist ideologies that are based on the idea that there are two 'natural' sexes.

Both slavery and *sexage* rely on a "naturalist false consciousness" by which the naturalized marks of racial and sexual difference are used to justify the social relationships that make these differences appear to be 'natural'. In this way, women are assigned the unpaid labor of caring for the young and the old *because* they are 'natural' caretakers, but they only appear to be 'natural' caretakers in the context of social relations that limit their possibilities to certain unpaid or low paying jobs. Guillaumin is not arguing against the existence of sexes or races, but, rather, against their appearance as innate and unchangeable facts of nature, and she asserts that these facts are meaningful only within the context of a web of social relations. Understanding the construction of such sexist and racist ideologies is necessary for gaining an understanding of the structures of social inequalities.

In "Race and Nature: The System of Marks," Guillaumin argues that the *idea* of race is not a 'natural' fact, but a sociohistorical one. The idea of race is ambiguous, referring both to bodily or physiological characteristics *and* to a culturally defined social group. Bodily traits are taken as evidence for the existence of cultural groups, in spite of the fact that 'natural' races have no existence at the level of the biological sciences. Indefensible as a fact of nature, the idea of race can be traced to the late eighteenth century, when the classification of humans into social groups produced the first social taxonomies. These social taxonomies combined with the belief in distinct, discrete, and self-reproducing groups (endogenous determinism) and increasingly came to be taken as taxonomies of endogenous or 'natural' groups, or as 'natural' taxonomies. The idea of 'natural' taxonomies historically coincides with the African slave trade and produces the modern idea of race. Guillaumin convincingly argues that the relationship between these facts has been inverted, in what she calls a "naturalistic false consciousness": the marks of race (and sex) that are attributed to 'nature' are used to justify the very sociohistorical relations that produced them. The racist ideologies precede (and not follow from) the idea of 'natural' groups or races. In short, the modern idea of race is an imaginary formulation that is institutionalized by law (such as apartheid and Jim Crow laws), whereupon it comes to have visible, material effects. These effects, racism and sexism, cannot be explained by an appeal to 'natural' differences.

Guillaumin offers a parallel analysis of the idea of sexual difference in "The Question of Difference." She begins by asserting that the concept of "sex" is not a fact of nature but a heterogeneous (and therefore ambiguous) notion that refers both to "anatomico-physiological givens" and "socio-mental phenomena." The slippage between these two meanings points to a false consciousness that masks the realities behind sexual difference. As a logical form, difference assumes sameness as its norm, so that women are different only in opposition to a male norm. As an empirical reality, women are subject to men's collective domination and appropriation—for example, they are pressured into marrying older, more experienced, men only to be discarded as objects themselves in old age.

Guillaumin argues that the celebration of difference, and the demand for the right to be different, are popular even with the dominant class precisely because they pose no real threat to the status quo. Such an attitude represents the admittance of weakness on the part of those who demand and of the authority of those to whom the demand is addressed. The rise of a feminist politics of "sexual difference" is an effective trap that reinforces women's position outside of social, cultural, and political norms and institutions. But even in this mistaken political attitude lies the possibility for a revolutionary consciousness, if only the question of "sexual difference" is turned into the consciousness of how different women really are from the myths of the feminine.

difference between myth/ reality

BIBLIOGRAPHY

Selected Primary Sources

1979. "Women and Cultural Values, Classes according to Sex and Their Relationship to Culture in Industrial Societies." *Cultures* 6, no. 1: 40–48.

1980. "The Idea of Race and Its Elevation to Autonomous Scientific and Legal Status." In *Sociological Theories: Race and Colonialism.* Edited by UNESCO. Paris: UNESCO Press.

1981. "The Practice of Power and Belief in Nature: Part I, the Appropriation of Women." Translated by Linda Murgatroyd. *Feminist Issues* 1, no. 2: 3–28. ["Practique du puvoir et idée de Nature: (I) L'Appropriation des femmes. *Questions féministes* (1978): 5–30.]

1981. "The Practice of Power and Belief in Nature: Part II: the Naturalist Discourse." Translated by Linda Murgatroyd. *Feminist Issues* 1, no. 3: 87–109. ["Practique du puvoir et idée de nature: (II) Le de la Nature." *Questions féministes* 3 (1978): 5–28.]

1982. "The Question of Difference." Translated by Hélène Vivienne Wenzel. *Feminist Issues* 2, no. 1: 33–52. ["Question de différence." *Questions féministes* 6 (1979): 3–21.]

"Herrings and Tigers: Animal Behavior and Human Society." Translated by Mary Jo Lakeland. *Feminist Issues* 3, no. 1: 45–59. ["Les Harengs et les tigres. Remarques sur l'éthologie." *Critique* 34, no. 375–6 (1978): 748–63.]

1984. "Women and Theories about Society: The Effects on Theory of the Anger of the

Oppressed." Translated by Mary Jo Lakeland. *Feminist Issues* 4, no. 1: 23–39. ["Femmes et théories de la société." *Sociologie et sociétés* 13, no. 2 (1981): 19–31.]

1988. "Race and Nature: The System of Marks." Translated by Mary Jo Lakeland. *Feminist Issues* 8, no. 2: 25–43. ["Race et nature: système de marques, idée de groupe naturel et rapports sociaux." *Pluriel-Débats* 11 (1977): 39–55.]

1988. "Sexism, a Right-Wing Constant of Any Discourse: A Theoretical Note." Translated by Caroline Kunstenaar. In *The Nature of the Right: A Feminist Analysis of Order Patterns*. Edited by G. Seidel. Amsterdam: John Benjamins Publishing Company.

1991. " 'Race' and Discourse." In *Race, Discourse and Power in France."* Edited by M. Silverman. Aldershot, Surrey: Avebury.

1993. "The Constructed Body." In *Reading the Social Body*. Edited by Catharine Burroughs and Jefferey Ehrenreich. Iowa City: University of Iowa Press.

1995. *Racism, Sexism, Power and Ideology*. New York: Routledge.

Selected Secondary Sources

Adkins, Lisa, and Diana Leonard. 1996. *Sex in Question: French Materialist Feminism*. Philadelphia: Taylor and Francis.

Juteau-Lee, Danielle. 1995. "Introduction (Re)constructing the Categories of 'Race' and 'Sex': The Work of a Precursor." In Colette Guillamin, *Racism, Sexism, Power and Ideology*. New York: Routledge.

Winter, Bronwyn. 1996. "Guillaumin, Colette." In *Feminist Writers*. Edited by Pamela Kester-Shelton. Detroit: St. James Press, pp. 213–15.

RACE AND NATURE: THE SYSTEM OF MARKS

THE IDEA OF RACE AND OF A 'NATURAL' GROUP

The idea of race

The idea of race. What is this self-evident notion, this 'fact of nature'? It is an ordinary historical fact—a social fact. I deliberately say *idea* of race: the belief that this category is a material phenomenon. For it is a heterogeneous intellectual

---

formulation, with one foot in the natural sciences and one foot in the social sciences. On the one hand, it is an aggregate of somatic and physiological characteristics—in short, race as conceived by the physical anthropologists and the biologists. On the other hand it is an aggregate of social characteristics that express a group—but a social group of a special type, a group *perceived as natural*, a group of people considered as materially specific in their bodies. This naturalness may be regarded by some people as fundamental (a natural group whose nature is expressed in social characteristics). Or it may be regarded by others as a secondary fact (a social group that 'furthermore' is natural). In any case, in the current state of opinion, this naturalness is always present in the approach which the social sciences take, and which the social system has crystallized and expressed under the name of 'race.'

So apparently it's all very simple. A purely 'material' approach to observed characteristics on the one hand; and on the other hand, a mixed approach, more interested in socio-symbolic traits than in somatic traits, all the while keeping the latter present in the mind, in the background in some way or another. But with no profound clash between the two approaches; it is indeed a matter of the same thing in both cases. And equilibrium seems assured with the natural sciences referring to physical forms and the classical social sciences referring to social forms.

Nevertheless, one might expect from the latter that their classifications and commentaries, even if they render discreet homage to the natural sciences, would still declare their specificity, first by defining with precision their concerns, and then by questioning the meaning in social terms of the fact that certain social categories are reputed to be natural. In fact, the social sciences are fascinated by the natural sciences, in which they hope to find a methodological model (which at the very least is debatable), but in which also (and this is the most serious matter) they believe they find an ultimate justification.[1] This attitude is not unrelated to the social reasons which lead to the usage of the idea of nature in the classification of social groups.

But, to proceed, let us accept for the moment that the division is effective and that equilibrium is realized between the disciplines, and let us take for established fact a separation between them, at least in their explicit concerns. So we have, on the one hand, a *supposedly natural* taxonomy, that of physical anthropology, population genetics, etc., declaring the existence of 'natural' groups of humans, finite and specific (whites, blacks, brachycephalics, dolichocephalics, etc.); and on the other hand, a *social* taxonomy, that of history and sociology, taking into account the relational and historical characteristics of groups (slaves, the nobility, the bourgeoisie, etc.). The two types of classification can overlap or not, can have common areas or have no meeting point.[2] An example of *non-overlap*:

The blacks of the American social (read racial) system obviously have nothing (or very little) to do with the blacks and whites of physical anthropology in the anthropological meaning of the term. An example of *overlap*: The whites and blacks of the apartheid system are indeed what anthropology designates them as. But let us note that this is only at the price of another category, which is, if you wish, non-existent, or out of consideration—the 'coloureds'—bringing together both an aggregate of socio-economic criteria (an aggregate without which and outside of which this group would literally not be *seen*) and an ideological *denial*—the denial of the non-existence of naturally finite groups. The denial is constructed as follows:

First step: The fantasizing initial position postulates that an unbreachable barrier separates human groups, that races are radically dissimilar from each other.

Second step: The reality nevertheless is that this barrier does not exist, since the continuity between groups is proven in action by individuals who, belonging to two (or several) 'races', show that there is only one.

Third step: Then comes the denial: 'I do not want to know that there is no barrier, because I assert that there is one, and I consider null and void any contradiction of that barrier. I don't see it, it doesn't exist'. In other words the constituting of a 'coloured' group says that *it is not true that there is no* unbreachable barrier between 'blacks' and 'whites'. By the creation of this non-group' no evidence exists of the continuity between groups, for the evidence of it is turned into a particular and independent entity. That class formed by people belonging in fact to one *and* the other group is declared to belong to neither the one nor the other, but to itself.[3] And thus the system proclaims that human groups are natural, and that in one's natural materiality one can belong to one *or* the other of these groups (or to some other *group*) but in no case to both one *and* the other. But the reality meanwhile is that people do belong to one *and* the other (or to some other groups).

A first questioning can already begin. The two preceding statements—that certain (social) blacks are whites (in the United States) and that a group belongs to both one *and* the other group (in South Africa)—are exactly the opposite of what is implied by the idea of race itself, which is supposed to be a *natural closed category*, and which thereby certifies the status of a group that is first of all fixed and secondly hereditary. In the impassioned proclamations of the social system there is the fantastic and *legalized* affirmation (we will return to this) that the boundaries between the groups are beyond the reach of, and anterior to, human beings—thus immutable. And, in addition, these boundaries are considered as obvious, as the very avowal of common sense ('You're not going to tell me there are no races—surely?' and 'It's plain for everyone to see!').[4] And on the other hand, one cannot but charge such affirmations with lack of reality when one looks at what actually goes on and when one tries to apply the most ordinary rules of logic to it. For what goes on is the opposite of the impossibility that they affirm to us—no barrier nor separation, but a close association, a deep social and material imbrication which far outstrips the simple somatic continuity between the groups so violently denied.

The idea of a 'natural' group

Material 'imbrication'? Social 'imbrication'? Yes, for supposedly 'natural' groups only exist by virtue of the fact that they are so interrelated that effectively each of the groups is a function of the other. In short, it is a matter of social relations within the same social formation. One does not care to assert naturalness when there is economic, spatial and other independence among groups. Only certain specific relations (of dependence, exploitation) lead to the postulation of the existence of 'natural heterogeneous entities'. Colonization by the appropriation of people (traffic in slaves, later in labourers) and of territories (that of the last two centuries) and the appropriation of the bodies of women (and not solely of their labour power) have led to the proclamation of the specific nature of the groups that endured or still endure these relations.

In fact, the groups concerned are *one and the same natural group* if one accepts this classification in terms of nature. The social idea of natural group rests on the ideological postulation that there is a closed unit, endo-determined [determined from within], hereditary and dissimilar to other social units. This unit, always empirically social, is supposed to reproduce itself and within itself. All this rests on the clever finding that whites bear whites and blacks bear blacks, that the former are the masters and the latter the slaves, that the masters bear masters and the slaves slaves, etc., and that nothing can happen, and that nothing does happen, to trouble this impeccable logic. The children of slaves are slaves, as we know, while the children of slaves can also be—and often are—the children of the master. What 'natural' group do they belong to? That of their mother? That of their father? That of their slave mother or that of their master father? In the United States in the eighteenth century the person who was on either side (the mother's or the father's) the child of a slave was a slave. The child of a slave man and a free woman was a slave (in Maryland as far back as the seventeenth century); the child of a slave woman and a free man was also a slave (in all the slave states). What 'natural' group did they belong to? It was said (this line of argument developed in the United States) that the child of a slave women was a slave 'because it is difficult to dissociate a child from its mother', but what becomes of this argument when the slave child is the child of a free woman? If it is 'difficult to dissociate a child from its mother', should it not be free? In Maryland a free woman who married a slave saw her children born slaves.

We can move one step further if we take into consideration the social relationships of sex in this matter. They clarify the relationships of 'race' (theoretically involved in slavery) better than considerations about 'maternity'. The child and the wife are the property of the husband-father, which is forgotten. A woman slave is the property of the master as a slave; her child is therefore the property of the master; a free woman is the property of her husband as a wife and—her husband being the property of the master as a slave—her children are the property of the master, thus slaves. She herself, moreover, was obliged to serve the master as long as her husband was living.

In addition, the sexed division of humanity is regarded as leading to and constituting two heterogeneous groups. The fantasy implies that men make men and women make women. In the case of the sexes, emphasis is more and more placed on intragroup homogeneity: men with men, women with women, in their quasi-speciation. This can be seen in the scientized expressions used in discussing parthenogenesis and in the half-reproving, half-condescending attitude which surrounds fathers who father 'only' girls. But, for the time being, men are the children of women (a fact which is well known, perhaps too well known). What is less known seems to be that women are the children of men. To what 'natural' group do they belong? Being a man or being a woman, being white or being black means to belong to a social group regarded as natural, but certainly not to a 'natural' group.

And moreover the American system—first a slave system, later transformed into a racial system in the nineteenth century with the abolition of slavery—has well and truly defined belonging to a 'race' according to class criteria, since the whites who had (or might have had) a supposed slave ancestor were (and still are) 'blacks'. Thus, a great-grandparent—that is, one out of eight direct genitors (since we have eight great-grandparents)—or even one ancestor out of sixteen makes you belong to a determined social group, under the mask of naturalness— the most adulterated naturalness in this case. For logically if one takes the suggestions of natural realism literally (and not figuratively), having seven white great-grandparents certainly means being white. But this is not so! You are not white, you are 'black', for it is the social system that decides. The social situation is that you are black because that is the way the (social) definitions have decided it. Why then speak of pre-social, outside-of-society, 'scientific' classification—in a word, of 'natural' classification? It is this which makes us ask ourselves about this 'natural' that claims to be natural while being something else than what it claims to be, a natural that defines a class by something other than that which is effectively at work in constituting a class. In short, beneath this single notion there stretches a network of relationships covered with a justifying mask—that of Nature, of our Mother Nature.

The denial of reality in the apartheid system illustrates this extraordinary operation of masking. This system claims—having found another, more subtle means of defining membership in a group—that there is no material mixing between groups. There are supposed to be two races, one white, the other black, each exhibiting its own characteristics and its own nature, *and* another race, completely different, without any relation to the preceding ones, a pure product in and of itself. Institutionally separate, the 'coloureds' constitute the 'other' race, the third element that renders any questioning of the system irrelevant.

These two examples of naturalist false consciousness have been taken from western industrial society and refer to two historical extreme points: the sequels of the period of capital accumulation (plantation slavery) and the contemporary technological society of South Africa. This is not by chance, for the development of the idea of race is co-extensive with that spatial and temporal zone. But it is more than doubtful that this idea still has spatial limits today.

THE SYSTEMS OF 'MARKS'

The conventional mark

During the two preceding centuries, the geographical localization of productive forces has been the determining factor in the *form* taken by the imputation of naturalness to social groups. The European labour force, in Europe itself, produced a certain number of products (metal ingots, cloth, weapons, etc.) which served as the means of exchange in Africa, especially in the Gulf of Guinea, for a labour force directly transported to the Americas (the South, the Caribbean and the North) to cultivate the land by 'industrial' (or intensive) exploitation. This agriculture, which at first had been extensive and devoted to luxury products (tobacco, indigo, etc.), rapidly became intensive, with the growing first of sugar-cane and then of cotton to be exported to Europe. This triangular traffic, as it is called, maintained the European labour force in Europe for mining and manufacturing, and exported the African labour force to America for the industrial-agricultural production of tropical products. But the recruitment of the labor force was not immediately so neatly divided. During the seventeenth century, the American agricultural slavery system recruited in both Europe and Africa; the indentured slaves of that period came from the two old continents.[5]

It is then as a by-product of, and in a manner dependent on, geographical origin that skin colour acquired a role, in so far as the occasion presented by the search for a labor force and the extension of the triangular traffic offered the possibility for 'marking'. For if the idea of naturalness is modern, written into the industrial-scientific society, it is not the same, on the other hand, for the socio-symbolic system of marks put on social groups. This latter system concerns a large number of historical and contemporary societies. It is not linked, as the race system will be, to the position of the dominated as such. It comes into play at all levels of the relationship, dominating and dominated, although the mark has specific characteristics according to the level, as we shall see.

Distinct from the idea of nature,[6] and even in a sense contrary to it, since it bears witness to the conventional and artificial inscription of social practices, the system of marks has been present for a very long time as the accompaniment of social cleavages. It still exists, although it is not always noticed, and in its most constant form it is too familiar to be seen. The fact that men and women dress differently, with clothes that are not cut in the same way (draping persists to some extent in women's clothes, while it has disappeared from men's) is an example of marking that continues to be generally recognized.

Nevertheless, people recognized the dress differentiation between the bourgeoisie and the nobility during the feudal period of the eighteenth century which gave the nobility the right to furs, jewels, bright colours and metallic cloth, and gave the bourgeoisie almost a monopoly on the wearing of black.[7] This distinction disappeared when the noble class melted into the bourgeoisie during the nineteenth century, after the bourgeois revolutions. These latter, by abolishing clothing prohibitions, are the source of so-called peasant 'regional' costumes, in which colour, lace and embroidery express a newly acquired right. It is well known that during the Middle Ages the members of non-dominant religions wore a clothing mark such as the yellow pointed hat or the yarmulke (varying according to regions and period) of the Jews, the yellow cross for the Cathars, etc. The nobles marked their various family groups (groups that, from the fifteenth to the eighteenth century, were called 'races') with 'coats of arms' on movable objects such as harnesses, shields, armour, vehicles, paintings, servants (objects like the others), or on their buildings, on the porticoes, gates, etc. In the sixteenth and seventeenth centuries, the galley slaves, the deported prostitutes, and then the slaves until the nineteenth century, were marked by an *immovable* sign, directly inscribed on the body (physical marking of slaves was abolished in 1833 for France), as in the twentieth century deportees were marked by the Nazi state; this same state imposed a cloth badge on Jews before it started to exterminate them. We know that today military personnel and street cleaners (among others) wear a uniform, but we have forgotten that only a short while ago (in the nineteenth century) a man's shaving his beard was a sign of being in domestic service; the tonsure of Catholic priests, ringlets of very orthodox Jews, and long hair for women and short for men were (or still are) some of the many signs and marks, either external or inscribed on the body, that expressed (and imprinted) the fact of belonging to a definite social group. And there is a very long list of such signs and marks.

The characteristics of the mark vary, and its indelibility, as well as its more or less close proximity to/association with the body, is a function of: (1) the assumed permanence of the position that it is a sign of; and (2) the degree of subjection that it symbolizes. The convict under the *ancien régime*, the contemporary concentration camp victim and the American slave bore the mark on their body (tattooed number or brand), a sign of the *permanence* of the power relationship. The dominating group imposes its fixed inscription on those who are materially subject to them. The mark of status is inscribed in a reversible fashion when it signifies *contractual* subordination: transitory bodily adaptions, such as shaving the beard or not (domestic services), the wearing of a wig (marriage), the tonsure (religious vows), the length of hair, etc. Marking by clothing, much more subject to change in one sense, is without doubt the zero expression of belonging to a *social station*,[8] or, if you prefer, the expression of place in social relations. It is only in the division between the sexes that the clothing mark persists in a permanent fashion today. For although a person puts on a uniform (professional, military or other) for work—that is, for a specified time and in a limited area—a person is, on the contrary, at every moment when dressed, and in all circumstances, in the uniform of sex. In short, the idea of visually making known the groups in a society is neither recent nor exceptional.

Naturalization of the system of marking and development of the idea of a natural group

However, the idea of classifying *according to* somatic/morphological criteria is recent and its date can be fixed: the eighteenth century. From a circumstantial association between economic relations and physical traits was born a new type of mark ('colour'), which had great success. Later developments turned it from the traditional status of a *symbol* to that of a *sign of a specific nature* of social actors. Then began the fabrication of taxonomies that were to be progressively qualified as 'natural'. This naturalness was not obvious at the beginning, when the concern for form unquestionably overshadowed it.[9] The taxonomies were transformed into classification systems based on a morphological mark, in which the latter is presumed to precede the classification, while social relationships created the group on which the mark—because of the social relationship—is going to be 'seen' and attached. The taxonomies thus served as anchoring for the development of the idea of race, but the idea of endo-determinism spread little by little onto the schema of marking, which was completely classical at its beginning.

However that may be, the morphological 'mark' does not precede the social relationship, any more than branding or the tattooing of a number do. I alluded above to the triangular traffic and to the role played by the spatial/temporal extension of this process. At the end of the seventeenth century and at the beginning of the eighteenth, the capture of a labor force for the Americas from just one region of the world—the Gulf of Guinea and East Africa—to the exclusion of Europe, played the role of catalyst in the formation of the idea of race, which was done through the means of the class 'mark'. The accidents of economic history furnished in this case a ready-made form. But in fact the process of the appropriation of slaves had already been going on for around a century when the first taxonomies that included somatic characteristics appeared: the mark *followed* slavery and in no way preceded the slave grouping. The slave system was already constituted when the inventing of the races was thought up.

This system developed from something completely different from the somatic appearance of its actors. It is heart-rending to hear so many well-intentioned people (then as now) question themselves about the reasons that could exist for 'reducing the blacks to slavery' (contempt, they think; visibility; who knows what else?). But no 'blacks' *per se* were reduced to slavery; slaves were made—which is very different. All these strange reasons are sought and advanced as if 'being black' existed in itself, outside of any social reason to construct such a form, as if the symbolic fact asserted itself and could be a cause. But the idea of 'reducing "the blacks" to slavery' is a modern idea which only came about at a specific historical juncture when the recruitment of slaves (who at the beginning were blacks *and* whites) was focalized. People were enslaved wherever they could be and as need dictated. Then at a certain historical moment, from the end of the seventeenth century on, slaves ceased to be recruited in Europe because their labor power from then on was needed there, with the development of industrialization. Consequently they were taken only from a specific and relatively limited region of the world, constituting one of the poles of the triangular traffic. During the period of European/African recruitment, there was not (not yet) a system of marking other than that used for this purpose (branding). So, *a fortiori*, neither was there any reflection about the somatic/physiological 'nature' of slaves. This reflection, moreover, only appeared after the marking by the somatic sign itself. The taxonomics preceded the racist theories.

The nature of the exploited

During the nineteenth and twentieth centuries there have been (and moreover still are) many scholars looking for a 'naturalness' in classes and exploited groups. For example, the presumption and affirmation of a genetic and biological particularity of the working class, expressed in the form of a lesser intelligence, was— and still remains—one of the strong points of the naturalist discourse. It must also be said that this approach is strongly opposed; it may even be censured. Nevertheless the censure only occurs when it is a matter of the white, male, urban part of the exploited class. All censure or hesitation disappears at the moment when it is a question of the female part, or the immigrant part, or the neocolonized part in the relations of exploitation. Nature is nature, isn't it?

The obsession with the natural mark (proclaimed as the 'origin' of social relationships) operates today with great effectiveness. It does not do so with the same facility in all circumstances. But whatever the twists and turns of the line of argument, the natural mark is presumed to be the intrinsic *cause* of the place that a group occupies in social relationships. As such this 'natural' mark differs from the dress mark or the mark inscribed on the body known by pre-modern societies. For the old mark was recognized as *imposed* by social relationships, known as one of their consequences, while the natural mark is not presumed to be a mark but the very *origin* of these relationships. It is supposed to be the internal (therefore natural) 'capacities' that determine social facts. This is a throwback to the idea of endogenous determinism in human relationships, an idea characteristic of mechanistic scientific thought.

In short, the modern idea of a natural group is the fluid synthesis of two systems: (1) the traditional system of the mark, purely *functional*, in which there is no endogenous implication and which is no different from the marking of livestock; and (2) the archaeo-scientific deterministic system which sees in any object whatever a substance which secretes its own causes, which is *in itself its own cause*. What interests us here is the social group, and its practices are supposed to be the product of its specific nature.

For example: 'It is the nature of women to clean up the shit', a statement that (practically throughout the world) means: 'Women are women; it's a natural fact; women clean up the shit; it's their nature that makes them do it; and besides, since this is a specialization of genetic origin, it doesn't disgust them, which is itself proof that for them it's natural'. In the same way (in the United States), 'It's the nature of blacks not to work' means: 'It's a natural fact; blacks are unemployed; that's the way their nature makes them; and moreover they are lazy and don't want to do a stroke of work, which shows very well that for them it's natural to be out of work'. Notwithstanding that women don't 'like' shit more than men do (which is to say, not at all) and that blacks don't 'like' to do less work than whites do (which is to say, neither more nor less), what we have here is an intentionally purely subjective critique of their states of mind. On the other hand, that which refers to the effective experiences of the groups of 'women' and 'blacks' (cleaning up, unemployment), that which refers to the facts is correct: women do clean up the shit, and being black condemns one to unemployment— but *the relationship between the facts is false.*

The spontaneous idea of nature[10] introduces an erroneous relationship between the facts; it changes the very character of these facts. And it does this in a particular way: Nature proclaims the permanence of the effects of certain social relations on dominated groups. Not the perpetuation of these relations themselves (on which no one cares to fix their eyes, and that is understandable; they are like the sun, they burn), but the permanence of their effects—the permanence of shit and of unemployment. The crux of the question really is: A *social relationship,* here a relationship of domination, of power, of exploitation, which secretes the idea of nature, is regarded as the product of traits internal to the object which endures the relationship, traits which are expressed and revealed in specific practices. To speak of a specificity of races or of sexes, to speak of a natural specificity of social groups is to say in a sophisticated way that a particular 'nature' is *directly productive* of a social practice and to bypass the *social relationship* that this practice brings into being. In short, it is a pseudo-materialism.

The idea of the nature of the groups concerned precludes recognition of the real relationship by concentrating attention first (with the explanation to follow) on isolated, fragmented traits, presumed to be intrinsic and permanent, which are supposed to be the direct causes of a practice which is itself purely mechanical. It is thus that slavery becomes an attribute of skin colour, that non-payment for domestic work becomes an attribute of the shape of sexual organs. Or more exactly, *each* of the numerous obligations imposed by the precise relationships of race and sex is supposed to be a natural trait, with the multiplicity of these natural traits becoming merged to indicate the specific nature of the social group that suffers the relationship of domination. At this precise point the idea of a natural group is invented—of 'race', of 'sex'—which inverts the reasoning.

CURRENT FORM OF THE IDEA OF NATURE IN SOCIAL RELATIONSHIPS

Some ideas of race and sex can be said to be imaginary formulations, legally sanctioned and materially effective. Let us look at these three points one after the other.

Natural groups: imaginary formulations

It is certainly not an accident that the classic arguments about the non-pertinence of the idea of race (I would say, moreover, more aptly, of the idea of a natural group) have been made about natural categories that are not very 'distinguishable', and have been made in the case of those where the quality of the mark is rather ambiguous and even wholly evanescent. Both Jean-Paul Sartre in the past in his *Réflexions sur la question juive* and Jacques Ruffié today in his *De la biologie à la culture* use the same subject to support in an immediately convincing fashion the fact that races do not exist. Although their perspectives are different, both of them refer to a group, the Jews, who, whatever the time and place, are not physically distinguished from the dominant group.[11] Showing that belief in the natural characteristics of sociality is illusory, that this belief has been built up by a coercive history, is certainly much easier in the case where no fallacious distraction in terms of physical evidence or visibility is possible. The absence of visual criteria, which might support a counter-attack by supporters of the natural inscription of social characteristics, helps considerably in arguing a case that is in itself extremely difficult.

But, all things considered, is it such a good tactic? I do not believe that one can overcome preconceived ideas and commonplace beliefs—which go hand in hand with a unanimous and naïve belief in 'races' and other natural groups—by a rational argument making appeal to the suspension of judgement and to waiting for an examination of the facts. It seems to me that, on the contrary, it would be more logical to treat the problem by what is most 'evident' about it to the eyes of the believers in naturalness, and not by what seems at first view to support the argument of the ideological character of naturalness. What is 'least visible' is a trap in this field. For one is not operating within a classical framework of discussion where the terms of the debate are common and the definitions approximately shared. One is well and truly in a situation of conflict. The idea of the endo-determined nature of groups is precisely *the* form taken by the antagonism between the very social groups which are concerned. First let us try to start from scratch and take another approach that calls into question, at their level of highest visibility, the ideas of visual evidence themselves.

No, it is not a matter of fact that the idea of race, since its historical appearance, is found both in common sense and in the sciences.[12] Although physical traits, elsewhere and in the past, have certainly drawn attention, this was done without making distinctions and with a non-classifying attitude that has become difficult for us to understand. In short, such traits were noticed little more than baldness, eye colour, or size are today—interesting certainly, but not the basis for discrimination.[13] Today we are confronted with fierce realities, which it is not enough to say don't exist. We see them, we draw conclusions—(1) classifying conclusions, and (2) conclusions about *nature*—stages which are historically and analytically distinct, as we have seen by following the passage from the conventional mark to the natural mark, but which today are mingled, almost syncretically. Moreover, these classifying conclusions are not false, since people do belong to a group, a social group which is defined by its practices within one relationship (among many).[14] It is not by virtue of its (constructed) membership that the group is defined, despite the perception imposed on us by a naturalist apprehension that places the somatic nature of social actors as the origin of classifications and practices.

So there is both truth and falsehood in these classifications—truth (a group), falsehood (the 'somatic nature' of the group)—and the falsehood lives on the truth. Appearance (colour, sex), furnishes very good information about work (and even about the jobs within a line of work), about pay (or non-pay), and even, if there is one, about the wage level. In 1977 (and still today) in France, for example, if one encounters a woman, one surely encounters someone who does domestic work gratis and probably someone also who without pay, or sometimes for pay, physically cleans the youngest and oldest people in a family or in public or private establishments. And there is a very good chance one will encounter one of those workers at the minimum wage or below who are women. This is not nature; it is a social relationship. In France, if one encounters a Mediterranean man—and it is by design that I do not use a word indicating nationality, because nationality has nothing to do with it, while the region of the world is the determining factor—there is a very good chance that one will encounter one of those workers with a specific type of contract or even one who risks having none at all, and maybe not even a residence permit, someone who works longer hours than other workers, and does this in a construction trade, the mines or heavy industry. In short, he is one piece of the very structural 'labour cushion', which also includes the 46 per cent of women who have access to a paid job. If one encounters in France a Caribbean or West Indian man or woman, it is very likely that one encounters someone employed in the service sector—in hospitals, transport, communications—and precisely someone employed in the public sector. In France, if one encounters a Mediterranean woman, one will very likely encounter someone who also works in the service industries, but not in the public sector; she will be working in the private sector, for an individual employer or a collective employer (a company)—a cleaning woman, a *concierge*, a kitchen employee, etc. One will encounter someone who, for less than the minimum wage (as a woman) does domestic work (as a Mediterranean person), and who does family domestic work (as a woman) gratis.

So here we have these obvious 'natural' groups, whose activities, presumed to

be 'natural' like those who do them, are only the actualization of a very social relationship. It is important to find out how these groups are reputed to be 'natural', and natural *first and foremost*. To find out how that is the 'logical consequence' of that nature to some people, who consider that one is born with a
precise place and task in life, or how it is an 'abominable injustice' to others, who
think it is cruel and unjustifiable to confine to the 'lower strata' or quasi-castes
the members of these groups, who, poor things, can do nothing about where
they naturally belong. Although the conception of what is wished for varies, the
perception of reality is the same—there are natural groups. It is indisputable
that nature, which serves us today as portable household god, is the ideological
form of a certain type of social relationship. But, stratum or caste ('nature', no
less!), it is also true that attention is focused on the subject in order to refuse to
see the relationship that constituted it.

The idea of the somatic-physiological internal specificity of the social groups
concerned is an imaginary formulation (in the sense that naturalness exists in the
mind) associated to a social relationship. This relationship is identifiable through
the criteria we have noted, which are completely material, historical, technological and economic. These traits are connected to a naturalist affirmation
whose contradictions, logical silences, and affirmations (all the more confident
because based on unclarified implications) demonstrate ambiguity and dubi-
ousness. And the imaginary character of a term of the connection is invisible—
thanks to Nature.

Imaginary formulation, legally sanctioned

Legally, and not, as has been claimed for a century, scientifically sanctioned.
And the two terms—*legal* and *scientific*—form a pair in the social system. In the
case of the natural, the legal plays the role of guarantee theoretically ascribed to
scientific fact.

The *institutionalization*, the transformation of the idea of a natural group into
a category sanctioned at the level of the state, was not done by the scientific community, despite all its efforts in that direction, but was in fact done by the legal
system. Race became an effective legal category *as a category of nature* (that is,
a category of non-divine, non-socio-human origin) at the end of the nineteenth
century in the United States (the Jim Crow law), in 1935 in Nazi Germany (the
Nuremberg laws), and in 1948 in South Africa (the apartheid laws). These discriminatory, interdictory, segregating laws, which touch practically all areas of
life (marriage, work, domicile, moving about, education, etc.), stipulate the interdictions as a function of racial criteria by *name*. It is not the fact of their being interdictions that is new—interdictions were not created yesterday—but the

fact that they write into the law the 'natural' membership of citizens in a group. The failure to devise logical naturalist categories by scientific means was only a superficial episode in a process that could do without them. The law came to furnish the socio-governmental, institutional sanction which had not been produced by the channel from which it had at first been expected, even though the scientific field itself had not given up pursuing it.

The gigantic and grotesque enterprise of physical anthropology that Nazism launched in order to enunciate 'scientifically' its racial-legal 'truth' was not an enigmatic dysfunction, but the result of a logic of previous social relationships. This scientific justification, unceasingly proclaimed and actively researched in all possible directions, proved to be as elusive as it was foreseeable. And particularly elusive, since, aiming at a *functionality* of the idea of race, they tried, looking for a legitimation of a natural order, to create indicators that could coincide with a previous definition of 'Aryans' and 'Jews' according to the Nazi system. Frenzy by the dominant group about the racial or sexual 'nature' of the groups concerned bursts out in periods of open conflict or explicit antagonism. Witness the works on the various human 'races' in the post-slavery United States,[15] or the Jews in Nazi Germany, on the particularities of sexual chromosomes in the whole industrial world since the 1960s, and on the chemophysiological or genetic nature of deviance in the contemporary USSR. Whether it be in the United States, in colonizing France, in Nazi Germany, or in the transnational patriarchal system, it remains impossible to claim—despite the efforts in which considerable means and great energy were (and are) invested—that human heterogeneity is demonstrated or demonstrable.

So then it is a legal category and a *natural* category of the law. For it is not at all true that when one leaves the domain of the natural sciences in order to enter the realm of the law, one renounces the idea of nature. Quite the contrary. What is involved is the same nature and a guarantee directed at the same objective. The law more than science came to serve as witness of and assurance for the strong usable belief in the endo-determined character of groups in a given society. This transference shows that race is a category peculiar to social relationships, springing from them and in turn orienting them. The actual relationships come to be expressed in one of the two possible superstructural forms: legal institutions or science.

Imaginary formulation, legally sanctioned, materially effective

The social sciences themselves have a strangely ambiguous relationship, both reluctant and submissive, with the idea of a natural group. They are reluctant in that they do not accept the thesis that races are, in so far as they are a natural category, an effective, non-mediated cause of social relationships (the proponents of the naturalist thesis are found mostly among physicists, physical anthropologists or psychologists). They are submissive in that they nevertheless accept the idea of a natural category, but as something dissociated from social relationships and somehow able to have a pure existence. This results in an untenable position. A total abstention from the idea of naturalness would be an easier position to maintain. But the ideological implications of the idea of nature and of natural groups *cannot be passed over*, and therefore it occupies—even if one is loath to see it—a central place in almost all social relations. Ideologically hidden (if the ideology is hidden beneath the 'obviousness' of it, as I think), the 'natural' form, whether it be common knowledge or already institutionalized, is at the center of the *technical means* used by the relationships of domination and power to impose themselves on dominated groups, and to go on using them.

As a technical/legal category, the proclamation of the existence of natural groups enters the order of material facts. The law is the expression of the ideology/*practical* techniques of the system of *domination*. One finds there the privileged guarantee of what is ideologically supposed not to need guarantee in social rules, since it is a fact of nature. Who can go against nature, the law of the world, the writing down of which can only be a nullity or a tautology? In affirming the specificity of groups, nature passes through legal inscription; it is affirmed as a social fact at the same time that it claims to be the origin of and the reason for human society. It is a sinister game of 'one is supposed to act as if . . .' and then, in fact, one does 'act as if'.

In fact, a natural characteristic (race, sex), being a legal category, intervenes in social relationships as a constraining and impelling trait. It inscribes the system of domination on the body of the individual assigning to the individual his/her place as a dominated person: but it does not assign any place to the dominator.[16] Membership in the dominant group, on the contrary, is legally marked by a convenient lack of interdiction, by unlimited possibilities. Let me explain: Legally nothing prevents a member of the dominant group (which, moreover, is only a 'natural' group by negation; it is 'neither' this 'nor' that) from taking up the activities of the dominated categories. Such a person can become a migrant farm worker, do home sewing, do the laundry gratis for a whole domestic group, be paid to do typing, not be paid to care for, wash and feed children. Outside of a low wage or none at all, this person would not encounter anything but sarcasm, contempt or indifference. In any case, there would be no barrier to doing it, but this person would not do it—it is just a theoretical possibility. For (1) while no one would prevent someone from doing it, (2) no one would require it. The two propositions are only meaningful in combination; each is important in itself *and when taken together*.

However, everything keeps the members of the dominated groups from (1) getting paid for jobs that are socially defined as being jobs performed without pay, and (2) becoming part of certain state or religious establishments. They are forbidden to them. And I am not even speaking here of the usual barriers so effective in barring access to high salaries, to personal independence, to freedom of movement. The dominated persons are in the symmetrical and inverse situation of the dominators, for (1) everything prohibits certain activities to them, and (2) on the contrary, everything requires them to do domestic work gratis, to be labourers, to work at (or below) the minimum wage level, etc. And this is done with an array of resources, including legal resources.

CONCLUSION

The invention of the idea of nature cannot be separated from domination and the appropriation of human beings. It unfolded within this precise type of relationship. But appropriation which treats human beings as things, and from that draws diverse ideological variations, is not enough in itself to lead to the modern idea of natural groups. Aristotle after all talked about the nature of slaves, but it was not with the meaning that we give today to this word. The word 'nature', applied to any object, fixed its purpose in the world order, an order which at the time was regulated by theology. In order for the modern meanings of the word to come into being there had to be another element, a factor internal to the object. Endogenous determinism, which ushers in scientific development, will come, by attaching itself to the 'purpose', to form this new idea of the 'natural group'. For beginning with the eighteenth century, rather than appealing to God to explain material phenomena, people turned to analysing mechanical causes in the study of phenomena, first physical phenomena, and then living phenomena. The stake, moreover, was the conception of Man, and the first materialism was to be mechanistic during this same century (see *L'Homme machine* by Julien Offray de La Mettrie).

If what is expressed by the term 'natural' is the pure materiality of the implicated objects, then there is nothing less natural than the groups in question, which precisely are constituted *by a precise type of* relationship: the relationship of power, a relationship which makes them into things (both destined to be things and mechanically oriented to be such), but which *makes* them, since they *only* exist as things within this relationship. This is the social relations in which they are involved (slavery, marriage, migrant labor) and which makes them such at every moment. Outside of these relations they don't exist, *they cannot even be imagined*. They are not givens of nature, but naturalized givens of social relationships.

NOTES

1. For a critical presentation of this position, see the collective work *Discours biologique et ordre social*, ed. Pierre Achard *et al.* (Paris: Seuil, 1977), which endeavours to demonstrate this fascination and constant reference at work.

2. In fact, the same problem arises in classical physical anthropology, for the 'natural' position is practically untenable. But it is with the social sciences that the present discussion is concerned.

3. At the time that the present article was written, an evening newspaper, in a review of recent books in French on South Africa, used the term *métis* (half-breed) to refer to the 'coloured' group. Correct in the logical sense, this is false in the social sense, the South African particularly. The word 'coloured' exists precisely in order to censor the word 'half-breed'. Everybody knows that half-breed is what is referred to— that is not the question—but *nobody wants to know it.*

4. But it would be pointless to keep resorting (as is the case) to reaffirmations of morphosomatic evidence if—as is often said (even among social scientists)—the somatic traits were 'striking' and 'obvious' and were, because of that the cause of racial prejudice, conflicts and power relations between groups.

5. On the process that separated the two strands of the recruitment of forced labor, the European and the African, see Eric Williams, *Capitalism and Slavery* (Chapel Hill: University of North Carolina Press, 1944).

6. I mean here the idea of 'nature' in the present scientific sense. The theological societies gave to this word the meaning of 'internal order', a meaning always present within the contemporary idea, but until the nineteenth century it *did not include* an endogenous determinism, which is a fundamental characteristic today.

7. An allusion to this practice can be found in Tallemant des Réaux (a leading member of a bourgeois banking family) in the seventeenth century: 'She called him over to a corner of the room to ask him if he didn't find that black suited me well. At that time young people didn't wear black so early in the day as one does now'.

8. I distinguish here between dependence and belonging. Belonging—'being' in a social station, in a religion—is supposed to be both permanent *and* subject to change. One could be ennobled or change one's religion in certain circumstances. Dependence implies a direct relationship, either contractual or coercive: The 'indentured' servant, the cleric bound by his vows, and the appropriated slave were considered to be in an irreversible situation for a specific term of time (which could be limited but which also could be for an entire lifetime).

9. Carl von Linné, the first great taxonomist of the human species, had, as in his vegetable classifications (which it may be noted in passing were, all the same, his essential preoccupation), a conception of method that did not place him at all within an empiricist perspective. His system is a set of statements of principle. He would probably have been very surprised if one had connected him to some endo-determinism, which today necessarily accompanies the idea of nature.

10. 'Spontaneous idea': that is, an idea which is tightly associated with—or indissociable from—a specific historical relationship, and which is always present at the heart of this relationship.

11. Even supposing that one accepts this kind of argument, one can also point out that the 'obvious distinction' between a Tunisian and a Dutch person is completely in-

visible to someone who is neither North African nor European, as I have been able to note on numerous occasions. In any case these distinctions are less than those that distinguish between social classes or the sexes, where weight, height, etc. are differentiated.

12. I take the liberty of referring to some of my own previous works: Colette Guillaumin, *L'Idéologie raciste. Genèse et langage actuel* (Paris: Mouton, 1972); and Chapters 1 and 2 of the present book, which originally appeared as 'Caractères spécifiques de l'idéologie raciste', *Cahiers internationaux de sociologie* (vol. LIII, 1972), and 'The Idea of Race and its Elevation to Autonomous Scientific and Legal Status', in *Sociological Theories: Race and Colonialism* (Paris: UNESCO, 1980).

13. One can only ask oneself why it is so frequently argued (and by important scholars) that the somatic—so-called racial—mark (in face, skin colour) is supposed to be so much more relevant than eye colour or hair colour and that it is supposed to have so much more value as a discriminating factor than the latter, which (I quote) 'can differ from parent to child'. It is forgotten curiously quickly that, as a matter of fact, racial characteristics such as skin colour can be *different between parents and children* (in the United States and the West Indies, for example, a white parent can have a black child). And this difference is more important than the shade of eye colour or hair colour not because it is more visible, but because it is socially proclaimed to be racial and assumes the characteristic of constraining violence. Here we have again an example of the lack of reality in the propositions that are presented as evidence of simple common sense.

14. For—let me repeat it—if there was not a *social* group, the physical trait (whatever it might be) would not be discriminating.

15. See, for example: John S. Haller, *Outcasts from Evolution: Scientific Attitudes of Racial Inferiority 1959–1900* (Urbana: University of Illinois Press, 1971); and Marvin Harris, *The Rise of Anthropological Theory* (New York: Crowell, 1968).

16. And it is at this precise point where we find the break with the traditional system of marks, which conventionally applied to all opposing groups. The groups of slaves, of deported prostitutes, of condemned criminals are in an intermediate classification, between those based on the conventional mark and the natural mark, in which the mark on the body was imposed only on the dominated persons.

THE QUESTION OF DIFFERENCE

RECALLING TIMES GONE BY—(GONE BY?)

A while back, in the good old days, a woman's worth was determined on the basis of her animal qualities. The amount of menstrual blood (that is important: the value of a woman is measured by the litre, like that of a milk cow), the num-

My God!

ber of children she had in marriage, the age at menopause (the closer you were to 60, the more valuable you were; a hectolitre of blood up past the age of 60 was the general goal).[1]

INTRODUCTION

The notion of difference, whose success among us is now prodigious—among us, as well as elsewhere—is both a heterogeneous and ambiguous notion. The one because of the other.

It is heterogeneous because it masks on the one hand anatomico-physiological givens, and on the other socio-mental phenomena. This permits a double-cross, conscious or not, and the use of the notion on one level or another depending upon the moment or the needs. It is ambiguous in that it is typically a manifestation of false consciousness (and politically disastrous) and *at the same time* the mask of a real *repressed* consciousness.

Its very ambiguity assures its success, for it permits the lumping together of antagonistic feminist political aims into a sort of superficial consensus. Difference appears to be gaining on all fronts.

This text seems to render these different levels of 'difference' understandable—levels which are inseparable because they are the consequences of each other, but which are none the less distinct in the analysis. I should like to show that difference is an *empirical reality*, that is to say that it manifests itself on a day-to-day basis in a material fashion; briefly, that it is something that happens in actual life. At the same time, difference is a *logical form*, that is, a certain form of reasoning, a way of understanding what happens in and around us; briefly, it is something which happens in our heads. Difference is also a *political attitude* in that it presents itself as a demand, a project; briefly, it is something which has consequences for our lives.

Finally, we cannot speak of 'difference' as if it occurred in a neutral world. In fact, since one speaks of 'woman's difference' so easily, it is because it is something which happens to women. And women are not milk cows ('females') but a defined social group ('women') whose fundamental characteristic is known to be the fact that they are appropriated. And they are appropriated as a group (and not only as individuals bound by personal ties). And it is known that this appropriation is collective: it is not limited to the private appropriation of some of us, by the father when one is a minor, by the husband (or concubine-keeper) when one is a wife. But every man (and not only fathers and husbands) has 'rights' over all women, and these rights are lessened only by the private appropriation of a woman by a particular man. And finally no woman, even if she has escaped private appropriation, has ownership of herself.

KNEEL AND YOU WILL BELIEVE

But, concretely, what is difference? These things become decidedly less clear. Today this demand for difference leans partly on classical anatomico-physiological traits which are clear and well defined. In this perspective, what do we possess that is different? Sexual organ, weight, height, reproductive physiology, speed. Difference also includes a group of feelings, habits and daily practices: attention to others, spontaneity, patience, the gift for making, or the taste for, preserves, etc.

But this notion implies, while it also hides, a certain number of facts which are more complex and removed from anatomical materiality or subjectivity: the use of space and time, longevity, clothing, wages, social and legal rights. In sum there must be as much difference between our world and the world of men as there is between Euclidean geometric space and curved space, or between classical and quantum mechanics.

Let us take several *reputedly superficial* (I am emphasizing deliberately) examples, of this famous difference—practices which we had all been led to believe, quite wrongly, to be in the process of disappearing in these last years:

(a) *Skirts*, destined to maintain women in a state of permanent sexual accessibility, make accidental falls (or simply atypical physical movements) more painful to one's dignity, and ensure a deeper-seated dependency based on the insidious fear (one does not think clearly here) that women have about maintaining their equilibrium and about risking any freedom of movement. Paying attention to one's own body is guaranteed, for it is in no way protected; on the contrary, it is offered up by this artful piece of clothing, this sort of flounce around the sexual organ, fastened at the waist like a lampshade.

(b) *High-heeled shoes*. We pity the feet of Chinese women of former days, yet we wear narrow spike heels or platforms which are akin to ice skates (and not so long ago buskins several centimetres high). These various shoes hinder running, twist ankles, render moving about with parcels or children, or both, extremely difficult; and they have a particular affinity for all kinds of gratings and escalators. The limitation of bodily independence is well assured by such prostheses. I do nevertheless recognize a certain superiority over bound feet; while one cannot take off one's feet, one can remove one's shoes.

(c) *Diverse prostheses of the lace-up family*. Belts, wasp-waist cinches, sus-

pender belts, girdles—there are no more corsets (however, it is not such an an-
tique article; I have seen them with my own eyes)—limit their effects to hin-
dering or reducing normal breathing. They make stretching difficult and distressing. Briefly, they do not let a woman forget her body. The veil, which has
such a clear significance, is an extreme case. There is a difference of degree, but
not of kind among all these instruments, whose common function is to remind
women that they are not men, that they must not confuse the two, and above all
that they must never, *for a moment*, forget it. (When we say 'men' here, it should
be understood that we mean human beings, of course, not males). To summa-
rize, then, it is a question of memory aids, of concrete reminders of 'difference'
which effectively wear down any tendencies a woman might have to think herself free—free as in 'a free man', or even 'one who decides for oneself', etc.

(d) *Diverse loads* (children, shopping bags, etc.) also mark difference quite effectively. Such loads accompany a good part of women's movement outside the
home, including on the way to work. For when one is a woman every movement
must be useful; nothing of our precious being must be lost. *Necessity alone never
suffices to justify what a woman does*; she must add utility to necessity, the necessary to the necessary; do the shopping while returning home from work, drop
the kid off on the way to work, knit while watching the children in the park, peel
vegetables while discussing all the family business or problems with any and all
members of the family, cook dinner while gobbling down her own breakfast, etc.
Briefly, never one thing at a time, and as far as possible, never with her arms
free-swinging at her sides, never with an unencumbered body, never with idle
empty hands.

Clearly we are speaking of *a comparison with* male activities, clothes and prostheses. (The people whose men and women share common clothes and hin-
drances obviously would teach us nothing about difference. For however discom-
forting or mutilating a custom might be, if it is practised by all persons it does not
indicate a relationship, a 'difference'!) In sharp outline I see long parades of men
in the streets, without skirts, without high-heeled shoes, arms swinging free, who
do not knit in the parks or in the underground but relax there (far from wishing to
censor this, I would prefer, on the contrary, that we all did the same thing), and
who return home at night not exactly fresh (everyone's tired, men too),[2] but at least
not on their last legs, and, in any case, in flat-heeled shoes.

There you have a collection of signs, considered minor by many people, and
which are anything but. They certainly indicate women's dependence, and we will
all agree on that score. But these signs do not merely indicate dependence. They
are also and above all the *technical means* for maintaining perpetual domination
of the bodies, and thus of the minds, of those who are so dominated—the means
for not allowing women to forget what they are. *More*, they are the means for pro-

viding women with minute-to-minute practical exercises in the maintenance of a state of dependency. Pascal was not an innovator when he stated: 'Make no mistake, we are as much automatons as we are mind . . . Custom . . . influences the automaton, which in turn influences the mind without its ever thinking about it' (Fragment 470 of Pascal's *Pensées*). Wearing a full, short or slit skirt, very high-heeled and pointed shoes, and carrying a full grocery bag are infallible means, among others, for teaching us over and over again our difference, what we are and what we must be. This is not done on a conscious level, but, as Pascal saw, through *ingrained bodily comportment*: identity in the process of being born. And thus a dependent identity is re-formed at every single moment.

This reminder in our dress, our movements creates a very unique habit of carrying ourselves, one to which we have, perhaps, not paid all the attention it merits.

(e) *The smile*, always hanging on our lips, the characteristic of an automaton, which we exhibit with the least word—and even when we are silent. Of course, not always, and not all of us (the same is true with high-heeled shoes and skirts), but only we women, do this. The smile, the traditional accompaniment of submission, obligatory and almost part of the contract in the professions of stewardess or saleswoman, is also demanded of female children and domestics. Required of wives performing their 'social duties' and in a general way of all subordinates of the female sex (which is a tautology), the smile has become a *reflex*. It is a reflective act which at every instant reminds us that we must yield and acquiesce whatever the circumstances, and reminds men that we are available and 'happy' to show our availability.

And with the smile comes that zone of evanescence, that halo where tenderness, spontaneity, warmth, graciousness, help, etc., create a mixed image of geisha and Virgin Mary, purported to be the quintessence of virtues for a woman (*Woman*). The virtues demanded of us today are no longer those of a Rachel, the strong women whose solid virtues guarantee the ease and luxury of her master; they are other virtues, but still 'different'. In this realm, that of the smile, of concocting potions, even of less delightful things like hysteria or the gift for poetry, there now arises the demand for 'difference', for the right to be different, for the minority culture and its respectability—woman's language, poetic or medical secrets, ravaging passions, table or bed manners, 'feminine culture'.

HEY! ME, I WANT . . . HEY! ME, I WANT . . .

We find ourselves in the strange situation of already possessing something (difference) and of demanding with hue and cry the possession of this very same thing. This could make someone think either that we do not have what we have, or that someone wants to deprive us of it. Well, the most dispassionate and least biased glance at our daily lives must reveal on the contrary that they accord us, that they give us—what am I saying?—that they throw! they force! 'difference' upon us. They do it in all areas and by all available means. So? What's going on? How is it that certain oppressed groups (and not only women) have at certain moments (and not just today) demanded 'difference'? At least something that we can today call 'difference'.

The expression 'the right to be different' made its appearance in the 1960s, in international organizations and anti-racist movements at first, then in the media. I recall my amazement at that time. It was visibly, in the political context, a *flight* of the oppressed (a flight which was accepted extremely favourably—understandably—by those who rule): a reticence, or more exactly a refusal to analyse the shortcomings of the battles for integration which had been fought within the legal system.[3]

The legal independence of previously colonized nations, the conquest of civil rights by Afro-Americans then appeared to have been accomplished. But these formal rights began to reveal their inadequacy to produce real equality; the distance between the hopes which had sustained the struggles, and the practical consequences of those struggles revealed itself to be very great, indeed. National legal independence is not yet real independence; civil rights are not yet real rights; constitutional equality is not yet equality. For example, we have the legal right to the same wage as men, *but we do not have the same wage.*

We have also seen this flight reaction in the course of the decade of the 1970s. Briefly, anxiety and the feeling that we have been had provoked a pulling back from political analysis, from the analysis of the *relationship* between the dominant and the dominated, and of the nature of that relationship. So much so that a sweet song arose from our ranks, and certain ones began to whisper the word 'difference'. This pleasing whisper really started something; one would have thought that it had been carried over loudspeakers. Suddenly we found ourselves surrounded with kindness, and even attention, and it became a race between which ones—the dominated or the dominators—would scream 'difference' the loudest.

The great unfolding of the idea of minority 'cultures' postulates that reggae or preserves, soul music or maternal tenderness are in and of themselves the justifications for our existence. And even more, that they are the virtues, the eternal, isolated virtues of those who produced them. We persist in considering them isolated from that which brought them into life, and from that which maintains them materially in their daily existence. For there is no maternal tenderness without the raising of children, without their being taken care of materially;

there are no preserves without domestic relationships, no reggae or soul music without unemployment.

It is striking that the 'demand for a culture'—whether it is 'blackism'[4] or the mystique of the witches, or any other of the many literary revivals—associates the tolerance of the dominant with the powerlessness of the dominated. Calypso or creativity most often only encounter amused, more or less condescending (and on the whole not very repressive) interest on the part of the dominant group. Let's dance in the moonlight, invoke the goddesses, glorify our ancestors, admire our beauty, jealously guard the secrets of our potions. What is there that is sometimes so consonant with the interests of the dominant group that they do not get all unnerved by certain cries? He who holds in his hands the material means to control the situation easily allows (although with sometimes abrupt fits and starts) these more or less visionary messianisms, which in any event do not have the perspective for winning the concrete means of independence.

What happens that seems so dangerous to the eyes of the dominant group that the paternalistic permissions and the interested (or amused) smiles change into threats and then into an exercise of force? The quest for and the acquisition of practical and concrete *means* for independence—wouldn't that create the dividing line? The harshness of conflicts in this area, whether they are collective or individual (as in divorce, for example) clearly show that what the dominant group fears above all is the *concrete autonomy* of the dominated, and even just its possible eventuality.

A WORLD IN ORDER

In the word *difference* all our 'specific' characteristics are pell-mell engulfed in a tidal wave. In this way difference joins up with the classical folk ideologies which, from 'noirisme' to femininity, have always claimed that they—the dominated—possess something particular, that everything about them is particular. (The others, the dominant group, are no doubt content to be general rather than particular.)

One can have a psychological appreciation of the demand to be different and discern there the desire for specificity, for particularity. This is not wrong, for we do say: we are not 'like something', we are 'ourselves'. And what could be more true or more deceptive? This kind of breathless chase after a fleeting identity, this hopeless desire for reunion with ourselves—this is no doubt what we call 'difference' and what we demand.

We experience the greatest difficulty in trying to unite ourselves into a single self. How not to be crushed by the multiple uses made of us? These uses do not

succeed in connecting with each other organically inside us, and for good reason! Much has been said about assembly lines in industry and their fragmented
tasks. But it seems that no one has deigned to devote an analysis, from this perspective, to that which, moreover, had not even been considered work until recently: work in the area of domestic relations (I am speaking here of 'housework'). Factory work, as fragmented as it is, is characteristically carried out in
one place and concretized by a wage. But, more importantly, it is done in the
framework of a transfer of labour power, that is, by the individuals who, *themselves*, sell something of themselves, but not their own bodies. This is not the
case with domestic work where *all* of one's individuality is alienated (yielded).
In this case there is no *place* where the *I* articulates itself socially—the *I* signifying one's own unity and determination (for men the body is this place). For a
woman the only unifying factor of her experience is in the person of the owner
of the things and the people to which her activity is applied. Apartment, nour-
ishment, fields, animals, children, business, store, etc. belong to the one who
possesses her as well. This is not to say that the only factor of unity is that same
one which transforms the woman (female, companion, wife, mother—'woman'
means *all* of these and *nothing but* them) into an object. That which for the class
of men may be divided into 'private' or 'public' based on their possession of
themselves, cannot be so for us; in a certain way *everything is exterior to us, including ourselves*. For us nothing is separated, it is we who are dispersed and in
pieces; there is no unity in us with which to be able to determine a private or a
public, an interior or an exterior.

The mystique of 'love' (which today tends to transform itself into a mystique
of sex: desire, sexual pleasure, climax, etc.) is an attempt to escape into some
minimal unity—sensation or feeling. It is an attempt to become a subject (I)
through the experiences of one's own body. But we do not succeed for all that,
because socially we do not have possession of our own bodies. Therefore there
is no place in which to reunite and repossess our various practical activities.
From this comes the extreme fragmentation of our acts, which have a reality not
as much in connection with us who perform them as in connection with a relationship within which we perform them. This relationship imposes upon us an
indefinite accumulation of acts applied to objects and ends of which we are not
the common denominator even if we mentally strain for it. For the taking back
of individual homogeneity is only possible when one is in a position of subjectivity, *which sexage*[5] deprives us of. We are 'used'.

In reality we are aiming at *originality*, not difference. The thirst to be recognized as unique and, no doubt more deeply, as irreplaceable, seems to be a powerful and tragic common feeling. But we women experience this feeling with
more intensity than many, to the very degree that existence is systematically and

institutionally refused and denied to members of our class, refused and denied to female individuals. I have always been struck at seeing in people of dominated classes, women and men alike, the desperate desire to be recognized as unique manifest itself in the form of the 'rare malady'. Let the doctor see in you a beautiful specimen, or a rare or exceptional form of illness, and this seems to be a powerful consolation in a life that is not exactly bursting with them; it seems to be the sign of an originality that augments existence and awakens in one a unique and individual identity. In our 'difference' there is a little of that, and it is one of the effects of domination.

Because the search for a personal originality is particularly strong in oppressed persons, it takes quasi-desperate, paradoxical forms in contrast to the dominant originality which goes without saying, like a gift of life conferred by birth. In the oppressed the desire to be recognized is a rarely stated thirst; they thus experience it much more painfully than the individuals of the dominant classes. In our cry for difference there is the passionate rage to signal to the dominators that we are not them, but that we are definitely us. The psychological impact of this 'demand' is thus considerable.

But the idea of characteristics 'appropriate' to a group relies heavily upon a completely mythic belief in the *independence* of the opposing groups, in their existence *per se*—an existence which would owe nothing to the other groups, to the other group. As if the groups of *men* and *women* could exist in themselves and show a permanence which would allow them to be defined outside of their relationship to each other. *It is an imaginary way* of affirming the independence of the dominated group, of guaranteeing its existence forever: to the extent that we ourselves will never be in danger since we exist absolutely, nothing really threatens us. This is a proposition which is very useful to the dominant group, because by affirming that we exist eternally in ourselves, in our essence, the fundamental questions are evaded. This proposition hinders us from seeing how we are concretely fabricated, how transitory we are, and how rooted in material facts and real power relationships. (Not imaginary, not symbolic, not eternal. And not to our advantage.) From this comes men's inevitable complicity, inevitable because it strengthens them in what is their *practice*: to make us into separate beings designated for all eternity to be tools.

In summary, somewhere behind all that there lurks a conception of the sexes in terms of BEING. 'Femininity' is a sort of being-all-alone, which occurs outside of social relationships. And even outside of supposed 'natural' relationships, because if the human species is anatomico-physiologically a sexed species, this implies precisely that there can be no women *per se*, any more than there can be men *per se* (but this latter error curiously does not get anyone excited; absolutely nothing at all is made of 'male reality').[6] The sexing of the human species, the fact that it concerns a species whose reproduction is sexual, implies by definition that the species is *one*, and that there do not exist two kinds of human beings.

But let us leave aside the 'natural', which is a socio-ideological category, and stick with the fact that human societies consider themselves to be divided into men and women. In this they are not wrong, without, however, being right, about the mode of existence of the two groups. For there do exist in fact two groups in the heart of the society in which we live, two classes which are born of a social relationship, and whose social existence is *masked* by anatomico-sexual division.

One thus makes short shrift of the analysis, and, in the short term, of the struggle as well. We believe that we will get away with a certificate of recognition of our originality, in good and due form, from our boss. This certificate will be obtained with reciprocal amenity and gentility, and at the moment of the exchange will give rise to a few discreet laughs and a complicity all in good taste. Just the kind of pleasant laughs and complicity which accompany—I have always noticed this with great surprise—theoretical exchanges between men and women on subjects as distinguished, pleasing and amusing as those of battered women, the abandonment and infanticide of girl children, the exceptionally high mortality rate of females, the double work day, etc. I note in passing that I have never met (I repeat, never) or heard even a hint of such laughter in mixed groups discussing men dying in war, in work-related accidents on construction sites or in heavy industry, or discussing executives' heart attacks, etc.

Here is the source of our hypocritical reasoning: We will not have to face the real problems. We will get away with symbolic considerations—the symbolic being a guarantee of a world in order where each one of us knows her place. We thus give ourselves the means to avoid confrontation—confrontation which frightens us even more in our heads than in our bodies. We have this insane hope that men will decide to stop dominating and using us, that they will make this altruistic decision themselves, that they will 'recognize' us, that they will *give* us permission to liberate ourselves, that they will give us freedom and, for good measure, that they will give us love. And they will do that, we believe, because if we are not 'like them' but 'different' they will have nothing to fear, but nothing, about what we are going to do or what we can do. When we think difference, *we* think: 'We'll not harm you, so spare us.' When *they* think difference, they think: 'They'll stay in their place'.

The demand for 'difference' is the expression of the fact that we are defenceless, and, furthermore, that we do not wish to defend ourselves, or to acquire the means to do so, but that we ask for esteem and love. In fact, it comes down to a

demand for weakness. But can the demand for dependency and weakness eliminate dependence and weakness?

FALSE CONSCIOUSNESS?

But we can also discern a political, or at least a proto-political, protest in this
demand for difference. For if it is a tactical error in judgement in that it serves
to distinguish our interests, if it is a manifestation of false consciousness, it is also
something else in its ambiguity. There is a great probability that a 'misunderstanding' explains the success of 'difference'. For, a veritable stroke of good luck
for the dominant class on the one hand, it is at the same time a *compromise* for
a great number of us. A compromise between the emergence of a political consciousness of what we really are as a class, and the repression of this emergence.
A political consciousness repressed at the same time that it is expressed by the
idea of difference. The latter is therefore—also—the beginning of a true consciousness, our consciousness, the one before which we hesitate because its development scares us. It may make us discover our existence as a class. For we
are in fact different. *But* we are not different FROM men (as false consciousness claims) *as we are different FROM THAT WHICH men claim that we are.*
This co-occurrence of two meanings (that we are different from you AND that
we are different from that which we are supposed to be) comes from the fact
that *we cannot not know somewhere*, even if it is hidden in our deepest recesses,
that a *use* is being made of us, from which comes the violence which surrounds
us, and the contempt which encircles us. I say violence and I say contempt, this
contempt which we cannot really endure because it signifies to us that we
are . . . No! We are something else, we are different, we are not that! I am not
even speaking of intense hatred; for if hatred is physically destructive, contempt
is psychologically destructive. It deprives us of self-esteem (which we know), but
it also deprives us of our intellectual and political strength by attempting to force
us into accepting and interiorizing the status of an appropriated object.

So we censor, we cover up, we say something else, we say we love children
and peace, we say that we do not give a damn about power—without specifying
what we mean by 'power', as if it were an object one could take or leave, as if it
were a thing in itself—*as if it were not a relationship*. In fact it is not obvious that
we so easily accept not being paid, doing the nasty jobs, being beaten or sexually harassed, etc., that we accept being without any means of real response.

No, we remain vague, defining neither 'power' nor 'difference'. What is the
goal of this demand, unformulated as to its objective and its modalities? On the

one hand there is the feminine mystique or neofemininity; on the other hand, the refusal of 'power' (but was it really ever offered to us?) and the horror of violence and contempt.

DIF-FERENCE

So let us talk about the right to be different, about the fact that we believe that it would be doing us wrong not to recognize this difference that we experience so strongly and which appears to us to be our own territory, our freedom in the face of permanent encroachment.

A short etymological but not useless comment at the beginning (those who say that words do not mean anything are either hypocrites or they are desperate), for no word is ever chosen at random. We know very well what words mean, something psychoanalysis and the fierce harshness of verbal relationships jointly teach us. *Difference* comes from a Latin verb (*fero*) which means 'to carry', 'to orient'. Dif-ference adds the idea of dispersion (di) to this orientation; we say 'to differ *from*'.What is important is this little *from*. We can certainly speak of difference *between* one thing and another, each term in this case being the point of reference to the other. But this is a rare usage. The kernel of the meaning is the distance from a centre, the distance from a referent (still *fero*). In practice one perhaps claims to mean: 'X and Y and different from each other'; but in reality one says 'X is different *from* Y'. Y is put in the position of the referent. If language offers the possibility of an egalitarian articulation (between), none the less it is hierarchy (from) which is the rule.

In short, difference is thought of (a) in a relationship, but (b) in a relationship of a particular type where there is a fixed point, a centre which orders everything around it, and by which all things are measured, in a word, a REFERENT. This is in fact the hidden reality of difference.

The ideological significance of difference is the distance from the referent. To speak of 'difference' is to articulate a rule, a law, a norm—briefly, an absolute which would be the measure, the origin, the fixed point of a relationship, by which the 'rest' would be defined. This is to suppose an immobile entity somewhere out there. And it is tantamount to acknowledging that there is no reciprocal action. It is quite simply the statement of the *effects* of a power relationship. There is a great realism hidden in the word 'difference': the knowledge that there exists a source of evaluation, a point of reference, an *origin of the definition*. And if there is an origin of the definition, it means precisely that this definition is not 'free'. The definition is seen for what it is: a fact of dependence and a fact of domination. From this comes logically the idea of a 'right' to be different.

THE RIGHT TO, THE RIGHT TO . . .

A right, whether in fact or in law, is something which is defined *in relation to*—in relation to a rule, a norm, a tradition. And therefore, by definition, a right refers to a request for power. To have the right is to be in a position decentred from the decision-making authority. A right *is obtained*, thus it is situated in a perspective of dependence, of a concession—not of negotiation or of exchange.

A member of the dominant group would obviously not claim the 'right to be different'; first of all because his practices and his ideal of existence are effectively the norm of society—what the dominator does goes without saying; then, because he considers himself, in as much as he is an individual in the bosom of his group, as exquisitely specific and distinguished; and because he exercises this distinction by right without having asked for, without ever having to ask for, anyone's authorization, individuality being a practical effect of the position of the dominator. On the contrary, the 'right' to be different is a recourse to authorization. Please give us the right to be otherwise than you are. Or even more clearly: You are the centre of the world. The proposition is tantamount to saying: 'You are the Law'. This drags us into the problematic of established orders, that is, of disorders guaranteed by power.

For the 'right to be different' occurs in a not at all undifferentiated, and in a not in the least bit neutral, relationship. In fact, in what circumstance do we speak of the 'right to be different'? We noted above: in the relationships between the 'developed' world and the exploited world, in the relationship which one can call that 'of race' and in the one which one can call that 'of sex'. It thus concerns determined human groups which have precise relationships between them, relationships precisely of domination and dependence. It concerns groups which are born of a relationship such that the existence of one draws its substance from the other, and where the existence of the other is at the mercy of the power of the one. To speak of a 'right to' is thus in some way or in some place to accept the status quo of the power relationships to which we are subject, to accept these relationships themselves. This is quite different from being aware of them. For want of being aware of them, in fact, we accept them. This puts us in a very bad position to combat and destroy them.

Contrary to what we are often told, there is no question of an alternative. 'Different/Same', there is no choice since we are in a determined place, that of difference. Zero options. The visible dichotomy hides from us a relationship which makes us, women, tools, instruments of survival or of luxury for the dominant class, men. In this relationship there is no choice. When they try to make us believe that there is a choice, they treat us like a child whose anger or bitterness one tries to divert by directing it (often very materially) toward a trap (Oh! the pretty flower), so that absorbed by another object than its own pain, the child ceases to see it, stops thinking about it, and in this way the object finally disappears from perception.

Thus there is no alternative 'Different/Same' with which we might be confronted. The one and the other are the two faces of a power relationship. Unless we adopt a mystical point of view and rally around the famous moral which claims that freedom is choosing what is imposed on you (the freedom of the slave is thus assured), the point of view of choice is absurd.

In addition to that, the fact of its having been presented as a real alternative (although there is only one place and no choice) hinders us from analysing the power relationship itself by turning our attention away from it. This also prevents us from thinking about *what is destroyed* by this power relationship, which probably includes diversity, the infinity of possibilities, etc. For we are deprived of those concrete elements which, in a determined society, are the *conditions*— material and therefore mental—of creation, of invention, of personal determination. Inside practical relationships, such as nutrition, space, relaxation, autonomy, etc., it is easy to see what that means.

THE PRICE OF BREAD

Let us look at the *material means of existence*, and let us see how 'difference' is a concrete relationship: the hierarchy of wages.

We know, for example, that the pressure to marry (that is, the passage from collective appropriation to private appropriation—or from one private appropriation to another) is transmitted through the hierarchy of wages. We know very well that this relationship (between a woman's wage and that of the head of the family) not only pressures women to marry and allows each man to acquire a unit of physical and affective material servicing of his person, but also leads women (statistically) to accept men older than themselves.[7] The hierarchy which gives the best wages to men who are settled down, and the worst to women as a whole (whatever their age) is a homogeneous mechanism which puts the private use of young women at the disposition of mature men (without however depriving the men of general usage of young women).[8] As a result there are not two distinct hierarchies, which would be that of sex and age, but one continuous hierarchy which is only visible when we put the two sex classes at the centre of the picture.

(1) This hierarchy results from, and guarantees, the physical material maintenance of one class, that of men (and the children of men), by another class, that of women. This means, as we are coming to know better and better, all material

maintenance: from shopping to cleaning, from cooking to the moral and physical supervision of children, from maintaining social ties—whether they are familial, professional, worldly or quite simply friendly—to being obliged to serve as the ornament of man in society.

(2) *And*, as a result, it also deprives women of the material means of existence in their middle years and *in their old age*. Abandoned, divorced, they are excluded from social rights (health insurance, pension) once they are no longer private property. Forced into unemployment or reduced then to the National Allocation of Funds, which may ('may', but not necessarily does) allow her to obtain as much as 1,000 francs a month (in 1978). Women are deprived of the means of existence in the most material and immediate sense of that word *when* they return solely to the status of *collective ownership*. They are then reduced to being beggars in the literal sense of the term: they no longer have the right to anything which had been assured them by the fact of being possessed by a particular man. Not only do they lose what that man's money can pay for, but also the very rights which are (in theory) guaranteed by the community to each of its members are taken away from them. It could not be established more clearly that a woman is not a member of the community, that she is only the property of her husband or of her companion. A woman, in so far as she is a woman, that is, without her own income, has no individual rights, no existence as a social subject.

From this there flows a number of 'womanly qualities' which may be considered unique and precious, likeable or fascinating—'feminine characteristics' which come to be ensconced in the famous 'difference': ties between human beings, inspiration in daily material life, attention to others (just between ourselves, we would prefer that this attention to others, for example, were a bit more shared out). Praised as such, these characteristics are the consequences—happy, value-laden, inestimable (all that one could wish for), but consequences all the same—of a material relationship, of a certain place in a classical relationship of exploitation.

This is true, unless one believes—a very convenient and very reassuring belief for all (dominant and dominated)—that 'whims', tenderness and preserves are directly inscribed in the genetic code of women, which in this way—an interesting novelty—reveals itself as distinct from that of men; and that in some way it is a question of our nature. In this case we would be right to defend it fiercely against the assaults of those who would want to traffic in 'our' genetic message and to make us against our will into men.

Into 'men'? There are two important things here:

(1) We have just surreptitiously changed terrain by ideological slippage in a vocabulary laced with traps. We are talking about females and males, not about women and men. This is not at all the same thing even though they constantly

try to make us believe it. For in one case we are talking about *physical characteristics appropriate to sexed reproduction*: all organized beings who reproduce
by cross-fertilization comprise a female and a male sex. In this regard human beings are not in any way particular; they possess both female and male. When we
speak of women and men, we are speaking of *social groups which maintain a determined relationship*, and which are constituted in the very heart of this relationship by specific practices. These practices affect the entire life of each of the
individuals concerned and rule her/his existence, from work to the laws which
govern her/him, from clothes to the mode of possession of the material means
of survival, etc.

(2)However—and this should not escape us—we do not have to defend ourselves against any aggression which aims at taking our youngest children away
from us,[9] against tenderness, against whims or against the detergent which
washes gently. On that front, we can even affirm that everything works together
to guarantee us precisely these privileges and the *material means to cultivate*
these exquisite characteristics. On that front, there is not the slightest danger on
the horizon. No, they will not deprive us of our children, nor of the aged, nor of
family relations, nor of laundry, housework, preparation of meals, and listening
to men's personal, professional, political and amorous problems. Thus they will
not take away from us those things which also make possible the 'bad characteristics' based on difference—hysteria, mythomania, anger, fatigue, despair, in-
sanity. No, they will not deprive us of the control constantly exercised over us at
home and in the street, of the harassment and self-conceit which surround us,
of the unfathomable self-centredness of the class of men. They will not deprive
us of the state of uncertainty in which the majority of us are institutionally kept:
He will come home, he won't come home. He will be drunk, he won't be drunk.
He will stay, he won't stay. He will give me money, he won't give me money.
They will not deprive us of silence and decisions made elsewhere without us.
Decidedly not. Let us not get agitated by an imaginary fear; they will not take
away from us that which makes us different. Let us not waste our time asking for
what we already have.

DIGNITY

This 'difference' which is being demanded is supposed to be an effort to take
back a little dignity for those who do not have any socially. Unfortunately, dignity is not fabricated only in one's head; it is first of all created in the reality of
facts. Thus to believe that a request for esteem and consideration will be able to
assure us this esteem and consideration is day-dreaming. Don't you remember

Mother's Day and the campaign for the 'rehabilitation' of manual labour? Let us talk about this campaign, where ´manual labour', photographed in huge posters on city walls, was incarnated in miners' hats, mechanics' hammers, builder's frames, cranes and men's faces. Manual labour is not bringing food to X number of persons, doing the wash, changing and bathing an infant, cleaning the family dwelling. No, that is not manual labour: that is women's mission—a fine distinction. But neither is it visibly assembling the pieces of an article of clothing, soldering an electric circuit, book-binding, or fruit-picking, and so not a single woman's face appeared. Only men work with their hands. Moreover, what did this publicity campaign resemble if not at best the atrocious length-of-service badges and the touching speeches about the good and faithful service of those loved in their place and, above all, nowhere else. Our place is 'difference'. They do not refuse it to us, and they even want to praise us for it at some festival celebrating procreative work. And even when we have passed beyond this kind of work, we can have a place almost right up to the end: when we are old, we are still useful for the 'little' chores where we are irreplaceable as grandmothers, cleaning women, or servants who form part of the family (not always part of the family, though, although old and servants just the same). It is truly when we no longer 'take care of' anybody but ourselves that we are ejected from the system to become a part of the oldsters (in fact, old hags) who in their absolute powerlessness none the less weigh down a society which does not stop moaning about what a burden they are and the threat that they pose to the national budget.

MYSTIQUE—OF DIFFERENCE (OR OF POWERLESSNESS?)

Mystique has very little to do with relationships of power. This is shown very clearly by the messianisms which, in the 'Third World' more than anywhere else, delude those groups most distanced from independence, from power and even from possible negotiations with their oppressors. And the dominant groups always have a tendency to see history as immobile, and eternity at the end of the road. One wonders how they would even be able to imagine that this could be otherwise, and even that it could have been different. The place of the dominant gives us an incomparably elevated view, where parasitic visions certainly do not trouble the luminosity of the perspective.

So to scream for wonderful difference is to accept the perennial existence of relationships of exploitation. It means, for us, thinking in terms of eternity. And perhaps more seriously, it means not seeing that we are in such a relationship, when we accept the spontaneous ideology according to which nature is nature.

Or else it means being so desperate that we act 'as if'. And this must well be the kind of behaviour we have acquired during long experience: Do not make too many waves because in the long run we could lose something. Play the mad-woman, the child; caprice goes over better than a bill of reckoning. Or play the hunchback, the idiot, the modest woman, the eternal one. Or, even better, play the diplomat, the sensible one, the one who will not go too far, who will not offend the exquisite sensitivity of the so, so fragile master.

But the history of humans is not immobile. The struggle to establish relationships which, by definition, *will not be able to be* the same as those which exist today (since it is these relations which we are in the process of destroying) gives us, moreover, the possibility of starting from scratch.

CONCLUSION

If domination divides us against ourselves because of the joint effects of the use that is made of us and internalization of our 'difference', it also brings with it the birth of our consciousness. The practices of the dominant class which fragment us oblige us to consider ourselves comprised of heterogeneous pieces. In a sort of patchwork of existences we are forced to live things as distinct and cut off from one another, to behave in a fragmented way. But our own existence, hidden beneath this fragmentation, is constantly being reborn in our corporeal unity and in our consciousness of that unity. Our resistance to the use that is made of us (resistance which grows when we analyse it) restores homogeneity to our existence.

Even if it is—and perhaps *because it is*—criss-crossed with *conflicts which are created in us by the very use that is made of us* at every moment of our daily lives, consciousness is the very expression of these conflicts. If we are torn and if we protest, it is because in us somewhere *the subject is discovering that it has been used as an object*. Permanent anxiety, so constant among us that it has become a tiresome banality, is the expression of being torn like this: it is to know that we (I), who are conscious subjects in our experience, are negated as subjects in the use that is made of us socially.

This conflict between the subject (that is, the experience of one's own acts) and the object (that is, the appropriation which splits us up) produces our consciousness. Today this consciousness is still often *individual*; it is that of particular experience, and not yet our class consciousness. In other words, it is our consciousness of ourselves as individuals, but not yet the knowledge that the relationship in which we are defined is a social relationship, that it is not an unfortunate accident or personal bad luck which has placed our person in this unliveable dilemma.

It is time for us to know ourselves for what we are: *ideologically split because employed for fragmented concrete uses.*

But we are unique and homogeneous as an appropriated class, as women conscious of being split by a power relationship, a class relationship which disperses us, distances us, *differentiates* us. With this consciousness we fight for our own class, our own life, a life not divisible.

NOTES

General note: This text does not have bibliographical notes. It is necessary, however, to indicate that it comes directly from an analysis of the 'three moments' of the feminist battle written by Nicole-Claude Mathieu in the editorial by the editors of *Questions féministes* entitled 'Variations on Some Common Themes' and published in *Feminist Issues* 1(1): 14–19. It also owes much to the article by Monique Plaza, "Phallomorphic" Power and the Psychology of "Woman" in the same issue (pp. 71–102).

1. I speak here of the popular culture (the only one which I know in this area of inquiry), that culture where a certain amount of admiring commiseration always accompanies commentary on excess, excessive quantity, excessive violence, etc.; that culture which is fascinated by the stud, the bossy woman, the big-mouth, the 'gorgeous guy' (180 pounds, 6 feet tall), stomping and slapping around, the moonlighters (doing two paid jobs, not like our double day), etc.

2. A thinly veiled allusion to a delightful French Communist Party poster (which disappeared very quickly, no doubt when the enormity of the gaffe became obvious to somebody): *We can all be happy, women too.* Not having taken notes at that time, I am not absolutely certain of the first page of the proposition, but I am completely certain of the 'women too'.

3. These stages of formal integration were necessary from several points of view: (a) as a consciousness-raiser of the political character of the situation of the dominated; (b) as a demonstration to the dominant of the existence of the dominated; and finally (c) for the *real practical benefits* gained through application of what had been obtained and for the possibilities for later struggles which these stages implied.

4. The terms *blackism* and *noirisme* designate a political and cultural attitude comparable to that previously designated by the term *négritude* in French colonized countries. *Blackism* is used in the English Caribbean area, and *noirisme* in Haiti.

5. T.n.: The author coins a word, *sexage*, on the model of *esclavage* (slavery) and *servage* (serfdom), and uses it to refer to a system of generalized appropriation of women.

6. Another thinly veiled allusion, this time to a recent book which discourses upon a supposed 'female reality'. We have left behind the 'female condition' but we have not got far beyond it. See Emmanuèle de Lesseps, 'Female Reality: Biology or Society?' *Feminist Issues* 1(2), Winter 1981: 77–102.

7. 'You're not going to marry him as long as he has no job (or position or skill)', and the man who will have the job will be two or four or ten years older than you. Inversely: 'Women age earlier than men'. This permits the recommendation of this age difference, which will then reinforce even more men's authority (as if there were any need to do so!). As to the psychology of the chase: between the man who 'courts' a woman with nice things, with fancy presents, with flowers, with vacation trips—as well as the irreplaceable seriousness presented by his expanding midriff—and the man who does not yet have the means to pay court, if a woman is supernormal she will think the first suitor better, more 'in love', more serious; if she is cynical and realistic, she will simply find that he has more money.

8. But the hierarchy of wages is not the sole factor to intervene in 'inciting' women to marry. Another considerable means of pressure is sexuality; it is one of the key points of the relationship, and crucial to it. Heterosexual sexuality *cannot be separated* by a simple mental operation from the domination and exploitation of women by men. Sexuality is women's problem. Men want to keep women in order to have a companion. Women do not only want a man because he is the main means of subsistence (something which is not always clearly conscious) and the guarantor of access to a recognized social existence, but also because he is the sole certain provider of sex. There is for women no socially guaranteed sexual exchange outside of companionship, *even a fleeting one.* This is not the case for men, who have shared women, whether in the framework of a monetary service, or in the framework of seizure and the use of force; either physical or persuasive.

9. T.n.: In the United States, men are, in fact, trying more and more to take their children away from women upon divorce.

5

A LESBIAN IS NOT A WOMAN

Monique Wittig

INTRODUCTION

by Doris Rita Alphonso

Monique Wittig was born in Alsace, France, in 1935. She studied Oriental languages, literature, philosophy, and history at the University of Paris IV, Sorbonne. Wittig's career as a writer was launched in 1964 when her first novel, *L'Opoponax*, was praised as a cutting-edge *nouveau roman* and awarded the *Prix Médicis*. A leading activist for the socialist and feminist movement, she became a part of the radical feminist group *Féministes Révolutionnaires* in 1970, and took part in the first actions of the *Mouvement de Libération des Femmes* (MLF). Immigrating to the United States in 1976, Wittig turned her attention to writing and lecturing on feminist theory. She nonetheless kept up with developments back home, actively participating in the *Questions féministes* collective from 1977 to 1980 (when it disbanded). At the University of California, Berkeley, Wittig served as editorial advisor for *Feminist Issues* from 1980 to 1991. In 1986, she earned her Ph.D. (from the Sorbonne) in literary language, and she has since returned to writing fiction and drama. She has been a visiting professor at the University of California, Berkeley, the University of Southern California, Duke University, Vassar College, and New York University. Currently, she is professor of French literature at the University of Arizona in Tucson.

Like the character in her *L'Opoponax*, Wittig began writing after having fallen in love with another girl, at the age of twelve. Early in her career, she was attracted to the subversive school of the *nouveaux romanciers*—to the attention they paid to the material and typographical form of texts, as well as to their rejection of visual or narrative linearity, their cinematic narrative techniques, and their self-reflexive writing style. Ideologically, Wittig's writings have a radical political force that is derived from the heady political context in which they were written. Wittig is part of a tendency in the French feminist movement, materialist feminism, that takes women to be a social class whose interests are opposed to those of men, in the context of patriarchal domination. A leader of the feminist movement, she was a founding member of various radical feminist groups, such as the Little Marguerites, the *Gouines Rouges*, and the well known Féministes Révolutionnaires. The latter, in solidarity with American feminists who were striking on behalf of women's rights, staged the march to the Arc de Triomphe that became the first action of the MLF.

Wittig's writing, like that of other materialist feminists, is influenced by Marxist theories of class solidarity and oppression and the Marxist critique of ideology. It is also influenced by the Enlightenment idea, borrowed from Rousseau, that society is founded by the people on the basis of a "social contract." What her writings and her activism seek is to bring about the signing of a new social contract. *Les Guérillères* was written in the wake of the socialist student revolts of May 1968, when Wittig was heavily involved in MLF campaigns. It was after immigrating to the United States that Wittig's attention was turned toward a systematic analysis of oppression, and she began to write in essay form. The theoretical essays of this time are influenced by the American radical feminist movement, including Adrienne Rich's groundbreaking "Compulsory Heterosexuality and Lesbian Experience" (1980) to which her own analysis is akin.

Monique Wittig's fiction, activism, and theory can all be characterized by their subversion of conventional forms—be they literary, political, social, or theoretical. Wittig's first novel, *L'Opoponax*, was widely praised for its subversion of the traditional autobiographical form, while one of her latest works, *Across the Archenon*, satirically reworks Dante's *Divine Comedy*. In the theoretical realm, she is best known for the idea that patriarchy (as a political system) must be subverted and overthrown and that this can best be achieved from the political position of the lesbian. Wittig theorizes a "materialist lesbian feminism" that puts into question the heterosexual assumption of early feminist analyses of patriarchy—that there are two sexes, women and men. Wittig argues that since women exist only in relation to men, lesbians cannot be considered women because their existence does not depend on men. Where women are a *class* defined by their subservient relationship to men, lesbians are "run aways" from the class of women. They alone escape the web of heterosexual relations that constitute patriarchy, and it is from their position outside the heterosexual categories of sex that it is possible to subvert patriarchy.

Wittig's use of language sets out to abolish the categories of "man" and "woman," upon which patriarchal domination depends, since language is the means by which the movement between conceptual and material realities is achieved. (Unlike English, French is a gendered language, and therefore marked through and through by heterosexual difference). Wittig coined the verb *to lesbianize* to denote the violent subversion of heterosexual and patriarchal forms through the figuration of lesbian identity in language. To lesbianize identity is to engage in a subjective cognitive practice, to embark on a constant journey of refiguration toward an as of yet unimaginable elsewhere. Her subversive use of the impersonal, genderless pronoun "one" and of inverted relational pronouns (*j/e*) allow for the emergence of an "I" or subject that is not bound by the terms of heterosexual systems of signification. Her attention to language has led some to assimilate her work with Hélène Cixous' project of *ecriture féminine*, but Wittig's work is incompatible with projects that rely on categories of sex and celebrate "sexual difference." Outside the categories of man/woman and masculine/feminine, Wittig establishes in language a lesbian identity for a new political system. The lesbian warriors of *Les Guérillères* open the space for forging a new social contract in which the differences between 'men' and 'women' no longer amount to patriarchal domination.

In "The Category of Sex," Wittig argues that 'man' and 'woman' are not 'natural' categories but the product of social relations. The category of sex establishes heterosexuality as the 'natural' basis for society, and further establishes a 'natural' division of labor that assigns to women a 'natural' reproductive role. Women's reproductive role is institutionalized by law through the marriage contract, which is used to enforce and justify the exploitation of women's labor. Economically exploited through marriage, women are thus bound to perform unpaid sexual, reproductive, and productive labor for an unlimited time. As an ideology, the category of sex marks women as sexually different from the male norm, so that it is women who are reduced to their biological sex and who are seen as lacking any public or political dimensions. As long as these differences are believed to be 'natural', their basis in social, economic, and political realities remains concealed, and the conflict necessary to bring about a more egalitarian society is neutralized.

"One Is Not Born a Woman" establishes a link between the denial of the 'natural' category of "woman" and the possibility for a feminist political movement in which women, as a class, fight for one another and for the destruction of sex categories. Women must first become conscious of themselves as an oppressed class through the "subjective cognitive practice" of abstracting themselves from the myth of woman, in its negative and positive aspects. For example, Wittig argues that the myth that women are superior to men because of their capacity to bear children (the myth of matriarchy) should be rejected because replacing patriarchy with matriarchy leaves intact the heterosexual category of sex and reinforces sexual inequality. What must be accomplished is the evacuation of heterosexuality. Wittig argues for a political lesbianism that puts into practice the theories of materialist feminism. Because lesbians are neither women nor men, they present a challenge to the 'natural' categories of sex in which social inequalities are attractively packaged. Lesbianism is the practice of materialist feminism that can bring about the destruction of heterosexuality as a sociopolitical system and provide the basis for imagining a more egalitarian society.

Wittig offers a critique of heterosexuality as a political system in "The Straight Mind." The straight mind is an interlocking system of discourses that assumes heterosexuality at the expense of true diversity. This system can only think of differences in terms of opposites, so that it finds it impossible to imagine a society not based on the heterosexual categories of man and woman. Even homosexuality can only be thought in terms of heterosexuality, which is compulsory to the straight mind. In "Homo Sum," Wittig traces the origins of totalizing systems to the dialectical method of Greek philosophy, in which a unity (Being) is assumed and normalized through its opposition to a negated plurality (non-being). It is from this perspective beyond dichotomous oppositions that the dominance of the same—the one, totalized unity—can be overcome. This is the perspective of the lesbian beyond heterosexuality. Neither the one nor the other sex, lesbians represent the possibility for true human diversity.

BIBLIOGRAPHY

Selected Primary Sources

1966. *The Opoponax*. New York: Simon and Schuster. [*The Opoponax*. Paris: Editions de Minuit, 1964.]

1971. *Les Guérillères*. New York: Viking. [*Les Guérillères*. Paris: Editions de Minuit, 1969.]

1975. *The Lesbian Body*. New York: William Morrow. *Le Corps lesbien*. Paris: Editions de Minuit, 1973.]

1979. *Lesbian Peoples: Materials for a Dictionary*. With Sande Zeig. New York: Avon. [*Brouillon pour un dictionnaire des amantes*. Paris: Grasset et Fasquelle, 1975.]

1980. "The Straight Mind." *Feminist Issues* 1, no. 1: 103–12. ["La pensée straight." *Questions féministes* 7 (1980): 21–26.]

1981. "One Is Not Born a Woman." *Feminist Issues* 1, no. 4: 47–54.

1982. "The Category of Sex." *Feminist Issues* 2, no. 2: 63–68.

1983. "The Point of View: Universal or Particular?" *Feminist Issues* 3, no. 2: 63–70.

1985. "The Mark of Sex." *Feminist Issues* 5, no. 2: 3–12.

1987. *Across the Acheron*. London: Peter Owen.

1990. "Homo Sum." *Feminist Issues* 10, no. 1: 3–11.

1992. *The Straight Mind and Other Essays*. Boston: Beacon Press.

Selected Secondary Sources

Butler, Judith. 1990. "Monique Wittig: Bodily Disintegration and Fictive Sex." In *Gender Trouble: Feminism and the Subversion of Identity*. New York: Routlege.

Cowder, Diane Griffin. 1991. "Monique Wittig." In *French Women Writers: A Bio-*

Bibliographical Source Book, ed. Eva Martin Sartori and Dorothy Wynne Zimmerman. Westport, Connecticut: Greenwood Press.
Ostrovsky, Erika. 1991. *A Constant Journey: The Fiction of Monique Wittig*. Carbondale: Southern Illinois University Press.
Sellers, Susan, 1991. "Monique Wittig." In *Language and Sexual Difference: Feminist Writing in France*. New York: Macmillan.
Wenzel, Hélène Vivienne. 1981. "The Text as Body/Politics: An Appreciation of Monique Wittig's Writings in Context." *Feminist Studies* 7, no. 2: 264–87.

THE CATEGORY OF SEX

O. expresses a virile idea. Virile or at least masculine. At last a woman who admits it! Who admits what? Something that women have always till now refused to admit (and today more than ever before). Something that men have always reproached them with: that they never cease obeying their nature, the call of their blood, that everything in them, even their minds, is sex.
—Jean Paulhan, "Happiness in Slavery,"
preface to *The Story of O*, by Pauline de Réage

In the course of the year 1838, the peaceful island of Barbados was rocked by a strange and bloody revolt. About two hundred Negroes of both sexes, all of whom had recently been emancipated by the Proclamation of March, came one morning to beg their former master, a certain Glenelg, to take them back into bondage. . . . I suspect . . . that Glenelg's slaves were in love with their master, that they couldn't bear to be without him.
—Jean Paulhan, *"Happiness in Slavery"*

What should I be getting married for? I find life good enough as it is. What do I need a wife for? . . . And what's so good about a woman?—A woman is a worker. A woman is a man's servant.—But what would I be needing a worker for?—That's just it. You like to have others pulling your chestnuts out of the fire. . . . Well, marry me off, if that's the case.
—Ivan Turgenev, *The Hunting Sketches*

The perenniality of the sexes and the perenniality of slaves and masters proceed from the same belief, and, as there are no slaves without masters, there are no women without men. The ideology of sexual difference functions as censorship in our culture by masking, on the ground of nature, the social opposition between men and women. Masculine/feminine, male/female are the categories which serve to conceal the fact that social differences always belong to an economic, political, ideological order. Every system of domination establishes divisions at the material and economic level. Furthermore, the divisions are abstracted and turned into concepts by the masters, and later on by the slaves when they rebel and start to struggle. The masters explain and justify the established divisions as a result of natural differences. The slaves, when they rebel and start to struggle, read social oppositions into the so-called natural differences.

For there is no sex. There is but sex that is oppressed and sex that oppresses. It is oppression that creates sex and not the contrary. The contrary would be to say that sex creates oppression, or to say that the cause (origin) of oppression is to be found in sex itself, in a natural division of the sexes preexisting (or outside of) society.

The primacy of difference so constitutes our thought that it prevents turning inward on itself to question itself, no matter how necessary that may be to apprehend the basis of that which precisely constitutes it. To apprehend a difference in dialectical terms is to make apparent the contradictory terms to be resolved. To understand social reality in dialectical materialist terms is to apprehend the oppositions between classes, term to term, and make them meet under the same copula (a conflict in the social order), which is also a resolution (an abolition in the social order) of the apparent contradictions.

The class struggle is precisely that which resolves the contradictions between two opposed classes by abolishing them at the same time that it constitutes and reveals them as classes. The class struggle between women and men, which should be undertaken by all women, is that which resolves the contradictions between the sexes, abolishing them at the same time that it makes them understood. We must notice that the contradictions always belong to a material order. The important idea for me is that before the conflict (rebellion, struggle) there are no categories of oppression but only of difference. And it is not until the struggle breaks out that the violent reality of the oppositions and the political nature of the differences become manifest. For as long as oppositions (differences) appear as given, already there, before all thought, "natural"—as long as there is no conflict and no struggle—there is no dialectic, there is no change, no movement. The dominant thought refuses to turn inward on itself to apprehend that which questions it.

And, indeed, as long as there is no women's struggle, there is no conflict between men and women. It is the fate of women to perform three-quarters of the work of society (in the public as well as in the private domain) plus the bodily work of reproduction according to a preestablished rate. Being murdered, mutilated, physically and mentally tortured and abused, being raped, being battered, and being forced to marry is the fate of women. And fate supposedly cannot be changed. Women do not know that they are totally dominated by men, and when they acknowledge the fact, they can "hardly believe it." And often, as a last recourse before the bare and crude reality, they refuse to "believe" that men dominate them with full knowledge (for oppression is far more hideous for the oppressed than for the oppressors). Men, on the other hand, know perfectly well that they are dominating women. ("We are the masters of women," said André Breton[1]) and are trained to do it. They do not need to express it all the time, for one can scarcely talk of domination over what one owns.

What is this thought which refuses to reverse itself, which never puts into question what primarily constitutes it? This thought is the dominant thought. It is a thought which affirms an "already there" of the sexes, something which is supposed to have come before all thought, before all society. This thought is the thought of those who rule over women.

> The ideas of the ruling class are in every epoch the ruling ideas, i.e. the class which is the ruling *material* force of society, is at the same time its ruling *intellectual* force. The class which has the means of material production at its disposal, has control at the same time over the means of mental production, so that thereby, generally speaking, the ideas of those who lack the means of mental production are subject to it. The ruling ideas are nothing more than the ideal expression of the dominant material relationships, the dominant material relationships grasped as ideas: hence of the relationships which make the one class the ruling one, therefore, the ideas of its dominance. (Marx and Engels, *The German Ideology*)

This thought based on the primacy of difference is the thought of domination.

Dominance provides women with a body of data, of givens, of a prioris, which, all the more for being questionable, form a huge political construct, a tight network that affects everything, our thoughts, our gestures, our acts, our work, our feelings, our relationships.

Dominance thus teaches us from all directions:

- that there are before all thinking, all society, "sexes" (two categories of individuals born) with a constitutive difference, a difference that has ontological consequences (the metaphysical approach),
- that there are before all thinking, all social order, "sexes" with a "natural" or "biological" or "hormonal" or "genetic" difference that has sociological consequences (the scientific approach),
- that there is before all thinking, all social order, a "natural division of labor in the family," a "division of labor [that] was originally nothing *but* the division of labor in the sexual act" (the Marxist approach).

Whatever the approach, the idea remains basically the same. The sexes, in spite
of their constitutive difference, must inevitably develop relationships from category to category. Belonging to the natural order, these relationships cannot be
spoken of as social relationships. This thought which impregnates all discourses,
including common-sense ones (Adam's rib or Adam *is*, Eve is Adam's rib), is the
thought of domination. Its body of discourses is constantly reinforced on all levels of social reality and conceals the political fact of the subjugation of one sex
by the other, the compulsory character of the category itself (which constitutes
the first definition of the social being in civil status). The category of sex does not
exist a priori, before all society. And as a category of dominance it cannot be a
product of natural dominance but of the social dominance of women by men,
for there is but social dominance.

 The category of sex is the political category that founds society as heterosexual. As such it does not concern being but relationships (for women and men are
the result of relationships), although the two aspects are always confused when
they are discussed. The category of sex is the one that rules as "natural" the relation that is at the base of (heterosexual) society and through which half of the
population, women, are "heterosexualized" (the making of women is like the
making of eunuchs, the breeding of slaves, of animals) and submitted to a heterosexual economy. For the category of sex is the product of a heterosexual society which imposes on women the rigid obligation of the reproduction of the
"species," that is, the reproduction of heterosexual society. The compulsory reproduction of the "species" by women is the system of exploitation on which heterosexuality is economically based. Reproduction is essentially that work, that
production by women, through which the appropriation by men of all the work
of women proceeds. One must include here the appropriation of work which is
associated "by nature" with reproduction, the raising of children and domestic
chores. This appropriation of the work of women is effected in the same way as
the appropriation of the work of the working class by the ruling class. It cannot
be said that one of these two productions (reproduction) is "natural" while the
other one is social. This argument is only the theoretical, ideological justification
of oppression, an argument to make women believe that before society and in
all societies they are subject to this obligation to reproduce. However, as we
know nothing about work, about social production, outside of the context of exploitation, we know nothing about the reproduction of society outside of its context of exploitation.

 The category of sex is the product of a heterosexual society in which men appropriate for themselves the reproduction and production of women and also
their physical persons by means of a contract called the marriage contract. Compare this contract with the contract that binds a worker to his employer. The con-

BOO! HISS!

tract binding the woman to the man is in principle a contract for life, which only law can break (divorce). It assigns the woman certain obligations, including unpaid work. The work (housework, raising children) and the obligations (surrender of her reproduction in the name of her husband, cohabitation by day and night, forced coitus, assignment of residence implied by the legal concept of "surrender of the conjugal domicile") mean in their terms a surrender by the women of her physical person to her husband. That the woman depends directly on her husband is implicit in the police's policy of not intervening when a husband beats his wife. The police intervene with the specific charge of assault and battery when one citizen beats another citizen. But a woman who has signed a marriage contract has thereby ceased to be an ordinary citizen (protected by law). The police openly express their aversion to getting involved in domestic affairs (as opposed to civil affairs), where the authority of the state does not have to intervene directly since it is relayed through that of the husband. One has to go to shelters for battered women to see how far this authority can be exercised.

GRR! this is changing (but not enough!)

The category of sex is the product of heterosexual society that turns half of the population into sexual beings, for sex is a category which women cannot be outside of. Wherever they are, whatever they do (including working in the public sector), they are seen (and made) sexually available to men, and they, breasts, buttocks, costume, must be visible. They must wear their yellow star, their constant smile, day and night. One might consider that every woman, married or not, has a period of forced sexual service, a sexual service which we may compare to the military one, and which can vary between a day, a year, or twenty-five years or more. Some lesbians and nuns escape, but they are very few, although the number is growing. Although women are very visible as sexual beings, as social beings they are totally invisible, and as such must appear as little as possible, and always with some kind of excuse if they do so. One only has to read interviews with outstanding women to hear them apologizing. And the newspapers still today report that "two students and a woman," "two lawyers and a woman," "three travelers and a woman" were seen doing this or that. For the category of sex is the category that sticks to women, for only they cannot be conceived of outside of it. Only *they* are sex, *the* sex, and sex they have been made in their minds, bodies, acts, gestures; even their murders and beatings are sexual. Indeed, the category of sex tightly holds women.

Beauvoir agrees

like Jews

for not being home enough!

Media

For the category of sex is a totalitarian one, which to prove true has its inquisitions, its courts, its tribunals, its body of laws, its terrors, its tortures, its mutilations, its executions, its police. It shapes the mind as well as the body since it controls all mental production. It grips our minds in such a way that we cannot think outside of it. That is why we must destroy it and start thinking beyond it if we want to start thinking at all, as we must destroy the sexes as a sociological re-

sex distinctions!

ality if we want to start to exist. The category of sex is the category that ordains slavery for women, and it works specifically, as it did for black slaves, through an operation of reduction, by taking the part for the whole, a part (color, sex) through which the whole human group has to pass as through a screen. Notice that in civil matters color as well as sex still must be "declared." However, because of the abolition of slavery, the "declaration" of "color" is now considered discriminatory. But that does not hold true for the "declaration" of "sex," which not even women dream of abolishing. I say: it is about time to do so.[2]

NOTES

1. André Breton, *Le Premier Manifeste du Surréalisme*, 1924.
2. Pleasure in sex is no more the subject of this paper than is happiness in slavery.

ONE IS NOT BORN A WOMAN

but race isn't nat. either!

A materialist feminist[1] approach to women's oppression destroys the idea that women are a "natural group" ("a racial group) of a special kind, a group perceived *as natural*, a group of men considered as materially specific in their bodies."[2] What the analysis accomplishes on the level of ideas, practice makes actual at the level of facts: by its very existence, lesbian society destroys the artificial (social) fact constituting women as a "natural group." A lesbian society[3] pragmatically reveals that the division from men of which women have been the object is a political one and shows that we have been ideologically rebuilt into a "natural group." In the case of women, ideology goes far since our bodies as well as our minds are the product of this manipulation. We have been compelled in our bodies and in our minds to correspond, feature by feature, with the *idea* of nature that has been established for us. Distorted to such an extent that our deformed body is what they call "natural," what is supposed to exist as such before oppression. Distorted to such an extent that in the end oppression seems to be a consequence of this "nature" within ourselves (a nature which is only an *idea*). What a materialist analysis does by reasoning, a lesbian society accomplishes practically: not only is there no natural group "women" (we lesbians are living proof of it), but as individuals as well we question "woman," which for us, as for

Ads! media again

---

we are aware of ambiguous/confused feelings about our sex

Simone de Beauvoir, is only a myth. She said: "One is not born, but becomes a woman. No biological, psychological, or economic fate determines the figure that the human female presents in society: it is civilization as a whole that produces this creature, intermediate between male and eunuch, which is described as feminine."[4]

However, most of the feminists and lesbian-feminists in America and elsewhere still believe that the basis of women's oppression *is biological as well* as *historical.* Some of them even claim to find their sources in Simone de Beauvoir.[5] The belief in mother right and in a "prehistory" when women created civilization (because of a biological predisposition) while the coarse and brutal men hunted (because of a biological predisposition) is symmetrical with the biologizing interpretation of history produced up to now by the class of men. It is still the same method of finding in women and men a biological explanation of their division, outside of social facts. For me this could never constitute a lesbian approach to women's oppression, since it assumes that the basis of society or the beginning of society lies in heterosexuality. Matriarchy is no less heterosexual than patriarchy: it is only the sex of the oppressor that changes. Furthermore, not only is this conception still imprisoned in the categories of sex (woman and man), but it holds onto the idea that the capacity to give birth (biology) is what defines a woman. Although practical facts and ways of living contradict this theory in lesbian society, there are lesbians who affirm that "women and men are different species or races (the words are used interchangeably): men are biologically inferior to women; male violence is a biological inevitability . . ."[6] By doing this, by admitting that there is a natural division between women and men, we naturalize history, we assume that "men" and "women" have always existed and will always exist. Not only do we naturalize history, but also consequently we naturalize the social phenomena which express our oppression, making change possible. For example, instead of seeing giving birth as a forced production, we see it as a "natural," "biological" process, forgetting that in our societies births are planned (demography), forgetting that we ourselves are programmed to produce children, while this is the only social activity "short of war"[7] that presents such a great danger of death. Thus, as long as we will be "unable to abandon by will or impulse a lifelong and centuries-old commitment to childbearing as *the* female creative act,"[8] gaining control of the production of children will mean much more than the mere control of the material means of this production: women will have to abstract themselves from the definition "woman" which is imposed upon them.

A materialist feminist approach shows that what we take for the cause or origin of oppression is in fact only the *mark*[9] imposed by the oppressor: the "myth of woman,"[10] plus its material effects and manifestations in the appropriated

not so?

Guillaumin

consciousness and bodies of women. Thus, this mark does not predate oppression: Colette Guillaumin has shown that before the socioeconomic reality of black slavery, the concept of race did not exist, at least not in its modern meaning, since it was applied to the lineage of families. However, now, race, exactly like sex, is taken as an "immediate given," a "sensible given," "physical features," belonging to a natural order. But what we believe to be a physical and direct perception is only a sophisticated and mythic construction, an "imaginary formation,"[11] which reinterprets physical features (in themselves as neutral as any others but marked by the social system) through the network of relationships in which they are perceived. (They are seen as *black*, therefore they *are* black; they are seen as *women*, therefore, they *are* women. But before being *seen* that way, they first had to be *made* that way.) Lesbians should always remember and acknowledge how "unnatural," compelling, totally oppressive, and destructive being "woman" was for us in the old days before the women's liberation movement. It was a political constraint, and those who resisted it were accused of not being "real" women. But then we were proud of it, since in the accusation there was already something like a shadow of victory: the avowal by the oppressor that "woman" is not something that goes without saying, since to be one, one has to be a "real" one. We were at the same time accused of wanting to be men. Today this double accusation has been taken up again with enthusiasm in the context of the women's liberation movement by some feminists and also, alas, by some lesbians whose political goal seems somehow to be becoming more and more "feminine." To refuse to be a woman, however, does not mean that one has to become a man. Besides, if we take as an example the perfect "butch," the classic example which provokes the most horror, whom Proust would have called a woman/man, how is her alienation different from that of someone who wants to become a woman? Tweedledum and Tweedledee. At least for a woman, wanting to become a man proves that she has escaped her initial programming. But even if she would like to, with all her strength, she cannot become a man. For becoming a man would demand from a woman not only a man's external appearance but his consciousness as well, that is, the consciousness of one who disposes by right of at least two "natural" slaves during his life span. This is impossible, and one feature of lesbian oppression consists precisely of making women out of reach for us, since women belong to men. Thus a lesbian *has* to be something else, a not-woman, a not-man, a product of society, not a product of nature, for there is no nature in society.

The refusal to become (or to remain) heterosexual always meant to refuse to become a man or a woman, consciously or not. For a lesbian this goes further than the refusal of the *role* "woman." It is the refusal of the economic, ideological, and political power of a man. This, we lesbians, and nonlesbians as well, knew before the beginning of the lesbian and feminist movement. However, as Andrea Dworkin emphasizes, many lesbians recently "have increasingly tried to transform the very ideology that has enslaved us into a dynamic, religious, psychologically compelling celebration of female biological potential."[12] Thus, some avenues of the feminist and lesbian movement lead us back to the myth of woman which was created by men especially for us, and with it we sink back into a natural group. Having stood up to fight for a sexless society,[13] we now find ourselves entrapped in the familiar deadlock of "woman is wonderful." Simone de Beauvoir underlined particularly the false consciousness which consists of selecting among the features of the myth (that women are different from men) those which look good and using them as a definition for women. What the concept "woman is wonderful" accomplishes is that it retains for defining women the best features (best according to whom?) which oppression has granted us, and it does not radically question the categories "man" and "woman," which are political categories and not natural givens. It puts us in a position of fighting within the class "women" not as the other classes do, for the disappearance of our class, but for the defense of "woman" and its reenforcement. It leads us to develop with complacency "new" theories about our specificity: thus, we call our passivity "nonviolence," when the main and emergent point for us is to fight our passivity (our fear, rather, a justified one). The ambiguity of the term "feminist" sums up the whole situation. What does "feminist" mean? Feminist is formed with the word "femme," "woman," and means: someone who fights for women. For many of us it means someone who fights for women as a class and for the disappearance of this class. For many others it means someone who fights for woman and her defense—for the myth, then, and its reenforcement. But why was the word "feminist" chosen if it retains the least ambiguity? We chose to call ourselves "feminists" ten years ago, not in order to support or reenforce the myth of woman, nor to identify ourselves with the oppressor's definition of us, but rather to affirm that our movement had a history and to emphasize the political link with the old feminist movement.

It is, then, this movement that we can put in question for the meaning that it gave to feminism. It so happens that feminism in the last century could never resolve its contradictions on the subject of nature/culture, woman/society. Women started to fight for themselves as a group and rightly considered that they shared common features as a result of oppression. But for them these features were natural and biological rather than social. They went so far as to adopt the Darwinist theory of evolution. They did not believe like Darwin, however, "that women were less evolved than men, but they did believe that male and female natures had diverged in the course of evolutionary development and that society at large

reflected this polarization."[14] "The failure of early feminism was that it only attacked the Darwinist charge of female inferiority, while accepting the foundations of this charge—namely, the view of woman as 'unique.' "[15] And finally it was
women scholars—and not feminists—who scientifically destroyed this theory.
But the early feminists had failed to regard history as a dynamic process which
develops from conflicts of interest. Furthermore, they still believed as men do
that the cause (origin) of their oppression lay within themselves. And therefore
after some astonishing victories the feminists of this first front found themselves
at an impasse out of a lack of reasons to fight. They upheld the illogical principle
of "equality in difference," an idea now being born again. They fell back into the
trap which threatens us once again: the myth of woman.

Thus it is our historical task, and only ours, to define what we call oppression
in materialist terms, to make it evident that women are a class, which is to say
that the category "woman" as well as the category "man" are political and economic categories not eternal ones. Our fight aims to suppress men as a class, not
through a genocidal, but a political struggle. Once the class "men" disappears,
"women" as a class will disappear as well, for there are no slaves without masters. Our first task, it seems, is to always thoroughly dissociate "women" (the
class within which we fight) and "woman," the myth. For "woman" does not exist for us: it is only an imaginary formation, while "women" is the product of a
social relationship. We felt this strongly when everywhere we refused to be
called a "woman's liberation movement." Furthermore, we have to destroy the
myth inside and outside ourselves. "Woman" is not each one of us, but the political and ideological formation which negates "women" (the product of a relation of exploitation). "Woman" is there to confuse us, to hide the reality
"women." In order to be aware of being a class and to become a class we first
have to kill the myth of "woman" including its most seductive aspects (I think
about Virginia Woolf when she said the first task of a woman writer is to kill "the
angel in the house"). But to become a class we do not have to suppress our individual selves, and since no individual can be reduced to her/his oppression we
are also confronted with the historical necessity of constituting ourselves as the
individual subjects of our history as well. I believe this is the reason why all these
attempts at "new" definitions of woman are blossoming now. What is at stake
(and of course not only for women) is an individual definition as well as a class
definition. For once one has acknowledged oppression, one needs to know and
experience the fact that one can constitute oneself as a subject (as opposed to an
object of oppression), that one can become *someone* in spite of oppression, that
one has one's own identity. There is no possible fight for someone deprived of
an identity, no internal motivation for fighting, since, although I can fight only
with others, first I fight for myself.

The question of the individual subject is historically a difficult one for everybody. Marxism, the last avatar of materialism, the science which has politically formed us, does not want to hear anything about a "subject." Marxism has rejected the transcendental subject, the subject as constitutive of knowledge, the "pure" consciousness. All that thinks per se, before all experience, has ended up in the garbage can of history, because it claimed to exist outside matter, prior to matter, and needed God, spirit, or soul to exist in such a way. This is what is called "idealism." As for individuals, they are only the product of social relations, therefore their consciousness can only be "alienated." (Marx, in *The German Ideology*, says precisely that individuals of the dominating class are also alienated, although they are the direct producers of the ideas that alienate the classes oppressed by them. But since they draw visible advantages from their own alienation they can bear it without too much suffering.) There exists such a thing as class consciousness, but a consciousness which does not refer to a particular subject, except as participating in general conditions of exploitation at the same time as the other subjects of their class, all sharing the same consciousness. As for the practical class problems—outside of the class problems as traditionally defined—that one could encounter (for example, sexual problems), they were considered "bourgeois" problems that would disappear with the final victory of the class struggle. "Individualistic," "subjectivist," "petit bourgeois," these were the labels given to any person who had shown problems which could not be reduced to the "class struggle" itself.

Thus Marxism has denied the members of oppressed classes the attribute of being a subject. In doing this, Marxism, because of the ideological and political power this "revolutionary science" immediately exercised upon the workers' movement and all other political groups, has prevented all categories of oppressed peoples from constituting themselves historically as subjects (subjects of their struggle, for example). This means that the "masses" did not fight for themselves but for the party or its organizations. And when an economic transformation took place (end of private property, constitution of the socialist state), no revolutionary change took place within the new society, because the people themselves did not change.

For women, Marxism had two results. It prevented them from being aware that they are a class and therefore from constituting themselves as a class for a very long time, by leaving the relation "women/men" outside of the social order, by turning it into a natural relation, doubtless for Marxists the only one, along with the relation of mothers to children, to be seen this way, and by hiding the class conflict between men and women behind a natural division of labor (*The German Ideology*). This concerns the theoretical (ideological) level. On the practical level, Lenin, *the* party, all the communist parties up to now, including *[handwritten annotations: "Women asserting themselves as subjects will result in the divisiveness of the working class [class dissent]" at top; left margin: "women writing placed under capital + politics", "rhetoric"]*

all the most radical political groups, have always reacted to any attempt on the part of women to reflect and form groups based on their own class problem with an accusation of divisiveness. By uniting, we women are dividing the strength of the people. This means that for the Marxists women *belong* either to the bourgeois class or to the proletariat class, in other words, to the men of these classes. In addition, Marxist theory does not allow women any more than other classes of oppressed people to constitute themselves as historical subjects, because Marxism does not take into account the fact that a class also consists of individuals one by one. Class consciousness is not enough. We must try to understand philosophically (politically) these concepts of "subject" and "class consciousness" and how they work in relation to our history. When we discover that women are the objects of oppression and appropriation, at the very moment that we become able to perceive this, we become subjects in the sense of cognitive subjects, through an operation of abstraction. Consciousness of oppression is not only a reaction to (fight against) oppression. It is also the whole conceptual reevaluation of the social world, its whole reorganization with new concepts, from the point of view of oppression. It is what I would call the science of oppression created by the oppressed. This operation of understanding reality has to be undertaken by every one of us: call it a subjective, cognitive practice. The movement back and forth between the levels of reality (the conceptual reality and the material reality of oppression, which are both social realities) is accomplished through language.

It is we who historically must undertake the task of defining the individual subject in materialist terms. This certainly seems to be an impossibility since materialism and subjectivity have always been mutually exclusive. Nevertheless, and rather than despairing of ever understanding, we must recognize the *need* to reach subjectivity in the abandonment by many of us to the myth "woman" (the myth of woman being only a snare that holds us up). This real necessity for everyone to exist as an individual, as well as a member of a class, is perhaps the first condition for the accomplishment of a revolution, without which there can be no real fight or transformation. But the opposite is also true; without class and class consciousness there are no real subjects, only alienated individuals. For women to answer the question of the individual subject in materialist terms is first to show, as the lesbians and feminists did, that supposedly "subjective," "individual," "private" problems are in fact social problems, class problems; that sexuality is not for women an individual and subjective expression, but a social institution of violence. But once we have shown that all so-called personal problems are in fact class problems, we will still be left with the question of the subject of each singular woman—not the myth, but each one of us. At this point, let us say that a new personal and subjective definition for all humankind can only be found beyond the categories of sex (woman and man) and that the advent of individual subjects demands first destroying the categories of sex, ending the use of them, and rejecting all sciences which still use these categories as their fundamentals (practically all social sciences).

To destroy "woman" does not mean that we aim, short of physical destruction, to destroy lesbianism simultaneously with the categories of sex, because lesbianism provides for the moment the only social form in which we can live freely. Lesbian is the only concept I know of which is beyond the categories of sex (woman and man), because the designated subject (lesbian) is *not* a woman, either economically, or politically, or ideologically. For what makes a woman is a specific social relation to a man, a relation that we have previously called servitude,[16] a relation which implies personal and physical obligation as well as economic obligation ("forced residence,"[17] domestic corvée, conjugal duties, unlimited production of children, etc.), a relation which lesbians escape by refusing to become or to stay heterosexual. We are escapees from our class in the same way as the American runaway slaves were when escaping slavery and becoming free. For us this is an absolute necessity; our survival demands that we contribute all our strength to the destruction of the class of women within which men appropriate women. This can be accomplished only the the destruction of heterosexuality as a social system which is based on the oppression of women by men and which produces the doctrine of the difference between the sexes to justify this oppression.

NOTES

1. Christine Delphy, "Pour un féminisme matérialiste," *L'Arc* 61 (1975). Translated as "For a Materialist Feminism," *Feminist Issues* 1, no. 2 (Winter 1981).
2. Colette Guillaumin, "Race et Nature: Système des marques, idée de groupe naturel et rapports sociaux," *Pluriel* no. 11 (1977). Translated as "Race and Nature: The System of Marks, the Idea of a Natural Group and Social Relationships," *Feminist Issues* 8, no. 2 (Fall 1988).
3. I use the word society with an extended anthropological meaning; strictly speaking, it does not refer to societies, in that lesbian societies do not exist completely autonomously from heterosexual social systems.
4. Simone de Beauvoir, *The Second Sex* (New York: Bantam, 1952), p. 249.
5. Redstockings, *Feminist Revolution* (New York: Random House, 1978), p. 18.
6. Andrea Dworkin, "Biological Superiority: The World's Most Dangerous and Deadly Idea," *Heresies* 6:46.
7. Ti-Grace Atkinson, *Amazon Odyssey* (New York: Links Books, 1974), p. 15.
8. Dworkin, op. cit.
9. Guillaumin, op. cit.

10. de Beauvoir, op. cit.
11. Guillaumin, op. cit.
12. Dworkin, op. cit.
13. Atkinson, p. 6: "If feminism has any logic at all, it must be working for a sexless society."
14. Rosalind Rosenberg, "In Search of Woman's Nature," *Feminist Studies* 3, no. 1/2 (1975): 144.
15. Ibid., p. 146.
16. In an article published in *L'Idiot International* (mai 1970), whose original title was "Pour un mouvement de libération des femmes" ("For a Women's Liberation Movement").
17. Christiane Rochefort, *Les stances á Sophie* (Paris: Grasset, 1963).

THE STRAIGHT MIND[1]

In recent years in Paris, language as a phenomenon has dominated modern theoretical systems and the social sciences and has entered the political discussions of the lesbian and women's liberation movements. This is because it relates to an important political field where what is at play is power, or more than that, a network of powers, since there is a multiplicity of languages that constantly act upon the social reality. The importance of language as such as a political stake has only recently been perceived.[2] But the gigantic development of linguistics, the multiplication of schools of linguistics, the advent of the sciences of communication, and the technicality of the metalanguages that these sciences utilize, represent the symptoms of the importance of what is politically at stake. The science of language has invaded other sciences, such as anthropology through Lévi-Strauss, psychoanalysis through Lacan, and all the disciplines which have developed from the basis of structuralism. The early semiology of Roland Barthes nearly escaped from linguistic domination to become a political analysis of the different systems of signs, to establish a relationship between this or that system of signs—for example, the myths of the petit bourgeois class—and the class struggle within capitalism that this system tends to conceal. We were almost saved, for political semiology is a weapon (a method) that we need to analyze what is called ideology. But the miracle did not last. Rather than introducing into semiology concepts which are for-

Semiology only one system among many

eign to it—in this case Marxist concepts—Barthes quickly stated that semiology was only a branch of linguistics and that language was its only object.

Thus, the entire world is only a great register where the most diverse languages come to have themselves recorded, such as the language of the Unconscious,[3] the language of fashion, the language of the exchange of women where human beings are literally the signs which are used to communicate. These languages, or rather these discourses, fit into one another, interpenetrate one another, support one another, reinforce one another, auto-engender, and engender one another. Linguistics engenders semiology and structural linguistics, structural linguistics engenders structuralism, which engenders the Structural Unconscious. The ensemble of these discourses produces a confusing static for the oppressed, which makes them lose sight of the material cause of their oppression and plunges them into a kind of ahistoric vacuum. *Hm!*

For they produce a scientific reading of the social reality in which human beings are given as invariants, untouched by history and unworked by class conflicts, with identical psyches because genetically programmed. This psyche, equally untouched by history and unworked by class conflicts, provides the specialists, from the beginning of the twentieth century, with a whole arsenal of invariants; the symbolic language which very advantageously functions with very few elements, since, like digits (0–9), the symbols "unconsciously" produced by the psyche are not very numerous. Therefore, these symbols are very easy to impose, through therapy and theorization, upon the collective and individual unconscious. We are taught that the Unconscious, with perfectly good taste, structures itself upon metaphors, for example, the name-of-the-father, the Oedipus complex, castration, the murder-or-death-of-the-father, the exchange of women, etc. If the Unconscious, however, is easy to control, it is not just by anybody. Similar to mystical revelations, the apparition of symbols in the psyche demands multiple interpretations. Only specialists can accomplish the deciphering of the Unconscious. Only they, the psychoanalysts, are allowed (authorized?) to organize and interpret psychic manifestations which will show the symbol in its full meaning. And while the symbolic language is extremely poor and essentially lacunary, the languages or metalanguages which interpret it are developing, each one of them, with a richness, a display, that only theological exegeses of the Bible have equalled. *A good ?!*

unc. all about metaphors

Who gave the psychoanalysts their knowledge? For example, for Lacan, what he calls the "psychoanalytic discourse," or the "analytical experience," both "teach" him what he already knows. And each one teaches him what the other one taught him. But can we deny that Lacan scientifically discovered, through the "analytical experience" (somehow an experiment), the structures of the Unconscious? Will we be irresponsible enough to disregard the discourses of the *thinks structuralism is a crock — this idea of "structure" is always put there by someone*

acting, reading questions etc.

psychoanalyzed people lying on their couches? In my opinion, there is no doubt that Lacan found in the Unconscious the structures he said he found there, since he had previously put them there. People who did not fall into the power of the psychoanalytical institution may experience an immeasurable feeling of sadness at the degree of oppression (of manipulation) that the psychoanalyzed discourses show. In the analytical experience there is an oppressed person, the psychoanalyzed, whose need for communication is exploited and who (in the same way as the witches could, under torture, only repeat the language that the inquisitors wanted to hear) has no other choice, (if s/he does not want to destroy the implicit contract which allows her/him to communicate and which s/he needs), than to attempt to say what s/he is supposed to say. They say that this can last for a lifetime—cruel contract which constrains a human being to display her/his misery to an oppressor who is directly responsible for it, who exploits her/him economically, politically, ideologically and whose interpretation reduces this misery to a few figures of speech.

But can the need to communicate that this contract implies only be satisfied in the psychoanalytical situation, in being cured or "experimented" with? If we believe recent testimonies[4] by lesbians, feminists, and gay men, this is not the case. All their testimonies emphasize the political significance of the impossibility that lesbians, feminists, and gay men face in the attempt to communicate in heterosexual society, other than with a psychoanalyst. When the general state of things is understood (one is not sick or to be cured, one has an enemy) the result is that the oppressed person breaks the psychoanalytical contract. This is what appears in the testimonies, along with the teaching that the psychoanalytical contract was not a contract of consent but a forced one.

The discourses which particularly oppress all of us, lesbians, women, and homosexual men, are those which take for granted that what founds society, any society, is heterosexuality.[5] These discourses speak about us and claim to say the truth in an apolitical field, as if anything of that which signifies could escape the political in this moment of history, and as if, in what concerns us, politically insignificant signs could exist. These discourses of heterosexuality oppress us in the sense that they prevent us from speaking unless we speak in their terms. Everything which puts them into question is at once disregarded as elementary. Our refusal of the totalizing interpretation of psychoanalysis makes the theoreticians say that we neglect the symbolic dimension. These discourses deny us every possibility of creating our own categories. But their most ferocious action is the unrelenting tyranny that they exert upon our physical and mental selves.

When we use the overgeneralizing term "ideology" to designate all the discourses of the dominating group, we relegate these discourses to the domain of Irreal Ideas; we forget the material (physical) violence that they directly do to

the oppressed people, a violence produced by the abstract and "scientific" discourses as well as by the discourses of the mass media. I would like to insist on
the material oppression of individuals by discourses, and I would like to underline its immediate effects through the example of pornography.
Pornographic images, films, magazine photos, publicity posters on the walls
of the cities, constitute a discourse, and this discourse covers our world with its
signs, and this discourse has a meaning: it signifies that women are dominated.
Semioticians can interpret the system of this discourse, describe its disposition.
What they read in that discourse are signs whose function is not to signify and
which have no *raison d'être* except to be elements of a certain system or disposition. But for us this discourse is not divorced from the real as it is for semioticians. Not only does it maintain very close relations with the social reality which
is our oppression (economically and politically), but also it is in itself real since
it is one of the aspects of oppression, since it exerts a precise power over us. The
pornographic discourse is one of the strategies of violence which are exercised
upon us: it humiliates, it degrades, it is a crime against our "humanity." As a ha-
rassing tactic it has another function, that of a warning. It orders us to stay in
line, and it keeps those who would tend to forget who they are in step; it calls
upon fear. These same experts in semiotics, referred to earlier, reproach us for
confusing, when we demonstrate against pornography, the discourses with the
reality. They do not see that this discourse *is* reality for us, one of the facets of
the reality of our oppression. They believe that we are mistaken in our level of
analysis.

I have chosen pornography as an example because its discourse is the most
symptomatic and the most demonstrative of the violence which is done to us
through discourses, as well as in the society at large. There is nothing abstract
about the power that sciences and theories have to act materially and actually
upon our bodies and our minds, even if the discourse that produces it is abstract.
It is one of the forms of domination, its very expression. I would say, rather, one
of its exercises. All of the oppressed know this power and have had to deal with
it. It is the one which says: you do not have the right to speech because your discourse is not scientific and not theoretical, you are on the wrong level of analysis, you are confusing discourse and reality, your discourse is naive, you misun-
derstand this or that science.

If the discourse of modern theoretical systems and social sciences exert a
power upon us, it is because it works with concepts which closely touch us. In
spite of the historic advent of the lesbian, feminist, and gay liberation movements, whose proceedings have already upset the philosophical and political categories of the discourses of the social sciences, their categories (thus brutally put
into question) are nevertheless utilized without examination by contemporary

science. They function like primitive concepts in a conglomerate of all kinds of disciplines, theories, and current ideas that I will call the straight mind. (See *The Savage Mind* by Claude Lévi-Strauss.) They concern "woman," "man," "sex," "difference," and all of the series of concepts which bear this mark, including such concepts as "history," "culture," and the "real." And although it has been accepted in recent years that there is no such thing as nature, that everything is culture, there remains within that culture a core of nature which resists examination, a relationship excluded from the social in the analysis—a relationship whose characteristic is ineluctability in culture, as well as in nature, and which is the heterosexual relationship. I will call it the obligatory social relationship between "man" and "woman." (Here I refer to Ti-Grace Atkinson and her analysis of sexual intercourse as an institution.[6]) With its ineluctability as knowledge, as an obvious principle, as a given prior to any science, the straight mind develops a totalizing interpretation of history, social reality, culture, language, and all the subjective phenomena at the same time. I can only underline the oppressive character that the straight mind is clothed in in its tendency to immediately universalize its production of concepts into general laws which claim to hold true for all societies, all epochs, all individuals. Thus one speaks of *the* exchange of women, *the* difference between the sexes, *the* symbolic order, *the* Unconscious, Desire, *Jouissance*, Culture, History, giving an absolute meaning to these concepts when they are only categories founded upon heterosexuality, or thought which produces the difference between the sexes as a political and philosophical dogma.

The consequence of this tendency toward universality is that the straight mind cannot conceive of a culture, a society where heterosexuality would not order not only all human relationships but also its very production of concepts and all the processes which escape consciousness, as well. Additionally, these unconscious processes are historically more and more imperative in what they teach us about ourselves through the instrumentality of specialists. The rhetoric which expresses them (and whose seduction I do not underestimate) envelopes itself in myths, resorts to enigma, proceeds by accumulating metaphors, and its function is to poeticize the obligatory character of the "you-will-be-straight-or-you-will-not-be."

In this thought, to reject the obligation of coitus and the institutions that this obligation has produced as necessary for the constitution of a society, is simply an impossibility, since to do this would mean to reject the possibility of the constitution of the other and to reject the "symbolic order," to make the constitution of meaning impossible, without which no one can maintain an internal coherence. Thus lesbianism, homosexuality, and the societies that we form cannot be thought of or spoken of, even though they have always existed. Thus, the straight mind continues to affirm that incest, and not homosexuality, represents its major interdiction. Thus, when thought by the straight mind, homosexuality is nothing but heterosexuality.

Yes, straight society is based on the necessity of the different/other at every level. It cannot work economically, symbolically, linguistically, or politically without this concept. This necessity of the different/other is an ontological one for the whole conglomerate of sciences and disciplines that I call the straight mind. But what is the different/other if not the dominated? For heterosexual society is the society which not only oppresses lesbians and gay men, it oppresses many different/others, it oppresses all women and many categories of men, all those who are in the position of the dominated. To constitute a difference and to control it is an "act of power, since it is essentially a normative act. Everybody tries to show the other as different. But not everybody succeeds in doing so. One has to be socially dominant to succeed in it."[7]

For example, the concept of difference between the sexes ontologically constitutes women into different/others. Men are not different, whites are not different, nor are the masters. But the blacks, as well as the slaves, are. This ontological characteristic of the difference between the sexes affects all the concepts which are part of the same conglomerate. But for us there is no such thing as being-woman or being-man. "Man" and "woman" are political concepts of opposition, and the copula which dialectically unites them is, at the same time, the one which abolishes them.[8] It is the class struggle between women and men which will abolish men and women.[9] The concept of difference has nothing ontological about it. It is only the way that the masters interpret a historical situation of domination. The function of difference is to mask at every level the conflicts of interest, including ideological ones.

In other words, for us, this means there cannot any longer be women and men, and that as classes and categories of thought or language they have to disappear, politically, economically, ideologically. If we, as lesbians and gay men, continue to speak of ourselves and to conceive of ourselves as women and as men, we are instrumental in maintaining heterosexuality. I am sure that an economic and political transformation will not dedramatize these categories of language. Can we redeem *slave*? Can we redeem *nigger, negress*? How is *woman* different. Will we continue to write *white, master, man*? The transformation of economic relationships will not suffice. We must produce a political transformation of the key concepts, that is of the concepts which are strategic for us. For there is another order of materiality, that of language, and language is worked upon from within by these strategic concepts. It is at the same time tightly connected to the political field, where everything that concerns language, science and thought refers to the person as subjectivity and to her/his relationship to society. And we cannot leave this within the power of the straight mind or the thought of domination.

If among all the productions of the straight mind I especially challenge the models of the Structural Unconscious, it is because: at the moment in history when the domination of social groups can no longer appear as a logical necessity to the dominated, because they revolt, because they question the differences, Lévi-Strauss, Lacan, and their epigones call upon necessities which escape the control of consciousness and therefore the responsibility of individuals.

They call upon unconscious processes, for example, which require the exchange of women as a necessary condition for every society. According to them, that is what the unconscious tells us with authority, and the symbolic order, without which there is no meaning, no language, no society, depends on it. But what does women being exchanged mean if not that they are dominated? No wonder then that there is only one Unconscious, and that it is heterosexual. It is an Unconscious which looks too consciously after the interests of the masters[10] in whom it lives for them to be dispossessed of their concepts so easily. Besides, domination is denied; there is no slavery of women, there is difference. To which I will answer with this statement made by a Rumanian peasant at a public meeting in 1848: "Why do the gentlemen say it was not slavery, for we know it to have been slavery, this sorrow that we have sorrowed." Yes, we know it, and this science of oppression cannot be taken away from us.

It is from this science that we must track down the "what-goes-without-saying" heterosexual, and (I paraphrase the early Roland Barthes) we must not hear "seeing Nature and History confused at every turn."[11] We must make it brutally apparent that psychoanalysis after Freud and particularly Lacan have rigidly turned their concepts into myths—Difference, Desire, the Name-of-the-father, etc. They have even "over-mythified" the myths, an operation that was necessary for them in order to systematically heterosexualize that personal dimension which suddenly emerged through the dominated individuals into the historical field, particularly through women, who started their struggle almost two centuries ago. And it has been done systematically, in a concert of interdisciplinarity, never more harmonious than since the heterosexual myths started to circulate with ease from one formal system to another, like sure values that can be invested in anthropology as well as in psychoanalysis and in all the social sciences.

This ensemble of heterosexual myths is a system of signs which uses figures of speech, and thus it can be politically studied from within the science of our oppression; "for-we-know-it-to-have-been-slavery" is the dynamic which introduces the diachronism of history into the fixed discourse of eternal essences. This undertaking should somehow be a political semiology, although with "this sorrow that we have sorrowed" we work also at the level of language/manifesto, of language/action, that which transforms, that which makes history.

In the meantime, in the systems that seemed so eternal and universal that laws could be extracted from them, laws that could be stuffed into computers, and in any case for the moment stuffed into the unconscious machinery, in these systems, thanks to our action and our language, shifts are happening. Such a model, as for example, the exchange of women, reengulfs history in so violent and brutal a way that the whole system, which was believed to be formal, topples over into another dimension of knowledge. This dimension of history belongs to us, since somehow we have been designated, and since, as Lévi-Strauss said, we talk, let us say that we break off the heterosexual contract.

So, this is what lesbians say everywhere in this country and in some others, if not with theories at least through their social practice, whose repercussions upon straight culture and society are still unenvisionable. An anthropologist might say that we have to wait for fifty years. Yes, if one wants to universalize the functioning of these societies and make their invariants appear. Meanwhile the straight concepts are undermined. What is woman? Panic, general alarm for an active defense. Frankly, it is a problem that the lesbians do not have because of a change of perspective, and it would be incorrect to say that lesbians associate, make love, live with women, for "woman" has meaning only in heterosexual systems of thought and heterosexual economic systems. Lesbians are not women.

NOTES

1. This text was first read in New York at the Modern Language Association Convention in 1978 and dedicated to American lesbians.
2. However, the classical Greeks knew that there was no political power without mastery of the art of rhetoric, especially in a democracy.
3. Throughout this paper, when Lacan's use of the term "the Unconscious" is referred to it is capitalized, following his style.
4. For example see Karla Jay and Allen Young, eds., *Out of the Closets* (New York: Links Books, 1972).
5. Heterosexuality: a word which first appears in the French language in 1911.
6. Ti-Grace Atkinson, *Amazon Odyssey* (New York: Links Books, 1974), pp. 13–23.
7. Claude Faugeron and Philippe Robert, *La Justice et son public et les représentations sociales du système pénal* (Paris: Masson, 1978).
8. See, for her definition of "social sex," Nicole-Claude Mathieu, "Notes pour une définition sociologique des catégories de sexe," *Epistémologie Sociologique* 11 (1971). Translated as *Ignored by Some, Denied by Others: The Social Sex Category in Sociology* (pamphlet), Explorations in Feminism 2 (London: Women's Research and Resources Centre Publications, 1977), pp. 16–37.

9. In the same way that in every other class struggle the categories of opposition are "reconciled" by the struggle whose goal is to make them disappear.
10. Are the millions of dollars a year made by the psychoanalysts symbolic?
11. Roland Barthes, *Mythologies* (New York: Hill and Wang, 1972), p. 11.

HOMO SUM

Homo sum; humani nihil a me alienum puto.
(Man am I; nothing human is alien to me.)
—Terence, *Heauton Timoroumenos, 25 (The Self-Tormentor)*

All of us have an abstract idea of what being "human" means, even if what we mean when we say "human" is still potential and virtual, has not yet been actualized. For indeed, for all its pretension to being universal, what has been until now considered "human" in our Western philosophy concerns only a small fringe of people: white men, proprietors of the means of production, along with the philosophers who theorized their point of view as the only and exclusively possible one. This is the reason why when we consider abstractly, from a philosophical point of view, the potentiality and virtuality of humanness, we need to do it, to see clearly, from an oblique point of view. Thus, being a lesbian, standing at the outposts of the human (of humankind) represents historically and paradoxically the most human point of view. This idea that from an extreme point of view one can criticize and modify the thought and the structures of society at large is not a new one. We owe it to Robespierre and Saint-Just. Marx and Engels in their *German Ideology* extended the idea by affirming the necessity for the most radical groups to show their point of view and their interests as general and universal, a stand that touches both the practical and philosophical (political) points of view.

The situation of lesbians here and now in society, whether they know it or not, is located philosophically (politically) beyond the categories of sex. Practically they have run away from their class (the class of women), even if only partially and precariously.

It is from this cultural and practical site, both extremely vulnerable and crucial, that I will raise the question of dialectics.

There is, on one side, the whole world in its massive assumption, its massive affirmation of heterosexuality as a must-be, and on the other side, there is only the dim, fugitive, sometimes illuminating and striking vision of heterosexuality as a trap, as a forced political regime, that is, with the possibility of escaping it as a fact.

Our political thought has been for more than a century shaped by dialectics. Those of us who have discovered dialectical thought through its most modern form, the Marxian and Engelsian one, that is, the producer of the theory of class struggle, had, in order to understand its mechanism, to refer to Hegel, particularly if they needed to comprehend the reversal which Marx and Engels inflicted on Hegel's dialectics. That is, briefly, a dynamization of the essentialist categories of Hegel, a transport from metaphysics to politics (to show that in the political and social field metaphysical terms had to be interpreted in terms of conflicts, and not anymore in terms of essential oppositions, and to show that the conflicts could be overcome and the categories of opposition reconciled).

A remark here: Marx and Engels, in summarizing all the social oppositions in terms of class struggle and class struggle only, reduced all the conflicts under two terms. This was an operation of reduction which did away with a series of conflicts that could be subsumed under the appellation of "capital's anachronisms." Racism, antisemitism and sexism have been hit by the Marxian reduction. The theory of conflict that they originated could be expressed by a paradigm that crossed all the Marxist "classes." They could not be interpreted exclusively in economic terms: that is, in terms of the bare appropriation of surplus value in a sociological context where all are equal in rights, but where the capitalists because they possess the means of production can appropriate most of the workers' production and work as far as it produces a value that is exchangeable in terms of money and the market. Every conflict whose forms could not be flattened to the two terms of the class struggle was supposed to be solved after the proletarian class assumed power.

We know that historically the theory of the class struggle did not win, and the world is still divided into capitalists (owners of the means of production) and workers (providers of work and labor strength and producers of surplus value). The consequence of the failure of the proletarian class to change the social relationships in all countries leads us to a dead end. In terms of dialectics the result is a freezing of the Marxian dynamics, the return to a metaphysical thought and the superimposition of essentialist terms onto the terms that were to be transformed through Marxian dialectics. In other words, we are still facing a capitalist versus a proletarian class, but this time, as though they had been struck by the wand of the Sleeping Beauty fairy, they are here to stay, they are struck by the coin of fate, immobilized, changed into essential terms, emptied of the dynamic relationship that could transform them.

For my purpose here there is no need to go into a deep reexamination of the Marxian approach, except to say in terms of the world equilibrium that what Marx called the anachronisms of capital, of the industrial world, cover up a mass of different people, half of humankind in the persons of women, the colonized, the third world and *le quart monde*,[1] and the peasants in the industrial world. Lenin and Mao Zedong had to face the problem with their masses early in the century.

From a lesbian political philosophical point of view, when one reflects on women's situation in history, one needs to interrogate dialectics further back than Hegelian dialectics, back to its originating locus; that is, one needs to go back to Aristotle and Plato to comprehend how the categories of opposition that have shaped us were born.

Of the first Greek philosophers, some were materialists and all were monists, which means that they did not see any division in Being. Being as being was one. According to Aristotle, we owe to the Pythagorean school the division in the process of thought and therefore in the thought of Being. Then, instead of thinking in terms of unity, philosophers introduced duality in thought, in the process of reasoning.

Consider the first table of opposites which history has handed down to us, as it has been recorded by Aristotle (*Metaphysics*, Book I, 5, 6):

Limited	Unlimited
Odd	Even
One	Many
Right	Left
Male	Female
Rest	Motion
Straight	Curved
Light	Dark
Good	Bad
Square	Oblong

We may observe that

right	left
male	female
light	dark
good	bad

are terms of judgment and evaluation, ethical concepts, that are foreign to the series from which I extracted them. The first series is a technical, instrumental series corresponding to a division needed by the tool for which it was created (a kind of carpenter's square called a gnomon). Since Pythagoras and the members of his school were mathematicians, one can comprehend their series. The second series is heterogeneous to the first one. So it so happens that as soon as the precious conceptual tools resting on division (variations, comparisons, differences) were created, they were immediately (or almost immediately by the successors of the school of Pythagoras) turned into a means of creating metaphysical and moral differentiation in Being.

There is then with Aristotle a displacement, a jump in the comprehension of these concepts, which he used for his historical approach to philosophy and what he called metaphysics. From being practical concepts they became abstract ones. From terms whose function had been to sort out, to classify, to make measurement possible (in itself a work of genius) they were translated into a metaphysical dimension, and pretty soon they got totally dissociated from their context. Furthermore, the evaluative and ethical terms (right, male, light, good) of the tabulation of opposites, as used within the metaphysical interpretation of Aristotle (and Plato), modified the meaning of technical terms like "One." Everything that was "good" belonged to the series of the One (as Being). Everything that was "many" (different) belonged to the series of the "bad," assimilated to nonbeing, to unrest, to everything that questions what is good. Thus we left the domain of deduction to enter the domain of interpretation.

In the dialectical field created by Plato and Aristotle we find a series of oppositions inspired by the first mathematical tabulation, but distorted. Thus under the series of the "One" (the absolute being nondivided, divinity itself) we have "male" (and "light") that were from then on never dislodged from their dominant position. Under the other series appear the unrestful: the common people, the females, the "slaves of the poor," the "dark" (barbarians who cannot distinguish between slaves and women), all reduced to the parameter of non-Being. For Being is being good, male, straight, one, in other words, godlike, while non-Being is being anything else (many), female: it means discord, unrest, dark, and bad. (See Aristotle's *Politics*).

Plato played with the terms One and the Same (as being God and the Good) and the Other (which is not the same as God which is non-Being, bad). Thus dialectics operates on a series of oppositions that basically have a metaphysical connotation: Being or non-Being. From our point of view, Hegel, in his dialectics of master versus slave, does not proceed very differently. Marx himself, although trying to historicize the oppositions into conflicts (social ones, practical ones), was a prisoner of the metaphysical series, of the dialectical series. Bourgeoisie is on the side of the One, of Being; Proletariat is on the side of the Other, the non-Being.

Thus the need, the necessity of questioning dialectics consists for us in the "dialecticizing" of dialectics, questioning it in relation to its terms or opposition as principles and also in its functioning. For if in the history of philosophy there was a jump from deduction to interpretation and contradiction, or, in other words, if from mathematical and instrumental categories we jumped to the normative and metaphysical categories, shouldn't we call attention to it?

Shouldn't we mention that the paradigm to which female, dark, bad, and unrest belong has also been augmented to slave, Other, different? Every philosopher of our modern age, including the linguists, the psychoanalysts, the anthropologists, will tell us that without the precise categories of opposition (of difference), one cannot reason or think or, even better, that outside of them meaning cannot shape itself, there is an impossibility of meaning as outside of society, in the asocial.

Certainly Marx intended to turn Hegel's dialectics upside down. The step forward for Marx was to show that dialectical categories such as the One and the Other, Master and Slave, were not there to stay and had nothing metaphysical or essential about them, but had to be read and understood in historical terms. With this gesture he was reestablishing the link between philosophy and politics. Thus the categories which are today called so solemnly categories of Difference (belonging to what I call the thought of Difference) were for Marx conflictual categories—categories of social conflicts—which throughout the class struggle were supposed to destroy each other. And, as it had to happen in such a struggle, in destroying (abolishing) the One, the Other was also going to destroy (abolish) itself. For as soon as the proletariat constituted itself as an economic class, it had to destroy itself as well as the bourgeoisie. The process of destruction consists in a double movement: destroying itself as a class (otherwise the bourgeoisie keeps the power) and destroying itself as a philosophical category (the category of the Other), for staying mentally in the category of the Other (of the slave) would mean a nonresolution in terms of Marxian dialectics. The resolution then tends toward a philosophical reevaluation of the two conflictual terms, which as soon as it makes clear that there is an economic force where there was before a nonforce (a nothing), this force has to deny itself on the side of the Other (slave) and to take over on the side of the One (master), but only to abolish both orders, thus reconciling them to make them the same and only one.

What has happened in history throughout the revolutions which we have known is that the Other (a category of others) has substituted itself for the One, keeping under it huge groups of oppressed peoples that would in turn become the Other of the ex-others, become by then the One. This happened already (before Marx) with the French Revolution, which could not deal very well with the questions of slavery and did not deal at all with the questions of women (Women, the eternal Other). To dialecticize dialectics seems to me to question what will really happen to the question of humanness once all categories of others will be transferred onto the side of the One, of Being, of the Subject. Will there be no transformation? For example, in terms of language will we be able to keep the terms "humanity," "human," "man," "*l'homme*," "*homo*," even though all these terms in the abstract mean first the human being (without distinction of sex)? Shall we keep these terms after they have been appropriated for so long by the dominant group (men over women) and after they have been used to mean both abstractly and concretely humanity as male? Mankind: Malekind. In other words a philosophical and political abuse.

This necessary transformation (a dialectical operation) was not dealt with by Marx and Engels. They were dealing (as usual with revolutions) with a substitution. For a good reason: because they were writing about the issue *before* the event of a proletarian revolution and could not determine before the fact what would happen. For a bad reason: the bearers of the Universal, of the General, of the Human, of the One, was the bourgeois class (see *The Communist Manifesto*), the yeast of history, the only class able to go beyond the national bounds. The proletarian class, although the climbing one, had stayed for them at the stage of limbo, a mass of ghosts that needed the direction of the Communist Party (its members themselves mostly bourgeois) to subsist and fight.

Thus perished our most perfect model of dialectics, of materialist dialectics, because the dice were loaded: the Other from the start was condemned to stay in the place where it was to be found at first in the relationship, that is, *essentially* in the Other's place, since the agency that was to achieve the class transformation (that is, to break down the categories of the One and the Other, and to turn them into something else) belonged to the parameter of the One, that is, to the bourgeoisie itself.

When it was upon the bourgeoisie by the means of its revolutionary fraction that Marxian dialectics imposed the demand of fighting itself and of reducing itself to nothing, through the reduction of both classes, could we expect them to do it? For the representatives of the Communist Party mostly did belong, did come from, the bourgeois class through its intellectuals.

This issue, even more crucial as far as women and men are concerned, is still in its infancy, barely questioned. It is scarcely possible to position women in relation to men. Who is actually reasonable enough to conceive that it is necessary, or that it will be necessary to destroy these categories as categories and to end the domination of the "One" over the Other? Which is not to say to substitute women for men (the Other for the One).

Actually, as of old, men are on one side and women are on the other. The

"Ones" dominate and possess everything, including women, the others are dominated and appropriated. What I believe in such a situation is that at the level of philosophy and politics women should do without the privilege of being different and above all never formulate this imposition of being different (relegated to the category of the Other) as a "right to be different," or never abandon themselves to the "pride of being different." Since politically and economically the matter seems to be very slow to get settled, it seems to me that philosophically one can be helped by the process of abstraction.

In the abstract, mankind, Man, is everybody—the Other, whatever its kind, is included. Once the possibility of abstraction becomes a fact among human beings, there are at this level certain facts that can be made clear.

There is no need when coming under the parameters of the oppressed to follow the Marxian design and to wait until the "final victory" to declare that the oppressed are human as well as the dominators, that women are human as well as men. Where is the obligation for us to go on bearing with a series of ontological, etymological, and linguistic *entourloupettes*[2] under the pretext that we do not have the power. It is part of our fight to unmask them, to say that one out of two men is a woman, that the universal belongs to us although we have been robbed and despoiled at this level as well as at the political and economic ones. At this point maybe the dialectical method that I have admired so much can do very little for us. For abstractly, in the order of reasoning, in the order of possibility and potentiality, in philosophy, the Other cannot essentially *be* different from the One, it *is* the Same, along the lines of what Voltaire called the Sameness (*la "Mêmeté"*, a neologism he coined, never used in French). No Thought of the Other or Thought of Difference should be possible for us, for "nothing human is alien" to the One or to the Other.

I believe we have not reached the end of what Reason can do for us. And I do not want to deny my Cartesian cast of mind, for I look back to the Enlightenment for the first glimmer of light that history has given us. By now, however, Reason has been turned into a representative of Order, Domination, Logocentrism. According to many of our contemporaries the only salvation is in a tremendous exaltation of what they call alterity under all of its forms: Jewish, Black, Red, Yellow, Female, Homosexual, Crazy. Far away from Reason (do they mean within Folly?), "Different," and proud of being so.

Both the figureheads of the dominators and of the dominated have adopted this point of view. Good is no more to be found in the parameter of the One, of Male, of Light, but in the parameter of the Other, of Female, Darkness. So long live Unreason, and let them be embarked anew in *la nef des fous*, the carnival, and so on. Never has the Other been magnified and celebrated to this extent. Other cultures, the mind of the Other, the Feminine brain, Feminine writing, and so on—we have during these last decades known everything as far as the Other is concerned.

I do not know who is going to profit from this abandonment of the oppressed to a trend that will make them more and more powerless, having lost the faculty of being subjects even before having gained it. I would say that we can renounce only what we have. And I would be glad to send the representatives of the dominators away back to back, whether they come from the party of the One or the party of the Other.

Naiveté, innocence, lack of doubt, certainty that everything is either black or white, certainty that when Reason is not sovereign then Unreason or Folly have the upper hand, belief that where there is Being there is also non-Being as a kind of refuse, and the most absurd of all things, the need and necessity in reaction to this evidence and these certainties to support and advocate, in contrast, a "right to Difference" (a right of difference) which by reversing everything corresponds to the Tweedledum and Tweedledee of Lewis Carroll—these are all the symptoms of what I have once called, out of exasperation, the straight mind. Sexes (gender), Difference between the sexes, man, woman, race, black, white, nature are at the core of its set of parameters. And they have shaped our concepts, our laws, our institutions, our history, our cultures.

They think they answer everything when they read metaphors in this double parameter, and to our analysis they object that there is a symbolic order, as though they were speaking of another dimension that would have nothing to do with domination. Alas for us, the symbolic order partakes of the same reality as the political and economic order. There is a continuum in their reality, a continuum where abstraction is imposed upon materiality and can shape the body as well as the mind of those it oppresses.

NOTES

1. We must add here the notion of the "fourth world" used in Europe to designate people who live in poverty in the Western industrialized world.
2. Nasty tricks, circumventing tricks.

6

MATERNITY, FEMINISM, AND LANGUAGE

Julia Kristeva

INTRODUCTION

by Kelly Oliver

Julia Kristeva was born in 1941 in Bulgaria. She was educated by French nuns, studied literature, and worked as a journalist before going to Paris in 1966 to do graduate work with Lucien Goldmann and Roland Barthes. While in Paris she finished her doctorate in French literature, became involved in the influential journal *Tel Quel*, and began psychoanalytic training. In 1979 she finished her training as a psychoanalyst. Currently, Kristeva is a professor of linguistics at the University of Paris VII and a regular visiting professor at Columbia University. In addition to her work as a practicing psychoanalyst and her theoretical writings, Kristeva is a novelist.

Kristeva's work reflects her diverse background. Her writing is an intersection between philosophy, psychoanalysis, linguistics, and cultural and literary theory. She developed the science of what she calls "semanalysis," which is a combination of Freud's psychoanalysis and Saussure's and Peirce's semiology. With this new science Kristeva challenges traditional psychoanalytic theory, linguistic theory, and philosophy.

Kristeva's most influential contribution to philosophy of language has been her distinction between the semiotic and the symbolic elements of signification. All signification is made up of these two elements in varying proportions. The semiotic element is the organization of drives in signifying practices. It is associated with rhythms and tones that are meaningful parts of language and yet do not represent or signify something. Rhythms and tones do not represent bodily drives; rather bodily drives are discharged through rhythms and tones. The symbolic element of language, on the other hand, is the domain of position and judgment. It is associated with the grammar or structure of language that enables it

— Individuation always requires a certain amount of disgust w/ the other, at an individual and cultural level

to signify something. The dialectical oscillation between the semiotic and the symbolic is what makes signification possible.

Kristeva criticizes the traditional Freudian account of how the infant enters the social because it is based on the threat of castration, which cannot adequately explain the child's move to signification. If motivations for the move to signification are threats and the pain of separation, then why would anyone make this move? Why not remain in the safe haven of the maternal body and refuse the social and signification with its threats? Kristeva maintains that separation also must be pleasurable and this explains the move away from the maternal body and into signification.

Kristeva's alternative account of the infant's entrance into signification complicates the traditional psychoanalytic accounts of both the paternal function and the maternal function. Kristeva maintains that individuation requires what she calls "abjection." The most powerful location of abjection in the development of any individual is the maternal body. In *Powers of Horror*, Kristeva describes the abject as that which calls into question borders; and in an individual's development, the maternal body poses the greatest threat to the border of the subject. For Kristeva, before the mother can become an object for the infant, she becomes an abject. Through this process of abjection the infant finds the maternal body disgusting, if still fascinating, and is able to leave it behind and enter the social.

In *Powers of Horror*, Kristeva argues that collective identity formation is analogous to individual identity formation. She claims that abjection is coextensive in both individual and collective identity, which operate according to the same logic of abjection. Just as an individual marks his difference from the maternal body through a process of abjection, society marks off its difference from animals through a process of abjection. In her analysis, however, the animal realm has been associated with the maternal, which ultimately represents the realm of nature from which human culture must separate to assert its humanity. Kristeva's analysis of the process of abjection from the maternal inherent in social formation is an elaboration of Freud's thesis that the social is founded on the murder of the father and the incest taboo. Kristeva's provocative reading of the incest taboo as the operation of abjection through which we attempt to guarantee the separation of culture from nature is useful to feminist theorists interested in the dynamics of marginalization and exclusion, especially insofar as Kristeva continually elaborates various ways that the repressed abject returns. The process of abjection is never completed. Rather, like everything repressed it is bound to return.

Although Kristeva maintains that all language and culture sets up separations and order by repressing maternal authority, she also insists that this repressed maternal authority returns in religious rituals, literature, and art. In fact, some of her work suggests that all art is the result of a sublimation of the repressed maternal relation; in other words, all art is a form of incest. While in *Powers of Horror* Kristeva does not address sexual difference in relation to abjection, in interviews and later work, including *Black Sun*, Kristeva indicates some of the ways in which the process of abjection works differently for males and females. We could say that the incest taboo affects men and women differently and therefore the repressed maternal returns differently in relation to men and women. Given that men can separate from the maternal body and enter the social, they can also return to it through art and literature without threatening their position within the social order. While the male artist can access this repressed maternal semiotic and still maintain his position within the social order, the female artist's return to the maternal semiotic threatens her social position which is always more precarious because of her identification with the abjected maternal body. So, it is more dangerous for a woman to articulate the excluded or repressed maternal body in her work because as a woman within a patriarchal culture she is already marginal. If a woman identifies with the semiotic in her work, she risks not being taken seriously by the social order. In terms of everyday experience, this means that men can be more experimental than women can be in their work and still be taken seriously.

On the other hand, women can take up the law in revolutionary ways. Kristeva suggests that from her marginal position within the social order, a woman can challenge the symbolic element of signification merely by embracing the law or reason as a woman. When a marginal person inserts herself into the subject position at the center of culture, she changes the effect of that position. This is why in "From One Identity to an Other" Kristeva claims that perhaps it takes a woman or another marginal figure to propel theoretical reason into infinite analysis of its own subject position as always a subject-in-process. Women also have a privileged access to the maternal body through childbirth. In "Stabat Mater" and "Motherhood according to Bellini" Kristeva makes the provocative claim that the desire to have children is a sublimated incestuous desire for reunion with the maternal body. While the artist gains access to the repressed maternal body through his work, the mother gains access to the repressed maternal body through childbirth, which is a type of reunion with her own mother.

Although Kristeva has an ambivalent, sometimes hostile, relationship to feminism and some aspects of the feminist movement in France, her theories provide some innovative approaches for feminist theory. One of her central contributions to feminist theory is her call for a new discourse of maternity. In "Stabat Mater," an essay in *Tales of Love*, she criticizes some of the traditional discourses of maternity in Western culture, specifically the myth of the Virgin Mary, be-

nature → social → ethical

cause they do not present the mother as primarily a speaking being. Without a
new discourse of maternity we cannot begin to conceive of ethics. If ethics is the
philosophy of our obligations to each other, then in order to theorize ethics we
need to analyze the structure of our relationships to each other. And if, as
Freudian psychoanalytic theory maintains, our relation with our mothers is the
model for all subsequent relations, then we need to analyze our relation with our
mothers. In Western culture, however, this relation has been figured as a relation to nature, a relation that threatens the social and any possibility of ethical
relations. In this view the relation with the mother is not a social relation and
therefore not a model for an ethical relation. In order to conceive of an ethical
relation, we need to conceive of a relation with the mother as a social relation
with a speaking social being.

    Kristeva suggests that women's oppression can be explained at least partially
as a misplaced abjection. It is necessary to abject the maternal body qua the ful-
filler of needs. But in Western culture woman, the feminine, and the mother
have all been reduced to the reproductive function of the maternal body. The
result is that when we abject the maternal body we also abject woman, the feminine, and the mother. We need a new discourse of maternity that can delineate
between these various aspects and functions of women. Kristeva has set the
stage by highlighting and complicating the maternal function. To view the
mother's relation to the developing infant as a function uncouples the activities
performed by the caretaker from the sex of the caretaker. Although Kristeva may
believe that the maternal function should be performed by women, she does use
the language of functions to separate caretaking functions from other activities
performed by women. Woman, the female, the feminine, and the mother cannot be reduced to the maternal function. Women and mothers are primarily
speaking social beings.

    In "Women's Time," Kristeva identifies two generations of feminism, both of
which she accuses of using "woman" as a religious ideal. The first (pre-1968)
feminism is the feminism of suffragettes and existentialists. It is a struggle over
the identity of woman as rational citizen, deserving of the "rights of man." The
ideal "woman" contains the same characteristics of the ideal "man," and the
struggle is to insert her in man's linear history. The second (post-1968) feminism
is the feminism of psychoanalysts and artists. It is a struggle against reducing the
identity of woman to the identity of man by inserting her into his linear time.
These feminists assert a unique essence of woman or the feminine that falls outside of phallic time and phallic discourse. Kristeva argues that this strategy not
only makes feminism into a religion but also traps women in an inferior and marginal position with regard to society. She embraces a radical individualism beyond the first two phases of feminism wherein each individual is considered

unique to the extreme that there are as many sexualities and "maladies of the soul" as there are individuals.

Like many intellectuals after May 1968, Kristeva became disillusioned with practical politics. She maintains that political interpretation, like religion, is a search for one transcendent Meaning. Insofar as they fix an ideal, even political interpretations with emancipatory goals can become totalitarian. This is Kristeva's complaint against contemporary feminist movements. In order for political movements to be emancipatory, they must acknowledge that their fixed ideals are built on exclusions and persecutions. They must admit that their ideals are illusions created in the contexts of particular psychic struggles. Kristeva claims that psychoanalysis cuts through the illusions of political interpretation.

BIBLIOGRAPHY

Selected Primary Texts

1977. *About Chinese Women*. Translated by Anita Barrows. New York: Marion Boyars. [*Des Chinoises*. Paris: Editions des Femmes, 1974.]

1980. *Desire in Language*. Translated by Thomas Gora, Alice Jardine, and Leon Roudiez; edited by Leon Roudiez. New York: Columbia University Press.

1982. *Powers of Horror*. Translated by Leon Roudiez. New York: Columbia University Press. [*Pouvoirs de l'horreur*. Paris: Editions du Seuil, 1980.]

1984. *Revolution in Poetic Language*. Translated by Margaret Waller. New York: Columbia University Press. [*La Revolution du langage poetique*. Paris: Seuil, 1974.]

1986. *The Kristeva Reader*. Edited by Toril Moi. New York: Columbia Press.

1987. *Tales of Love*. Translated by Leon Roudiez. New York: Columbia University Press. [*Histoires d'amour*. Paris: Editions Denöel, 1983.]

1989. *Black Sun: Depression and Melancholy*. Translated by Leon Roudiez. New York: Columbia University Press. [*Soleil Noir: Depression et Melancolie*. Paris: Gallimard, 1987.]

1991. *Strangers to Ourselves*. Translated by Leon Roudiez. New York: Columbia University Press. [*Etrangers à nous mêmes*. Paris: Fayard, 1989.]

1995. *New Maladies of the Soul*. Translated by Ross Guberman. New York: Columbia University Press. [*Les Nouvelles maladies de l'ame*. Paris: Fayard, 1993.]

1996. *Julia Kristeva Interviews*. Edited by Ross Guberman. New York: Columbia University Press.

1996. *Time and Sense: Proust and the Experience of Literature*. Translated by Ross Guberman. New York: Columbia University Press. [*Le temps sensible: Proust et l'expérience littéraire*. Paris: Gallimard, 1994.]

1998. *The Portable Kristeva*. Edited by Kelly Oliver. New York: Columbia University Press.

Selected Secondary Texts

Benjamin, Andrew, and John Fletcher, eds. 1990. *Abjection, Melancholia and Love: The Work of Julia Kristeva*. London: Routledge.
Crownfield, David, ed. 1992. *Body/Text in Julia Kristeva: Religion, Women and Psychoanalysis*. Albany: SUNY Press.
Lechte, John. *Julia Kristeva*. 1990. London: Routledge.
Oliver, Kelly. 1993. *Reading Kristeva: Unraveling the Double-bind*. Bloomington: Indiana University Press.
———, ed. 1993. *Ethics, Politics and Difference in Julia Kristeva's Writings*. New York: Routledge.
———. *Subjectivity without Subjects*. 1998. Lanham, Md.: Rowman & Littlefield.
Smith, Anna. 1996. *Julia Kristeva: Readings of Exile and Estrangement*. New York: St. Martins.
Smith, Anna-Marie. 1998. *Julia Kristeva: Speaking the Unspeakable*. New York: Stylus Press.

FROM ONE IDENTITY TO AN OTHER

. . . [O]ne should begin by positing that there is within poetic language (and therefore, although in a less pronounced manner, within any language) a *heterogeneousness* to meaning and signification. This *heterogeneousness*, detected genetically in the first echolalias of infants as rhythms and intonations anterior to the first phonemes, morphemes, lexemes, and sentences; this heterogeneousness, which is later reactivated as rhythms, intonations, glossalalias in psychotic discourse, serving as ultimate support of the speaking subject threatened by the collapse of the signifying function; this heterogeneousness to signification operates through, despite, and in excess of it and produces in poetic language "musical" but also nonsense effects that destroy not only accepted beliefs and significations, but, in radical experiments, syntax itself, that guarantee of thetic consciousness (of the signified object and ego)—for example, carnivalesque discourse, Artaud, a number of texts by Mallarmé, certain Dadaist and Surrealist experiments. The notion of *heterogeneity* is indispensable, for though articulate, precise, organized, and complying with constraints and rules (especially, like the rule of *repetition*, which articulates the units of a particular rhythm or intonation), this signifying disposition is not that of meaning or signification: no sign, no predication, no signified object and therefore no operating consciousness of a transcendental ego.

We shall call this disposition *semiotic (le sémiotique)*, meaning, according to the etymology of the Greek *sémeion* (σημεῖον), a distinctive mark, trace, index, the premonitory sign, the proof, engraved mark, imprint—in short, a *distinctiveness* admitting of an uncertain and indeterminate articulation because it does not yet refer (for young children) or no longer refers (in psychotic discourse) to a signified object for a thetic consciousness (this side of, or through, both object and consciousness). Plato's *Timeus* speaks of a *chora* (χώρα), receptacle (ὑποδοχεῖον), unnamable, improbable, hybrid, anterior to naming, to the One, to the father, and consequently, maternally connoted to such an extent that it merits "not even the rank of syllable." One can describe more precisely than did philosophical intuition the particularities of this signifying disposition that I have just named semiotic—a term which quite clearly designates that we are dealing with a disposition that is definitely heterogeneous to meaning but always in sight of it or in either a negative or surplus relationship to it. Research I have recently undertaken on child language acquisition in the prephonological, one could say prepredicative stages, or anterior to the "mirror stage," as well as another concomitant study on particularities of psychotic discourse aim notably at describing as precisely as possible—with the help of, for example, modern phonoacoustics—these semiotic operations (rhythm, intonation) and their dependence vis-à-vis the body's drives observable through muscular contractions and the libidinal or sublimated cathexis that accompany vocalizations. It goes without saying that, concerning a *signifying practice*, that is, a socially communicable discourse like poetic language, this semiotic heterogeneity posited by theory is inseparable from what I shall call, to distinguish it from the latter, the *symbolic* function of significance. The symbolic *(le symbolique)*, as opposed to the semiotic, is this inevitable attribute of meaning, sign, and the signified object for the consciousness of Husserl's transcendental ego. Language as social practice necessarily presupposes these two dispositions, though combined in different ways to constitute *types of discourse*, types of signifying practices. Scientific discourse, for example, aspiring to the status of metalanguage, tends to reduce as much as possible the semiotic component. On the contrary, the signifying economy of poetic language is specific in that the semiotic is not only a constraint as is the symbolic, but it tends to gain the upper hand at the expense of the thetic and predicative constraints of the ego's judging consciousness. Thus in any poetic language, not only do the rhythmic constraints, for example, perform an organizing function that could go so far as to violate certain grammatical rules of a national language and often neglect the importance of an ideatory message, but in recent texts, these semiotic constraints (rhythm, phonic, vocalic timbres in Symbolist work, but also graphic disposition on the page) are accompanied by nonrecoverable syntactic elisions; it is impossible to reconstitute the particular elided syntactic category (object or verb), which makes the meaning of the utterance undecidable (for example, the nonrecoverable elisions in *Un Coup de Dés*).[1] However elided, attacked, or corrupted the symbolic function might be in poetic language, due to the impact of semiotic processes, the symbolic function nonetheless maintains its presence. It is for this reason that it is a language. First, it persists as an internal limit of this bipolar economy, since a multiple and sometimes even uncomprehensible signified is nevertheless communicated; secondly, it persists also because the semiotic processes themselves, far from being set adrift (as they would be in insane discourse), set up a new formal construct: a so-called new formal or ideological "writer's universe," the never-finished, undefined production of a new space of significance. Husserl's "thetic function" of the signifying act is thus re-assumed, but in different form: though poetic language unsettled the position of the signified and the transcendental ego, it nonetheless posits a thesis, not of a particular being or meaning, but of a signifying apparatus; it posits its own process as an undecidable process between sense and nonsense, between *language* and *rhythm* (in the sense of linkage that the word "rhythm" had for Aeschylus's *Prometheus* according to Heidegger's reading), between the symbolic and semiotic.

For a theory attuned to this kind of functioning, the language object itself appears quite differently than it would from a phenomenological perspective. Thus, a phoneme, as distinctive element of meaning, belongs to language as symbolic. But this same phoneme is involved in rhythmic, intonational repetitions; it thereby tends towards autonomy from meaning so as to maintain itself in a semiotic disposition near the instinctual drives' body; it is a sonorous distinctiveness, which therefore is no longer either a phoneme or a part of the symbolic system—one might say that its belonging to the set of the language is indefinite, between zero and one. Nevertheless, the set to which it thus belongs exists with this indefinition, with this fuzziness.

It is poetic language that awakens our attention to this undecidable character of any so-called natural language, a feature that univocal, rational, scientific discourse tends to hide—and this implies considerable consequences for its subject. The support of this signifying economy could not be the transcendental ego alone. If it is true that there would unavoidably be a speaking *subject* since the signifying set exists, it is nonetheless evident that this subject, in order to tally with its heterogeneity, must be, let us say, a questionable *subject-in-process*. It is of course Freud's theory of the unconscious that allows the apprehension of such a subject; for through the surgery it practiced in the operating consciousness of the transcendental ego, Freudian and Lacanian psychoanalysis did allow, not for (as certain simplifications would have it) a few typologies or structures that might accommodate the same phenomenological reason, but rather for heterogeneity, which, known as the unconscious, shapes the signifying function. In light of these statements, I shall now make a few remarks on the questionable subject-in-process of poetic language.

1. The semiotic activity, which introduces wandering or fuzziness into language, and *a fortiori*, into poetic language is, from a synchronic point of view, a mark of the workings of drives (appropriate/rejection, orality/anality, love/hate, life/death) and, from a diachronic point of view, stems from the archaisms of the semiotic body. Before recognizing itself as identical in a mirror and, consequently, as signifying, this body is dependent vis-à-vis the mother. At the same time instinctual and maternal, semiotic processes prepare the future speaker for entrance into meaning and signification (the symbolic). But the symbolic (i.e., language as nomination, sign, and syntax) constitutes itself only by breaking with this anteriority, which is retrieved as "signifier," "primary processes," displacement and condensation, metaphor and metonymy, rhetorical figures—but which always remains subordinate—subjacent to the principal function of naming-predicating. Language as symbolic function constitutes itself at the cost of repressing instinctual drive and continuous relation to the mother. On the contrary, the unsettled and questionable subject of poetic language (for whom the word is never uniquely sign) maintains itself at the cost of reactivating this repressed instinctual, maternal element. If it is true that the prohibition of incest constitutes, at the same time, language as communicative code and women as exchange objects in order for a society to be established, *poetic language would be* for its questionable subject-in-process the *equivalent of incest*: it is within the economy of signification itself that the questionable subject-in-process appropriates to itself this archaic, instinctual, and maternal territory; thus it simultaneously prevents the word from becoming mere sign and the mother from becoming an object like any other—forbidden. This passage into and through the forbidden, which constitutes the sign and is correlative to the prohibition of incest, is often explicit as such (Sade: "Unless he becomes his mother's lover from the day she has brought him into the world, let him not bother to write, for we shall not read him,"—*Idée sur les romans*; Artaud, identifying with his "daughters"; Joyce and his daughter at the end of *Finnegans Wake*; Céline who takes as pseudonym his grandmother's first name; and innumerable identifications with women, or dancers, that waver between fetishization and homosexuality). I stress this point for three reasons:

(*a*) To emphasize that the dominance of semiotic constraint in poetic language cannot be solely interpreted, as formalist poetics would have it, as a preoccupation with the "sign," or with the "signifier" at the expense of the "message"; rather, it is more deeply indicative of the instinctual drives' activity relative to the first structurations (constitution of the body as self) and identifications (with the mother).

(b) To elucidate the intrinsic connection between literature and breaking up social concord: because it utters incest, poetic language is linked with "evil"; "literature and evil" (I refer to a title by Georges Bataille) should be understood, beyond the resonances of Christian ethics, as the social body's self-defense against the discourse of incest as destroyer and generator of any language and sociality. This applies all the more as "great literature," which has mobilized unconsciousnesses for centuries, has nothing to do with the hypostasis of incest (a petty game of fetishists at the end of an era, priesthood of a would-be enigma—the forbidden mother); on the contrary, this incestuous relation, exploding in language, embracing it from top to bottom in such a *singular* fashion that it defies *generalizations*, still has this common feature in all outstanding cases: it presents itself as demystified, even disappointed, deprived of its hallowed function as support of the law, in order to become the cause of a permanent trial of the speaking subject, a cause of that agility, of that analytic "competency" that legend attributes to Ulysses.

(c) It is of course possible, as Lévi-Strauss pointed out to Dr. André Green, to ignore the mother-child relationship within a given anthropological vision of society; now, given not only the thematization of this relationship, but especially the mutations in the very economy of discourse attributable to it, one must, in discussing poetic language, consider what this presymbolic and trans-symbolic relationship to the mother introduces as aimless wandering within the identity of the speaker and the economy of its very discourse. Moreover, this relationship of the speaker to the mother is probably one of the most important factors producing interplay within the structure of meaning as well as a questioning process of subject and history.

2. And yet, this reinstatement of maternal territory into the very economy of language does not lead its questioned subject-in-process to repudiate its symbolic disposition. Formulator—logothete, as Roland Barthes would say— the subject of poetic language continually but never definitively assumes the thetic function of naming, establishing meaning and signification, which the paternal function represents within reproductive relation. Son permanently at war with father, not in order to take his place, nor even to endure it, erased from reality, as a symbolic, divine menace and salvation in the manner of *Senatspräsident* Schreber. But rather, to signify what is untenable in the symbolic, nominal, paternal function. If symbolic and social cohesion are maintained by virtue of a sacrifice (which makes of a *soma* a sign towards an unnamable transcendence, so that only thus are signifying and social structures clinched even though they are ignorant of this sacrifice) and if the paternal function repre-

sents this sacrificial function, then it is not up to the poet to adjust to it. Fearing its rule but sufficiently aware of the legislation of language not to be able
to turn away from this sacrificial-paternal function, he takes it by storm and
from the flank. In *Maldoror,* Lautréamont struggles against the Omnipotent.
After the death of his son Anatole, Mallarmé writes a *Tombeau*, thanks to
which a book replaces not only the dead son, his own father, mother, and fi-
ancée at the same time, but also hallowed humanism and the "instinct of
heaven" itself. The most analytical of them all, the Marquis de Sade, gives up
this battle with, or for, the symbolic legislation represented by the father, in
order to attack the power represented by a woman, Madame de Montreuil, visible figurehead of a dynasty of matrons toward whom he usurps, through writing, the role of father and incestuous son; here, the transgression is carried out
and the transsymbolic, transpaternal function of poetic language reaches its
thematic end by staging a simultaneously impossible, sacrificial, and orgastic
society—never one without the other.

Here we must clearly distinguish two positions: that of the rhetorician and
that of the writer in the strongest sense of the word; that is, as Céline puts it, one
who has "style." The rhetorician does not invent a language; fascinated by the
symbolic function of paternal discourse, he *seduces* it in the Latin sense of the
verb—he "leads it astray," inflicts it with a few anomalies generally taken from
writers of the past, thus miming a father who remembers having been a son and
even a daughter of his father, but not to the point of leaving cover. This is indeed what is happening to the discourse of contemporary philosophers, in
France particularly, when, hemmed in by the breakthroughs in social sciences
on the one hand, and social upheavals on the other, the philosopher begins performing literary tricks, thus arrogating to himself a power over imaginations: a
power which, though minor in appearance, is more fetching than that of the
transcendental consciousness. The stylist's adventure is totally different; he no
longer needs to seduce the father by rhetorical affectations. As winner of the battle, he may even drop the name of the father to take a pseudonym (Céline signs
with his grandmother's first name), and thus, in the place of the father, assume
a different discourse; neither imaginary discourse of the self, nor discourse of
transcendental knowledge, but a permanent go-between from one to the other,
a pulsation of sign and rhythm, of consciousness and instinctual drive. "I am the
father of my imaginative creations," writes Mallarmé at the birth of Geneviève.
"I am my father, my mother, my son, and me," Artaud claims. Stylists all, they
sound a dissonance within the thetic, paternal function of language.

3. Psychosis and fetishism represent the two abysses that threaten the unstable subject of poetic language, as twentieth-century literature has only too
clearly demonstrated. As to *psychosis*, symbolic legality is wiped out in favor of

arbitrariness of an instinctual drive without meaning and communication; pan-icking at the loss of all reference, the subject goes through fantasies of omnipo-tence or identification with a totalitarian leader. On the other hand, where *fetishism* is concerned, constantly dodging the paternal, sacrificial function pro-duces an objectification of the pure signifier, more and more emptied of mean-ing—an insipid formalism. Nevertheless, far from thus becoming an unpleasant or negligible accident within the firm progress of symbolic process (which, in the footsteps of science, would eventually find signified elements for all signifiers, as rationalists believe), these borderline experiences, which contemporary poetic language has undergone, perhaps more dramatically than before or elsewhere, show not only that the Saussurian cleavage (signifier/signified) is forever un-bridgeable, but also that it is reinforced by another, even more radical one be-tween an instinctual, semioticizing body, heterogeneous to signification, and this very signification based on prohibition (of incest), sign, and thetic signification establishing signified object and transcendental ego. Through the permanent contradiction between these two dispositions (semiotic/symbolic), of which the internal setting off of the sign (signifier/signified) is merely a witness, poetic lan-guage, in its most disruptive form (unreadable for meaning, dangerous for the subject), shows the constraints of a civilization dominated by transcendental ra-tionality. Consequently, it is a means of overriding this constraint. And if in so doing it sometimes falls in with deeds brought about by the same rationality, as is, for example, the instinctual determination of fascism—demonstrated as such by Wilhelm Reich—poetic language is also there to forestall such translations into action.

This means that if poetic economy has always borne witness to crises and im-possibilities of transcendental symbolics, in our time it is coupled with crises of social institutions (state, family, religion), and, more profoundly, a turning point in the relationship of man to meaning. Transcendental mastery over discourse is possible, but repressive; such a position is necessary, but only as a limit to con-stant challenge; this relief with respect to repression—establishing meaning—is no longer possible under the incarnate appearance of a providential, historical, or even rationalist, humanist ego (in the manner of Renan), but through a *dis-cordance* in the symbolic function and consequently within the identity of the transcendental ego itself: this is what the literary experience of our century inti-mates to theoretical reason, thereby taking its place with other phenomena of symbolic and social unrest (youth, drugs, women). . . .

Faced with this poetic language that defies knowledge, many of us are rather tempted to leave our shelter to deal with literature only by miming its mean-derings, rather than by positing it as an object of knowledge. We let ourselves be taken in by this mimeticism: fictional, para-philosophical, para-scientific writings. It is probably necessary to be a woman (ultimate guarantee of sociality beyond the wreckage of the paternal symbolic function, as well as the inexhaustible generator of its renewal, of its expansion) not to renounce theoretical reason but to compel it to increase its power by giving it an object beyond its limits. Such a position, it seems to me, provides a possible basis for a theory of signification, which, confronted with poetic language, could not in any way account for it, but would rather use it as an indication of what is heterogeneous to meaning (to sign and predication): instinctual economies, always and at the same time open to bio-physiological sociohistorical constraints.

This kind of heterogeneous economy and its questionable subject-in-process thus calls for a linguistics other than the one descended from the phenomenological heavens; a linguistics capable, within its language object, of accounting for a nonetheless articulated *instinctual drive*, across and through the constitutive and insurmountable frontier of *meaning*. This instinctual drive, however, located in the matrix of the sign, refers back to an instinctual body (to which psychoanalysis has turned its attention), which ciphers the language with rhythmic, intonational, and other arrangements, nonreducible to the position of the transcendental ego even though always within sights of its thesis.

The development of this theory of signification is in itself regulated by Husserlian precepts, because it inevitably makes an *object* even of that which departs from meaning. But, even though abetting the law of signifying structure as well as of all sociality, this expanded theory of signification cannot give itself new objects except by positing itself as nonuniversal: that is, by presupposing that a questionable subject-in-process exists in an economy of discourse other than that of thetic consciousness. And this requires that subjects of the theory must be themselves subjects in infinite analysis; this is what Husserl could not imagine, what Céline could not know, but what a woman, among others, can finally admit, aware as she is of the inanity of Being.

When it avoids the risks that lie in wait for it, literary experience remains nevertheless something other than this analytical theory, which it never stops challenging. Against knowing thought, poetic language pursues an effect of *singular truth*, and thus accomplishes, perhaps, for the modern community, this solitary practice that the materialists of antiquity unsuccessfully championed against the ascendance of theoretical reason.

NOTE

1. See Kristeva, *La Révolution du language poétique* (Paris: Seuil, 1974), pp. 274ff. [Ed.]

FROM FILTH TO DEFILEMENT

*Abjection [. . .] is merely the inability to assume with sufficient
strength the imperative act of excluding abject things
(and that act establishes the foundations of collective existence.)
[. . .] The act of exclusion has the same meaning
as social or divine sovereignty, but it is not located on the same level; it is
precisely located in the domain of things and not, like sovereignty,
in the domain of persons. It differs from the latter in the
same way that anal eroticism differs from sadism.*
—Georges Bataille, *Essais de sociologie*

[handwritten: level of thing to / level of personhood]

MOTHER-PHOBIA AND THE MURDER OF THE FATHER

In psychoanalysis as in anthropology one commonly links the sacred and the establishment of the religious bond that it presupposes with *sacrifice*. Freud tied the sacred to taboo and totemism,[1] and concluded that, "we consider ourselves justified in substituting the father for the totem animal in the male's formula of totemism."[2] We are all familiar with that Freudian thesis as to the murder of the father and, more specifically, with the one he develops in *Moses and Monotheism*: in connection with Judaic religion the archaic father and master of the primeval horde is killed by the conspiring sons who, later seized with a sense of guilt for an act that was upon the whole inspired by ambivalent feelings, end up restoring paternal authority, no longer as an arbitrary power but as a right; thus renouncing the possession of all women in their turn, they establish at one stroke the sacred, exogamy, and society.

There is nevertheless a strange slippage in the Freudian argument, one that has not been sufficiently noticed. Relying on numerous readings in ethnology and the history of religions, more specifically on Frazer and Robertson Smith, Freud notes that the morality of man starts with "the two taboos of totemism"—*murder* and *incest*.[3] *Totem and Taboo* begins with an evocation of the "dread of incest," and Freud discusses it at length in connection with taboo, totemism, and more specifically with food and sex prohibitions. The woman- or mother-image haunts a large part of that book and keeps shaping its background even when, relying on the testimony of obsessional neurotics, Freud slips from dread (p. 23: "His incest dread"; p. 24: "the incest dread of savages"; p. 161: "The interpretation of incest dread," "This dread of incest") to the inclusion of dread symptom in obsessional neurosis. At the same time he leaves off speculating on incest ("we do not know the origin of incest dread and do not even know how to guess at it,"

[handwritten: dread ?]

p. 162) in order to center his conclusion in the second taboo, the one against murder, which he reveals to be the murder of the father.

That such a murderous event could be as much mythical as endowed with founding properties, that it should be both the keystone to the desire henceforth known as Oedipal and a severance that sets up a signifier admitting of logical concatenation, analytic attention now knows only too well. Divergences from and even contradictions with this Freudian thesis[4] are finally no more than variants and confirmations. What will concern me here is not that aspect of the Freudian position, which I shall consider to have been logically established. I shall attempt to question the other side of the religious phenomenon, the one that Freud points to when he brings up dread, incest, and the mother; one that, even though it is presented as the second taboo founding religion, nevertheless disappears during the final elucidation of the problem.

THE TWO-SIDED SACRED

Could the sacred be, whatever its variants, a two-sided formation? One aspect founded by murder and the social bond made up of murder's guilt-ridden atonement, with all the projective mechanisms and obsessive rituals that accompany it; and another aspect, like a lining, more secret still and invisible, nonrepresentable, oriented toward those uncertain spaces of unstable identity, toward the fragility—both threatening and fusional—of the archaic dyad, toward the non-separation of subject/object, on which language has no hold but one woven of fright and repulsion? One aspect is defensive and socializing, the other shows fear and indifferentiation. The similarities that Freud delineates between religion and obsessional neurosis would then involve the defensive side of the sacred. Now, to throw light on the subjective economy of its other side, it is phobia as such, and its drifting toward psychosis, that one would need to tackle head on.

That, at any rate, will be my point of departure. For we shall see, in a large number of rituals and discourses involved in making up the sacred—notably those dealing with *defilement* and its derivations in different religions—an attempt at *coding* the other taboo that the earliest ethnologists and psychoanalysts viewed as presiding over social formations: beside death, *incest*. Lévi-Strauss' structural anthropology has shown how all systems of knowledge in so-called primitive societies, and myths in particular, are a later elaboration, within stages of symbolicity, of the prohibition that weighs on incest and founds the signifying function as well as the social aggregate. What will concern me here is not the socially productive value of the son-mother incest *prohibition* but the alter-

ations, within subjectivity and within the very symbolic competence, implied by
the *confrontation with the feminine* and the way in which societies code themselves in order to accompany as far as possible the speaking subject on that journey. Abjection, or the journey to the end of the night.

End of the womb, perhaps?

PROHIBITED INCEST VS. COMING FACE TO FACE
WITH THE UNNAMABLE

What we designate as "feminine," far from being a primeval essence, will be
seen as an "other" without a name, which subjective experience confronts when
it does not stop at the appearance of its identity. Assuming that any Other is ap-
pended to the triangulating function of the paternal prohibition, what will be
dealt with here, beyond and through the paternal function, is a coming face to
face with an unnamable otherness—the solid rock of jouissance and writing as
well.

I shall set aside in this essay a different version of the confrontation with the
feminine, one that, going beyond abjection and fright, is enunciated as ecstatic.
"The light-suffused face of the young Persian god" Freud refers to, and similarly,
in a more secular fashion, Mallarmé's claim to be that "startled hero," "merry"
for having overcome the "dishevelled tuft"—both point to another manner of
coming to terms with the unnamable. That kind of confrontation appears, where
our civilization is concerned, only in a few rare flashes of writing. Céline's laughter, beyond horror, also comes close to it, perhaps. . . .

THE FUNDAMENTAL WORK OF MARY DOUGLAS

Anthropologists, since Sir James George Frazer, W. Robertson Smith, Arnold
von Gennep, and Alfred Reginald Radcliff-Brown, or Rudolf Steiner, have
noted that secular "filth," which has become sacred "defilement," is the *excluded*
on the basis of which religious prohibition is made up. In a number of primitive
societies religious rites are purification rites whose function is to separate this or
that social, sexual, or age group from another one, by means of prohibiting a
filthy, defiling element. It is as if dividing lines were built up between society
and a certain nature, as well as within the social aggregate, on the basis of the
simple logic of *excluding filth*, which, promoted to the ritual level of *defilement*,
founded the "self and clean" of each social group if not of each subject.

The purification rite appears then as that essential ridge, which, prohibiting
the filthy object, extracts it from the secular order and lines it at once with a sa-

teen abstinence: religious camps where CDs are burned, defiled

cred facet. Because it is excluded as a possible object, asserted to be a non-object of desire, abominated as ab-ject, as abjection, filth becomes defilement and founds on the henceforth released side of the "self and clean" the order that is thus only (and therefore, always already) sacred.

Defilement is what is jettisoned from the "symbolic system." It is what escapes that social rationality, that logical order on which a social aggregate is based, which then becomes differentiated from a temporary agglomeration of individuals and, in short, constitutes a *classification system* or a *structure*.

The British anthropologist Mary Douglas begins by construing the "symbolic system" of religious prohibitions as a reflection of social divisions or even contradictions. As if the social being, coextensive with a "symbolic system," were always present to itself through its religious structures, which transfer its contradictions to the level of rituals. And yet, at a second stage of her thinking, Mary Douglas seems to find in the human body the prototype of that translucid being constituted by a society as symbolic system. As a matter of fact, the explanation she gives of defilement assigns in turn different statuses to the human body: as ultimate cause of the socio-economic causality, or simply as metaphor of that socio-symbolic being constituted by the human universe always present to itself. In so doing, however, Mary Douglas introduces willy-nilly the possibility of a subjective dimension within anthropological thought on religions. Where then lies the subjective value of those demarcations, exclusions, and prohibitions that establish the social organism as a "symbolic system"? The anthropological analysis of these phenomena was for Mary Douglas essentially *syntactic* at first: defilement is an element connected with the boundary, the margin, etc., of an order. Henceforth she finds herself led to *semantic* problems: what is the *meaning* of such a border-element assumes in other psychological, economic, etc., systems? At this moment of her thinking there emerges a concern to integrate Freudian data as semantic values connected with the psychosomatic functioning of the speaking subject. But a hasty assimilation of such data leads Mary Douglas naively to *reject* Freudian premises.

Finally, such a conception disregards both *subjective dynamics* (if one wishes to consider the social set in its utmost particularization) and *language as common and universal code* (if one wishes to consider the aggregate and the social aggregates in their greatest generality). Lévi-Strauss' structural anthropology had one advantage among others; it linked a classification system, this is, a symbolic system, within a given society, to the order of language in its universality (binary aspects of phonology, signifier-signified dependencies and autonomies, etc.). In thus attaining universal truth, it nevertheless neglected the subjective dimension and/or the diachronic and synchronic implication of the speaking subject in the universal order of language.

Consequently, when I speak of *symbolic order*, I shall imply the dependence and articulation of the speaking subject in the order of language, such as they appear diachronically in the advent of each speaking being, and as analytic listening discovers them synchronically in the speech of analysands. I shall consider as an established fact the analytic finding that different subjective structures are possible within that symbolic order, even if the different types presently recorded seem subject to discussion and refinement, if not reevaluation.

One might advance the hypothesis that a (social) symbolic system *corresponds* to a specific structuration of the speaking subject in the *symbolic order*. To say that it "corresponds" leaves out questions of cause and effect; is the social determined by the subjective, or is it the other way around? The subjective-symbolic dimension that I am introducing does not therefore reinstate some deep or primary causality in the social *symbolic system*. It merely presents the *effects* and especially the *benefits* that accrue to the speaking subject from a precise symbolic organization; perhaps it explains what desiring motives are required in order to maintain a given social symbolics. Furthermore, it seems to me that such a statement of the problem has the advantage of not turning the "symbolic system" into a secular replica of the "preestablished harmony" or the "divine order"; rather, it roots it, as a *possible variant*, within the only concrete universality that defines the speaking being—the signifying process.

IN THE SAME FASHION AS INCEST PROHIBITION

We are now in a position to recall what was suggested earlier concerning that border of subjectivity where the object no longer has, or does not yet have a correlative function bonding the subject. On that location, to the contrary, the vacillating, fascinating, threatening, and dangerous object is silhouetted as nonbeing—as the abjection into which the speaking being is permanently engulfed.

Defilement, by means of the rituals that consecrate it, is perhaps, for a social aggregate, only one of the possible foundings of abjection bordering the frail identity of the speaking being. In this sense, abjection is coextensive with social and symbolic order, on the individual as well as on the collective level. By virtue of this, abjection, just like *prohibition of incest*, is a universal phenomenon; one encounters it as soon as the symbolic and/or social dimension of man is constituted, and this throughout the course of civilization. But abjection assumes specific shapes and different codings according to the various "symbolic systems." I shall attempt to examine some of its variants: *defilement, food taboo*, and *sin*.

Socio-historical considerations can be brought in at a second stage. They will allow us to understand why that demarcating imperative, which is subjectively experienced as abjection, varies according to time and space, even though it is universal. I shall nevertheless stick to a typological argument. Prohibitions and conflicts that are specific to a given subject and ritualized by religion for a given type of body will appear as isomorphic with the prohibitions and conflicts of the social group within which they happen. Leaving aside the question of the priority of one over the other (the social does not represent the subjective any more than the subjective represents the social), I shall posit that they both follow the same logic, with no other goal than the survival of both group and subject.

My reflections will make their way through anthropological domains and analyses in order to aim at a deep psycho-symbolic economy: the general, logical determination that underlies anthropological variants (social structures, marriage rules, religious rites) and evinces a specific economy of the speaking subject, no matter what its historical manifestations may be. In short, an economy that analytic listening and semanalytic deciphering discover in our contemporaries. Such a procedure seems to me to be directly in keeping with Freudian utilization of anthropological data. It inevitably entails a share of *disappointment* for the empirically minded ethnologist. It does not unfold without a share of *fiction*, the nucleus of which, drawn from actuality and the subjective experience of the one who writes, is projected upon data collected from the life of other cultures, less to justify itself than to throw light on them by means of an interpretation to which they obviously offer resistance.

THE MARGIN OF A FLOATING STRUCTURE

Taking a closer look at defilement, as Mary Douglas has done, one ascertains the following. In the first place, filth is not a quality in itself, but it applies only to what relates to a *boundary* and, more particularly, represents the object jettisoned out of that boundary, its other side, a margin.

> Matter issuing from them [the orifices of the body] is marginal stuff of the most obvious kind. Spittle, blood, milk, urine, faeces or tears by simply issuing forth have traversed the boundary of the body. [. . .] The mistake is to treat bodily margins in isolation from all other margins.[5]

The potency of pollution is therefore not an inherent one; it is proportional to the potency of the prohibition that founds it.

> It follows from this that pollution is a type of danger which is not likely to occur except where the lines of structure, cosmic or social, are clearly defined.[6]

Finally, even if human beings are involved with it, the dangers entailed by defilement are not within the power to deal with but depend on a power "inhering in the structure of ideas."[7] Let us posit that defilement is an objective evil undergone by the subject. Or, to put it another way, the danger of filth represents for the subject the risk to which the very symbolic order is permanently exposed, to the extent that it is a device of discriminations, of differences. But from where and from what does the threat issue? From nothing else but an equally objective reason, even if individuals can contribute to it, and which would be, in a way, the frailty of the symbolic order itself. A threat issued from the prohibitions that found the inner and outer borders in which and through which the speaking subject is constituted—borders also determined by the phonological and semantic differences that articulate the syntax of language.

And yet, in the light of this structural-functional X-ray of defilement, which draws on the major anthropological works of modern times, from Robertson Smith to Marcel Mauss, from Emile Durkheim to Lévi-Strauss, one question remains unanswered. Why does *corporeal waste*, menstrual blood and excrement, or everything that is assimilated to them, from nail-parings to decay, represent—like a metaphor that would have become incarnate—the objective frailty of symbolic order?

One might be tempted at first to seek the answer in a type of society where defilement takes the place of supreme danger or absolute evil.

BETWEEN TWO POWERS

Nevertheless, no matter what differences there may be among societies where religious prohibitions, which are above all behavior prohibitions, are supposed to afford protection from defilement, one sees everywhere the importance, both social and symbolic, of women and particularly the mother. In societies where it occurs, ritualization of defilement is accompanied by a strong concern for separating the sexes, and this means giving men rights over women. The latter, apparently put in the position of passive objects, are none the less felt to be wily powers, "baleful schemers" from whom rightful beneficiaries must protect themselves. It is as if, lacking a central authoritarian power that would settle the definitive supremacy of one sex—or lacking a legal establishment that would balance the prerogatives of both sexes—two powers attempted to share out society. One of them, the masculine, apparently victorious, confesses through its very relentlessness against the other, the feminine, that it is threatened by an asymmetrical, irrational, wily, uncontrollable power. Is this a survival of a matrilineal society or the specific particularity of a structure (without the incidence of diachrony)? The question of the origins of such a handling of sexual difference remains moot. But whether it be within the highly hierarchical society of India or the Lele in Africa[8] it is always to be noticed that the attempt to establish a male, phallic power is vigorously threatened by the no less virulent power of the other sex, which is oppressed (recently? or not sufficiently for the survival needs of society?). That other sex, the feminine, becomes synonymous with a radical evil that is to be suppressed.[9]

Let us keep that fact in mind; I shall return to it later on for the interpretation of defilement and its rites. In the meantime I turn to the particulars—the prohibited objects and the symbolic devices that accompany those prohibitions.

EXCREMENTS AND MENSTRUAL BLOOD

While they always relate to corporeal orifices as to so many landmarks parceling-constituting the body's territory, polluting objects fall, schematically, into two types: excremental and menstrual. Neither tears nor sperm, for instance, although they belong to borders of the body, have any polluting value.

Excrement and its equivalents (decay, infection, disease, corpse, etc.) stand for the danger to identity that comes from without: the ego threatened by the non-ego, society threatened by its outside, life by death. Menstrual blood, on the contrary, stands for the danger issuing from within the identity (social or sexual); it threatens the relationship between the sexes within a social aggregate and, through internalization, the identity of each sex in the face of sexual difference.

MATERNAL AUTHORITY AS TRUSTEE OF THE SELF'S CLEAN AND PROPER BODY

What can the two types of defilement have in common? Without having recourse to anal eroticism or the fear of castration—one cannot help *hearing* the reticence of anthropologies when confronted with that explanation—it might be suggested, by means of another psychoanalytic approach, that those *two* defilements stem from the *maternal* and/or the feminine, of which the maternal is the real support. That goes without saying where menstrual blood signifies sexual difference. But what about excrement? It will be remembered that the anal penis is also the phallus with which infantile imagination provides the feminine sex and that, on the other hand, maternal authority is experienced first and above all, after the first essentially oral frustrations, as sphincteral training. It is as if, while having been forever immersed in the symbolics of language, the human being experienced, in addition, an *authority* that was a—chronologically and logically immediate—repetition of the *laws* of language. Through frustrations and prohibitions, this authority shapes the body into a *territory* having areas, orifices, points and lines, surfaces and hollows, where the archaic power of mastery and neglect, of the differentiation of proper-clean and improper-dirty, possible and impossible, is impressed and exerted. It is a "binary logic," a primal mapping of the body that I call semiotic to say that, while being the precondition of language, it is dependent upon meaning, but in a way that is not that of *linguistic* signs nor of the *symbolic* order they found. Maternal authority is the trustee of that mapping of the self's clean and proper body; it is distinguished from paternal laws within which, with the phallic phase and acquisition of language, the destiny of man will take shape.

If language, like culture, sets up a separation and, starting with discrete elements, concatenates an order, it does so precisely by repressing maternal authority and the corporeal mapping that abuts against them. It is then appropriate to ask what happens to such a repressed item when the legal, phallic, linguistic symbolic establishment does not carry out the separation in radical fashion—or else, more basically, when the speaking being attempts to think through its advent in order better to establish its effectiveness. . . .

FEAR OF WOMEN—FEAR OF PROCREATION

Fear of the archaic mother turns out to be essentially fear of her generative power. It is this power, a dreaded one, that patrilineal filiation has the burden of subduing. It is thus not surprising to see pollution rituals proliferating in societies where patrilineal power is poorly secured, as if the latter sought, by means of purification, a support against excessive matrilineality.

Thus, in a society where religious prohibitions correspond to the sexual prohibitions intended to separate men from women and insure the power of the former over the latter, it has been possible to note—as with the Gidjingali in Australia—the considerable sway of maternal authority over the sons. On the other hand, with the neighboring Aranda, where paternal control is much more important than with the Gidjingali, there is no connection between sexual and religious prohibitions.[10]

The instance of the Nuer, analyzed by Evans Pritchard and again by Mary Douglas, is very significant in that respect. It involves a society that is dominated, at least among the aristocrats, by the agnatic principle and in which women are a divisive factor; essential for reproduction, they nevertheless endanger the ideal norms of the agnatic group, the more so as cohabitation with maternal relatives seems common. Menstrual pollution, as well as prohibition of incest with the mother, considered the most dangerous of all, can be interpreted as the symbolic equivalent of that conflict.[11]

A loathing of defilement as protection against the poorly controlled power of mothers seems even clearer with the Bemba. Ritually impure and contaminating, menstrual defilement wields with them, in addition, a cataclysmic power such that one is led to speak, under the circumstances, not only of *ritual impurity* but also of the *power of pollution*. Thus, if a woman undergoing her period touches fire (a masculine and patrilineal symbol), food cooked on that fire makes her ill and threatens her with death. Now, among the Bemba, power is in the hands of men, but filiation is matrilineal and residence, after marriage, is matrilocal. There is a great contradiction between male rule and matrilocal residence; the young bridegroom is subjected to the authority of the bride's family, and he must override it through personal excellence during his maturity. He remains nevertheless, because of matrilineality, in conflict with the maternal uncle who is the legal guardian of the children especially when they are growing up.[12] The power of pollution (the threat of illness or death through the conjunction blood-fire) thus transposes, on the symbolic level, the permanent conflict resulting from an unsettled separation between masculine and feminine power at the level of social institutions. Non-separation would threaten the whole society with disintegration.

Here is a significant fact. Again as protection against the generative power of women, pollution rites arise within societies that are afraid of overpopulation (in barren regions, for instance). One thus finds them, as part of a whole system of restraining procreation, along with incest taboo, etc., among the Enga of New Guinea. On the other hand, with their Fore neighbors, the desire to procreate, encouraged for opposite ecological reasons, entails, one might say symmetrically, the disappearance of incest taboo and pollution rites. Such a relaxation of prohibitions among the Fore, for the sake of a single objective—reproduction at any cost—is accompanied by such a lack of the "clean and proper" and hence of the "abject" that cannibalism of the dead seems to be current practice. Contrariwise the Enga, heedful of pollution and subjected to fear of procreation, are not acquainted with cannibalism.[13]

Is that parallel sufficient to suggest that defilement reveals, at the same time as an attempt to throttle matrilineality, an attempt at separating the speaking being from his body in order that the latter accede to the status of clean and proper body, that is to say, non-assimilable, uneatable, abject? It is only at such a cost that the body is capable of being defended, protected—and also, eventually, sublimated. Fear of the uncontrollable generative mother repels me from the body; I give up cannibalism because abjection (of the mother) leads me toward respect for the body of the other, my fellow man, my brother. . . .

NOTES

1. In *Totem and Taboo* (1913), in vol. 13 of *Complete Works*. References will be to the Vintage Book edition published by Random House.
2. *Totem and Taboo*, p. 170.
3. *Totem and Taboo*, p. 185.
4. See René Girard, *Des Choses cachées depuis la fondation du monde* (Paris: Grasset, 1978).
5. Mary Douglas, *Purity and Danger* (London, Boston, and Henley: Routledge and Kegan Paul, 1969), p. 121.
6. Douglas, p. 113.
7. Douglas, p. 113.
8. See Douglas, pp. 149ff.
9. "For the Lele evil is not to be included in the total system of the world, but to be expunged without compromise" (Douglas, p. 171).
10. See K. Maddock, "Dangerous Proximities and Their Analogues," *Mankind* (1974), 5(3):206–217.
11. See K. Gouph, "Nuer Kinship: A Re-examination," in T. O. Beidelman, ed., *The Translation of Culture* (London: Tavistock, 1971), p. 91.
12. See L. N. Rosen, "Contagion and Cataclysm: A Theoretical Approach to the Study of Ritual Pollution Beliefs," *African Studies* (1973), 32(4):229–246.
13. See S. Lindenbaum, "Sorcerers, Ghosts, and Polluting Women: An Analysis of Religious Belief and Population Control," *Journal of Geography* (1972), 11(3):241.

MOTHERHOOD [ACCORDING TO GIOVANNI BELLINI]

THE MATERNAL BODY

Cells fuse, split, and proliferate; volumes grow, tissues stretch, and body fluids change rhythm, speeding up or slowing down. Within the body, growing as a graft, indomitable, there is an other. And no one is present, within that simultaneously dual and alien space, to signify what is going on. "It happens, but I'm not here." "I cannot realize it, but it goes on." Motherhood's impossible syllogism. This becoming-a-mother, this gestation, can possibly be accounted for by means of only two discourses. There is *science*; but as an objective discourse, science is not concerned with the subject, the mother as site of her proceedings. There is *Christian theology* (especially canonical theology); but theology defines maternity only as an impossible elsewhere, a sacred beyond, a vessel of divinity, a spiritual tie with the ineffable godhead, and transcendence's ultimate support—necessarily virginal and committed to assumption. Such are the wiles of

Christian reason (Christianity's still matchless rationalism, or at least its ratio-
nalizing power, finally become clear); through the maternal body (in a state of
virginity and "dormition"[1] before Assumption), it thus establishes a sort of subject at the point where the subject and its speech split apart, fragment, and van-
ish. Lay humanism took over the configuration of that subject through the cult
of the mother; tenderness, love, and seat of social conservation.

And yet, if we presume that *someone* exists throughout the process of cells, mol-
ecules, and atoms accumulating, dividing, and multiplying without any *identity*
(biological or socio-symbolical) having been formed so far, are we not positing an
animism that reflects the inherent psychosis of the speaking Being? So, if we suppose that a *mother* is the subject of gestation, in other words the *master* of a
process that science, despite its effective devices, acknowledges it cannot now and
perhaps never will be able to take away from her; if we suppose her to be *master*
of a process that is prior to the social-symbolic-linguistic contract of the group,
then we acknowledge the risk of losing identity at the same time as we ward it off.
We recognize on the one hand that biology jolts us by means of unsymbolized instinctual drives and that this phenomenon eludes social intercourse, the representation of preexisting objects, and the contract of desire. On the other hand, we
immediately deny it; we say there can be no escape, for mamma is there, she embodies this phenomenon; she warrants that *everything is*, and that it is repre-
sentable. In a double-barreled move, psychotic tendencies are acknowledged, but
at the same time they are settled, quieted, and bestowed upon the mother in order to maintain the ultimate guarantee: symbolic coherence.

This move, however, also reveals, better than any mother ever could, that the
maternal body is the place of a splitting, which, even though hypostatized by
Christianity, nonetheless remains a constant factor of social reality. Through a
body, destined to insure reproduction of the species, the woman-subject, although under the sway of the paternal function (as symbolizing, speaking subject and like all others), more of a *filter* than anyone else—a thoroughfare, a
threshold where "nature" confronts "culture." To imagine that there is *someone*
in that filter—such is the source of religious mystifications, the font that nourishes them: the fantasy of the so-called "Phallic" Mother. Because if, on the contrary, there were no one on this threshold, if the mother were not, that is, if she
were not phallic, then every speaker would be led to conceive of its Being in relation to some void, a nothingness asymetrically opposed to this Being, a permanent threat against, first, its mastery, and ultimately, its stability.

The discourse of analysis proves that the *desire* for motherhood is without fail
a desire to bear a child of the father (a child of her own father) who, as a result,
is often assimilated to the baby itself and thus returned to its place as *devalorized
man*, summoned only to accomplish his function, which is to originate and jus-

tify reproductive desire. Only through these phantasmatic nuptials can the father-daughter incest be carried out and the baby come to exist. At that, the incest is too far removed, bringing peace only to those who firmly adhere to the paternal symbolic axis. Otherwise, once the object is produced, once the fruit is detached, the ceremony loses its effect unless it be repeated forever.

And yet, through and with this desire, motherhood seems to be impelled *also* by a nonsymbolic, nonpaternal causality. Only Ferenczi, Freud, and, later, Marie Bonaparte, have spoken about this, evoking the biological destiny of each differentiated sex. Material compulsion, spasm of a memory belonging to the species that either binds together or splits apart to perpetuate itself, series of markers with no other significance than the eternal return of the life-death biological cycle. How can we verbalize this prelinguistic, unrepresentable memory? Heraclitus' flux, Epicurus' atoms, the whirling dust of cabalic, Arab, and Indian mystics, and the stippled drawings of psychedelics—all seem better metaphors than the theories of Being, the logos, and its laws.

Such an excursion to the limits of primal regression can be phantasmatically experienced as the reunion of a woman-mother with the body of *her* mother. The body of her mother is always the same Master-Mother of instinctual drive, a ruler over psychosis, a subject of biology, but also, one toward which women aspire all the more passionately simply because it lacks a penis: that body cannot penetrate her as can a man when possessing his wife. By giving birth, the woman enters into contact with her mother; she becomes, she is her own mother; they are the same continuity differentiating itself. She thus actualizes the homosexual facet of motherhood, through which a woman is simultaneously closer to her instinctual memory, more open to her own psychosis, and consequently, more negatory of the social, symbolic bond.

The symbolic paternal facet relieves feminine aphasia present within the desire to bear the father's child. It is an appeasement that turns into melancholy as soon as the child becomes an object, a gift to others, neither self nor part of the self, an object destined to be a subject, an other. Melancholy readjusts the paranoia that drives to action (often violent) and to discourse (essentially parental, object-oriented, and pragmatic discourse) the feminine, verbal scarcity so prevalent in our culture.

The homosexual-maternal facet is a whirl of words, a complete absence of meaning and seeing; it is feeling, displacement, rhythm, sound, flashes, and fantasied clinging to the maternal body as a screen against the plunge. Perversion slows down the schizophrenia that collapsing identities and the delights of the well-known and oft-solicited (by some women) pantheist fusion both brush up against.

Those afflicted or affected by psychosis have put up in its place the image of the Mother: for women, a paradise lost but seemingly close at hand, for men, a hidden god but constantly present through occult fantasy. And even psychoanalysts believe in it.

Yet, swaying between these two positions can only mean, for the woman involved, that she is within an "enceinte" separating her from the world of everyone else.[2] Enclosed in this "elsewhere," an "enceinte" woman loses communital meaning, which suddenly appears to her as worthless, absurd, or at best, comic—a surface agitation severed from its impossible foundations. Oriental nothingness probably better sums up what, in the eyes of a Westerner, can only be regression. And yet it is jouissance, but like a negative of the one, tied to an object, that is borne by the unfailingly masculine libido. Here, alterity becomes nuance, contradiction becomes a variant, tension becomes passage, and discharge becomes peace. This tendency towards equalization, which is seen as a regressive extinction of symbolic capabilities, does not, however, reduce differences; it resides within the smallest, most archaic, and most uncertain of differences. It is powerful sublimation and indwelling of the symbolic within instinctual drives. It affects this series of "little differences-resemblances" (as the Chinese logicians of antiquity would say). Before founding society in the same stroke as signs and communication, they are the precondition of the latter's existence, as they constitute the living entity within its species, with its needs, its elementary apperceptions and communications, distinguishing between the instinctual drives of life and death. It affects primal repression. An ultimate danger for identity, but also supreme power of symbolic instance thus returning to matters of its concern. Sublimation here is both eroticizing without residue and a disappearance of eroticism as it returns to its source.

The speaker reaches this limit, this requisite of sociality, only by virtue of a particular, discursive practice called "art." A woman also attains it (and in our society, *especially*) through the strange form of split symbolization (threshold of language and instinctual drive, of the "symbolic" and the "semiotic") of which the act of giving birth consists. As the archaic process of socialization, one might even say civilization, it causes the childbearing woman to cathect, immediately and unwittingly, the physiological operations and instinctual drives dividing and multiplying her, first, in a biological, and finally, a social teleology. The maternal body slips away from the discursive hold and immediately conceals a cipher that must be taken into account biologically and socially. This ciphering of the species, however, this pre- and transsymbolic memory, makes the mother mistress of neither begetting nor instinctual drive (such a fantasy underlies the cult of any ultimately feminine deity); it does make of the maternal body the stakes of a natural and "objective" control, independent of any individual consciousness; it inscribes both biological operations and their instinctual echoes into this necessary and hazardous *program* constituting every species. The maternal body is the module of a biosocial program. Its jouissance, which is mute, is nothing more than a recording, on the screen of the preconscious, of both the messages that consciousness, in its analytical course, picks up from this ciphering process and their classifications as empty foundation, as a subjective lining of our rational exchanges as social beings. If it is true that every national language has its own dream language and unconscious, then each of the sexes—a division so much more archaic and fundamental than the one into languages—would have its own unconscious wherein the biological and social program of the species would be ciphered in confrontation with language, exposed to its influence, but independent from it. The symbolic destiny of the speaking animal, which is essential although it comes second, being superimposed upon the biological—this destiny *seals off* (and in women, in order to preserve the homology of the group, it *censures*) that archaic basis and the special jouissance it procures in being transferred to the symbolic. Privileged, "psychotic" moments, or whatever induces them naturally, thus become necessary. Among such "natural" inducements, maternity is needed for this sexual modality to surface, this fragile, secretly guarded and incommunicable modality, quickly stifled by standard palliatives (by viril and "rational" censorship, or by the sentimentality of "maternal" tenderness toward a substitute-object for everything). This process is quite rightly understood as the demand for a penis. Fantasy indeed has no other sign, no other way to imagine that the speaker is capable of reaching the Mother, and thus, of unsettling its own limits. And, as long as there is language-symbolism-paternity, there will never be any other way to represent, to objectify, and to explain this unsettling of the symbolic stratum, this nature/culture threshold, this instilling the subjectless biological program into the very body of a symbolizing subject, this event called motherhood.

In other words, from the point of view of social coherence, which is where legislators, grammarians, and even psychoanalysts have their seat; which is where every body is made homologous to a male speaking body, motherhood would be nothing more than a phallic attempt to reach the Mother who is presumed to exist at the very place where (social and biological) identity recedes. If it is true that idealist ideologies develop along these lines, urging women to satisfy this presumed demand and to maintain the ensuing order, then, on the other hand, any negation of this utilitarian, social, and symbolic aspect of motherhood plunges into regression—but a particular regression whose currently recognized manifestations lead to the hypostasis of blind substance, to the negation of symbolic position, and to a justification of this regression under the aegis of the same Phallic Mother–screen.

The language of art, too, follows (but differently and more closely) the other aspect of maternal jouissance, the sublimation taking place at the very moment of primal repression within the mother's body, arising perhaps unwittingly out of her marginal position. At the intersection of sign and rhythm, of representation and light, of the symbolic and the semiotic, the artist speaks from a place where she is not, where she knows not. He delineates what, in her, is a body rejoicing [*jouissant*]. The very existence of aesthetic practice makes clear that the Mother as subject is a delusion, just as the negation of the so-called poetic dimension of language leads one to believe in the existence of the Mother, and consequently, of transcendence. Because, through a symbiosis of meaning and nonmeaning, of representation and interplay of differences, the artist lodges into language, and through his identification with the mother (fetishism or incest— we shall return to this problem), his own specific jouissance, thus traversing both sign and object. Thus, before all other speakers, he bears witness to what the unconscious (through the screen of the mother) records of those clashes that occur between the biological and social programs of the species. This means that through and across secondary repression (founding of signs), aesthetic practice touches upon primal repression (founding biological series and the laws of the species). At the place where it obscurely succeeds within the maternal body, every artist tries his hand, but rarely with equal success. . . .

NOTES

1. "Dormition" refers to the period of the Virgin Mary's death, which is viewed merely as a period of sleep, before she was carried to heaven (Assumption). The word originated in the *Transitus Maria*, a fifth-century Byzantine apocrypha. [Ed.]
2. The French word "enceinte" has been kept as the only way to preserve the pun: "enceinte" is a protective wall around a town; "femme enceinte" is a pregnant woman. [Ed.]

WOMEN'S TIME

NATIONAL AND EUROPEAN WOMEN

The nation, which was the dream and the reality of the nineteenth century, seems to have reached both its peak and its limit with the 1929 crash and the National Socialist apocalypse. We have witnessed the destruction of its very foundation—economic homogeneity, historical tradition, and linguistic unity.

World War II, which was fought in the name of national values, brought an end
to the reality of the nation, which it turned into a mere illusion that has been preserved for ideological or strictly political purposes ever since. Even if the resur-
gence of nations and nationalists may warrant hope or fear, the social and philosophical coherence of the nation has already reached its limit.

The search for economic *homogeneity* has given way to *interdependence*
when it has not yielded to the economic superpowers of the world. In like manner, *historical* tradition and *linguistic* unity have been molded into a broader and
deeper denominator that we might call a *symbolic denominator*: a cultural and
religious memory shaped by a combination of historical and geographical influences. This memory generates national territories determined by the ever-di-
minishing but still widespread conflicts between political parties. At the same
time, this common "symbolic denominator" is a means not only to globalization
and economic standardization, but also to entities that are greater than any one
nation, and that *sometimes* embrace the boundaries of an entire continent.

In this way, a "common symbolic denominator" can lead to a new social grouping that is greater than the nation, though it enables the nation to retain and
build upon its characteristics instead of losing them. This transformation occurs,
however, within a paradoxical temporal structure, a sort of "future perfect" in
which the most deeply repressed and transnational past gives a distinctive character to programmed uniformity. For the memory in question (the common
symbolic denominator) is linked to the solution that spatially and temporally
united human groupings have offered less for the problems of the *production* of
material goods (which is the domain of economics, human relations, and politics)—than of *reproduction*—the survival of the species, life and death, the
body, sex, and the symbol. If it is true, for instance, that Europe represents this
sort of sociocultural grouping, its existence stems more from its "symbolic denominator" of art, philosophy, and religion than from its economic profile. Of
course, economics is a function of collective memory, but its characteristics are
easily modified by pressures from one's partners in the world.

Therefore, we see that this sort of social grouping is endowed with a *solidity*
rooted in the various modes of reproduction and its representations by which
the biological species is placed within a temporally determined humanity. Yet,
it is also tainted with a certain *fragility*, for the symbolic denominator can no
longer aspire to universality and endure the influences and assaults inflicted by
other sociocultural memories. Hence, Europe, which is still fairly inconstant, is
obliged to identify with the cultural, artistic, philosophical, and religious manifestations of other supranational groupings. Such identifications are of no surprise when the entities in question share a historical connection, like Europe and

North America, or Europe and Latin America. They also occur, however, when the universality of this symbolic denominator juxtaposes two modes of production and reproduction that may seem incongruous, like those of Europe and the Arab world, Europe and India, Europe and China, and so forth.

In short, when dealing with the sociocultural groupings of the "European" type, we are forever faced with two major issues: first, that of *identity*, which is brought about by historical sedimentation, and second, the *loss of identity*, which is caused by memory links that bypass history in favor of anthropology. In other words, we are confronted with two temporal dimensions: the time of linear, *cursive* history, and the time of another history, that is, another time, a *monumental* time (the nomenclature comes from Nietzsche) that incorporates these supranational sociocultural groupings within even larger entities.

I would like to draw attention to certain formations that seem to embody the dynamics of this sort of sociocultural organism. I am speaking of groups we call "sociocultural" because they are defined by their role in production, but also (and especially) because of their role in the mode of reproduction and its representations. Although these groups share all the traits of the sociocultural formation in question, they *transcend* it and link it to other sociocultural formations. I am thinking specifically of sociocultural groups that we summarily define according to age categories (for instance, "European youth"), or gender divisions (for instance, "European women"), and so forth. Clearly, European youth and European women have a particularity of their own, and it is no less obvious that what defines them as "youth" or "women" is concomitant with their "European" origin and shared by their counterparts in North America and China, among others. Insofar as they participate in "monumental history," they are not merely European "youth" or "women." In a most specific way, they will mirror the universal features of their structural position with regard to reproduction and its representations.

In the pages that follow, I would like to place the problematics of European women in the context of an inquiry into time, that is, the time that the feminist movement has not only inherited but altered. Then, I shall delimit two phases or two generations of women, whose respective demands cause them to be directly universalist or cosmopolitan, though they still can be distinguished from each other. The first generation is particularly linked to national concerns, and the second, which tends to be determined by the "symbolic denominator," is European and trans-European. Finally, I shall attempt to use the problems I am addressing and the type of analysis I am proposing to show that against the backdrop of what has become a global generality, a European stance (or at least a stance taken by a European woman) has emerged.

WHICH TIME?

Joyce said "Father's time, mother's species," and it seems indeed that the evocation of women's name and fate privileges the *space* that *generates* the human species more than it does *time*, destiny, or history. Modern studies of subjectivity—of its genealogy or its accidents—have reaffirmed this separation, which may result from sociohistorical circumstances. After listening to his patients' dreams and fantasies, Freud grew to believe that "hysteria was linked to place."[1] Subsequent studies on children's acquisition of the symbolic function have shown that the permanency and quality of maternal love pave the way for the earliest spatial references, which give rise to childhood laughter and then prepare the whole array of symbolic manifestations that permit sign and syntax.[2]

Before endowing the patient with a capacity for transference and communication, do not both anti-psychiatry and applied psychoanalysis (when applied to the treatment of psychoses) purport to mark out new places that serve as gratifying and healing substitutes for long-standing deficiencies of maternal space? The examples of this are many, but they all converge upon the problematics of space, which so many religions with a matriarchal bent attribute to "the woman," and which Plato, who echoed the atomists of antiquity within his own system, referred to as the aporia of the *chora*, a matrixlike space that is nourishing, unnameable, prior to the One and to God, and that thus defies metaphysics.[3]

As for time, female subjectivity seems to offer it a specific concept of measurement that essentially retains *repetition* and *eternity* out of the many modalities that appear throughout the history of civilization. On the one hand, this measure preserves cycles, gestation, and the eternal return of biological rhythm that is similar to the rhythm of nature. Its predictability can be shocking, but its simultaneity with what is experienced as extra-subjective and cosmic time is a source of resplendent visions and unnameable jouissance. On the other hand, it preserves a solid temporality that is faultless and impenetrable, one that has so little to do with linear time that the very term "temporality" seems inappropriate. All-encompassing and infinite, like imaginary space, it reminds us of Hesiod's Kronos, the incestuous son who smothered Gaea with his entire being in order to take her away from Ouranos the father. It also recalls the myths of resurrection in the various traditions that have perpetuated the trace of a maternal cult through its most recent manifestation within Christianity. In Christianity, the body of the Virgin Mother does not die, but travels from one space to another within the same time frame, whether by dormition (according to the Orthodox faith) or assumption (according to Catholicism).[4]

These two types of temporality—cyclical and monumental—are traditionally associated with female subjectivity, when female subjectivity is considered to be innately maternal. We must not forget, however, that repetition and eternity serve as fundamental conceptions of time in numerous experiences, notably mystical ones.[5] That the modern feminist movement has identified with these experiences suggests that it is not intrinsically incompatible with "masculine" values.

On the other hand, female subjectivity poses a problem only with respect to a certain conception of time, that of time as planning, as teleology, as linear and prospective development—the time of departure, of transport and arrival, that is, the time of history. It has been amply demonstrated that this sort of temporality is inherent in the logical and ontological values of any given civilization. We can assume that it explains a rupture, a waiting period, or an anxiety that other temporalities hide from our view. This sort of time is that of language, of the enunciation of sentences (noun phrase and verb phrase, linguistic topic and comment, beginning and end), and it is maintained through its outer limit—death. A psychoanalyst would call it obsessional time, for the very structure of the slave can be found within the mastery of this time. A male or female hysteric (who suffers from reminiscences, according to Freud) would identify, rather, with prior temporal modalities—the cyclical, the monumental.

Within the bounds of a given civilization, however, this antinomy of psychic structures becomes an antinomy among social groups and ideologies. Indeed, the radical viewpoints of certain feminists are akin to the discourse of marginal spiritual or mystic groups, as well as, interestingly enough, to the concerns of modern science. Is it not true that the problematics of a time indissociable from space—of a space-time placed in an infinite expansion or articulated by accidents and catastrophes—are of great interest to space science as well as genetics? And in a different way, is it not true that the media revolution that has manifested itself as the information age suggests that time is frozen or exploded according to the fortuity of demand? Is it a time that returns to its source but cannot be mastered, that inexorably overwhelms its subject and restricts those who assimilate it to only two concerns: who will wield power over the origin (its programming) and the end (its use)?

The reader may be struck by these fluctuating points of reference—mother, woman, hysteric. Although the seemingly coherent use of the word "woman" in current ideology may have a "popular" or "shock" effect, it eradicates the differences among the various functions and structures that operate beneath this word. The time may have come, in fact, to celebrate the *multiplicity* of female perspectives and preoccupations. In a more accurate, honest, and less self-serving way, we must guarantee that the *fundamental difference* between the sexes arises out of the network of these differences. Feminism has accomplished a formidable task by making this difference a *painful* one, which means it is able to generate contingency and symbolic life in a civilization that has nothing to do besides playing the stock market and waging war.

We cannot speak about Europe or about "women in Europe" without defining the history that encompasses this sociocultural reality. It is true that a feminine sensibility has been in existence for more than a century now, but it is likely that by introducing its notion of time, it clashes with the idea of an "Eternal Europe," or perhaps even a "Modern Europe." Feminine sensibility, rather, would look for its own trans-European temporality by way of the European past and present as well as the European "ensemble," defined as the storehouse of memory. We can contend, however, that European feminist movements have displayed three attitudes toward this conception of linear temporality—a temporality that we readily deem to be masculine, and that is as "civilizational" as it is obsessional.

TWO GENERATIONS

When the women's movement began as the struggle of suffragists and existential feminists, it sought to stake out its place in the linear time of planning and history. As a result, although the movement was universalist from the start, it was deeply rooted in the sociopolitical life of nations. The political demands of women, their struggles for equal pay for equal work and for the right to the same opportunities as men have, as well as the rejection of feminine or maternal traits considered incompatible with participation in such a history all stem from the *logic of identification* with values that are not ideological (such values have been rightly criticized as too reactionary) but logical and ontological with regard to the dominant rationality of the nation and the state.

It is unnecessary to enumerate all the benefits that this logic of identification and spirited protest have offered and still offer to women (abortion rights, contraception, equal pay, professional recognition, and others). These benefits have had or will soon prove to have even more significant effects than those of the Industrial Revolution. This current of feminism, which is universalist in scope, *globalizes* the problems of women of various social categories, ages, civilizations, or simply psychic structures under the banner of Universal Woman. In this world, a reflection about *generations* of women could only be conceived of as a succession, a progression that sought to implement the program set out by its founding members.

A second phase is associated with women who have come to feminism since May 1968 and who have brought their aesthetic or psychoanalytic experiences with them. This phase is characterized by a quasi-universal rejection of linear temporality and by a highly pronounced mistrust of political life. Although it is true that this current of feminism still has an allegiance to its founding members and still focuses (by necessity) on the struggle for the sociocultural recognition of women, in a *qualitative* sense, it sees itself in a different light than did the prior generation of feminists.

The "second phase" women, who are primarily interested in the specificity of feminine psychology and its symbolic manifestations, seek a language for their corporeal and intersubjective experiences, which have been silenced by the cultures of the past. As artists or writers, they have undertaken a veritable exploration of the *dynamics of signs*. At least on the level of its intentions, their exploration is comparable to the most ambitious projects for religious and artistic upheaval. Attributing this experience to a new generation does not merely imply that new concerns have been added to the earlier demands of sociopolitical identity, for it also means that by requiring that we recognize an irreducible and self-sufficient singularity that is multifaceted, flowing, and in some ways nonidentical, feminism is currently situated outside the linear time of identities that communicate through projections and demands. Today, feminism is returning to an archaic (mythic) memory as well as to the cyclical or monumental temporality of marginal movements. It is clearly not by chance that the European and trans-European problem has manifested itself at the same time as this new phase of feminism.

What sociopolitical processes or events have led to this mutation? What are its problems, its contributions, its limits?

SOCIALISM AND FREUDIANISM

It could be maintained that this new generation of women has a more pronounced presence in Western Europe than in the United States, which may be attributed to the *rupture* in social relations and attitudes that has been caused by socialism and Freudianism. Although *socialism* as an egalitarian doctrine is presently experiencing a profound crisis, it still remains that governments and political parties of all persuasions expand solidarity by redistributing wealth and allowing free access to culture. *Freudianism*, which serves as an internal mechanism of the social realm, challenges egalitarianism by exploring sexual differences as well as the singularity of subjects who preserve their individuality.

Western socialism, shaken from its beginnings by the egalitarian or differential demands made by its women (Flora Tristan, for instance), has not hesitated to rid itself of those women who want us to recognize the specificity of the female role in culture and society. In the spirit of the egalitarian and universalist context of Enlightenment humanism, the only idea that socialism has held to is the notion that identity between the sexes is the only way to liberate the "second sex." For the moment, I shall refrain from pursuing the fact that this "ideal of equality" has not really been adopted by the actual movements and political parties that lay claims to socialism, and that since May 1968, the new generation of Western European women has been inspired, to some extent, by a revolt against the reality of the situation. Let me simply note that in theory (and in practice, in the case of Eastern Europe), socialist ideology, which is founded on the idea that human beings are determined by their relation to *production*, has ignored the role of the human being in *reproduction* and the *symbolic order*. As a result, socialist ideology has been compelled, in its totalizing, if not totalitarian, spirit,[6] to believe that the specific nature of women is unimportant, if not nonexistent. We have begun to realize, moreover, that Enlightenment humanism and even socialism have imposed this same egalitarian and censuring treatment onto individual religious groups, especially Jewish ones.[7]

Nevertheless, the effects of this attitude are of paramount importance for women. Let us take the example of the evolution of women's destiny in the socialist countries of Eastern Europe. It would only be a slight exaggeration to say that in these countries, the demands of the suffragists and existential feminists have been met, at least to a large degree. What is more, in Eastern Europe, various blunders and vacillations have not prevented three of the most important demands of the early feminist movement from being answered to: the demands of economic, political, and professional equality. The fourth demand, sexual equality, which would require permissiveness in sexual relationships as well as abortion and contraceptive rights, remains inhibited by a certain Marxist ethics as well as by the reason of state. Thus, it is the fourth equal right that poses a problem and seems *vital* to the struggle of the new generation. This may be true, but because of the successful socialist agenda (which has been quite disappointing, in reality), this struggle will no longer aim specifically for equality. At this point in its journey, the new generation is coming up against what I have called the *symbolic* question.

Sexual, biological, physiological, and reproductive difference reflects a difference in the relation between subjects and the symbolic contract—that is, the social contract. It is a matter of clarifying the difference between men and women as concerns their respective relationships to power, language, and meaning. The most subtle aspects of the new generation's feminist subversion will be directed toward this issue in the future. This focus will combine the sexual with the symbolic in order to discover first the specificity of the feminine [*le féminin*] and then the specificity of each woman.

The saturation of socialist ideology and the exhaustion of its plan in favor of a new social contract has made way for Freudianism. I am not unaware, however, that militant women have seen Freud as an annoying male chauvinist from a Vienna that was at once puritanical and decadent, as someone who believed women were submen, castrated men.

CASTRATED OR SUBJECT TO LANGUAGE

Before we bypass Freud in order to propose a more accurate vision of women, let us first attempt to understand his notion of castration. The founder of psychoanalysis posited a castration *anxiety* or *fear* and a correlative penis *envy*, both of which are *imaginary* constructs peculiar to the *discourse* of neurotic *men as well as women*. A close reading of Freud that goes beyond the biological and mechanical models of his day enables us to delve into these issues more deeply.

First, the castration fantasy and its correlative penis envy are like the "primal scene" in that they are all *hypotheses, a priori* judgments intrinsic to psychoanalytic theory itself. These notions represent logical necessities that are relegated to the "origin" in order to explain that which never fails to function in neurotic discourse. In other words, neurotic discourse (in men as well as women) can only be understood in terms of its own logic if we acknowledge its fundamental sources—the primal scene and castration fantasy—even if these are never present in reality itself. The reality of castration is as real as the supposed "big bang" at the origin of the universe, yet we are much less shocked when this sort of intellectual process concerns inanimate matter than when it is applied to our own subjectivity and to the fundamental mechanism of our epistemic thought.

Furthermore, certain Freudian texts (like *The Interpretation of Dreams*, but especially those of the second topology, in particular the *Metapsychology*) as well as their recent elaborations (notably by Jacques Lacan), suggest that castration is an imaginary construction stemming from a psychic mechanism that constitutes the symbolic field as well as anyone who enters it. Castration, then, would be the advent of sign and of syntax, that is, of language as a *separation* from a fusion state of pleasure. In this way, the institution of an *articulated network of differences*, which refers to objects separated from a subject, forms *meaning*. This logical operation of separation, which has been described by child psychology and psycholinguistics, anticipates the syntactic links of language for boys as well as girls. Freud offers a new approach to this notion by postulating that certain biological or familial conditions prompt some women (notably hysterics) to deny this logical operation of separation and the language that ensues, whereas some men (notably obsessional neurotics) glorify this separation and language while trying, petrified as they are, to master them.

Analytic practice has shown that in fantasies, the penis becomes the primary referent of this operation of separation and gives full meaning to the *lack* or *desire* that constitutes subjects when they join the order of language. In order for this operation, which constitutes the symbolic and social orders, to reveal its truth and be accepted by both sexes, it would be wise to add to it the entire series of deprivations and exclusion that accompany the fear of losing one's penis, and impose the loss of wholeness and completeness. Castration, then, would be the ensemble of "cuts" that are indispensable to the advent of the symbolic.

LIVING THE SACRIFICE

Whether or not women are aware of the mutations that have generated or accompanied their awakening, the question they are asking themselves today could be formulated as follows: *what is our place in the social contract?* If this contract, whose terms do not treat everyone in an equal fashion, bases itself upon an ultimately sacrificial relationship of separation and articulation of differences that serves to create a meaning that can be communicated, what is our place in the order of sacrifice and/or language? Since we no longer wish to be excluded from this order, and we are no longer satisfied with our perpetually assigned role of maintaining, developing, and preserving this sociosymbolic contract as mothers, wives, nurses, doctors, teachers, and so forth, how might we appropriate our own space, a space that is passed down through tradition and that we would like to modify?

It is difficult to enumerate with certainty the aspects of the current relationship between women and the symbolic that stem from sociohistorical circumstances (including patriarchal, Christian, humanist, and socialist ideologies, among others), or from a structure. We can only speak of a structure observed in a sociohistorical context, that of Western Christian civilization and its secular ramifications. At the interior of this psychosymbolic structure, women feel rejected from language and the social bond, in which they discover neither the affects nor the meanings of the relationships they enjoy with nature, their bodies, their children's bodies, another woman, or a man. The accompanying frustration, which is also experienced by some men, is the quintessence of the new feminist ideology. Consequently, it is difficult, if not impossible, for women to adhere to the sacrificial logic of separation and syntactic links upon which language and the social code are based, and this can eventually lead to a rejection of the of the symbolic that is experienced as a rejection of the paternal function and may result in psychosis.

Faced with this situation, some women have sought to develop a new perspective—through new objects and new analyses—for anthropology, psycho-analysis, linguistics, and other disciplines that explore the symbolic dimension.[8] Other, more subjective women, who have come forth in the wake of contemporary art, have attempted to modify language and other codes of expression through a style that remains closer to the body and to emotion. I am not referring to "female language,"[9] whose existence as a particular syntactic style is problematic, and whose apparent lexical specificity may be less a product of sexual difference than of social marginality. I am also not speaking of the aesthetic value of creations by women, most of which mirror a more or less euphoric and depressed romanticism, on the one hand, and stage an explosion of an ego that lacks narcissistic gratification, on the other. This leads me to believe that the primary focus of the new generation of women has become the sociosymbolic contract as a sacrificial contract.

For more than a century, anthropologists and sociologists have attracted our attention to the society-sacrifice that works behind "savage thought," wars, dream discourse, or great writers. In so doing, these scholars have reformulated and analyzed the metaphysical question of evil. If society is truly founded on a communal murder, the realization that castration provides the basis for the sociosymbolic is what will enable human beings to postpone murder. We symbolize murder (and ourselves), and thus have an opportunity to transform baleful chaos into an optimal sociosymbolic order.

Today's women have proclaimed that this sacrificial contract imposes itself against their will, which has compelled them to attempt a revolt that they perceive to be a resurrection. Society as a whole, however, considers this revolt to be a refusal and it can result in violence between the sexes (a murderous hatred, the break-up of the couple and the family) or in cultural innovation. In fact, it probably leads to them both. In any event, that is where the stakes are, and they are of enormous consequence. By fighting against evil, we reproduce it, this time at the core of the social bond—the bond between men and women.

THE TERROR OF POWER OR THE POWER OF TERRORISM

First in the former socialist countries (such as the former Soviet Union and China) and later, increasingly, in Western democracies, feminist movements have enabled women to attain positions of leadership in the worlds of business, industry, and culture. Even if various forms of unfair discrimination and persecution continue to hold sway, the struggle against these is a struggle against the ways of the past. Even if the cause has been made known and the principles accepted, there still are obstacles that need to be overcome. Thus, although the

ensuing struggle remains one of the major *preoccupations* of the new generation, in a strict sense of the word, it is no longer its primary *problem*. With respect to *power*, however, its problem could be stated as follows: What occurs
when women attain power and identify with it? What occurs when they reject
power but create an analogous society, a counterpower that ranges from a co-
terie of ideas to terrorist commandos?

That women have assumed commercial, industrial, and cultural power has not
changed the nature of this power, which can be clearly seen in the case of Eastern Europe. The women who have been promoted to positions of leadership and
who have suddenly obtained economic (as well as narcissistic) advantages that
had been refused to them for thousands of years are the same women who become the strongest supporters of the current regimes, the guardians of the status quo, and the most fervent protectors of the established order.[10] This identification between women and a power that they once found frustrating,
oppressive, or unattainable has often been used to the advantage of such totalitarian regimes as the German National Socialists or the Chilean junta.[11] One
possible explanation of this troubling phenomenon might be that it results from
a paranoid counterinvestment (in the psychoanalytic sense) of an initially denied
symbolic order. Even so, this does not prevent its massive propagation around
the world, sometimes in more subtle forms than the totalitarian ones I have
mentioned. In any event, all these forms share an interest in equalization, stability, and conformity, though this comes at a cost: the eradication of each individual's uniqueness, of personal experiences, and of the vagaries of life.

Some may regret that the rise of a libertarian movement such as feminism
may wind up reinforcing conformity, and others will celebrate this consequence
and use it to their advantage. Electoral campaigns and political life never fail to
bet on the latter alternative. Experience has shown that even the antiestablish-
ment or innovative initiatives led by women dragged in by power (when they do
not readily submit to it) are quickly attributed to "the system." The self-pro-
claimed democratization of institutions that pride themselves on accepting
women most often means that they simply add a few female "bosses" to their
ranks.

The various feminist currents, which tend to be more radical in approach, reject the powers that be and make the second sex into a *countersociety*, a sort of
alter ego of official society that harbors hopes for pleasure. This female society
can be opposed to the sacrificial and frustrating sociosymbolic contract: a countersociety imagined to be harmonious, permissive, free, and blissful. In our modern societies, which do not acknowledge an afterlife, the countersociety is the
only refuge for jouissance, for it is precisely an anti-utopia, a place outside the
law, yet a path to utopia.

Like all societies, the countersociety bases itself upon the expulsion of an already excluded element. The scapegoat deemed responsible for evil thus keeps it away from the established community,[12] which is thereby exonerated of any responsibility for it. Modern protest movements have often reproduced this model by designating a guilty party that shields them from criticism, whether it be the foreigner, money, another religion, or the other sex. If we take this logic at face value, does feminism not become a sort of reverse sexism?

In our world, the various marginal groups of sex, age, religion, ethnic origin, and ideology represent a refuge of hope, that is, a secular transcendence. All the same, insofar as the number of women affected by these problems has increased (albeit in a less dramatic way than was the case a few years ago), the problem of the countersociety is becoming an enormous one, no more and no less important than "half the sky."

It is not the case that protest movements, including feminism, are "libertarian at first" and then dogmatic only later. They do not fall into the abyss of defeated models through the fault of some internal deviation or external maneuver. The particular structure of the logic of counterpower and countersociety is what lies behind its essence as an image of defeated society or power. In such a perspective, which is most likely too Hegelian, modern feminism would be a single moment in an ongoing process—the process of becoming aware of the implacable violence (of separation and castration) that underlies *any* symbolic contract.

The large number of women participating in terrorist groups like the Palestinian commandos, the Baader-Meinhoff Gang, and the Red Brigades, has been noted. Exploitation of women is still far too frequent, and the traditional prejudices against women are so fierce that we cannot evaluate this phenomenon in an objective manner, though we may rightfully claim that it stems from a negation of the sociosymbolic contract as well as its counterinvestment. This paranoid mechanism is at the base of all forms of political commitment and it can generate various humanizing attitudes. Yet when a woman feels ruthlessly isolated and becomes aware of her affective experience as a woman or her status as a social being who remains unknown to the discourse and the powers that be (everything from her own family to the social institutions of the world), she can make herself into a "possessed" agent through the counterinvestment of the violence she encounters. She fights against her frustration, then, with weapons that may appear extreme at first glance, but that are justifiable and understandable once the narcissistic suffering that elicits their use is recognized.

This terrorist violence, which is inevitably directed against the regimes of current bourgeois democracies, assigns itself a program of liberation that consists of an order even more repressive and sacrificial than the one it is fighting. Indeed, the object of female terrorists groups' aggression is not the various totali-

tarian regimes, but the liberal regimes that are becoming increasingly democratic. Their mobilization comes about in the name of a nation, an oppressed
group, or what is believed to be a good and sound human essence, that is, the
fantasy of an archaic fulfillment that would be disturbed by an arbitrary, abstract,
and thus undesirable order. Although this order has been accused of being oppressive, is our primary criticism not that it is weak? That it does not stand up to
a substance believed to be pure and good but that is lost forever, a substance
that the marginalized woman hopes to recover?

Anthropologists have affirmed that the social order is a sacrificial one, yet sacrifice stops violence and develops into its own order (through prayer or social
well-being). If we reject it, we subject ourselves to the explosion of the so-called
good substance that uncontrollably erupts outside the bounds of law and rights,
like an absolute arbitrariness.

As a result of the crisis of monotheism, two centuries of revolutions (most recently materialized as Fascism and Stalinism) have staged the tragedy of the
logic of oppressed goodwill that winds up as a massacre. Are women more able
than other social groups to invest in the implacable terrorist mechanism? Perhaps one might merely note that ever since the dawn of feminism (and even before), women who fall outside the norm have often gained power through murder, conspiracy, or assassination. Eternal debt toward the mother has made her
more vulnerable to the symbolic order, more fragile when she suffers from it,
and more virulent when she protects herself. If the archetypal belief in a good
and sound chimerical substance is essentially a belief in the omnipotence of an
archaic, fulfilled, complete, all-encompassing mother who is not frustrated, not
separated, and who lacks the "cut" that permits symbolism (that is, who lacks
castration), the ensuing violence would be impossible to defuse without challenging the very myth of the archaic mother. It has been noted that feminist
movements have been invaded by paranoia,[13] and we may remember Lacan's
scandalous pronouncement that "There is no such thing as Woman." Indeed,
she does not exist with a capital "W," as a holder of a mythical plenitude, a
supreme power upon which the terror of power as well as terrorism as the desire for power base themselves. All the same, talk about a forceful subversion!
Talk about playing with fire!

CREATORS: MALE AND FEMALE

The desire to be a mother, which the previous generation of feminists held to
be alienating or reactionary, has not become a standard for the current generation. Nevertheless, there is a growing number of women who find maternity to

be compatible with their professional careers (this is also due to such improve-
ments in living conditions as the increase of daycare centers and nursery schools,
the more active participation of men in domestic life, and so forth). Furthermore, women are finding that maternity is vital to the richness of female experience, with its many joys and sorrows. This trend is illustrated to its fullest extent in lesbian mothers or in certain single mothers who reject the paternal
function. The latter cases exemplify one of the most dramatic examples of the
rejection of the symbolic order to which I referred earlier on, and they also exhibit an ardent deification of maternal power.

Hegel distinguishes between female right (familial and religious) and male
law (civil and political). Although our societies are very well acquainted with the
uses and abuses of this male law, we must admit that for the moment, female
right appears to be a void. If these practices of fatherless maternity were to become the norm, it would become absolutely necessary to develop appropriate
laws that could diminish the violence that might be inflicted on the child and the
father. Are women equipped for this psychological and legal responsibility? That
is one of the most profound questions that the members of this new generation
of women are coming up against, especially when they refuse to confront such
questions because they are gripped with a rage against the order and its law that
victimizes them.

Faced with this situation, feminist groups are becoming increasingly aware
(especially when they try to broaden their audience) that refusing maternity cannot be their primary political approach. The majority of women today feel that
they have a mission to put a child into the world. This brings up a question for
the new generation that the preceding one repudiated: what lies behind this desire to be a mother? Unable to answer this question, feminist ideology opens the
door to a return of religion, which may serve to pacify anxiety, suffering, and maternal expectations. Although we can only offer a partial adherence to Freud's
belief that the desire to have a child is the desire to have a penis, and is thus a
replacement for phallic and symbolic power, we still must pay close attention to
what today's women have to say about this experience. Pregnancy is a dramatic
ordeal: a splitting of the body, the division and coexistence of self and other, of
nature and awareness, of physiology and speech. This fundamental challenge to
identity is accompanied by a fantasy of wholeness of narcissistic self-contain-
ment. Pregnancy is a sort of institutionalized, socialized, and natural psychosis.
The arrival of the child, on the other hand, guides the mother through a
labyrinth of a rare experience: the love for another person, as opposed to love
for herself, for a mirror image, or especially for another person with which the
"I" becomes merged (through amorous or sexual passion). It is rather a slow, difficult, and delightful process of becoming attentive, tender, and self-effacing. If

maternity is to be guilt-free, this journey needs to be undertaken without masochism and without annihilating one's affective, intellectual, and professional personality, either. In this way, maternity becomes a true *creative act*, something that we have not yet been able to imagine.

At the same time, women's desire for affirmation has emerged as a longing for artistic and especially literary creation. Why the emphasis on literature? Is it because when literature is in conflict with social norms, it diffuses knowledge and occasionally the truth about a repressed, secret, and unconscious universe? Is it because literature intensifies the social contract by exposing the uncanny nature of that which remains unsaid? Is it because it plays with the abstract and frustrating order of social signs, of the words of everyday communication, and thus creates a place for fantasy and pleasure?

Flaubert said, "*Madame Bovary, c'est moi.*" These days, some women think, "*Flaubert, c'est moi.*" This claim points not only to an identification with the power of the imaginary, but also to women's desire to lift the sacrificial weight of the social contract and to furnish our societies with a freer and more flexible discourse that is able to give a name to that which has not yet been an object of widespread circulation: the mysteries of the body, secret joys, shames, hate displayed toward the second sex.

For this reason, women's writing has recently attracted a great deal of attention from "specialists" as well as the media. Nevertheless, the stumbling blocks that it must overcome are not inconsequential. Does women's writing not consist of a morose rejection of the very "male literature" that serves as a model for so much of women's writing? Thanks to the stamp of feminism, do we not sell many books whose naïve whining or commercialized romanticism would normally be scoffed at? Do female writers not make phantasmatic attacks against Language and the Sign, which are accused of being the ultimate mainstays of male chauvinist power, in the name of a body deprived of meaning and whose truth would only be "gestural" or "musical"?

Nevertheless, however questionable the results of women's artistic productions may be, the symptom has been made clear: women *are* writing. And we are eagerly awaiting to find out what *new material* they will offer us.

IN THE NAME OF THE FATHER, THE SON—AND THE WOMAN?

These few characteristic features of the new generation of women in Europe show that these women are placed within the same framework as the religious crisis of contemporary civilization. In my view, religion is our phantasmatic necessity to procure a *representation* (which could be animal, feminine, masculine, or parental, among others) that replaces the element that makes us what we are—our capacity to form symbols. Feminism today seems to constitute exactly this sort of *representation*, one that complements the frustration that women feel when faced with the Christian tradition and its variation—secular humanism. That this new ideology has some affinities with so-called matriarchal beliefs does not obliterate its radical innovation, for it participates in the anti-sacrificial trend that drives our culture. Although this ideology contests these constraints, it still remains vulnerable to the hazards of violence and terrorism. When radicalism goes this far, it challenges the very notion of social exchange.

Some contemporary thinkers maintain that modernity is the first era in human history in which human beings have attempted to live without religion. As it stands today, is feminism not about to become a sort of religion? Or will it manage to rid itself of its belief in Woman, Her power, and Her writing and support instead the singularity of each woman, her complexities, her many languages, at the cost of a single horizon, of a single perspective, of faith?

Is it a matter of ultimate solidarity, or a matter of analysis?

Is it an imaginary support in a technocratic era that frustrates narcissistic personalities, or a measurement of the time in which the cosmos, atoms, and cells—our true contemporaries—call for the formation of a free and flowing subjectivity?

ANOTHER GENERATION IS ANOTHER SPACE

It is now becoming possible to have a more objective perspective on the two preceding generations of women. I am suggesting, then, that a *third one* is taking shape, at least in Europe. I am thinking neither of a new age group (although its importance is far from negligible) nor of a new "mass feminist movement" that would follow in the footsteps of the second generation. The meaning I am attributing to the word "generation" suggests less a chronology than a *signifying* space, a mental space that is at once corporeal and desirous.

For this third generation, which I strongly support (which I am imagining?), the dichotomy between man and woman as an opposition of two rival entities is *a problem for metaphysics*. What does "identity" and even "sexual identity" mean in a theoretical and scientific space in which the notion of "identity" itself is challenged?[14] I am not simply alluding to bisexuality, which most often reveals a desire for totality, a desire for the eradication of difference. I am thinking more specifically of subduing the "fight to the finish" between rival groups, not in hopes of reconciliation—since at the very least, feminism can be lauded for bringing to light that which is irreducible and even lethal in the social contract—but in the hopes that the violence occurs with the utmost mobility within individual and sexual identity, and not through a rejection of the other.

As a result, both individual equilibrium and social equilibrium (which emerges through the homeostasis of aggressive forces typical of social, national, and religious groups) are made vulnerable. All the same, does not the unbearable tension that underlies this "equilibrium" lead those who suffer from it to avoid it, to seek another way of regulating *difference*?

Despite the apparent indifference that has been shown toward the militancy of the first and second generations of women, I have generally found sexism to be less pronounced than before.

With the exception of the proclaimed rights of male and female homosexuals, sex has an evershrinking hold on subjective interest. This "desexualization" goes as far as challenging not only humanism, but also the anthropomorphism that serves as a basis for our society. For this reason, "the man and the woman" are less of a fulcrum for social interest than they once were. The paroxysmal narcissism and egoism of our contemporaries only seem to contradict the retreat from anthropomorphism, for when anthropomorphism does not fall into technological supremacy or a general state of automation, it is forced to look to spirituality. Could the sexual revolution and feminism have merely been transitions into spiritualism?

That spiritualism turns to evasion or to conformist repression should not obscure the radical nature of the process, which comes forth as an *interiorization of the fundamental separation of the sociosymbolic contract*. From that point on, the other is neither an evil being foreign to me nor a scapegoat from the outside, that is, of another sex, class, race, or nation. I am *at once the attacker and the victim*, the same *and* the other, identical *and* foreign. I simply have to analyze incessantly the fundamental separation of my own untenable identity.

Religion is willing to accept this European awareness of *intrinsic evil*, which emerges from the ideological accomplishments and impasses of the feminist experience. Is any other discourse able to support it? Along with psychoanalysis, the role of aesthetic practices needs to be augmented, not only to counterbalance the mass-production and uniformity of the information age, but also to demystify the idea that the community of language is a universal, all inclusive, and equalizing tool. Each artistic experience can also highlight the diversity of our identifications and the relativity of our symbolic and biological existence.

Understood as such, aesthetics takes on the question of morality. The imaginary helps to outline an ethics that remains invisible, as the outbreak of the imposture and of hatred wreaks havoc on societies freed from dogmas and laws. As restriction and as play, the imaginary enables us to envision an ethics aware of its own sacrificial order and that thus retains part of the burden for each of its adherents, whom the imaginary pronounces guilty and responsible, though it offers them the direct possibility of jouissance, of various aesthetic productions, of having a life filled with trials and differences. This would be a utopian ethics, but is any other kind possible?

In this sense, we might return to Spinoza's question: are women subject to ethics? Women are probably not subject to the ethics laid out by classical philosophy, with which generations of feminists have had a dangerously precarious relationship. Nevertheless, do women not participate in the upheaval that our society is experiencing on several levels (war, drugs, artificial insemination), an upheaval that will require a new ethics? If we consider feminism to be a *moment* in the thought pertaining to the anthropomorphic identity that has diminished the freedom of our species, we will only be able to answer this question in the affirmative once this moment has come to a close. And what is the meaning of the current "politically correct" movement that has swept across the United States? European consciousness has surpassed such concerns, thanks, in some respects, to the dissatisfaction and creativity of its women.

NOTES

1. See *The Freud/Jung Letters*, Ralph Manheim and R. F. C. Hull, tr. (Princeton, N.J.: Princeton University Press, 1974).
2. See René Spitz, *The First Year of Life: A Psychoanalytic Study of Normal and Deviant Development of Object Relations* (New York: International Universities Press, 1966); D. W. Winnicott, *Playing and Reality* (New York: Basic Books, 1971); Julia Kristeva, "Place Names," *Desire in Language: A Semiotic Approach to Literature and Art*, Thomas Gora, Alice Jardine, Léon S. Roudiez, tr. (New York: Columbia University Press, 1980), pp. 271–95.
3. See Plato, *Timaeus*, Francis M. Cornford, tr. (New York: Harcourt, Brace 1937): "Space, which is everlasting, not admitting destruction; providing a situation for all things that come into being but itself apprehended without the senses by a sort of bastard reasoning, and hardly an object of belief. This, indeed, is that which we look upon as in a dream and say that anything that is must needs be in some place and occupy some room" (52a–52b). See my remarks on the chora in *Revolution in Poetic Language*, Margaret Waller, tr. (New York: Columbia University Press, 1984).
4. See Julia Kristeva, "Stabat Mater," in *Tales of Love*, Léon S. Roudiez, tr. (New York: Columbia University Press, 1983).
5. See H. C. Puech, *La Gnose et le temps* (Paris: Gallimard, 1977).
6. See D. Desanti, "L'autre sexe des bolcheviks," *Tel Quel 76* (1978); and Julia Kristeva, *About Chinese Women*, Anita Barrows, tr. (London: Marion Boyars, 1977).
7. See Arthur Hertzberg, *The French Enlightenment and the Jews* (New York: Columbia University Press, 1968); and *Les Juifs et la révolution française*, B. Blumenkranz and A. Soboul, ed. (Paris: Editions Privat, 1976).
8. From time to time, this work is published in various academic women's journals, one of the most prestigious being *Signs: Journal of Women in Culture and Society*, University of Chicago Press. Also of note are the special issue of the *Revue des sciences*

humaines 4 (1977) entitled "Écriture, féminité, féminisme" and "Les femmes et la philosophie" in *Le Doctrinal de sapience* 3 (1977).

9. See the various linguistic studies on "female language," such as Robin Lakoff, *Language and Women's Place* (New York: Harper & Row, 1974); Mary R. Key, *Male/Female Language* (Metuchen, N.J.: Scarecrow Press, 1973); and A. M. Houdebine, "Les femmes et la langue," *Tel Quel* 74 (1977): 84–95.

10. See Julia Kristeva, *About Chinese Women*.

11. See M. A. Macciocchi, *Éléments pour une analyse du fascisme* (Paris: 10/18, 1976); Michèle Mattelart, "Le coup d'état au féminin," *Les Temps modernes* (January 1975).

12. The principles of a "sacrificial anthropology" have been laid out by René Girard in *Violence and the Sacred*, Patrick Gregory, tr. (Baltimore: Johns Hopkins University Press, 1977); and especially in *Things Hidden Since the Foundation of the World*, Stephen Bann and Michael Metteer, tr. (Palo Alto: Stanford University Press, 1987).

13. See Micheline Enriquez, "Fantasmes paranoïaques: différences de sexes, homosexualité, loi du père," *Topiques* 13 (1974).

14. See Claude Lévi-Strauss et al., *L'Identité: séminaire interdisciplinaire* (Paris: Grasset & Fasquelle, 1977).

7

THERE ARE TWO SEXES, NOT ONE

Luce Irigaray

INTRODUCTION

by Jennifer Hansen

Luce Irigaray was born in the 1930s in Belgium. She holds numerous advanced degrees: doctorates in philosophy, psychoanalysis, and linguistics and advanced degrees in psychology, psychopathology, and literature. She attended the University of Louvain where she received a master's degree in philosophy and literature (*Maîtrise en philosophie et lettres*) in 1955. She then taught high school in Brussels until 1959, when she moved to Paris to study psychology.

She attended the University of Paris from 1959 to 1962, receiving first a master's degree in psychology in 1961 and then a diploma in psychopathology in 1962. After completing her work in psychology, Irigaray returned to Belgium where she worked at the *Foundation Nationale de la Recherche Scientifique* from 1962 to 1964. In 1964 she returned to Paris to begin work at the *Centre National de la Recherche Scientifique* (CNRS) as an assistant researcher on an interdisciplinary team of linguists, neurologists, logicians, psychiatrists, and philosophers in the Psychology Commission. In 1986 she transferred to the Philosophy Commission, where she currently works and has earned herself the prestigious position of director of research.

Upon her return to Paris in 1964, Irigaray also began her two doctorates. She was awarded her doctorate in linguistics in 1968 upon completing her dissertation, *Le Langage des Déments* (The Language of the Demented) at the University of Paris X, Nanterre. In her dissertation, she studied how patients with senile dementia used grammar and language, which sparked her interest in the ways in which men and women use language differently and the language of female hysteria. Her controversial second dissertation, *Speculum de l'autre femme* (Speculum of the Other Woman) at the University of Paris VIII, Vincennes, in 1974 was for her Ph.D.s in philosophy and psychoanalysis. She was trained as an analyst at the *École freudienne* and from 1970 to 1974 she taught in the Department of Psychoanalysis at Vincennes as part of her training. Though Irigaray received the highest honors for *Speculum*, she alienated herself from both the more traditional academics in France and the Lacanians, who perceived her work to be an attack on Lacan himself. She was relieved of her teaching position at Vincennes as well as generally blackballed from teaching in Parisian universities. She has never enjoyed as much scholarly attention in Paris as she has internationally. Despite the controversy surrounding her early work, Irigaray succeeded in winning teaching positions both in Paris and internationally, including positions at the University of Rotterdam and the University of Toronto.

In addition to her work at the CNRS and her academic posts, Irigaray has been a grassroots activist. She participated in the feminist movement of the 1970s in Paris, never allying herself with either of the main feminist groups, *Psychanalyse et Politique* (Psych et Po) or *Mouvement de Libération des Femmes* (MLF). She demonstrated for the legalization of abortion and contraceptives. Irigaray also participated in women's movement internationally, notably in Italy, where her work profoundly influences Italian feminism. She also contributes to the communist party paper *Unità*, in Italy, and spoke publicly with a communist party politician, Renzo Imbeni, to whom she dedicated her 1992 book, *J'amie à toi*.

The influences on Irigaray's work are wide-ranging and a reflection of her interdisciplinary formation. The four principal influences to her work are the post-1968 women's movement in France; avant-garde writers; French philosophers such as Jacques Lacan, Jacques Derrida, and Emmanuel Levinas; and the German philosophers G. W. F. Hegel, Friedrich Nietzsche, and Martin Heidegger. Irigaray credits the work of Simone de Beauvoir as particularly inspirational to her own work, and Irigaray's consideration of how Western culture produces 'Woman' as Other is a reworking and augmentation of Beauvoir's own work in *The Second Sex*.

In the late 1960s Derrida demonstrated how binary oppositions structure our language in ways that privilege one term at the expense of the other term. Irigaray argues that man is privileged at woman's expense. The opposites *man* and *woman* are not symmetrical, but clearly hierarchical. For example, woman is not the opposite of man, but the negation of man. Man *alone* is the paradigmatic metaphysical concept of human beings, and women are merely inferior instances of this concept. The operation of binary oppositions in culture works insidiously to shape our psyches so that we learn that *man* is the Universal, while *woman* is contingent, particular, and deficient.

In *Speculum*, Irigaray challenged the philosophical canon: Plato, Aristotle,

Much it does

Plotinus, Freud, and implicitly Jacques Lacan, as solely privileging and elaborating the masculine subject. She shows that the Western canon functions like a mirror (*speculum mundi* in Latin) which reflects back man as the master of the universe, and the universe and God in the image of man, while distorting the image of woman as imperfect, lacking, or a hysterical subject. Irigaray also plays upon another meaning of *speculum* in her text, namely the instrument (*trml*) used by the gynecologist to reveal the interior sex of a woman. Using such a metaphor, she attempts to use this tool or mirror to open or reflect sexual difference and the feminine so as to interrupt the disfiguring images of women in Western culture.

In her close reading of the Western canon, Irigaray reveals that at the core of each thinker's texts is a fundamental matricide and continued repression of sexual difference. For example, in the myths of origin, it is not the mother who brings forward life, but rather a self-originating male principle, or life force. Woman, in this scenario, is derived from man and then serves merely to reproduce the species. She is the 'envelope', as Irigaray often calls her; she is merely a womb in which male subjects gestate. And finally, woman's purpose is to nurture men, both nutritionally and spiritually, to enable them to one day leave her behind and participate in the social realm.

Irigaray's own philosophical work makes use of different strategies of writing, notably a mimetic voice, in order to open up a space within patriarchy through writing to enable the representation of sexual difference outside of it. In *Questions I*, Irigaray explains how she 'mimes' the texts she reads as a mode of deconstructing their authority. She plays on the double meaning of miming as an act of poking fun at something and as a symptom of hysteria (a disease patriarchy diagnoses women with) to reveal the patriarchal operations of Western thought to create the whole world, including women, in the image of men. She often repeats verbatim the words of philosophers—though supplying some critique between their lines—in order to compel the reader to recognize the absurdity of their presumptions concerning 'Woman', 'Nature', and femininity. By miming sections of these texts and placing them in a feminist context, she compels the reader to recognize how thoroughly patriarchal repression of women and female sexuality is in Western culture.

This repression of women leads not only to their madness, as she points out in "Body against Body: In Relation to the Mother," but to the phobia, disgust, and fear that men associate with female sexuality. Likewise, Irigaray shows that by turning women and nature into the raw materials that fuel men's projects, patriarchy treats women and nature as slavish to man's desires and sexual needs. In "Each Sex Must Have Its Own Rights," Irigaray argues that until we establish a truly ethical relationship between the sexes and honor sexual difference as a productive fact of culture, humanity will be plagued by illness, madness, wars, and technological disasters such as global nuclear war. If sexual difference only represents the difference between nature and culture, where women's bodies reproduce the future leaders of society, nurturing and satisfying the needs of male others, then natural entities come to represent exploitable matter. In such a logic, the planet, whose fate is linked to the perception of women and sexual difference, becomes a scarcer and scarcer commodity, overrun with pollution.

Irigaray argues that this destructive attitude toward nature and women's bodies derives from male sexuality that follows a model of tension and release. The tempo of male sexuality structures the technology that we build in our projects of taming the unruliness of nature and forces our bodies to endure the stress of endless workdays, high-speed transportation, noise pollution, and so on with the reward of orgasmic release once work is over. We build with an eye to the satisfaction of sexual and biological needs, but our vision does not yet extend beyond these immediate goals. If, however, we begin to revision nature and sexual difference in terms of the rich possibilities and creative energy these facts offer us, then we might begin to see a new stage of human development. This new stage requires transforming our attitudes toward difference (whether sexual, racial, or the mysteries of nature) from a desire to tame chaos in order to satisfy our basic animal needs to seeing difference as empowering us to reach new heights.

One concrete way in which we can achieve a new culture of sexual difference is by revising our legal code. First, argues Irigaray, the legal code operates with the masculine sex as its norm, insidiously protecting male bodies and desires while ignoring the needs and contributions of the other sex. The legal code, furthermore, only works to ensure that one's property and right to satisfaction are not infringed upon by the state. Laws function as negative rights. Laws should function as positive rights, empowering men and women to achieve to their fullest capacities. Furthermore, laws ought to reflect the unique capacities of the different sexes rather than treat them homogeneously. In her later works such as *I Love to You*, Irigaray actually offers examples of how these laws could be worded. Irigaray's legal suggestions are formed in reaction to the civil code legal system of France and not the common law of the United States. Strong assumptions inform the civil code about what human beings are—assumptions that Irigaray claims take the masculine sex as the generic civil subject. Irigaray maintains that to combat these assumptions the code must acknowledge at the very minimum that sexual difference exists.

For Irigaray, subjectivity is not a thing but a process bounded by and enhanced by historical and embodied limitations. Each subject ought to be free, argues Irigaray, to pursue the unique possibilities of his or *her* subjective identity in ways that do not subordinate their differences to a hierarchical, patriarchal economy. That is, for Irigaray, until sexual difference exists as a positive fact of humanity, rather than a marker of human deficiency, no subjects are free to become (an argument similar to Beauvoir's in *Ethics of Ambiguity*). Hence, Irigaray does not believe that women are destined to be inferior due to their different biology, nor does she believe that any subject is solely determined by his or her biology.

BIBLIOGRAPHY

Selected Primary Sources

1985. *Speculum of the Other Woman.* Translated by Gillian C. Gill. Ithaca: Cornell University Press. [*Speculum de l'autre femme.* Paris: Éditions de Minuit, 1974.]

1985. *This Sex Which Is Not One.* Translated by Catherine Porter. Ithaca: Cornell University Press. [*Ce sexe qui n'est pas un.* Paris: Éditions de Minuit, 1977.]

1991. *Marine Lover.* Translated by Gillian Gill. New York: Columbia University Press. [*Amante marine. De Friedrich Nietzsche.* Paris: Éditions de Minuit, 1980.]

1992. *Elemental Passions.* Translated by J. Collie and J. Still. New York: Routledge. [*Passions élémentaires.* Paris: Éditions de Minuit, 1981.]

1993. *An Ethics of Sexual Difference.* Translated by Carolyn Burke and Gillian C. Gill. Ithaca: Cornell University Press. [*L'Ethique de la différence sexuelle.* Paris: Éditions de Minuit, 1984.]

1993. *Sexes and Genealogies.* Translated by Gillian C. Gill. New York: Columbia University Press. [*Sexes et parentés* Paris: Éditions de Minuit, 1987.]

1993. *Je, Tu, Nous: Toward a Culture of Difference.* Translated by A. Martin. New York: Routledge. [*je, tu, nous.* Paris: Grasset & Fasquelle, 1990.]

1994. *Thinking the Difference.* Translated by A. Martin. New York: Routledge. [*Le Temps de la différence.* Paris: Éditions Hachette, 1989.]

1996. *I Love to You.* Translated by A. Martin. New York: Routledge. [*J'aime à toi: esquisse d'une félicité dans l'historie.* Paris: Bernard Grasset, 1992.]

1997. *Être Deus.* Paris: Bernard Grasset.

1999. *The Forgetting of Air in Martin Heidegger.* Translated by Mary Beth Mader. Austin: University of Texas Press. [*L'oubli de l'air chez Martin Heidegger.* Paris: Les Editions de Minuit, 1983.]

Selected Secondary Sources

Burke, Carolyn, Naomi Schor, and Margaret Whitford, eds. 1994. *Engaging with Irigaray: Feminist Philosophy and Modern European Thought.* New York: Columbia University Press.

Chanter, Tina. 1995. *Ethics of Eros: Irigaray's Rewriting of the Philosophers*. London: Routledge.

De Lauretis, Teresa. 1984. *Alice Doesn't: Feminism, Semiotics, Cinema*. Bloomington: Indiana University Press.

Gallop, Jane. 1982. *The Daughter's Seduction: Feminism and Psychoanalysis*. Ithaca: Cornell University Press.

Grosz, Elizabeth. 1989. *Sexual Subversions*. Boston: Allen and Unwin.

Hirsh, Elizabeth, and Gary A. Olson. 1995. " 'Je—Luce Irigaray': A Meeting with Luce Irigaray." Feminist Ethics and Social Policy, Part II, special issue of *Hypatia* 10, no. 2: 93–114.

Whitford, Margaret. 1991. *Luce Irigaray: Philosophy in the Feminine*. London: Routledge, 93–114.

THIS SEX WHICH IS NOT ONE

Questions I[1]

What motivation has promoted and sustained the pursuit of your work?

I am a woman. I am a being sexualized as feminine. I am sexualized female. The motivation of my work lies in the impossibility of articulating such a statement; in the fact that its utterance is in some way senseless, inappropriate, indecent. Either because *woman* is never the attribute of the verb *to be* nor *sexualized female* a quality of *being*, or because *am a woman* is not predicated of *I*, or because *I am sexualized* excludes the feminine gender.

In other words, the articulation of the reality of my sex is impossible in discourse, and for a structural, eidetic reason. My sex is removed, at least as the property of a subject, from the predicative mechanism that assures discursive coherence.

I can thus speak intelligently as sexualized male (whether I recognize this or not) or as asexualized. Otherwise, I shall succumb to the illogicality that is proverbially attributed to women. All the statements I make are thus either borrowed from a model that leaves my sex aside—implying a continuous discrepancy between the presuppositions of my enunciation and my utterances, and signifying furthermore that, mimicking what does not correspond to my own "idea" or "model" (which moreover I don't even have), I must be quite inferior to someone who has ideas or models on his own account—or else my utterances are unintelligible according to the code in force. In that case they are likely to be labeled abnormal, even pathological.

This aporia of discourse as to the female sex—whether it is envisaged as a limit of rationality itself, or as women's powerlessness to speak coherently—raises a question and even provokes a crisis, which may be analyzed in various specific areas, but which, in order to be interpreted, have to pass through the master discourse: the one that prescribes, in the last analysis, the organization of language, the one that lays down the law to the others, including even the discourse held on the subject of these others: the discourse on discourses, philosophical discourse. In order to interrogate its stranglehold on history, its historical domination.

But this philosophical mastery—which is the issue dealt with in *Speculum*—cannot simply be approached head on, nor simply within the realm of the philosophical itself. Thus it was necessary to deploy other languages—without forgetting their own debt to philosophical language—and even to accept the condition of silence, of aphasia as a symptom—historico-hysterical, hysterico-historical—so that something of the feminine as the limit of the philosophical might finally be heard.

What method have you adopted for this research?

A delicate question. For isn't it the method, the path to knowledge, that has always also led us away, led us astray, by fraud and artifice, from woman's path, and to the point of consecrating its oblivion? This second interpretation of the term method—as detour, fraud, and artifice—is moreover its second possible translation. In order to reopen woman's path, in particular in and through language, it was therefore necessary to note the way in which the method is never as simple as it purports to be, the way in which the teleological project—the teleologically constructive project—the method takes on is always a project, conscious or not, of turning away, of deviation, and of reduction, in the artifice of sameness, of otherness. In other words, speaking at the greatest level of generality so far as philosophical methods are concerned: of the feminine.

❅ ❅ ❅

Thus it was necessary to destroy, but, as René Char wrote, with nuptial tools. The tool is not a feminine attribute. But woman may re-utilize its marks on her, in her. To put it another way: the option left to me was to *have a fling with the* philosophers—which is easier said than done . . . for what path can one take to get back inside their ever so coherent systems?

imitation of man

In a first phase, there is perhaps only one path, and in any case it is the one to which the female condition is assigned: that of *mimicry.* But the mimetic role itself is complex, for it presupposes that one can lend oneself to everything, if not to everyone. That one can *copy* anything at all, anyone at all, can receive all impressions, *without appropriating them to oneself, and without adding any.* That is, can be nothing but a possibility that the philosopher may exploit for (self-) reflection. Like the Platonic *chora,* but also the mirror of the subject.

why not appropriate?

To go back inside the philosopher's house requires, too, that one be able to fulfill the role of *matter*—mother or sister. That is, what always begins anew to nourish speculation, what functions as the *resource* of reflection—the red blood of resemblance—but also as its *waste,* as the discard that shunts what resists transparency—madness—to the outside. *menstrual*

Having a fling with the philosopher also entails safeguarding *those components of the mirror that cannot reflect themselves*: its backing, its brilliancy, thus its dazzlements, its ecstasies. Reproductive material and duplicating mirror, the philosopher's wife also has to underwrite that *narcissism which often extends onto a transcendental dimension.* Certainly without saying so, without knowing it. That secret in particular must never be disclosed. This role is only possible because of its ultimate avoidance of self-exploration: it entails a virginity incapable of self-reflection. And a pleasure that is wholly "divine."

mirror, mirrored by narcissism

hm?

Ha!

The philosopher's wife must also, though in a secondary way, be beautiful, and *exhibit all the attractions of femininity,* in order to distract a gaze too often carried away by theoretical contemplations. *funny*

That woman—and, since philosophical discourse dominates history in general, *that wife/woman of every man*—is thus pledged to the service of the "philosopher's" "self" in all forms. And as far as the wedding celebration is concerned, she is in danger of being no more than the requisite mediator for the philosopher's celebrations with himself, and with his fellows.

If she can play that role so well, if it does not kill her, quite, it is because she keeps something in reserve with respect to this function. Because she still subsists, otherwise and elsewhere than there where she mimes so well what is asked of her. Because her own "self" remains foreign to the whole staging. But she doubtless needs to reenact it in order to remember what that staging has probably metabolized so thoroughly that *she* has forgotten it: her own sex. Her sex is heterogeneous to this whole economy of representation, but it is capable of interpreting that economy precisely because it has remained "outside." Because it does not postulate oneness, or sameness, or reproduction, or even representation. Because it remains somewhere else than in that general repetition where it is taken up only as *the otherness of sameness*.

By this token, woman stands indeed, as Hegel has written, for the eternal irony of the community—of men. Provided that she does not will to be their equal. That she does not enter into a discourse whose systematicity is based on her reduction into sameness.

◦ ◦ ◦

What are the conclusions of your work?

In conclusion, then, I come to what might be presented as propositions:

1. The fact that Freud took sexuality as the object of his discourse does not necessarily imply that he interpreted the role of sexualization in discourse itself, his own in particular. He did not carry out an analysis of the presuppositions that bear upon the production of discourse insofar as sexual difference is concerned. Or again: the questions that Freud's practice and theory raise for the scene of representation—questions about what it represses in the form of what he designates as unconscious, questions about what it neglects as effects of overdetermination, of deferred action, "death instinct," and so on, questions about the utterances of the subject—these questions do not go so far as to include the question of the sexualized determination of that scene. Lacking such an interpretation, Freud's discourse remains caught up in a meta-physical economy.

2. From a more strictly philosophical viewpoint, one may wonder whether taking into account the sexualization of discourse does not open up the possibility of a different relation to the transcendental. Neither simply subjective nor simply objective, neither univocally centered nor decentered, neither unique nor plural, but as the place—up to now always collapsed in an ek-stasis—of what I would call the *copula*. Which requires the interpretation of being as having always already taken on (again) the role of copula in a discursive economy that denies the copulative operation between the sexes in language.

3. That place may only emerge if the feminine is granted its own "specificity" in its relation to language. Which implies a logic other than the one imposed by discursive coherence. I have attempted to practice that other "logic" in the writ-

ing of *Speculum*; I have also begun to indicate certain of its elements in "L'in-contournable volume."[2] Let us say that it would reject all closure or circularity in discourse—any constitution of *archè* or of *télos;* that it would privilege the "near" rather than the "proper," but a "near" not (re)captured in the spatio-temporal economy of philosophical tradition; that it would entail a different relation to unity, to identity with self, to truth, to the same and thus to alterity, to repetition and thus to temporality; that it would retraverse "differently" the matter/form dyad, the power/act dyad, and so on. Since for the feminine, the other lies in the one [*l'un(e)*]—without any possibility of equality, identity, subordination, appropriation . . . of that one in its relation to the other. An economy of exchange in all of its modalities that has yet to be put into play.

All of this requires going back through the processes of specula(riza)tion that subtend our social and cultural organization. For relations among subjects have always had recourse, explicitly or more often implicitly, to the *flat mirror*, that is, to what privileges the relation of man to his fellow man. A flat mirror has always already subtended and traversed speculation. What effects of linear projection, of circular turning back onto the self-(as the) same, what eruptions in signifying-points of identity has it entailed? What "subject" has ever found in it, finally, its due? What "other" has been reduced by it to the hard-to-represent function of the negative? A function enveloped in that glass—and also in its void of reflections—where the historical development of discourse has been projected and reassured. Or again, a function assigned to the role of "matter," an opaque and silent matrix, a reserve for specula(riza)tions to come, a pole of a certain opposition whose fetishist dues have still not all been paid. To interpret the mirror's intervention, to discover what it may have kept suspended in an un-reflected blaze of its brilliance, what it may have congealed in its decisive cut, what it may have frozen of the "other"'s flowing, and vice versa of course: this is what is at stake.

Thus it was necessary both to reexamine the domination of the specular and the speculative over history and also—since the specular is one of the irreducible dimensions of the speaking animal—to put into place a mode of specularization that allows for the relation of woman to "herself" and to her like. Which presupposes *a curved mirror*, but also one that is *folded back on itself*, with its impossible reappropriation "on the inside" of the mind, of thought, of subjectivity. Whence the *intervention of the speculum and of the concave mirror*, which disturb the staging of representation according to too-exclusively masculine parameters. For these latter exclude women from participation in exchange, except as objects or the possibility of transactions among men.

[handwritten: must transform language (others agree)]

4. This brings to mind the political stake—in the restricted or generalized sense—of this work. The fact that women's "liberation" requires transforming the economic realm, and thus necessarily transforming culture and its operative agency, language. Without such an interpretation of a general grammar of culture, the feminine will never take place in history, except as a reservoir of matter and of speculation. And as Antigone has already told us, "between her and him, nothing can ever be said." *[handwritten: Oedipus & mom?]*

[handwritten: in between (as in between the two binary forces?)??]

NOTES

1. These three questions were raised, explicitly or implicitly, by members of the jury during a doctoral thesis defense in the Philosophy Department of the University of Vincennes, on October 2, 1974.
2. In *Speculum de l'autre femme* (Paris, 1974), pp. 282–298.

WOMEN ON THE MARKET

The society we know, our own culture, is based upon the exchange of women. Without the exchange of women, we are told, we would fall back into the anarchy (?) of the natural world, the randomness (?) of the animal kingdom. The passage into the social order, into the symbolic order, into order as such, is assured by the fact that men, or groups of men, circulate women among themselves, according to a rule known as the incest taboo. *[handwritten: HOW?]*

Whatever familial form this prohibition may take in a given state of society, its signification has a much broader impact. It assures the foundation of the economic, social, and cultural order that has been ours for centuries.

Why exchange women? Because they are "scarce [commodities] . . . essential to the life of the group," the anthropologist tells us.[1] Why this characteristic scarcity, given the biological equilibrium between male and female births? Because the "deep polygamous tendency, which exists among all men, always makes the number of available women seem insufficient. Let us add that, even if there were as many women as men, these women would not all be equally desirable . . . and that, by definition . . . , the most desirable women must form a minority."[2] *[handwritten: Who are they?]* *[handwritten: Wow! Interp Claim!]*

Are men all equally desirable? Do women have no tendency toward polygamy? The good anthropologist does not raise such questions. *A fortiori*: why are men not objects of exchange among women? It is because women's bod-

[handwritten: but men are supposed to be equally desirable, seen as equally desirable (or women's desire is not seen to figure in)]

ies—through their use, consumption, and circulation—provide for the condition making social life and culture possible, although they remain an unknown "infrastructure" of the elaboration of that social life and culture. The exploitation of the matter that has been sexualized female is so integral a part of our sociocultural horizon that there is no way to interpret it except within this horizon.

In still other words: all the systems of exchange that organize patriarchal societies and all the modalities of productive work that are recognized, valued, and rewarded in these societies are men's business. The production of women, signs, and commodities is always referred back to men (when a man buys a girl, he "pays" the father or the brother, not the mother . . .), and they always pass from one man to another, from one group of men to another. The work force is thus always assumed to be masculine, and "products" are objects to be used, objects of transaction among men alone.

Which means that the possibility of our social life, of our culture, depends upon a (ho(m)mo-sexual monopoly? The law that orders our society is the exclusive valorization of men's needs/desires, of exchanges among men. What the anthropologist calls the passage from nature to culture thus amounts to the institution of the reign of hom(m)o-sexuality. Not in an "immediate" practice, but in its "social" mediation. From this point on, patriarchal societies might be interpreted as societies functioning in the mode of "semblance." The value of symbolic and imaginary productions is superimposed upon, and even substituted for, the value of relations of material, natural, and corporal (re)production.

In this new matrix of History, in which man begets man as his own likeness, wives, daughters, and sisters have value only in that they serve as the possibility of, and potential benefit in, relations among men. The use of and traffic in women subtend and uphold the reign of masculine hom(m)o-sexuality, even while they maintain that hom(m)o-sexuality in speculations, mirror games, identifications, and more or less rivalrous appropriations, which defer its real practice. Reigning everywhere, although prohibited in practice, hom(m)o-sexuality is played out through the bodies of women, matter, or sign, and heterosexuality has been up to now just an alibi for the smooth workings of man's relations with himself, of relations among men. Whose "sociocultural endogamy" excludes the participation of that other, so foreign to the social order: woman. Exogamy doubtless requires that one leave one's family, tribe, or clan, in order to make alliances. All the same, it does not tolerate marriage with populations that are too far away, too far removed from the prevailing cultural rules. A sociocultural endogamy would thus forbid commerce *with* women. Men make commerce *of* them, but they do not enter into any exchanges *with* them. Is this perhaps all the

more true because exogamy is an economic issue, perhaps even subtends economy as such? The exchange of women as goods accompanies and stimulates exchanges of other "wealth" among groups of men. The economy—in both the
narrow and the broad sense—that is in place in our societies thus requires that
women lend themselves to alienation in consumption, and to exchanges in which
they do not participate, and that men be exempt from being used and circulated
like commodities.

o o o

will you alienate yourself from yourself and become my commodity?

Marx's analysis of commodities as the elementary form of capitalist wealth can
thus be understood as an interpretation of the status of women in so-called patriarchal societies. The organization of such societies, and the operation of the
symbolic system on which this organization is based—a symbolic system whose
instrument and representative is the proper name: the name of the father, the
name of God—contain in a nuclear form the developments that Marx defines as
characteristic of a capitalist regime: the submission of "nature" to a "labor" on
the part of men who thus constitute "nature" as use value and exchange value;
the division of labor among private producer-owners who exchange their
women-commodities among themselves, but also among producers and ex-
ploiters or exploitees of the social order; the standardization of women according to proper names that determine their equivalences; a tendency to accumulate wealth, that is, a tendency for the representatives of the most "proper"
names—the leaders—to capitalize more women than the others; a progression
of the social work of the symbolic toward greater and greater abstraction; and
so forth.

To be sure, the means of production have evolved, new techniques have been
developed, but it does seem that as soon as the father-man was assured of his reproductive power and had marked his products with his name, that is, from the
very origin of private property and the patriarchal family, social exploitation occurred. In other words, all the social regimes of "History" are based upon the exploitation of one "class" of producers, namely, women. Whose reproductive use
value (reproductive of children and of the labor force) and whose constitution
as exchange value underwrite the symbolic order as such, without any compensation would imply a double system of exchange, that is, a shattering of the mo-
nopolization of the proper name (and of what it signifies as appropriative power)
by father-men.

Thus the social body would be redistributed into producer-subjects no longer
functioning as commodities because they provided the standard of value for

commodities, and into commodity-objects that ensured the circulation of exchange without participating in it as subjects.

✴ ✴ ✴

Let us now reconsider a few points[3] in Marx's analysis of value that seem to describe the social status of women.

Wealth amounts to a subordination of the use of things to their accumulation. Then would *the way women are used matter less than their number?* The possession of a woman is certainly indispensable to man for the reproductive use value that she represents; but what he desires is to have them all. To "accumulate" them, to be able to count off his conquests, seductions, possessions, both sequentially and cumulatively, as measure or standard(s).

All but one? For if the series could be closed, value might well lie, as Marx says, in the relation among them rather than in the relation to a standard that remains external to them—whether gold or phallus.

The use made of women is thus of less value than their appropriation one by one. And their "usefulness" is not what counts the most. Woman's price is not determined by the "properties" of her body—although her body constitutes the *material* support of that price.

But when women are exchanged, woman's body must be treated as an *abstraction.* The exchange operation cannot take place in terms of some intrinsic, immanent value of the commodity. It can only come about when two objects—two women—are in a relation of equality with a third term that is neither the one nor the other. It is thus not as "women" that they are exchanged, but as women reduced to some common feature—their current price in gold, or phalluses—and of which they would represent a plus or minus quantity. Not a plus or a minus of feminine qualities, obviously. Since these qualities are abandoned in the long run to the needs of the consumer, *woman has value on the market by virtue of one single quality: that of being a product of man's "labor."*

On this basis, each one looks exactly like every other. They all have the same phantom-like reality. Metamorphosed in identical *sublimations,* samples of the same indistinguishable work, all these objects now manifest just one thing, namely, that in their production a force of human labor has been expended, that labor has accumulated in them. In their role as crystals of that common social substance, they are deemed to have value.

As *commodities, women are thus two things at once: utilitarian objects and bearers of value.* "They manifest themselves therefore as commodities, or have the form of commodities, only in so far as they have two forms, a physical or natural form, and a value form" (p. 55).

But "the reality of the value of commodities differs in this respect from Dame Quickly, that we don't know 'where to have it'" (ibid). *Woman, object of exchange, differs from woman, use value, in that one doesn't know how to take (hold of) her,* for since "the value of commodities is the very opposite of the coarse materiality of their substance, not an atom of matter enters into its composition. Turn and examine a single commodity, by itself, as we will. Yet in so far as it remains an object of value, it seems impossible to grasp it" (ibid). The value of a woman always escapes: black continent, hole in the symbolic, breach in discourse . . . It is only in the operation of exchange among women that something of this—something enigmatic, to be sure—can be felt. *Woman thus has value only in that she can be exchanged.* In the passage from one to the other, something else finally exists beside the possible utility of the "coarseness" of her body. But this value is not found, is not recaptured in her. It is only her measurement against a third term that remains external to her, and that makes it possible to compare her with another woman, that permits her to have a relation to another commodity in terms of an equivalence that remains foreign to both.

Women-as-commodities are thus subject to a schism that divides them into the categories of usefulness and exchange value; into matter-body and an envelope that is precious but impenetrable, ungraspable, and not susceptible to appropriation by women themselves; into private use and social use.

In order to have a *relative value* a commodity has to be confronted with another commodity that serves as its equivalent. Its value is never found to lie within itself. And the fact that it is worth more or less is not its own doing but comes from that to which it may be equivalent. Its value is *transcendent* to itself, *super-natural, ek-static.*

In other words, for the commodity, there is no mirror that copies it so that it may be at once itself and its "own" reflection. One commodity cannot be mirrored in another, as man is mirrored in his fellow man. For when we are dealing with commodities the self-same, mirrored, is not "its" own likeness, contains nothing of its properties, its qualities, its "skin and hair." The likeness here is only a measure expressing the ~~fabricated~~ character of the commodity, its trans-formation by man's (social, symbolic) "labor." The mirror that envelops and paralyzes the commodity specularizes, speculates (on) man's "labor." *Commodities, women, are a mirror of value of and for man.* In order to serve as such, they give up their bodies to men as the supporting material of specularization, of speculation. They yield to him their natural and social value as a locus of imprints, marks, and mirage of his activity.

Commodities among themselves are thus not equal, nor alike, nor different. They only become so when they are compared by and for man. And *the prosopopoeia of the relation of commodities among themselves is a projection* through which producers-exchangers make them reenact before their eyes their operations of specula(riza)tion. Forgetting that in order to reflect (oneself), to speculate (oneself), it is necessary to be a "subject," and that matter can serve as a support for speculation but cannot itself speculate in any way.

Thus, starting with the simplest relation of equivalence between commodities, starting with the possible exchange of women, the entire enigma of the money form—of the phallic function—is implied. That is, the appropriation-disappropriation by man, for man, of nature and its productive forces, insofar as a certain mirror now divides and travesties both nature and labor. Man endows the commodities he produces with a narcissism that blurs the seriousness of utility, of use. Desire, as soon as there is exchange, "perverts" need. But that perversion will be attributed to commodities and to their alleged relations. Whereas they can have no relationships except from the perspective of speculating third parties.

The economy of exchange—of desire—is man's business. For two reasons: the exchange takes place between masculine subjects, and it requires a *plus-value* added to the body of the commodity, a supplement which gives it a valuable form. That supplement will be found, Marx writes, in another commodity, whose use value becomes, from that point on, a standard of value.

But that surplus-value enjoyed by one of the commodities might vary: "just as many a man strutting about in a gorgeous uniform counts for more than when in mufti" (p. 60). Or just as "A, for instance, cannot be 'your majesty' to B, unless at the same time majesty in B's eyes assume the bodily form of A, and, what is more, with every new father of the people, changes its features, hair, and many other things besides" (ibid.). Commodities—"things" produced—would thus have the respect due the uniform, majesty, paternal authority. And even God. "The fact that it is value, is made manifest by its equality with the coat, just as the sheep's nature of a Christian is shown in his resemblance to the Lamb of God" (ibid.).

Commodities thus share in the cult of the father, and never stop striving to resemble, to copy, the one who is his representative. It is from that resemblance, from that imitation of what represents paternal authority, that commodities draw their value—for men. But it is upon commodities that the producers-exchangers bring to bear this power play. "We see, then, all that our analysis of the value of commodities has already told us, is told us by the linen itself, so soon as it comes into communication with another commodity, the coat. Only it betrays its thoughts in that language with which alone it is familiar, the language of commodities. In order to tell us that its own value is created by labour in its abstract character of human labour, it says that the coat, in so far as it is worth as much as the linen, and therefore is value, consists of the same labour as the linen. In order to inform us that its sublime reality as value is not the same as its buckram body, it says that value has the appearance of a coat, and consequently that so far as the linen is value, it and the coat are as like as two peas. We may here remark, that the language of commodities has, besides Hebrew, many other more or less correct dialects. The German 'werthsein,' to be worth, for instance, expresses in a less striking manner than the Romance verbs 'valere,' 'valer,' 'valoir,' that the equating of commodity B to commodity A, is commodity A's own mode of expressing its value. *Paris vaut bien une messe*" (pp. 60–61).

So *commodities speak. To be sure, mostly dialects and patois, languages hard for "subjects" to understand.* The important thing is that they be preoccupied with their respective values, that their remarks confirm the exchangers' plans for them.

The body of a commodity thus becomes, for another such commodity, a mirror of its value. Contingent upon a bodily *supplement*. A supplement *opposed* to use value, a supplement representing the commodity's *super-natural* quality (an imprint that is purely social in nature), a supplement completely different from the body itself, and from its properties, a supplement that nevertheless exists only on condition that one commodity agrees to relate itself to another considered as equivalent: "For instance, one man is king only because other men stand in the relation of subjects to him" (p. 66, n. 1).

This supplement of equivalency translates concrete work into abstract work. In other words, in order to be able to incorporate itself into a mirror of value, it is necessary that the work itself reflect only its property of human labour: that the body of a commodity be nothing more than the materialization of an abstract human labor. That is, that it have no more body, matter, nature, but that it be objectivization, a crystallization as visible object, a man's activity.

In order to become equivalent, a commodity changes bodies. A super-natural, metaphysical origin is substituted for its material origin. Thus its body becomes a transparent body, *pure phenomenality of value.* But this transparency constitutes a supplement to the material opacity of the commodity.

Once again there is a schism between the two. Two sides, two poles, nature and society are divided, like the perceptible and the intelligible, matter and form, the empirical and the transcendental . . . The commodity, like the sign, suffers from metaphysical dichotomies. Its value, its truth, lies in the social element. But this social element is added on to its nature, to its matter, and the social subordinates it as a lesser value, indeed as nonvalue. Participation in society requires that the body submit itself to a specularization, a speculation, that transforms it into a value-bearing object, a standardized sign, an exchangeable signifier, a "likeness" with reference to an authoritative model. *A commodity—a woman—is divided into two irreconcilable "bodies":* her "natural" body and her socially valued, exchangeable body, which is a particularly mimetic expression of masculine values. No doubt these values also express "nature," that is, the expenditure of physical force. But this latter—essentially masculine, moreover—serves for the fabrication, the transformation, the technicization of natural productions. And it is this *super*-natural property that comes to constitute the value of the product. Analyzing value in this way, Marx exposes the meta-physical character of social operations.

The commodity is thus a dual entity as soon as its value comes to possess a phenomenal form of its own, distinct from its natural form: that of exchange value. And it never possesses this form if it is considered in isolation. A commodity has this phenomenal form added on to its nature only in relation to another commodity.

As among signs, value appears only when a relationship has been established. It remains the case that the establishment of relationships cannot be accomplished by the commodities themselves, but depends upon the operation of two exchangers. The exchange value of two signs, two commodities, two women, is a representation of the needs/desires of consumer-exchanger subjects: in no way is it the "property" of the signs/articles/women themselves. At the most, the commodities—or rather the relationships among them—are the material alibi for the desire for relations among men. To this end, the commodity is disinvested of its body and reclothed in a form that makes it suitable for exchange among men.

But, in this value-bearing form, the desire for that exchange, and the reflection of his own value and that of his fellow man that man seeks in it, are ekstasized. In that suspension in the commodity of the relationship among men, producer-consumer-exchanger subjects are alienated. In order that they might "bear" and support that alienation, commodities for their part have always been dispossessed of their specific value. On this basis, one may affirm that the value of the commodity takes on *indifferently* any given form of use value. The price of the articles, in fact, no longer comes from *their* natural form, from *their* bodies, *their* language, but from the fact that they mirror the need/desire for exchanges among men. To do this, the commodity obviously cannot exist alone, but there is no such thing as a commodity, either, so long as there are not *at least two men* to make an exchange. In order for a product—a woman?—to have value, two men, at least, have to invest (in) her.

The general equivalent of a commodity no longer functions as a commodity itself. A preeminent mirror, transcending the world of merchandise, it guarantees the possibility of universal exchange among commodities. Each commodity may become equivalent to every other from the viewpoint of that sublime standard, but the fact that the judgment of their value depends upon some transcendental element renders them provisionally incapable of being directly exchanged for each other. They are exchanged by means of the general equivalent—as Christians love each other in God, to borrow a theological metaphor dear to Marx. That ek-static reference separates them radically from each other. *An abstract and universal value preserves them from use and exchange among themselves.* They are, as it were, transformed into value-invested idealities. Their concrete forms, their specific qualities, and all the possibilities of "real" relations with them or among them are reduced to their common character as products of man's labor and desire.

We must emphasize also that *the general equivalent*, since it is no longer a commodity, *is no longer useful. The standard as such is exempt from use.*

Though a commodity may at first appear to be "a very trivial thing, and easily understood, . . . it is, in reality, a very queer thing, abounding in metaphysical subtleties and theological niceties" (p. 81). No doubt, "so far as it is a value in use, there is nothing mysterious about it. . . . But, so soon as [a wooden table, for example] steps forth as a commodity, it is changed into something transcendent. It not only stands with its feet on the ground, but, in relation to all other commodities, it stands on its head, and evolves out of its wooden brain grotesque ideas, far more wonderful than 'table-turning' ever was" (pp. 81–82).

"The mystical character of commodities does not originate, therefore, in their use value. Just as little does it proceed from the nature of the determining factors of value. For, in the first place, however varied the useful kinds of labour, or productive activities, may be, it is a physiological fact, that they are functions of the human organism" (p. 82), which, for Marx, does not seem to constitute a mystery in any way . . . The material contribution and support of bodies in societal operations pose no problems for him, except as production and expenditure of energy. Where, then, does the enigmatic character of the product of labor come from, as soon as this product takes on the form of a commodity? It comes, obviously, from that form itself. *Then where does the enigmatic character of women come from?* Or even that of their supposed relations among themselves? Obviously, from the "form" of the needs/desires of man, needs/desires that women bring to light although men do not recognize them in that form. That form, those women, are always enveloped, veiled.

In any case, "the existence of things *qua* commodities, and the value relation between the products of labour which stamps them as commodities, have absolutely no connection with their physical properties and with the material relations arising therefrom. [With commodities] it is a definite social relation between men, that assumes, in their eyes, the fantastic form of a relation between things" (p. 83). *This phenomenon has no analogy except in the religious world.* In that world the productions of the human brain appear as independent beings endowed with life, and entering into relation both with one another and the human race. So it is in the world of commodities with the products of men's hands" (ibid.). Hence the fetishism attached to these products of labor as soon as they present themselves as commodities.

Hence *women's role as fetish-objects*, inasmuch as, in exchanges, they are the manifestation and the circulation of a power of the Phallus, establishing relationships of men with each other?

❋ ❋ ❋

Hence the following remarks:

ON VALUE.

It represents the equivalent of labor force, of an expenditure of energy, of toil. In order to be measured, these latter must be *abstracted* from all immediately natural qualities, from any concrete individual. A process of generalization and of universalization imposes itself in the operation of social exchanges. Hence the reduction of man to a "concept"—that of his labor force—and the reduction of his product to an "object," the visible, material correlative of that concept.

The characteristics of "sexual pleasure" corresponding to such a social state are thus the following: its productivity, but one that is necessarily laborious, even painful; its abstract form; its need/desire to crystallize in a transcendental element of wealth the standard of all value; its need for a material support where the relation of appropriation to and of that standard is measured; its exchange relationships—always rivalrous—among men alone, and so on.

Are not these modalities the ones that might define the economy of (so-called) *masculine sexuality?* And is libido not another name for the abstraction of "energy" in a productive power? For the work of nature? Another name for the desire to accumulate goods? Another name for the subordination of the specific qualities of bodies to a—neutral?—power that aims above all to transform them in order to process them? Does pleasure, for masculine sexuality, consist in anything other than the appropriation of nature, in the desire to make it (re)produce, and in exchange of its/these products with other members of society? An essentially *economic* pleasure.

Thus the following question: *what needs/desires of (so-called) masculine sexuality have presided over the evolution of a certain social order*, from its primitive form, private property, to its developed form, capital? But also: *to what extent are these needs/desires the effect of a social mechanism*, in part autonomous, that produces them as such?

ON THE STATUS OF WOMEN IN SUCH A SOCIAL ORDER.

What makes such an order possible, what assures its foundation is thus *the exchange of women*. The circulation of women among men is what establishes the operations of society, at least of patriarchal society. Whose presuppositions include the following: the appropriation of nature by man; the transformation of nature according to "human" criteria, defined by men alone; the submission of nature to labor and technology; the reduction of its material, corporeal, perceptible qualities to man's practical concrete activity; the equality of women among themselves, but in terms of laws of equivalence that remain external to them; the constitution of women as "objects" that emblematize the materialization of relations among men, and so on.

In such a social order, women thus represent a natural value, and a social value. Their "development" lies in the passage from one to the other. But this passage never takes place simply.

As mother, woman remains on the side of (re-productive) *nature* and, because of this, man can never fully transcend his relation to the "natural." His social existence, his economic structures and his sexuality are always tied to the work of nature: these structures thus always remain at the level of the earliest appropriation, that of the constitution of nature as landed property, and of the earliest labor, which is agricultural. But this relationship to productive nature, an insurmountable one, has to be denied so that relations among men may prevail. This means that mothers, reproductive instruments marked with the name of the father and enclosed in his house, must be private property, excluded from exchange. The *incest taboo* represents this refusal to allow productive nature to enter into exchanges among men. As both natural value and use value, mothers cannot circulate in the form of commodities without threatening the very existence of the social order. Mothers are essential to its (re)production (particularly inasmuch as they are [re]productive of children and of the labor force: through maternity, child-rearing, and domestic maintenance in general). Their responsibility is to maintain the social order without intervening so as to change it. Their products are legal tender in that order, moreover, only if they are marked with the name of the father, only if they are recognized within his law: that is, only insofar as they are appropriated by him. Society is the place where man engenders himself, where man produces himself as man, where man is born into "human," "super-natural" existence.

The virginal woman, on the other hand, is pure exchange value. She is nothing but the possibility, the place, the sign of relations among men. In and of herself, she does not exist: she is a simple envelope veiling what is really at stake in social exchange. In this sense, her natural body disappears into its representative function. *Red blood* remains on the mother's side, but it has no price, as such, in the social order; woman, for her part, as medium of exchange, is no longer anything but *semblance*. The ritualized passage from woman to mother is accomplished by the *violation of an envelope*: the hymen, which has taken on the value of *taboo*, the taboo of virginity. Once deflowered, woman is relegated to the status of use value, to her entrapment in private property; she is removed from exchange among men.

The *prostitute* remains to be considered. Explicitly condemned by the social order, she is implicitly tolerated. No doubt because the break between usage and exchange is, in her case, less clearcut? In her case, the qualities of woman's body are "useful." However, these qualities have "value" only because they have already been appropriated by a man, and because they serve as the locus of relations—hidden ones—between men. Prostitution amounts to *usage that is exchanged*. Usage that is not merely potential: it has already been realized. The woman's body is valuable because it has already been used. In the extreme case, the more it has served, the more it is worth. Not because its natural assets have been put to use this way, but, on the contrary, because its nature has been "used up," and has become once again no more than a vehicle for relations among men.

Mother, virgin, prostitute; these are the social roles imposed on women. The characteristics of (so-called) feminine sexuality derive from them: the valorization of reproduction and nursing; faithfulness; modesty, ignorance of and even lack of interest in sexual pleasure; a passive acceptance of men's "activity"; seductiveness, in order to arouse the consumers' desire while offering herself as its material support without getting pleasure herself . . . *Neither as mother nor as virgin nor as prostitute has woman any right to her own pleasure.*

Who? Freud?

Of course the theoreticians of sexuality are sometimes astonished by women's frigidity. But, according to them, this frigidity is explained more by an impotence inherent to feminine "nature" than by the submission of that nature to a certain type of society. However, *what is required of a "normal" feminine sexuality is oddly evocative of the characteristics of the status of a commodity.* With references to and rejections of the "natural"—physiological and organic nature, and so on—that are equally ambiguous.

And, in addition:

- just as nature has to be subjected to man in order to become a commodity, so, it appears, does "the development of a normal woman." A development that amounts, for the feminine, to subordination to the forms and laws of masculine activity. The rejection of the mother—imputed to woman—would find its "cause" here;

- just as, in commodities, natural utility is overridden by the exchange function, so the properties of a woman's body have to be suppressed and subordinated to the exigencies of its transformation into an object of circulation among men;

- just as a commodity has no mirror it can use to reflect itself, so woman serves as reflection, as image of and for man, but lacks specific qualities of her own. Her value-invested form amounts to what man inscribes in and on its matter: that is, her body;

- just as commodities cannot make exchanges among themselves without the intervention of a subject that measures them against a standard, so it is with women. Distinguished, divided, separated, classified as like and unlike, according to whether they have been judged exchangeable. In themselves, among themselves, they are amorphous and confused: natural body, maternal body, doubtless useful to the consumer, but without any possible identity or communicable value;

- just as commodities, despite their resistance, become more or less autonomous repositories for the value of human work, so, as mirrors of and for man, women more or less unwittingly come to represent the danger of a disappropriation of masculine power: the phallic mirage;

- just as a commodity finds the expression of its value in an equivalent—in the last analysis, a general one—that necessarily remains external to it, so woman derives her price from her relation to the male sex, constituted as a transcendental value: the phallus. And indeed the enigma of "value" lies in the most elementary relation among commodities. Among women. For, uprooted from their "nature," they no longer relate to each other except in terms of what they represent in men's desire, and according to the "forms" that this imposes upon them. Among themselves, they are separated by his speculations.

This means that the division of "labor"—sexual labor in particular—requires that woman maintain in her own body the material substratum of the object of desire, but that she herself never have access to desire. The economy of desire—of exchange—is man's business. And that economy subjects women to a schism that is necessary to symbolic operations: red blood/semblance; body/value-invested envelope; matter/medium of exchange; (re)productive nature/fabricated femininity . . . That schism—characteristic of all speaking nature, someone will surely object— is experienced by women without any possible profit to them. And without any way for them to transcend it. They are not even "conscious" of it. The symbolic system that cuts them in two this way is in no way appropriate to them. In them, "semblance" remains external, foreign to "nature." *Socially*, they are "objects" for and among men and furthermore they cannot do anything but mimic a "language" that they have not produced; *naturally*, they remain amorphous, suffering from drives without any possible representatives or representations. For them, the transformation of the natural into the social does not take place, except to the extent that they function as components of private property, or as commodities.

CHARACTERISTICS OF THIS SOCIAL ORDER

This type of social system can be interpreted as *the practical realization of the meta-physical*. As the *practical destiny* of the meta-physical, it would also represent its *most fully realized form*. Operating in such a way, moreover, that subjects themselves, being implicated in it through and through, being produced in it as concepts, would lack the means to analyze it. Except in an after-the-fact way whose delays are yet to be fully measured . . .

This practical realization of the meta-physical has as its founding operation the appropriation of woman's body by the father or his substitutes. It is marked by women's submission to a system of general equivalents, the proper name representing the father's monopoly of power. It is from this standardization that women receive their value, as they pass from the state of nature to the status of social object. This trans-formation of women's bodies into use values and exchange values inaugurates the symbolic order. But that order depends upon a *nearly pure added value*. Women, animals endowed with speech like men, assure the possibility of the use and circulation of the symbolic without being recipients of it. Their nonaccess to the symbolic is what has established the social order. Putting men in touch with each other, in relations among themselves, women only fulfill this role by relinquishing their right to speech and even to animality. No longer in the natural order, not yet in the social order that they nonetheless maintain, women are the symptom of the exploitation of individuals by a society that remunerates them only partially, or even not at all, for their "work." Unless subordination to a system that utilizes you and oppresses you should be considered as sufficient compensation . . . ? Unless the fact that women are branded with the proper name—of the "father"—should be viewed as the symbolic payment awarded them for sustaining the social order with their bodies?

But by submitting women's bodies to a general equivalent, to a transcendent, super-natural value, men have drawn the social structure into an ever greater process of abstraction, to the point where they themselves are produced in it as pure concepts: having surmounted all their "perceptible" qualities and individual differences, they are finally reduced to the average productivity of their labor. The power of this practical economy of the meta-physical comes from the fact that "physiological" energy is transformed into abstract value without the mediation of an intelligible elaboration. No individual subject can be credited any longer with bringing about this transformation. It is only after the fact that the subject might possibly be able to analyze his determination as such by the social structure. And even then it is not certain that his love of gold would not make him give up everything else before he would renounce the cult of this fetish. "The saver thus sacrifices to this fetish all the penchants of his flesh. No one takes the gospel of renunciation more seriously than he."

Fortunately—if we may say so—women/commodities would remain, as simple "objects" of transaction among men. Their situation of specific exploitation in exchange operations—sexual exchange, and economic, social, and cultural exchanges in general—might lead them to offer a new critique of the political economy." *A critique that would no longer avoid that of discourse, and more generally of the symbolic system, in which it is realized.* Which would lead to interpreting in a different way the impact of symbolic social labor in the analysis of relations of production.

For, without the exploitation of women, what would become of the social order? What modifications would it undergo if women left behind their condition as commodities—subject to being produced, consumed, valorized, circulated,

and so on, by men alone—and took part in elaborating and carrying out exchanges? Not by reproducing, by copying, the "phallocratic" models that have
the force of law today, but by socializing in a different way the relation to nature,
matter, the body, language, and desire.

NOTES

1. Claude Lévi-Strauss, *The Elementary Structures of Kinship (Les Structures élémentaires de la Parenté*, 1949, rev. 1967), trans. James Harle Bell, John Richard von
Sturmer, and Rodney Needham (Boston, 1969), p. 36.
2. Ibid., p. 38.
3. All the quotations in the remainder of this chapter are excerpted from Marx's *Capital*, section 1, chapter 1. (The page numbers given in the text refer to the Modern
Library edition, trans. Samuel Moore and Edward Aveling, ed. Frederick Engels,
rev. Ernest Untermann [New York, 1906].) Will it be objected that this interpretation is analogical by nature? I accept the question, on condition that it be addressed
also, and in the first place, to Marx's analysis of commodities. Did not Aristotle, a
"great thinker" according to Marx, determine the relation of form to matter by analogy with the relation between masculine and feminine? Returning to the question of
the difference between the sexes would amount instead, then, to going back through
analogism.

AN ETHICS OF SEXUAL DIFFERENCE

Sexual difference is one of the major philosophical issues, if not the issue, of our
age. According to Heidegger, each age has one issue to think through, and one
only. Sexual difference is probably the issue in our time which could be our "salvation" if we thought it through.

But, whether I turn to philosophy, to science, or to religion, I find this underlying issue still cries out in vain for our attention. Think of it as an approach that
would allow us to check the many forms that destruction takes in our world, to
counteract a nihilism that merely affirms the reversal or the repetitive prolifera-
tion of status quo values—whether you call them the consumer society, the circularity of discourse, the more or less cancerous diseases of our age, the unreliabil-
ity of words, the end of philosophy, religious despair or regression to religiosity,
scientistic or technical imperialism that fails to consider the living subject.

Sexual difference would constitute the horizon of worlds more fecund than
any known to date—at least in the West—and without reducing fecundity to the
reproduction of bodies and flesh. For loving partners this would be a fecundity

of birth and regeneration, but also the production of a new age of thought, art, poetry, and language: the creation of a new *poetics*.

Both in theory and in practice, everything resists the discovery and affirmation of such an advent or event. In theory, philosophy wants to be literature or rhetoric, wishing either to break with ontology or to regress to the ontological. Using the same ground and the same framework as "first philosophy," working toward its disintegration but without proposing any other goals that might assure new foundations and new works.

In politics, some overtures have been made to the world of women. But these overtures remain partial and local: some concessions have been made by those in power, but no new values have been established. Rarely have these measures been thought through and affirmed by women themselves, who consequently remain at the level of critical demands. Has a worldwide erosion of the gains won in women's struggles occurred because of the failure to lay foundations different from those on which the world of men is constructed? Psychoanalytic theory and therapy, the scenes of sexuality as such, are a long way from having effected their revolution. And with a few exceptions, sexual practice today is often divided between two parallel worlds: the world of men and the world of women. A nontraditional, fecund encounter between the sexes barely exists. It does not voice its demands publicly, except through certain kinds of silence and polemics.

A revolution in thought and ethics is needed if the work of sexual difference is to take place. We need to reinterpret everything concerning the relations between the subject and discourse, the subject and the world, the subject and the cosmic, the microcosmic and the macrocosmic. Everything, beginning with the way in which the subject has always been written in the masculine form, as *man*, even when it claimed to be universal or neutral. Despite the fact that *man*—at least in French—rather than being neutral, is sexed.

Man has been the subject of discourse, whether in theory, morality, or politics. And the gender of God, the guardian of every subject and every discourse, is always *masculine and paternal*, in the West. To women are left the so-called minor arts: cooking, knitting, embroidery, and sewing; and, in exceptional cases, poetry, painting, and music. Whatever their importance, these arts do not currently make the rules, at least not overtly.

Of course, we are witnessing a certain reversal of values: manual labor and art are being revalued. But the relation of these arts to sexual difference is never really thought through and properly apportioned. At best, it is related to the class struggle.

In order to make it possible to think through, and live, this difference, we must reconsider the whole problematic of *space* and *time*.

In the beginning there was space and the creation of space, as is said in all theogonies. The gods, God, first create *space*. And time is there, more or less in the service of space. On the first day, the first days, the gods, God, make a world by separating the elements. This world is then peopled, and a rhythm is established among its inhabitants. God would be time itself, lavishing or exteriorizing itself in its action in space, in places.

Philosophy then confirms the genealogy of the task of the gods or God. Time becomes the *interiority* of the subject itself, and space, its *exteriority* (this problematic is developed by Kant in the *Critique of Pure Reason*). The subject, the master of time, becomes the axis of the world's ordering, with its something beyond the moment and eternity: God. He effects the passage between time and space.

Which would be inverted in sexual difference? Where the feminine is experienced as space, but often with connotations of the abyss and night (God being space and light?), while the masculine is experienced as time.

The transition to a new age requires a change in our perception and conception of *space-time*, the *inhabiting of places*, and of *containers*, or *envelopes of identity*. It assumes and entails an evolution or a transformation of forms, of the relations of *matter* and *form* and of the interval *between*: the trilogy of the constitution of place. Each age inscribes a limit to this trinitary configuration: *matter, form, interval*, or *power [puissance], act, intermediary-interval*.

Desire occupies or designates the place of the *interval*. Giving it a permanent definition would amount to suppressing it as desire. Desire demands a sense of attraction: a change in the interval, the displacement of the subject or of the object in their relations of nearness or distance.

The transition to a new age comes at the same time as a change in the economy of desire. A new age signifies a different relation between:

- man and god(s),
- man and man,
- man and world,
- man and woman.

Our age, which is often thought to be one in which the problematic of desire has been brought forward, frequently theorizes this desire on the basis of observations of a moment of tension, or a moment in history, whereas desire ought to be thought of as a changing dynamic whose outlines can be described in the past, sometimes in the present, but never definitively predicted. Our age will have failed to realize the full dynamic reserve signified by desire if it is referred back to the economy of the *interval*, if it is situated in the attractions, tensions, and actions occurring between *form* and *matter*, but also in the *remainder* that subsists after each creation of work, *between* what has already been identified and what has still to be identified, and so on.

In order to imagine such an economy of desire, one must reinterpret what Freud implies by *sublimation* and observe that he does not speak of the sublimation of genitality (except in reproduction? But, if this were a successful form of sublimation, Freud would not be so pessimistic about parental child-rearing practices) or of the sublimation of the *partial drives in relation to the feminine* but rather of their repression (little girls speak earlier and more skillfully than little boys; they have a better relationship to the social; and so on—qualities or aptitudes that disappear without leaving any creative achievements that capitalize on their energy, except for the task of becoming a woman: an object of attraction?)[1]

In this possible nonsublimation of herself, and by herself, woman always tends *toward* without any return to herself as the place where something positive can be elaborated. In terms of contemporary physics, it could be said that she remains on the side of the electron, with all that this implies for her, for man, for their encounter. If there is no double desire, the positive and negative poles divide themselves between the two sexes instead of establishing a chiasmus or a double loop in which each can go toward the other and come back to itself.

If these positive and negative poles are not found in both, the same one always attracts, while the other remains in motion but lacks a "proper" place. What is missing is the double pole of attraction and support, which excludes disintegration or rejection, attraction and decomposition, but which instead ensures the separation that articulates every encounter and makes possible speech, promises, alliances.

In order to distance oneself, must one be able to take? To speak? Which in a certain way comes to the same thing. Perhaps in order to take, one needs a fixed container or place? A soul? Or a spirit? Mourning nothing is the most difficult. Mourning the self in the other is almost impossible. I search for myself, as if I had been assimilated into maleness. I ought to reconstitute myself on the basis of a disassimilation. . . .[2] Rise again from the traces of a culture, of works already produced by the other. Searching through what is in them—for what is not there. What allowed them to be, for what is not there. Their conditions of possibility, for what is not there.

Woman ought to be able to find herself, among other things, through the images of herself already deposited in history and the conditions of production of the work of man, and not on the basis of his work, his genealogy.

If traditionally, and as a mother, woman represents *place* for man, such a limit means that she becomes a *thing*, with some possibility of change from one historical period to another. She finds herself delineated as a thing. Moreover, the maternal-feminine also serves as an *envelope*, a *container*, the starting point from which man limits his things. The *relationship between envelope and things* constitutes one of the aporias, or the aporia, of Aristotelianism and of the philosophical systems derived from it.

In our terminologies, which derive from this economy of thought but are impregnated with a psychologism unaware of its sources, it is said, for example, that the woman-mother it *castrating*. Which means that, since her status as envelope and as thing(s) has not been interpreted, she remains inseparable from the work or act of man, notably insofar as he defines her and creates *his* identity with her as his starting point or, correlatively, with this determination of her being. If after all this, she is still alive, she continuously undoes his work—distinguishing herself from both the envelope and the thing, ceaselessly creating there some interval, play, something in motion and un-limited which disturbs his perspective, his world, and his/its limits. But, because he fails to leave her a subjective life, and to be on occasion her place and her thing in an intersubjective dynamic, man remains within a master-slave dialectic. The slave, ultimately, of a God on whom he bestows the characteristics of an absolute master. Secretly or obscurely, a slave to the power of the maternal-feminine which he diminishes or destroys.

The maternal-feminine remains the *place separated from "its" own place*, deprived of "its" place. She is or ceaselessly becomes the place of the other who cannot separate himself from it. Without her knowing or willing it, she is then threatening because of what she lacks: a "proper" place. She would have to re-envelop herself with herself, and do so at least twice: as a woman and as a mother. Which would presuppose a change in the whole economy of space-time.

In the meantime, this ethical question comes into play in matters of *nudity* and *perversity*. Woman must be nude because she is not situated, does not situate herself in her place. Her clothes, her makeup, and her jewels are the things with which she tries to create her container(s), her envelope(s). She cannot make use of the envelope that she is, and must create artificial ones.

Freud's statement that woman is identified with orality is meaningful, but it still exiles her from her most archaic and constituent site. No doubt orality is an especially significant measure for her: morphologically, she has two mouths and two pairs of lips. But she can act on this morphology or make something of it only if she preserves her relation to *spatiality* and to the *fetal*. Although she needs these dimensions to create a space for herself (as well as to maintain a receptive place for the other), they are traditionally taken from her to constitute man's nostalgia and everything that he constructs in memory of this first and ultimate dwelling place. An obscure commemoration. . . . Centuries will perhaps have been needed for man to interpret the meaning of his work(s): the endless construction of a number of substitutes for his prenatal home. From the depths of the earth to the highest skies? Again and again, taking from the feminine the tissue or texture of spatiality. In exchange—but it isn't a real one—he buys her a house, even shuts her up in it, places limits on her that are the opposite of the unlimited site in which he unwittingly situates her. He contains or envelops her with walls while enveloping himself and his things with her flesh. The nature of these envelopes is not the same: on the one hand, invisibly alive, but with barely perceivable limits; on the other, visibly limiting or sheltering, but at the risk of being prison-like or murderous if the threshold is not left open.

We must, therefore, reconsider the whole question of our conception of place, both in order to move on to another age of difference (each age of thought corresponds to a particular time of meditation on difference), and in order to construct an ethics of the passions. We need to change the relations between form, matter, interval, and limit, an issue that has never been considered in a way that allows for a relationship between two loving subjects of different sexes.

Once there was the enveloping body and the enveloped body, the latter being the more mobile through what Aristotle termed *locomotion* (since maternity does not look much like "motion"). The one who offers or allows desire moves and envelops, engulfing the other. It is moreover a danger if no third term exists. Not only to serve as a limitation. This third term can occur within the one who contains as a relation of the latter to his or her own limit(s): relation to the divine, to death, to the social, to the cosmic. If a third term does not exist within and for the container, he or she becomes *all-powerful*.

Therefore, to deprive one pole of sexual difference, women, of a third term also amounts to putting them in the position of omnipotence: this is a danger for men, especially in that it suppresses an interval that is both entrance and space between.[3] A place for both to enter and exit the envelope (and on the same side, so as not to perforate the envelope or assimilate it into the digestive process); for both, a possibility of unhindered movement, of peaceful immobility without the risk of imprisonment.

✿ ✿ ✿

To arrive at the constitution of an ethics of sexual difference, we must at least return to what is for Descartes the first passion: *wonder*. This passion has no opposite or contradiction and exists always as though for the first time. Thus man and woman, woman and man are always meeting as though for the first time because they cannot be substituted one for the other. I will never be in a man's place, never will a man be in mine. Whatever identifications are possible, one will never exactly occupy the place of the other—they are irreducible one to the other.

"When the first encounter with some object surprises us, and we judge it to be new, or very different from what we formerly knew, or from what we supposed that it ought to be, that causes us to wonder and be surprised; and because that may happen before we in any way know whether this object is agreeable to us or is not so, it appears to me that wonder is the first of all the passions; and it has no opposite, because if the object which presents itself has nothing in it that surprises us, we are in nowise moved regarding it, and we consider it without passion." (René Descartes, *The Passions of the Soul*, article 53).[4]

Who or what the other is, I never know. But the other who is forever unknowable is the one who differs from me sexually. This feeling of surprise, astonishment, and wonder in the face of the unknowable ought to be returned to its locus: that of sexual difference. The passions have either been repressed, stifled, or reduced, or reserved for God. Sometimes a space for wonder is left to works of art. But it is never found to reside in this locus: *between man and woman*. Into this place came attraction, greed, possession, consummation, disgust, and so on. But not that wonder which beholds what it sees always as if for the first time, never taking hold of the other as its object. It does not try to seize, possess, or reduce this object, but leaves it subjective, still free.

This has never existed between the sexes since wonder maintains their autonomy within their statutory difference, keeping a space of freedom and attraction between them, a possibility of separation and alliance.

This might take place at the time of the first meeting, even prior to the betrothal, and remain as a permanent proof of difference. The *interval* would never be *crossed*. Consummation would never take place, the idea itself being a delusion. One sex is not entirely consumable by the other. There is always a *remainder*.

Up until now this remainder has been entrusted to or reserved for *God*. Sometimes a portion was incarnated in the *child*. Or was thought of as being *neuter*. This neuter (in a different way, like the child or God?) suggests the possibility of an encounter but puts it off, deferring it until later, even when it is a question of a secondary revision [*après-coup*]. It always stays at an insurmountable distance, a respectful or deadly sort of no-man's-land:[5] no alliance is forged; nothing is celebrated. The immediacy of the encounter is annihilated or deferred to a future that never comes.

Of course, the neuter might signify an alchemical site of the sublimation of "genitality," and the possibility of generation, of the creation of and between different genders and genres. But it would still have to be receptive to the advent of difference, and be understood as an anticipation from this side and not as a beyond, especially an ethical one. Generally the phrase *there is* upholds the present but defers celebration. There is not, there will not be the moment of wonder of the *wedding*, an ecstasy that remains *in-stant*.[6] The *there is* remains a present that may be subject to pressure by the god, but it does not form a foundation for the triumph of sexual fecundity. Only certain oriental traditions speak of the energizing, aesthetic, and religious fecundity of the sexual act: the two sexes give each other the seed of life and eternity, the growing generation of and between them both.

We must reexamine our own history thoroughly to understand why this sexual difference has not had its chance to develop, either empirically or transcendentally. Why it has failed to have its own ethics, aesthetic, logic, religion, or the micro- and macrocosmic realization of its coming into being or its destiny.

It is surely a question of the dissociation of body and soul, of sexuality and spirituality, of the lack of a passage for the spirit, for the god, between the inside and the outside, the outside and the inside, and of their distribution between the sexes in the sexual act. Everything is constructed in such a way that these realities remain separate, even opposed to one another. So that they neither mix, marry, nor form an alliance. Their wedding is always being put off to a beyond, a future life, or else devalued, felt and thought to be less worthy in comparison to the marriage between the mind and God in a transcendental realm where all ties to the world of sensation have been severed.

The consequences of the nonfulfillment of the sexual act remain, and there are many. To take up only the most beautiful, as yet to be made manifest in the realm of time and space, there are *angels*. These messengers who never remain enclosed in a place, who are also never immobile. Between God, as the perfectly immobile act, man, who is surrounded and enclosed by the world of his work, and woman, whose task would be to take care of nature and procreation, *angels* would circulate as mediators of that which has not yet happened, of what is still going to happen, of what is on the horizon. Endlessly, reopening the enclosure of the universe, of universes, identities, the unfolding of actions, of history.

The angel is that which unceasingly *passes through the envelope(s)* or *container(s)*, goes from one side to the other, reworking every deadline, changing every decision, thwarting all repetition. Angels destroy the monstrous, that which hampers the possibility of a new age; they come to herald the arrival of a new birth, a new morning.

They are not unrelated to sex. There is of course Gabriel, the angel of the annunciation. But other angels announce the consummation of marriage, notably all the angels in the Apocalypse and many in the Old Testament. As if the angel were a representation of a sexuality that has never been incarnated. A light, divine gesture (or tale) of flesh that has not yet acted or flourished. Always fallen or still awaiting parousia. The fate of a love still torn between here and elsewhere. The work of a love that is the original sinner, since the first garden, the lost earthly paradise? The fate of all flesh which is, moreover, attributable to God![7]

These swift angelic messengers, who transgress all enclosures in their speed, tell of the passage between the envelope of God and that of the world as micro- or macrocosm. They proclaim that such a journey can be made by the body of man, and above all the body of woman. They represent and tell of another incarnation, another parousia of the body. Irreducible to philosophy, theology, morality, angels appear as the messengers of ethics evoked by art—sculpture, painting, or music—without its being possible to say anything more than the gesture that represents them.

They speak like messengers, but gesture seems to be their "nature." Movement, posture, the coming-and-going between the two. They move—or stir up?—the paralysis or *apatheia* of the body, or the soul, or the world. They set trances or convulsions to music, or give them harmony.

Their touch—when they touch—resembles that of gods. They are imperious in their grace even as they remain imperceptible.

One of the questions which arises about them is whether they can be found together in the same place. The traditional answer is no. This question, which is similar to and different from that of the co-location of bodies, comes back to the question of sexual ethics. The mucous should no doubt be pictured as related to the angel, whereas the inertia of the body deprived of its relation to the mucous and its gesture is linked to the fallen body or the corpse.

A sexual or carnal ethics would require that both angel and body be found together. This is a world that must be constructed or reconstructed. A genesis of love between the sexes has yet to come about in all dimensions, from the smallest to the greatest, from the most intimate to the most political. A world that must be created or re-created so that man and woman may once again or at last live together, meet, and sometimes inhabit the same place.

✿ ✿ ✿

The link uniting or reuniting masculine and feminine must be horizontal and vertical, terrestrial and heavenly. As Heidegger, among others, has written, it must forge an alliance between the divine and the mortal, such that the sexual encounter would be a festive celebration and not a disguised or polemical form of the master-slave relationship. Nor a meeting in the shadow or orbit of a Father-God who alone lays down the law, who is the immutable spokesman of a single sex.

Of course, the most extreme progression and regression goes under the name of God. I can only strive toward the absolute or regress to infinity under the guarantee of God's existence. This is what tradition has taught us, and its imperatives have not yet been overcome, since their destruction brings about terrible abandonments and pathological states, unless one has exceptional love partners. And even then . . . Unhappiness is sometimes all the more inescapable when it lacks the horizon of the divine, of the gods, of an opening onto a beyond, but also a *limit* that the other may or may not penetrate.

How can we mark this limit of a place, of place in general, if not through sexual difference? But, in order for an ethics of sexual difference to come into being, we must constitute a possible place for each sex, body, and flesh to inhabit. Which presupposes a memory of the past, a hope for the future, memory bridging the present and disconcerting the mirror symmetry that annihilates the difference of identity.

To do this requires time, both space and time. Perhaps we are passing through an era when *time must redeploy space*? A new morning of and for the world? A remaking of immanence and transcendence, notably through this *threshold* which has never been examined as such: the female sex. The threshold that gives access to the *mucous*. Beyond classical oppositions of love and hate, liquid and ice—a threshold that is always *half-open*. The threshold of the *lips*, which are strangers to dichotomy and oppositions. Gathered one against the other but without any possible suture, at least of a real kind. They do not absorb the world into or through themselves, provided they are not misused and reduced to a means of consumption or consummation. They offer a shape of welcome but do not assimilate, reduce, or swallow up. A sort of doorway to voluptuousness? They are not useful, except as that which designates *a place*, the very place of uselessness, at least as it is habitually understood. Strictly speaking, they serve neither conception nor jouissance. Is this the mystery of feminine identity? Of its self-contemplation, of this very strange word of silence? Both the threshold and reception of exchange, the sealed-up secret of wisdom, belief, and faith in all truths?

(Two sets of lips that, moreover, cross over each other like the arms of the cross, the prototype of the crossroads *between*. The mouth lips and the genital lips do not point in the same direction. In some way they point in the direction opposite from the one you would expect, with the "lower" ones forming the vertical.)

In this approach, where the borders of the body are wed in an embrace that transcends all limits—without, however, risking engulfment, thanks to the fecundity of the porous—in the most extreme experience of sensation, which is also always in the future, each one discovers the self in that experience which is inexpressible yet forms the supple grounding of life and language.

For this, "God" is necessary, or a love so attentive that it is divine. Which has never taken place? Love always postpones its transcendence beyond the here and now, except in certain experiences of God. And desire fails to act sufficiently on the porous nature of the body, omitting the communion that takes place through the most intimate mucous membranes. In this exchange, what is communicated is so subtle that one needs great perseverance to keep it from falling into oblivion, intermittency, deterioration, illness, or death.

This communion is often left to the child, as the symbol of the union. But there are other signs of union which precede the child—the space where the lovers give each other life or death? Regeneration or degeneration: both are possible. The intensity of desire and the filiation of both lovers are engaged.

And if the divine is present as the mystery that animates the copula, the *is* and the *being* in sexual difference, can the force of desire overcome the avatars of genealogical destiny? How does it manage this? With what power [*puissance*] does it reckon, while remaining nevertheless incarnate? Between the idealistic fluidity of an unborn body that is untrue to its birth and genetic determinism, how do we take the measure of a love that changes our condition from mortal to immortal? Certain figures of gods become men, of God become man, and of twice-born beings indicate the path of love.

Has something of the achievement of sexual difference still not been said or transmitted? Has something been held in reserve within the silence of a history in the feminine: an energy, a morphology, a growth and flourishing still to come from the female realm? An overture to a future that is still and always open? Given that the world has remained aporetic about this strange advent.

NOTES

1. Cf. Luce Irigaray, *Speculum, de l'autre femme* (Paris: Minuit, 1984), pp. 9–162; trans. Gillian C. Gill, under the title *Speculum of the Other Woman* (Ithaca: Cornell University Press, 1985), pp. 11–129.
2. (All ellipses occur in the original French text and do not indicate omissions in the translation.—Tr.)
3. (Irigaray plays on the double sense of *entre*, meaning both "enter" and "between."—Tr.)
4. *The Philosophical Works of Descartes*, trans. E. S. Haldane and G. R. T. Ross (Cambridge: Cambridge University Press, 1931; reprinted Dover, 1955), 1:358.
5. (In English in the original text.—Tr.)
6. (*Instance* is rendered here as "in-stant" to underscore Irigaray's emphasis on the term's root meaning, standing within the self, as opposed to "ecstasy," standing outside the self.—Tr.)
7. See Luce Irigaray, "Epistle to the Last Christians," in *Marine Lover of Friedrich Nietzsche*, trans. Gillian C. Gill (New York: Columbia University Press, 1991).

SEXES AND GENEALOGIES: EACH SEX
MUST HAVE ITS OWN RIGHTS

In the field of law, one sector that is currently mutating is the relationship between the male and female sexes, particularly insofar as the family and its relation to reproduction are concerned. Our cultures are seeing changes in the laws relating to the obligation to bear children, the right to contraception and abortion, the choice of name for women and children within the marriage, freedom to choose a domicile for the members of the couple, the relevance of paying a salary for housework, length of maternity leaves, protection for women in the workplace, etc. These measures cut across lines of natural law, penal codes, civil codes, religious law. Little thought is given to what the whole field represented by these different parts might mean.

Hegel did take on the project of interpreting how a whole society or culture might function. His aim was to describe and work out how the *Geist* or spirit of man as individual and as citizen functioned. The weakest link in his system seems to lie in his interpretation of spirit and right within the family. Even though he consistently sought to break up undifferentiated units, Hegel is unable to think of the family as anything but a single substance within which particular individuals lose their rights. Except the right to life, perhaps? Which is not that simple. . . .

THE ORIGIN OF THE FAMILY . . .

In the chapter of *The Phenomenology of Mind* that deals with the family, Hegel concentrates the first part of his analysis on the relation of man to spirit in culture. The chapter initially concerns the issue of ethics and their relation to morality. In this passage Hegel says something very important about the right of genders. Yet this seems to have been lost in the implications Hegel draws about the spirit of the people (*Volk*) and of peoples.

What is the issue here? In the analyses he devotes to the family as it relates to the state, Hegel explains that the daughter who remains faithful to the laws relating to her mother has to be cast out of the city, out of society. She cannot be violently killed, but she must be imprisoned, deprived of liberty, air, light, love, marriage, children. In other words, she is condemned to a slow and lonely death. The character Antigone represents that daughter. Hegel's analysis is supported by the content of Sophocles's tragedies.

What is the nature of the laws that Antigone respects? They are religious laws relating to the burial of her brother who has been killed in a war among men.

These laws have to do with the cultural obligations owed to the mother's blood, the blood shared by the brothers and sisters of the family. The duty to this blood will be denied and outlawed as the culture becomes patriarchal. This tragic episode in life—and in war—between the genders represents the passage into patriarchy. The daughter is forbidden to respect the blood bonds with her mother. From the spiritual viewpoint, these bonds have a religious quality, they move in consonance with the fertility of the earth and its flowers and fruits, they protect love in its bodily dimension, they keep watch over female fruitfulness within and without marriage (depending on whether the kingdom of Aphrodite or of Demeter is invoked), they correspond to times of peace.

Under the rule of patriarchy the girl is separated from her mother and from her family in general. She is transplanted into the genealogy of her husband; she must live with him, carry his name, bear his children, etc. The first time that this takes place, the move is recorded as the abduction of a woman by a man-lover. A war breaks out among men to recapture the stolen woman and bring her back to her community of origin.

Our code of morality today is still derived from those very ancient events. This means that the love between mother and daughter, which the patriarchal regime has made impossible (as Freud in fact reinforces for our benefit), has been transformed into the woman's obligation to devote herself to the cult of the children of her legal husband and to the husband himself as a male child. In fact, despite the incest taboo, there seems little indication that man has sublimated the natural immediately of his relationship to the mother. Rather, man has transferred that relationship to his wife as mother substitute. In this way the man-woman couple is always out of phase by a generation, since male and female genealogies are collapsed into a single genealogy: that of the *husband*.

THE DOUBLE MEANING OF THE WORD NATURE

The achievements recorded by recent movements for women's liberation have failed to establish a new *ethics* of sexuality. They nonetheless serve notice to us that ethics is the crucial issue because they have released so much violent, undirected energy, desperate for an outlet. They fall back into unmediated naturalness: the obligation to give birth, violence barely channeled into sado-masochistic scenarios, regression to animality (with no display?) in the erotic act, fear and destructiveness between the sexes. . . .

Obviously, I am not advocating a return to a more repressive, moralizing, conception of sexuality. On the contrary, what we need is to work out an art of the

sexual, a sexed culture, instead of merely using our bodies to release neuropsy-
chic tensions and produce babies.

When women are forced to bear children within the genealogy of the husband, this historically marks the beginning of a *failure of respect for nature*. A
new notion or concept of nature is set up, which takes the place of earth's fertility, abandons its religious quality, its link to the divinity of women and to the
mother-daughter relation. Paradoxically, the cult of the mother in our cultures
today is often associated with a scorn or neglect of nature. It is true that in patriarchal genealogy we are dealing with the cult of the *son's mother*, to the detri-
ment of the daughter's mother. The cult of the son's mother ties our tradition
into the whole mother-son incest issue and the taboo upon it. Our societies forget fascination with that incest leads us to neglect the genealogy of the woman,
which has been collapsed inside the man's.

Once one genealogy has been reduced to the other's, it becomes impossible
or at least difficult for the casual thinker to define two different genders or sexes.
Man takes his orientation from his relation to his father insofar as his name and
property are concerned and from his mother in relation to unmediated nature.
Woman must submit to her husband and to reproduction. This means that gender as sexuality is never sublimated. *Gender is confused with species.* Gender
becomes the human race, human nature, etc., as defined from within patriarchal
culture. Gender thus defined corresponds to a race of men (*un peuple
d'hommes*) who refuse, whether consciously or not, the possibility of another
gender: the female. All that is left is the human race/gender (*le genre humain*)
for which the only real value of sex is to reproduce the species. From this point
of view, *gender is always subservient to kinship*. Man and woman would not
come to maturity with a thinking and a culture relative to the sexual difference
of each. They would be more or less sexed children and adolescents, and then
reproductive adults. In this perspective, the family serves the interests of property, of material patrimony, and of the reproduction of children. The family is
not a small unit in which individual differences can be respected and cultivated.

As for life, the conclusion is inevitable that rights are unequally distributed
and frequently turn into duties, especially for women: the duty to bear children,
sexual duties. No legislation offers women protection. This anomaly is often accounted for by the power of religious morality in questions of social practice and
reproduction. This influence, which is the residue of ancient gynocratic traditions, is marked today by patriarchal imperatives: give property to the husband,
children to the State. . . .

We need to reinterpret the idea of nature that underlies such imperatives. Often, it is less a question of life than of an idea of life and of a valid lifestyle. But

value, and values, have been codified in the men's camp: they are not appropriate to women, or not appropriated by them. The law has not been written to defend the life and property of women. A few partial changes in rights for women
have been won in recent times. But even these are subject to recall. They are
won by partial and local pressures whereas what is needed is a full-scale rethinking of the law's duty to offer justice to *two genders that differ* in their needs,
their desires, their properties.

SEX AS AN ETHICAL DIMENSION

When faced by questions such as these, many men and women start talking
about *love*. But love is only possible when there are two parties and in a relationship that is not submissive to one gender, not subject to reproduction. It
requires that the rights of both male and female be written into the legal code.
If the rights of the couple were indeed written into the legal code, this would
serve to convert individual morality into collective ethics, to transform the relations of the genders within the family or its substitute into rights and duties
that involve the culture as a whole. Religion can then rediscover how each gender interprets its relation to the divine—a religion freed from its role of
guardian of a single gender and financial trustee for the property of one gender more than of the other. Hardly a godly role! Furthermore, once the rights
of each gender have been written into the legal documents representing society or culture, this will mean that natural law is no longer separate from civil
law, and that a concrete private law is set up that takes the daily needs of each
one of us into account. What does the right to private property mean when excessive noise and odor pollution and the organized violence of the media, etc.,
destroy the sense *perceptions* indispensable for life and mind? Such a law is
merely an abstract demand, based on money and careless of the bodies, love,
and intelligence of the men and women who share an often limited and ex-
pensive living space.

Such living conditions do not contribute to the development of human peoples. How often our nerves are set on edge. We are driven to compete in the rat
race of modern life—so maddened and overwhelmed by the pace of existence
that we embrace war as a means of regaining some measure of order and opening some new space onto the future. This was often true in the past. It will continue to be so if we fail to set up an ethics of the couple as an intermediary place
between individuals, peoples, States. Wars break out when peoples move too far
from their natural possibilities, when abstract energy builds up so much that it
can no longer be controlled by subjects or reduced to one or more concrete re-

sponsibilities. Collective madness, then, is the name we give to the concrete, sacrificial goal we set in order to reduce the rising tide of abstraction.

In the exercise of a social and cultural ethics that acknowledged sexual difference, History might find a more continuous course of development, one less
subject to periodic expansions and reductions that defy society's control.

BODY AGAINST BODY: IN RELATION
TO THE MOTHER

I should like to begin by thanking the organizing committee of the conference
on mental health for choosing "Women and Madness" as the theme of this meeting and for thus playing some part in breaking the silence and invisibility that af-
flict so many women.

I am surprised—and, sadly, am not at all surprised! but I prefer to keep on
being surprised—that so few male practitioners have come to the conference today to hear what women have to say about their madness. Most women are
treated by male physicians, and the absence of these men already tells us something about their practice, particularly their psychiatric practice. They seem to
have so little interest in what women say. To establish a diagnosis and prescribe
a treatment, men need only each other. Why bother listening to the female patient? This attitude goes far to explain the therapeutic choices available to these
male doctors.

Yet how often have I heard men say how annoying it is that women get together for meetings and how much they, the men, would like to be able to at-
tend and find out what is going on. So their absence here today is all the more
significant. They were not excluded from this conference, at which women
speakers would be in the majority. Why hasn't their curiosity brought them
here? The few men who are in attendance today should make an effort to try and
understand how and why they come to be exceptions!

Could it be that those other men, the majority of practitioners, have re-
frained from coming because of the power issue? Men are not leading this conference. Or are they simply ashamed to make an appearance, in light of the
statistics offered this morning on the frightening number of women committed to psychiatric institutions (usually committed by their families, with the
hospital serving as a place of incarceration) who are then treated with chemotherapy, not psychotherapy? Unless it is all a matter of professional disdain for
a conference organized by and for women? Or of sexual indifference? I leave
the interpretation open.

In any case, the absence of male doctors is, in and of itself, one explanation of

madness in women: their words are not heard. Women and their words are not
given the keys to the city when it comes to developing the diagnosis and therapeutic decisions that concern them. Serious scientific discourse and practice remain the privilege of men who have control of politics in general as well as of
our most private sphere as women. Everywhere, in everything, men's speech,
men's values, dreams, and desires are law. Everywhere and in everything men
define the function and the social role of women, right down to the sexual identity that women are to have—or not to have. Men know, men have access to the
truth, not us. We barely, at times, have access to fiction!

Rather to his own surprise, one particularly "honest" male friend admitted to
me not long ago: "You know, you're right. I always thought that all women were
mad." And he added: "Obviously that was one way of avoiding the issue of my
own madness."

This is in fact how the question needs to be posed. Each sex has a relation to
madness. Every desire has a relation to madness. But it would seem that one desire has been taken as wisdom, moderation, truth, leaving to the other sex the
weight of a madness that cannot be acknowledged or accommodated.

This relation of desire to madness works in a privileged manner in the relation to the mother, for man as well as for woman. But all too often man rids himself of that madness and unloads it upon woman—or women.

The relation to the mother is a mad desire, because it is the "dark continent"
par excellence. It remains in the shadow of our culture, it is night and hell. But
men cannot do without it anymore than—or perhaps less than—women can.
And if today's society is so polarized by the issues of contraception and abortion,
surely this reflects the need to escape the question of the imaginary and symbolic relation to the mother, to the woman-mother. What is woman, apart from
her social and material function in reproducing children, nursing, renewing the
work force?

The maternal function underlies the social order as well as the order of desire, but it is always restricted to the dimension of need. Once individual and collective needs have been met there is often nothing left of maternal female potency to satisfy desire, particularly in its religious dimension.

Her desire, the desire she has, that is what the law of the father, of all fathers,
moves to prohibit: the fathers of families, fathers in religion, father teachers, father doctors, father lovers, etc. Whether moral or immoral, all these fathers intervene to censure, repress, the mother's desire. For them, it's a matter of good
sense, good health, or even of virtue and holiness!

mothers with desire ° must
repress!

Perhaps we have reached a period in history when this question of the father's dominance can no longer be avoided. The prominence of this question is the result, at least in part, of several factors. Contraception and abortion raise the issue of the meaning of motherhood, and women (notably because they have gained access to the market) are in search of their sexual identity and are beginning to emerge from silence and anonymity.

One thing is plain, not only in everyday events but in the whole social scene: our society and our culture operate on the basis of an original matricide.

When Freud, notably in *Totem and Taboo*, describes and theorizes about the murder of the father as the founding act for the primal horde, he is forgetting an even more ancient murder, that of the woman-mother, which was necessary to the foundation of a specific order in the city.

With a few additions and subtractions, our imaginary still works according to the schema set in place by Greek mythology and tragedy. I shall therefore take the example of Clytemnestra's murder in the *Oresteia*.

Quite obviously, Clytemnestra does not conform to that image of the virgin-mother which has been promoted as our ideal for centuries. She is still passionately a lover. She will in fact go so far as to kill for love: she will kill her husband. But why?

For years and years her husband has been away from home, off with other men to recapture the fair Helen. This is perhaps the prototype of war among men. In order to secure his military and amorous expedition, Agamemnon sacrificed Iphigenia, the adolescent daughter he had with Clytemnestra. When he returns home, it is with another girl by his side, Cassandra, his slave and, no doubt, the latest in his string of mistresses.

Clytemnestra, for her part, has taken a lover. But she believed her husband was dead, since she had been without news of him for many years. When Agamemnon returns in triumph with his mistress she kills him. She kills him out of jealousy, out of fear perhaps, and because she has been dissatisfied and frustrated for so long. She also kills him because he has sacrificed their daughter in the cause of male conflicts, though this motive is often forgotten by the authors of tragedy.

But the new order decrees that she be killed in her turn by her son, who is inspired to do so by the oracle of Apollo, beloved son of Zeus: the God-Father. Orestes kills his mother because the empire of the God-Father, who has seized and taken for his own the ancient powers (*puissances*)[1] of the earth-mother, demands it. He kills his mother and is driven mad, as is his sister Electra.

Electra, the daughter, will remain mad. The matricidal son, on the other hand, must be saved from madness so that he can found the patriarchal order. The fair

Apollo, lover of men rather than women, narcissistic lover of their bodies and their words, a lover who in fact does not make love much more often than his sister in Zeus, Athena, helps Orestes shake off his madness.

Madness is in fact represented in the shape of a horde of angry women, the Erinnyes, who pursue Orestes, haunting him at every step, almost like ghosts of his mother. These women howl for revenge. Together they hunt down the son who has killed his mother. They are women in rebellion, types of hysterical revolutionaries who rise up against the patriarchal power that is being established.

As you will have noticed, this whole story is extremely topical. The mythology that underlies patriarchy has not changed. Everything described in the *Oresteia* is still taking place. Here and there we still see the emergence of some useful Athenas, who spring whole from the brain of the Father-King, dedicated solely to his service and that of the men in power. They bury the women who fight patriarchy under the sanctuary so as to eliminate troublesome challenge to the new order laid down for households, the order of the city-state, the only order from now on. These useful Athenas, perfect models of femininity, always veiled and clothed from head to toe, very respectable, can be recognized by this sign: they are extraordinarily attractive—which doesn't mean they attract—but they really aren't interested in making love.

Thus the murder of the mother is rewarded by letting the son go scot free, by burying the madness of women—and burying women in madness—and by introducing the image of the virgin goddess, born of the Father, obedient to his laws at the expense of the mother.

In fact, when Oedipus makes love to his mother one might say that he does so at first with impunity. On the other hand, he will become blind or mad as soon as he knows that it was his mother: whom he has already killed, according to the mythology, in obedience to the verdict of the Father of the gods.

This is a possible interpretation, although it is never offered. Inevitably the theory is accounted for in terms of taking the place of the father and the symbolic murder of the father. Yet, Oedipus clearly reactualizes the madness of Orestes. He is afraid of his mother when she reveals herself to him as his mother. His original crime is echoed back to him, he fears and loathes his act, and the woman who was the target of that act. Only on a secondary level does he infringe upon the law of the father.

Every history and practice derived from psychoanalysis seems to be based upon the ambivalence that Oedipus feels toward his father. An ambivalence that aims at the father but is projected retroactively upon the primitive relation to the mother's body. Now, it is true that, in so far as it takes account of the drives, analysis does have things to tell us about the mother's breast, about the milk she offers, about the feces she takes away (a "gift" she is more or less interested in), and even about her gaze and her voice. But analysis shows too little interest in these things. Furthermore, isn't it true that all this wrestling (*corps-à-corps*) with the mother, which has difficulties of its own, is part of a postoedipal phantasy projected backward into the Oedipus phase? When the mother is cut up in stages, when each part of her body has to be cathected and then decathected if the child is to grow, she has already been torn to pieces by the hatred of Oedipus. And when Freud talks about the father being torn apart by the sons in the primeval horde, isn't he, out of full-scale denial and misunderstanding, forgetting the woman who has been torn between son and father, among sons?

The *partial* drives, in fact, seem to refer especially to the body that brought us *whole* into the world. The genital drive is theoretically that drive by which the phallic penis captures the mother's power to give birth, nourish, inhabit, center. Doesn't the phallic erection occur at the place where the umbilical cord once was? The phallus becomes the organizer of the world through the man-father at the very place where the umbilical cord, that primal link to the mother, once gave birth to man and woman. All that had taken place within an originary womb, the first nourishing earth, first waters, first sheaths, first membranes in which the *whole* child was held, as well as the *whole* mother, through the mediation of her blood. According to a relationship that is obviously not symmetrical, mother and child are linked in a way that precedes all dissociations, all tearing of their bodies into pieces.

This primary experience is very unpopular with psychoanalysts: in fact they refuse to see it. They allude to a fetal situation or fetal regression and find nothing to say about it. A vague sort of taboo is in force. There would be a danger of fusion, death, lethal sleep, if the father did not intervene to sever this uncomfortably close link to the original matrix. Does the father replace the womb with the matrix of his language? But the exclusivity of his law refuses all representation to that first body, that first home, that first love. These are sacrificed and provide matter for an empire of language that so privileges the male sex as to confuse it with the human race.

The order of this empire decrees that when a proper name (*nom*) is given to a child, it substitutes for the most irreducible mark of birth, the navel (*nombril*). The family name, and even the first or given name, always stand at one remove from that most elemental identity tag: the scar where the umbilical cord was cut. The family name, and even the first name, slip over the body like clothes, like identity tags—outside the body.

Nonetheless, in psychoanalysis however much use is made of the law, of the symbolic, of language, and of the family name (the father's name), the analyst in therapy generally sits behind the analysand, like the mother toward whom the analysand is forbidden to turn. The patient must move forward, ahead, out, by forgetting the mother. And if he did turn around, perhaps she might have disappeared? Perhaps he has annihilated her?

The social order, our culture, psychoanalysis itself, are all insistent that the mother must remain silent, outlawed. The father forbids any *corps-à-corps* with the mother.

I am tempted to add: if only this were really true! We would be more at peace with our bodies if it were, and men need peace to feed their libido as well as their life and culture. For the ban does not prevent a certain number of failures of compliance, a certain blindness.

And where are we to find the imaginary and symbolic of life in the womb and the first *corps-à-corps* with the mother? In what darkness, what madness, do they lie abandoned?

And the relation to the placenta, that first home that surrounds us and whose aura accompanies our every step, like a primary safety zone, how is that presented to us in our culture? No image has been formed for the placenta and hence we are constantly in danger of retreating into the original matrix, of seeking refuge in any open body, and forever nestling into the body of other women.

In this way the opening of the mother, the opening to the mother, appears as threats of contagion, contamination, falling into sickness, madness, death. Obviously, there is nothing available that can allow us to move forward firmly without risk. No Jacob's ladder is there to help us climb back to the mother. Jacob's ladder always moves up to heaven, toward the father and his kingdom.

And who in fact would credit the innocence of this bond with the mother, since anyone who seeks to reestablish that bond with her will be accused of the crime that has repeatedly been committed against her?

The devouring monster we have turned the mother into is an inverted reflection of the blind consumption that she is forced to submit to. Her womb, sometimes her breast, gape open as a result of the gestation, the birthing, the life which have issued from them, without reciprocity. Unless murder, whether real or cultural, serves to erase the debt? forget the dependency? destroy the power (*puissance*)?

The insatiable character of what we in psychotherapy call orality, the unquenchable thirst, the desire for the mother to fill us to the brim, is the subject of much discussion in analysis, and may make certain cures impossible. Yet is this characterization of the infant's mouth—or the woman's sex—as a bottomless pit not a thought or a phantasy derived from oedipal hatred? There is no real reason to believe that an infant's thirst or a woman's sexuality is insatiable. All the evidence is to the contrary. But that mouth cavity of the child, like any desire, becomes a bottomless pit if the time spent in utero is a taboo issue and if no attempt is made to interpret and come to terms with the losses and the scars involved in our separation from that primary home and that first name. The child demands that the breast offer him everything. The everything that he once received in his mother's womb: life, home, both the home of his own body and of the mother's body that he inhabits, food, air, warmth, movement, etc. This everything is displaced into oral avidity because there is no way to place it in its space, its time, and the exile from both. The wound we can never heal, never cure, opens up when the umbilical cord is severed. When the father or the mother threaten Oedipus with scissors or knife, they forget that the cord, already, has been cut and that all that is needed is to take cognizance of that fact.

The problem is that when the father refuses to allow the mother her power of giving birth and seeks to be the sole creator, then according to our culture he superimposes upon our ancient world of flesh and blood a universe of language and symbols that has no roots in the flesh and drills a hole through the female womb and through the place of female identity. A stake, an axis is thus driven into the earth in order to mark out the boundaries of the sacred space in many patriarchal traditions. It defines a meeting place for men that is based upon an immolation. Women will in the end be allowed to enter that space, provided that they do so as nonparticipants.

The fertility of the earth is sacrificed in order to establish the cultural domain of the father's language (which is called, incorrectly, the mother tongue). But this is never spoken of. Just as the scar of the navel is forgotten, so, correspondingly, a hole appears in the texture of the language.

Some men and women would prefer to identify maternal power, the phallic mother, as an ensnaring net. But such attribution occurs only as a defensive mesh that the man-father or his sons casts over the chasms of a silent and threatening womb. Threatening because it is silent, perhaps? *no language*

The womb is never thought of as the primal place in which we become body. Therefore for many men it is variously phantasized as a devouring mouth, as a sewer in which anal and urethral waste is poured, as a threat to the phallus or, at best, as a reproductive organ. And the womb is mistaken for all the female sexual organs since no valid representations of female sexuality exist.

The only words we have for women's sexuality are filthy, mutilating words. Consequently, the feelings associated with women's sexuality will be anxiety, phobia, disgust, and the haunting fear of castration.

How are any other feelings possible when we are asked to move back toward something that has always been negated, denied, sacrificed for the construction of an exclusively male symbolic world?

Is it possible that castration anxiety is an unconscious reminder of the sacrifice that consecrated the phallic erection as unique sexual value? But neither the postulation nor the name of the father suffices to guarantee that the son's penis will remain erect. And it is not the murder of the father that both sustains and threatens the phallic erection, despite the claims made by patriarchal tradition in a kind of act of faith.

Unless—but this never crosses the threshold of thought—this murder of the father means not a desire to take the father's place as rival and competitor, but a desire instead to do away with the one who has artificially severed the bond with the mother in order to take over the power of creating any world, particularly a female one.

According to this interpretation, phallic erection, far from being all-powerful, would be the masculine version of the umbilical cord. If phallic erection respected the life of the mother—of the mother in every women and of the woman in every mother—it would repeat the living bond to the mother. At the very place where there once had been the cord, then the breast, would in due time appear, for the man, the penis which reconnects, gives life, feeds and recenters the bodies. The penis evokes something of the life within the womb as it stiffens, touches, and spills out, passing beyond the skin and the will. As it softens and falls, it evokes the end, mourning, the ever open wound. Men would be performing an act of anticipatory repetition, a return to the world that allows them to become sexual adults capable of eroticism and reciprocity in the flesh.

This return to the world is also necessary for women. It can take place only if woman is released from the archaic projections man lays upon her and if an autonomous and positive representation of female sexuality exists in the culture.

 Woman has no cause to envy the penis or the phallus. But because of the failure to establish a sexual identity for both sexes—man, and the race of men, has transformed the male organ into an instrument of power with which to master maternal power (*puissance*).

What is useful to women in all these descriptions? When we are able to understand and interpret all of this, we are empowered to leave a world of madness that is not our own, cease to fear the night, the unidentifiable, a fear of an ordinary murder that is culturally not ours. I think it is very important to take cognizance of all this, because we are still defined by these projections even today. Even today we become the slaves of those phantasies, of that ambivalence, that madness, which is not ours. Let us rather take new hold of our own madness and leave men theirs!

Our urgent task is to refuse to submit to a desubjectivized social role, the role of mother, which is dictated by an order subject to the division of labor—he produces, she reproduces—that walls us up in the ghetto of a single function. When did society ever ask fathers to choose between being men or citizens? We don't have to give up being women to be mothers.

One other point, since my purpose is to set out a number of issues to open up discussion. We also need to discover and declare that we are always mothers just by being women. We bring many things into the world apart from children, we give birth to many other things apart from children: love, desire, language, art, social things, political things, religious things, but this kind of creativity has been forbidden to us for centuries. We must take back this maternal creative dimension that is our birthright as women.

If birthing is not to become traumatizing and pathological, the question of having or not having children should always be raised in the context of another birthing, a creation of images and symbols. Both women and their children would benefit enormously from this.

We need to be careful in one other respect: not again to kill the mother who was immolated at the birth of our culture. Our task is to give life back to that mother, to the mother who lives within us and among us. We must refuse to allow her desire to be swallowed up in the law of the father. We must give her the right to pleasure, to sexual experience, to passion, give her back the right to speak, or even to shriek and rage aloud.

We also need to find, rediscover, invent the words, the sentences that speak of the most ancient and most current relationship we know—the relationship to the mother's body, to our body—sentences that translate the bond between our body, her body, the body of our daughter. We need to discover a language that is not a substitute for the experience of *corps-à-corps* as the paternal language seeks to be, but which accompanies that bodily experience, clothing it in words that do not erase the body but speak the body.

It is crucial that we keep our bodies even as we bring them out of silence and servitude. Historically we are the guardians of the flesh. We should not give up that role, but identify it as our own, by inviting men not to make us into body for their benefit, not to make us into guarantees that their body exists. All too often

the male libido needs some woman (wife-mother) to guard the male body. This
is why men need a wife in the home, even when they have a mistress elsewhere.
This is a very important issue, even if it seems harmless.

Thus it is desirable that we should speak as we are making love. We should
also speak as we feed a baby so that the child does not feel that the milk is being stuffed down his or her throat, in a kind of rape. It is equally important for
us to speak as we caress another body. Silence is all the more alive when words
exist. Let us not become the guardians of dumb silence, of dead silence.

If we are not to be accomplices in the murder of the mother we also need to
assert that there is a genealogy of women. Each of us has a female family tree:
we have a mother, a maternal grandmother and great-grandmothers, we have
daughters. Because we have been exiled into the house of our husbands, it is easy
to forget the special quality of the female genealogy; we might even come to
deny it. Let us try to situate ourselves within that female genealogy so that we
can win and hold on to our identity. Let us not forget, moreover, that we already
have a history, that certain women, despite all the cultural obstacles, have made
their mark upon history and all too often have been forgotten by us.

What this amounts to is that we need above all (though there's no one thing
that has to be done before another) to discover our sexual identity, the special-
ness of our desires, of our autoeroticism, our narcissism, our heterosexuality, our
homosexuality. In this context it is important to remind ourselves that, since the
first body we as women had to relate to was a woman's body and our first love is
love of the mother, women always have an ancient and primary relationship to
what is called homosexuality. Men, on the other hand, always have an ancient
relationship to heterosexuality, since their first love object is a woman.

When analytic theory claims that the little girl must give up her love for and
of the mother, abandon the desire for and of her mother, if she is to enter into
desire for the father, woman is thereby subjected to a normative heterosexuality, common in our societies, but nonetheless completely pathogenic and pathological. Neither the little girl nor the woman needs to give up the love for her
mother. To do so is to sever women from the roots of their identity and their
subjectivity.

Let us also try to discover the special character of our love for other women.
This could be called (though I hate labels), between lots of quotation marks:
""" secondary homosexuality.""" I am trying in this way to make a distinction
between the ancient love for the mother and the love for sister-women. This love
is essential if we are to quit our common situation and cease being the slaves of

This is so cynical; assumes we can't have any relations w/ men; that they can't be better than this!

the phallic cult, commodities to be used and exchanged by men, competing objects in the marketplace.

We need to discover what makes our experience of sexual pleasure special. Obviously, it is possible for a woman to use the phallic model of sexual pleasure and there's no lack of men or pornographers to tell women that they can achieve extraordinary sexual pleasure within that phallic economy. The question remains: doesn't that economy draw women out of themselves and leave them without energy, perceptions, affects, gestures, and images that refer to their own identity? There are at least two modes of sexual pleasure for women. The first is programmed into a male libidinal economy and obeys a certain phallic order. Another is much more in harmony with what women are, with their sexual identity. Many women feel guilty, unhappy, frozen, and claim to be frigid because they are unable to live their affects, their sexuality, in the framework of a phallocractic economy. These same women would no longer be frigid if they tried to reconnect with a sexual pleasure more suited to their bodies and their sexual resources. This does not mean that women should always and instantly give up the other. I have no wish to force any woman to make choices that risk becoming repressive in their turn. But I think it is important, if we are to discover our female identity, for us to know that another relation to sexual pleasure is available apart from the phallic model.

We have a great deal to do. But how much better to have a future in front of us, rather than some new version of the past. Let us not wait for the god Phallus to give us his grace. The god Phallus, indeed, because even though many people go around saying God is dead, few would question the fact that the Phallus is alive and well. And don't many of the bearers of the said phallus walk around today claiming to be gods no less? They are everywhere, even—and here I shall raise my final question—in the holy Roman Catholic church where the Holy Father the Pope believes it right to forbid us once again: contraception, abortion, extramarital relations, homosexuality, etc. And yet, when the minister of that one and only God, that God-Father, pronounces the words of the Eucharist: "This is my body, this is my blood," according to the rite that celebrates the sharing of food and that has been ours for centuries, perhaps we might remind him that he would not be there if our body and our blood had not given him life, love, spirit. And that he is also serving us up, we women-mothers, on his communion plate. But this is something that must not be known. That is why women cannot celebrate the Eucharist. . . . If they were to do so, something of the truth that is hidden in the communion rite would be brutally unmasked.

At the same moment the human race would be absolved of a great offense. If a woman were to celebrate the Eucharist with her mother, giving her a share of

Men can be better than this: time to think about that

"ancient and primary relationship to what is called homosexuality"—WHY?

the fruits of the earth blessed by them both, she might be freed from all hatred or ingratitude toward her maternal genealogy, and be hallowed in her identity as a woman.

[handwritten note: — Essentialist: assumes a uniform identity "beneath" surface oppression...]

NOTES

The title of this speech or essay, "Le corps-à-corps avec la mère," has no simple translation in English. The expression *corps-à-corps*, which recurs throughout the text, usually denotes armed combat between two warriors—hand-to-hand fighting. However, it is the word *corps* (body) that is crucial to Irigaray, who is looking to some new relationship between mother and child that accepts the body of both parties and moves toward a new imaginary and a new symbolic.—Tr.

1. Modern French has two more or less interchangeable words for *power: le pouvoir* and *la puissance*. Irigaray makes a practice of distinguishing the two. *Le pouvoir* in her work is used for power in general and associated with patriarchy. *La puissance* is associated with women, is used for ancient female authority and tradition as well as for the possible new, feminized, world order, and has positive connotations. As English has no equivalent pairing, the French will appear parenthetically when Irigaray uses *puissance*.—Tr.

8

FEMININE WRITING AND WOMEN'S DIFFERENCE

Hélène Cixous

INTRODUCTION

by Doris Rita Alphonso

Hélène Cixous was born in Oran, Algeria, on June 5, 1937. The daughter of a physician of Sephardic (Spanish Jewish) descent and a midwife of Austro-Czechoslovakian and German descent, Cixous grew up speaking French and German at home and was also exposed to Arabic and Spanish. Such a polyglot environment nourished her budding passion for languages. Cixous departed for France in 1955 to study English literature, receiving her doctorate in 1968 from the University of Paris IV, Sorbonne. She won the *Prix Médicis* for her first (autobiographical) novel, *Dedans* (Inside), in 1969. In the same year, she cofounded the journal *Revue de Théorie et D'Analyse Littéraire: Poétique*. In 1974, Cixous created the *Centre de Recherches en Études Féminines* and developed a doctorate in women's studies at the University of Paris VIII, Vincennes (later St. Denis)—an experimental university that she helped to found after the student revolts of May 1968. A prolific writer, with more than fifty novels, essays, and plays to her name to date, Cixous was awarded the Southern Cross of Brazil in 1989 and both the *Legion d'Honneur* and the *Prix des Critiques* in 1984. She holds honorary doctorates in Canada, England, South Africa, and the United States, and she has lectured at universities worldwide.

Cixous writes between the genres of literature, poetry, mythology, and philosophy. Her influences are multifarious, and include the writers Samuel Beckett, Jean Genet, James Joyce, Clarice Lispector, and Shakespeare. An early influence on Cixous was James Joyce, on whom she wrote her doctoral thesis, "The Exile of James Joyce or the Art of Replacement." In Joyce, she found language transformed and transformative, and she gained an appreciation for the musicality of language.

Cixous' involvement since the late 1960s with Antoinette Fouque, the leader of a feminist tendency called *Psychanalyse et Politique* (Psych et Po) and founder of the publishing house *Editions des femmes*, has proved crucial to Cixous' success as a writer. It was through *des femmes* that Cixous' often controversial ideas found an audience, in France as well as abroad. Her more recent collaborations with Ariane Mnouchkine, the director of the experimental *Théâtre du Soleil*, mark the beginning of Cixous' focus on questions of collective resistance and a critique of neocolonialism. In collaboration with Mnouchkine, Cixous has written several historical plays (on Cambodia, India, South African apartheid, and the German and Russian World War II death camps) that relate history from the perspective of the oppressed. The collaboration has provided the opportunity for Cixous' writings to take on a wider political dimension. In recent works, Cixous has returned to examine her Jewish roots and to the autobiographical form.

In France and throughout Europe, Cixous is known as the award-winning author of novels and plays and, more recently, as an activist for justice worldwide. In the United States, however, her name immediately recalls the theory of *ecriture féminine*, a popular writing and reading strategy. The theory arose from Cixous' deconstructive reading of Western metaphysics in *The Newly Born Woman* (1975, with Catherine Clément). Cixous' critique of a symbolic economy that is driven by opposition and exclusions led her to conclude that both writing and woman are the excluded grounds for Western metaphysics. She coined the term *ecriture féminine* (feminine writing) to describe that which has been erased through the privileging of the (masculine/speech) one over the (feminine/writing) other.

For Cixous, *ecriture féminine* was never reserved for women alone, in part because she envisioned the writer as radically bisexual. She offers the term "bisexual" in the context of the androgyny prevailing in feminist circles of the time, an androgyny that sought to obliterate sexual difference. As a third alternative, bisexuality was meant to put into question the discrete categories of masculine and feminine. Cixous' rendition of bisexuality depicts the diffusion of multiple erogenous zones, and at the same time, contests the phallologocentric delimitation of desire in an Oedipal economy. Both men and women, according to Cixous, can surpass the reduction of the erotic to the phallus, and through the practice of writing a feminine, diffuse erotogeneity. Because the term "bisexuality" works also to neutralize difference, multiplicity, and alterity, however, Cixous more recently abandoned her idea of bisexuality, in favor of a "poetics of sexual difference."

Also in the name of sexual difference, Cixous has refused to call herself a feminist because this term specifically designates a reformist political tendency to which she stands opposed; where feminists demand equality, she deems it necessary to affirm sexual difference. For Cixous, this takes the form of expressing, in writing, the radical alterity of the feminine sexual economy—in terms of its fluidity, openness, multiplicity, and sheer abundance. In her critique of the phallocentric economies of exchange and debt versus gift economies, Cixous formulates the feminine economy in terms of giving and a characteristic feminine generosity. The feminine gives of herself continually without losing herself in the exchange, and hers is not an exploitative desire, but a desire-that-gives. In this way, the feminine provides an alternative to the masculine economy that makes the gift impossible because it demands that all gifts be returned, in some form, to their senders—thus obliterating the generous intent, and replacing it with debts owed. This is a theme that is presented in *Newly Born Women* (1986) and continued in "Castration or Decapitation?" (1981), both originally written in the same intellectual period.

Cixous begins to develop her theory of *ecriture féminine* in "The Laugh of Medusa." She calls for women to return to their bodies in writing the feminine, to write their overflowing abundance, their profusion, their prodigious and multiple erotogeneity. *Ecriture féminine* is opposed to the thrift of a masculine libidinal economy that is centered on the phallus and discretely bounded. Indeed, *ecriture féminine* cannot fail to subvert the proper, phallocentric reason because, in putting her body forward, woman wields the force of the repressed. Repressed within patriarchal cultures, woman's speech resonates with a song that opens onto a volcanic laughter—shaking the old grounds of logic, overturning the heaps of reason, blowing the law to pieces, and making rubble of man's property. In an unforgettable image, Cixous writes that if one dares to look at Medusa (the figurehead of the repressed and feared feminine), one will see that she is laughing, and beautiful.

In "Castration or Decapitation?" Cixous argues that the masculine fear of castration leads to a backlash against woman that figures her repeated decapitation in literature, philosophy, and history. Unlike man who can sublimate his fear of castration, woman lives with the threat of the loss of her head without recourse to mourning, in the silence of the hysteric. But woman must affirm difference until her strangeness to the system of property exchange is made apparent. To woman falls the task of overturning patriarchal history by writing the sexual difference that marks her. Feminine writing is primarily tactile, bodily, and interior in the extreme. In an outpouring like menstrual blood, or mother's milk, *ecriture féminine* does the necessary work of mourning. Cixous characterizes *ecriture féminine* as the property of neither woman nor man, but a way of writing that embodies a giving without taking back and without the expectation of return. *Ecriture féminine* is the only way *anyone* will get to keep their heads. Another metalanguage, *ecriture féminine* is hard to follow because it is not linear but begins from all sides at once—allowing for a new departure in history, wandering through the unknown elsewhere, across detachment and boundaries, crossing categories, and opening onto a certain laughter. Clarice Lispector's *The Hour of the Star*, in its explorations of the relationship between life and writing, provided a vivid example of the *ecriture féminine* (woman's writing) that Cixous had been theorizing.

In some of her later work, Cixous theorizes being between masculine and feminine as between-two (*entredeux*), the cite of radical alterity. In *Rootprints*, she explains that through intense suffering and joy, we are exiled from ourselves and enter into the immense landscape between (*trans-*), also a passage to and from the other. In moving from the one to the other, identity (a relational "I") and sexual difference emerge. Sexual difference is the differential that arises between the two, or the very exchange that occurs between them. In Cixous' poetic tongue, she depicts sexual difference as the contact between two impossibilities and the exchange of the inexchangeable. Not a visible thing, sexual difference can nonetheless be felt—in a wondrous curiosity for the other, in the first stirrings of desire. The other furnishes the opportunity and desire to find the necessary words and, thus, the need to write is aroused.

BIBLIOGRAPHY

Selected Primary Sources

1972. *The Exile of James Joyce or the Art of Replacement*. Translated by Sally Purcell. New York: David Lewis. [*L'Exil de James Joyce: ou l'art du remplacement*. Paris: Grasset, 1968.]

1976. "The Laugh of Medusa." *Signs* 1, no. 4: 875–99. ["Le rire de la méduse." *L'arc* (1975): 39–54.]

1981. "Castration or Decapitation?" *Signs* 7, no. 1: 41–55. [Le Sexe ou la tête?" *Les Cahiers du GRIF*, no. 13 (1976): 5–15.

1986. *Inside*. Translated by Carol Barko. New York: Schocken Books. [*Dedans*. Paris: Grasser et Fasquelle, 1969; Paris: Editions des femmes, 1986.]

1986, with Catherine Clément. *The Newly Born Woman*. Translated by Betsy Wing. Minneapolis: Minnesota University Press. [*La Jeune Née*. Paris: Union Générale d'Editions, 1975.]

1990. *Reading With Clarice Lispector*. Translated by Verena Andermatt Conley. Minneapolis: Minnesota University Press.

1991. *The Book of Promethea*. Translated by Betsy Wing. Lincoln: University of Nebraska Press. [*Le Livre de Promethea*. Paris: Gallimard, 1983.]

1991. *"Coming to Writing" and Other Essays*. Translated by Sarah Cornell et al. Cambridge, MA.: Harvard University Press.

1993. *Three Steps on the Ladder of Writing*. Translated by Sarah Cornell and Susan Sellers. New York: Columbia University Press.

1994. *The Hélène Cixous Reader*. Edited by Susan Sellers. New York: Routlege.

1997, with Mirelle Calle-Gruber. *Hélène Cixous Rootprints: Memory and Life Writing*. Translated by Eric Prenowitz. New York: Routledge. [*Photos de racine*. Paris: Editions des femmes, 1994.]

1998. *Stigmata: Surviving Texts*. New York: Routledge.

Selected Secondary Sources

Conley, Verena Andermatt. 1992. *Hélène Cixous*. New York: Harvester and Wheatsheaf.

Moi, Toril. 1985. "Hélène Cixous. In *Sexual/Textual Politics: Feminist Literary Theory*. New York: Methuen.

Sellers, Susan. 1995. *Hélène Cixous: Authorship, Autobiography, and Love*. Cambridge, Mass.: Blackwell.

Shiach, Morag. 1991. *Hélène Cixous: A Politics of Writing*. New York: Routledge.

Wilcox, Helen, Keith McWatters, Ann Thomson, and Linda R. Williams, eds. 1990. *The Body and the Text: Hélène Cixous, Reading and Teaching*. New York: St. Martin's Press.

THE LAUGH OF THE MEDUSA

I shall speak about women's writing: about *what it will do*. Woman must write her self: must write about women and bring women to writing, from which they have been driven away as violently as from their bodies—for the same reasons, by the same law, with the same fatal goal. Woman must put herself into the text—as into the world and into history—by her own movement.

The future must no longer be determined by the past. I do not deny that the effects of the past are still with us. But I refuse to strengthen them by repeating them, to confer upon them an irremovability the equivalent of destiny, to confuse the biological and the cultural. Anticipation is imperative.

Since these reflections are taking shape in an area just on the point of being discovered, they necessarily bear the mark of our time—a time during which the new breaks away from the old, and, more precisely, the (feminine) new from the old (*la nouvelle de l'ancien*). Thus, as there are no grounds for establishing a discourse, but rather an arid millennial ground to break, what I say has at least two sides and two aims: to break up, to destroy; and to foresee the unforeseeable, to project.

I write this as a woman, toward women. When I say "woman," I'm speaking of woman in her inevitable struggle against conventional man; and of a universal woman subject who must bring women to their senses and to their meaning in history. But first it must be said that in spite of the enormity of the repression that has kept them in the "dark"—that dark which people have been trying to make them accept as their attribute—there is, at this time, no general woman, no one typical woman. What they have *in common* I will say. But what strikes me is the infinite richness of their individual constitutions: you can't talk about *a* female sexuality, uniform, homogeneous, classifiable into codes—any more than you can talk about one unconscious resembling another. Women's imaginary is inexhaustible, like music, painting, writing: their stream of phantasms is incredible.

I have been amazed more than once by a description a woman gave me of a world all her own which she had been secretly haunting since early childhood. A world of searching, the elaboration of a knowledge, on the basis of a systematic experimentation with the bodily functions, a passionate and precise interrogation of her erotogeneity. This practice, extraordinarily rich and inventive, in particular as concerns masturbation, is prolonged or accompanied by a production of forms, a veritable aesthetic activity, each stage of rapture inscribing a resonant vision, a composition, something beautiful. Beauty will no longer be forbidden.

I wished that that woman would write and proclaim this unique empire so that other women, other unacknowledged sovereigns, might exclaim: I, too, overflow; my desires have invented new desires, my body knows unheard-of songs. Time and again I, too, have felt so full of luminous torrents that I could burst—burst with forms much more beautiful than those which are put up in frames and sold for a stinking fortune. And I, too, said nothing, showed nothing. I didn't open my mouth, I didn't repaint my half of the world. I was ashamed. I was afraid, and I swallowed my shame and my fear. I said to myself: You are mad! What's the meaning of these waves, these floods, these outbursts? Where is the ebullient, infinite woman who, immersed as she was in her naiveté, kept in the dark about herself, led into self-disdain by the great arm of parental-conjugal phallocentrism, hasn't been ashamed of her strength? Who, surprised and horrified by the fantastic tumult of her drives (for she was made to believe that a well-adjusted normal woman has a . . . divine composure), hasn't accused herself of being a monster? Who, feeling a funny desire sitting inside her (to sing, to write, to dare to speak, in short, to bring out something new), hasn't thought she was sick? Well, her shameful sickness is that she resists death, that she makes trouble.

And why don't you write? Write! Writing is for you, you are for you; your body is yours, take it. I know why you haven't written. (And why I didn't write before the age of twenty-seven.) Because writing is at once too high, too great for you, it's reserved for the great—that is for "great men"; and it's "silly." Besides, you've written a little, but in secret. And it wasn't good, because it was in secret, and because you punished yourself for writing, because you didn't go all the way, or because you wrote, irresistibly, as when we would masturbate in secret, not to go further, but to attenuate the tension a bit, just enough to take the edge off. And then as soon as we come, we go and make ourselves feel guilty—so as to be forgiven; or to forget, to bury it until the next time.

Write, let no one hold you back, let nothing stop you: not man; not the imbecilic capitalist machinery, in which publishing houses are the crafty, obsequious relayers of imperatives handed down by an economy that works against us and off our backs; and not *yourself*. Smug-faced readers, managing editors, and big bosses don't like the true texts of women—female-sexed tests. That kind scares them.

I write woman: woman must write woman. And man, man. So only an oblique consideration will be found here of man; it's up to him to say where his masculinity and femininity are at: this will concern us once men have opened their eyes and seen themselves clearly.[1]

Now women return from afar, from always: from "without," from the heath where witches are kept alive; from below, from beyond "culture"; from their childhood which men have been trying desperately to make them forget, condemning it to "eternal rest." The little girls and their "ill-mannered" bodies immured, well-preserved, intact unto themselves, in the mirror. Frigidified. But are they ever seething underneath! What an effort it takes—there's no end to it—for the sex cops to bar their threatening return. Such a display of forces on both sides that the struggle has for centuries been immobilized in the trembling equilibrium of a deadlock.

Here they are, returning, arriving over and again, because the unconscious is impregnable. They have wandered around in circles, confined to the narrow room in which they've been given a deadly brainwashing. You can incarcerate them, slow them down, get away with the old Apartheid routine, but for a time only. As soon as they begin to speak, at the same time as they're taught their name, they can be taught that their territory is black: because you are Africa, you are black. Your continent is dark. Dark is dangerous. You can't see anything in the dark, you're afraid. Don't move, you might fall. Most of all, don't go into the forest. And so we have internalized this horror of the dark.

Men have committed the greatest crime against women. Insidiously, violently, they have led them to hate women, to be their own enemies, to mobilize their immense strength against themselves, to be the executants of their virile needs. They have made women an antinarcissism! A narcissism which loves itself only to be loved for what women haven't got! They have constructed the infamous logic of antilove.

We the precocious, we the repressed of culture, our lovely mouths gagged with pollen, our wind knocked out of us, we the labyrinths, the ladders, the tramped spaces, the bevies—we are black and we are beautiful.

We're stormy, and that which is ours breaks loose from us without our fearing any debilitation. Our glances, our smiles, are spent; laughs exude from all our mouths; our blood flows and we extend ourselves without ever reaching an end; we never hold back our thoughts, our signs, our writing; and we're not afraid of lacking.

What happiness for us who are omitted, brushed aside at the scene of inheritances; we inspire ourselves and we expire without running out of breath, we are everywhere!

From now on, who, if we say so, can say no to us? We've come back from always.

It is time to liberate the New Woman from the Old by coming to know her—by loving her for getting by, for getting beyond the Old without delay, by going out ahead of what the New Woman will be, as an arrow quits the bow with a movement that gathers and separates the vibrations musically, in order to be more than her self.

I say that we must, for, with a few rare exceptions, there has not yet been any writing that inscribes femininity; exceptions so rare, in fact, that, after plowing through literature across languages, cultures, and ages,[2] one can only be startled at this vain scouting mission. It is well known that the number of women writers (while having increased very slightly from the nineteenth century on) has always been ridiculously small. This is a useless and deceptive fact unless from their species of female writers we do not first deduct the immense majority whose workmanship is in no way different from male writing, and which either obscures women or reproduces the classic representations of women (as sensitive—intuitive—dreamy, etc.).[3]

Let me insert here a parenthetical remark. I mean it when I speak of male writing. I maintain unequivocally that there is such a thing as *marked* writing; that, until now, far more extensively and repressively than is ever suspected or admitted, writing has been run by a libidinal and cultural—hence political, typically masculine—economy; that this is a locus where the repression of women has been perpetuated, over and over, more or less consciously, and in a manner that's frightening since it's often hidden or adorned with the mystifying charms of fiction; that this locus has grossly exaggerated all the signs of sexual opposition (and not sexual difference), where woman has never *her* turn to speak—this being all the more serious and unpardonable in that writing is precisely *the very possibility of change*, the space that can serve as a springboard for subversive thought, the precursory movement of a transformation of social and cultural structures.

Nearly the entire history of writing is confounded with the history of reason, of which it is at once the effect, the support, and one of the privileged alibis. It has been one with the phallocentric tradition. It is indeed that same self-admiring, self-stimulating, self-congratulatory phallocentrism.

With some exceptions, for there have been failures—and if it weren't for them, I wouldn't be writing (I-woman, escapee)—in that enormous machine that has been operating and turning out its "truth" for centuries. There have been poets who would go to any lengths to slip something by at odds with tradition—men capable of loving love and hence capable of loving others and of wanting them, of imagining the woman who would hold out against oppression and constitute herself as a superb, equal, hence, "impossible" subject, untenable in a real social framework. Such a woman the poet could desire only by breaking the codes that negate her. Her appearance would necessarily bring on, if not revolution—for the bastion was supposed to be immutable—at least harrowing explosions. At times it is in the fissure caused by an earthquake, through that radical mutation of things brought on by a material upheaval when every structure is for a moment thrown off balance and an ephemeral wildness sweeps order away, that the poet slips something by, for a brief span, of woman. Thus did Kleist expend himself in his yearning for the existence of sister-lovers, maternal daughters, mother-sisters, who never hung their heads in shame. Once the palace of magistrates is restored, it's time to pay: immediate bloody death to the uncontrollable elements.

But only the poets—not the novelists, allies of representationalism. Because poetry involves gaining strength through the unconscious and because the unconscious, that other limitless country, is the place where the repressed manage to survive: women, or as Hoffmann would say, fairies.

She must write her self, because this is the invention of a *new insurgent* writing which, when the moment of her liberation has come, will allow her to carry out the indispensable ruptures and transformations in her history, first at two levels that cannot be separated.

a) Individually. By writing her self, woman will return to the body which has been more than confiscated from her, which has been turned into the uncanny stranger on display—the ailing or dead figure, which so often turns out to be the nasty companion, the cause and location of inhibitions. Censor the body and you censor breath and speech at the same time.

Write your self. Your body must be heard. Only then will the immense resources of the unconscious spring forth. Our naphtha will spread, throughout the world, without dollars—black or gold—nonassessed values that will change the rules of the old game.

To write. An act which will not only "realize" the decensored relation of woman to her sexuality, to her womanly being, giving her access to her native strength; it will give her back her goods, her pleasures, her organs, her immense bodily territories which have been kept under seal; it will tear her away from the superegoized structure in which she has always occupied the place reserved for the guilty (guilty of everything, guilty at every turn: for having desires, for not having any; for being frigid, for being "too hot"; for not being both at once; for being too motherly and not enough; for having children and for not having any; for nursing and for not nursing . . .)—tear her away by means of this research, this job of analysis and illumination, this emancipation of the marvelous text of her self that she must urgently learn to speak. A woman without a body, dumb, blind, can't possibly be a good fighter. She is reduced to being the servant of the militant male, his shadow. We must kill the false woman who is preventing the live one from breathing. Inscribe the breath of the whole woman.

b) An act that will also be marked by woman's *seizing* the occasion to *speak*, hence her shattering entry into history, which has always been based *on her suppression.* To write and thus to forge for herself the antilogos weapon. To become *at will* the taker and initiator, for her own right, in every symbolic system, in every political process.

It is time for women to start scoring their feats in written and oral language.

Every woman has known the torment of getting up to speak. Her heart racing, at times entirely lost for words, ground and language slipping away—that's how daring a feat, how great a transgression it is for a woman to speak—even just open her mouth—in public. A double distress, for even if she transgresses, her words fall almost always upon the deaf male ear, which hears in language only that which speaks in the masculine.

It is by writing, from and toward women, and by taking up the challenge of speech which has been governed by the phallus, that women will confirm women in a place other than that which is reserved in and by the symbolic, that is, in a place other than silence. Women should break out of the snare of silence. They shouldn't be conned into accepting a domain which is the margin or the harem.

Listen to a woman speak at a public gathering (if she hasn't painfully lost her wind). She doesn't "speak," she throws her trembling body forward; she lets go of herself, she flies; all of her passes into her voice, and it's with her body that she vitally supports the "logic" of her speech. Her flesh speaks true. She lays herself bare. In fact, she physically materializes what she's thinking; she signifies it with her body. In a certain way she *inscribes* what she's saying, because she doesn't deny her drives the intractable and impassioned part they have in speaking. Her speech, even when "theoretical" or political, is never simple or linear or "objectified," generalized: she draws her story into history.

There is not that scission, that division made by the common man between the logic of oral speech and the logic of the text, bound as he is by his antiquated relation—servile, calculating—to mastery. From which proceeds the niggardly lip service which engages only the tiniest part of the body, plus the mask.

In women's speech, as in their writing, that element which never stops resonating, which, once we've been permeated by it, profoundly and imperceptibly touched by it, retains the power of moving us—that element is the song: first music from the first voice of love which is alive in every woman. Why this privileged relationship with the voice? Because no woman stockpiles as many defenses for countering the drives as does a man. You don't build walls around yourself, you don't forgo pleasure as "wisely" as he. Even if phallic mystification has generally contaminated good relationships, a woman is never far from "mother" (I mean outside her role functions: the "mother" as nonname and as source of goods). There is always within her at least a little of that good mother's milk. She writes in white ink.

Woman for women.—There always remains in woman that force which produces/is produced by the other—in particular, the other woman. In her, matrix, cradler; herself giver as her mother and child; she is her own sister-daughter. You might object, "What about she who is the hysterical offspring of a bad mother?" Everything will be changed once woman gives to the other woman. There is hidden and always ready in woman the source; the locus for the other. The mother, too, is a metaphor. It is necessary and sufficient that the best of herself be given to woman by another woman for her to be able to love herself and return in love the body that was "born" to her. Touch me, caress me, you the living no-name, give me my self as myself. The relation to the "mother," in terms of intense pleasure and violence, is curtailed no more than the relation to childhood (the child that she was, that she is, that she makes, remakes, undoes, there at the point where, the same, she mothers herself). Text: my body—shot through with streams of song; I don't mean the overbearing, clutchy "mother" but, rather, what touches you, the equivoice that affects you, fills your breast with an urge to come to language and launches your force; the rhythm that laughs you; the intimate recipient who makes all metaphors possible and desirable; body (body? bodies?), no more describable than god, the soul, or the Other; that part of you that leaves a space between yourself and urges you to inscribe in language your woman's style. In women there is always more or less of the mother who makes everything all right, who nourishes, and who stands up against separation; a force that will not be cut off but will knock the wind out of the codes. We will rethink womankind beginning with every form and every period of her body. The Americans remind us, "We are all Lesbians"; that is, don't denigrate woman, don't make of her what men have made of you.

Because the "economy" of her drives is prodigious, she cannot fail, in seizing the occasion to speak, to transform directly and indirectly *all* systems of exchange based on masculine thrift. Her libido will produce far more radical effects of political and social change than some might like to think.

Because she arrives, vibrant, over and again, we are at the beginning of a new history, or rather of a process of becoming in which several histories intersect with one another. As subject for history, woman always occurs simultaneously in several places. Woman un-thinks[4] the unifying, regulating history that homogenizes and channels forces, herding contradictions into a single battlefield. In woman, personal history blends together with the history of all women, as well as national and world history. As a militant, she is an integral part of all liberations. She must be farsighted, not limited to a blow-by-blow interaction. She foresees that her liberation will do more than modify power relations or toss the ball over to the other camp; she will bring about a mutation in human relations, in thought, in all praxis: hers is not simply a class struggle, which she carries forward into a much vaster movement. Not that in order to be a woman-in-struggle(s) you have to leave the class struggle or repudiate it; but you have to split it open, spread it out, push it forward, fill it with the fundamental struggle so as to prevent the class struggle, or any other struggle for the liberation of a class or people, from operating as a form of repression, pretext for postponing the inevitable, the staggering alteration in power relations and in the production of individualities. This alteration is already upon us—in the United States, for example, where millions of night crawlers are in the process of undermining the family and disintegrating the whole of American sociality.

The new history is coming; it's not a dream, though it does extend beyond men's imagination, and for good reason. It's going to deprive them of their conceptual orthopedics, beginning with the destruction of their enticement machine.

It is impossible to *define* a feminine practice of writing, and this is an impossibility that will remain, for this practice can never be theorized, enclosed, coded—which doesn't mean that it doesn't exist. But it will always surpass the discourse that regulates the phallocentric system; it does and will take place in areas other than those subordinated to philosophico-theoretical domination. It will be conceived of only by subjects who are breakers of automatisms, by peripheral figures that no authority can ever subjugate.

Hence the necessity to affirm the flourishes of this writing, to give form to its movement, its near and distant byways. Bear in mind to begin with (1) that sexual opposition, which has always worked for man's profit to the point of reducing writing, too, to his laws, is only a historico-cultural limit. There is, there will be more and more rapidly pervasive now, a fiction that produces irreducible effects of femininity. (2) That it is through ignorance that most readers, critics, and writers of both sexes hesitate to admit or deny outright the possibility or the pertinence of a distinction between feminine and masculine writing. It will usually be said, thus disposing of sexual difference: either that all writing, to the extent that it materializes, is feminine; or, inversely—but it comes to the same thing—that the act of writing is equivalent to masculine masturbation (and so the woman who writes cuts herself out a paper penis); or that writing is bisexual, hence neuter, which again does away with differentiation. To admit that writing is precisely working (in) the in-between, inspecting the process of the same and of the other without which nothing can live, undoing the work of death—to admit this is first to want the two, as well as both, the ensemble of the one and the other, not fixed in sequences of struggle and expulsion or some other form of death but infinitely dynamized by an incessant process of exchange from one subject to another. A process of different subjects knowing one another and beginning one another anew only from the living boundaries of the other: a multiple and inexhaustible course with millions of encounters and transformations of the same into the other and into the in-between, from which woman takes her forms (and man, in his turn; but that's his other history).

In saying "bisexual, hence neuter," I am referring to the classic conception of bisexuality, which, squashed under the emblem of castration fear and along with the fantasy of a "total" being (though composed of two halves), would do away with the difference experienced as to operation incurring loss, as the mark of dreaded sectility.

To this self-effacing, merger-type bisexuality, which would conjure away castration (the writer who puts up his sign: "bisexual written here, come and see," when the odds are good that it's neither one nor the other), I oppose the *other bisexuality* on which every subject not enclosed in the false theater of phallocentric representationalism has founded his/her erotic universe. Bisexuality: that is, each one's location in self (*repérage en soi*) of the presence—variously manifest and insistent, according to each person, male or female—of both sexes, nonexclusion either of the difference or of one sex, and, from this "self-permission," multiplication of the effects of the inscription of desire, over all parts of my body and the other body.

Now it happens that at present, for historico-cultural reasons, it is women who are opening up to and benefiting from this vatic bisexuality which doesn't annul differences but stirs them up, pursues them, increases their number. In a certain way, "woman is bisexual"; man—it's a secret to no one—being poised to keep glorious phallic monosexuality in view. By virtue of affirming the primacy of the phallus and of bringing it into play, phallocratic ideology has claimed more than one victim. As a woman, I've been clouded over by the great shadow of the scepter and been told: idolize it, that which you cannot brandish. But at the same time, man has been handed that grotesque and scarcely enviable destiny (just imagine) of being reduced to a single idol with clay balls. And consumed, as Freud and his followers note, by a fear of being a woman! For, if psychoanalysis was constituted from woman, to repress femininity (and not so successful a repression at that—men have made it clear), its account of masculine sexuality is now hardly refutable; as with all the "human" sciences, it reproduces the masculine view, of which it is one of the effects.

Here we encounter the inevitable man-with-rock, standing erect in his old Freudian realm, in the way that, to take the figure back to the point where linguistics is conceptualizing it "anew," Lacan preserves it in the sanctuary of the phallos (φ) "sheltered" from *castration's lack!* Their "symbolic" exists, it holds power—we, the sowers of disorder, know it only too well. But we are in no way obliged to deposit our lives in their banks of lack, to consider the constitution of the subject in terms of a drama manglingly restaged, to reinstate again and again the religion of the father. Because we don't want that. We don't fawn around the supreme hole. We have no womanly reason to pledge allegiance to the negative. The feminine (as the poets suspected) affirms: ". . . And yes," says Molly, carrying *Ulysses* off beyond any book and toward the new writing; "I said yes, I will Yes."

The Dark Continent is neither dark nor unexplorable.—It is still unexplored only because we've been made to believe that it was too dark to be explorable. And because they want to make us believe that what interests us is the white continent, with its monuments to Lack. And we believed. They riveted us between two horrifying myths: between the Medusa and the abyss. That would be enough to set half the world laughing, except that it's still going on. For the phallologocentric sublation[5] is with us, and it's militant, regenerating the old patterns, anchored in the dogma of castration. They haven't changed a thing: they've theorized their desire for reality! Let the priests tremble, we're going to show them our sexts!

Too bad for them if they fall apart upon discovering that women aren't men, or that the mother doesn't have one. But isn't this fear convenient for them? Wouldn't the worst be, isn't the worst, in truth, that women aren't castrated, that they have only to stop listening to the Sirens (for the Sirens were men) for history to change its meaning? You only have to look at the Medusa straight on to see her. And she's not deadly. She's beautiful and she's laughing.

Men say that there are two unrepresentable things: death and the feminine sex. That's because they need femininity to be associated with death; it's the jitters that give them a hard-on! for themselves! They need to be afraid of us. Look at the trembling Perseuses moving backward toward us, clad in apotropes. What lovely backs! Not another minute to lose. Let's get out of here.

Let's hurry: the continent is not impenetrably dark. I've been there often. I was overjoyed one day to run into Jean Genet. It was in *Pompes funèbres.*[6] He had come there led by his Jean. There are some men (all too few) who aren't afraid of femininity.

Almost everything is yet to be written by women about femininity: about their sexuality, that is, its infinite and mobile complexity, about their eroticization, sudden turn-ons of a certain miniscule-immense area of their bodies; not about destiny, but about the adventure of such and such a drive, about trips, crossings, trudges, abrupt and gradual awakenings, discoveries of a zone at one time timorous and soon to be forthright. A woman's body, with its thousand and one thresholds of ardor—once, by smashing yokes and censors, she lets it articulate the profusion of meanings that run through it in every direction—will make the old single-grooved mother tongue reverberate with more than one language.

We've been turned away from our bodies, shamefully taught to ignore them, to strike them with that stupid sexual modesty; we've been made victims of the old fool's game: each one will love the other sex. I'll give you your body and you'll give me mine. But who are the men who give women the body that women blindly yield to them? Why so few texts? Because so few women have as yet won back their body. Women must write through their bodies, they must invent the impregnable language that will wreck partitions, classes, and rhetorics, regulations and codes, they must submerge, cut through, get beyond the ultimate reserve-discourse, including the one that laughs at the very idea of pronouncing the word "silence," the one that, aiming for the impossible, stops short before the word "impossible" and writes it as "the end."

Such is the strength of women that, sweeping away syntax, breaking that famous thread (just a tiny little thread, they say) which acts for men as a surrogate umbilical cord, assuring them—otherwise they couldn't come—that the old lady is always right behind them, watching them make phallus, women will go right up to the impossible.

When the "repressed" of their culture and their society returns, it's an explosive, *utterly* destructive, staggering return, with a force never yet unleashed and equal to the most forbidding of suppressions. For when the Phallic period comes to an end, women will have been either annihilated or borne up to the highest and most violent incandescence. Muffled throughout their history, they have lived in dreams, in bodies (though muted), in silences, in aphonic revolts.

And with such force in their fragility; a fragility, a vulnerability, equal to their incomparable intensity. Fortunately, they haven't sublimated; they've saved their skin, their energy. They haven't worked at liquidating the impasse of lives without futures. They have furiously inhabited these sumptuous bodies: admirable hysterics who made Freud succumb to many voluptuous moments impossible to confess, bombarding his Mosaic statue with their carnal and passionate body words, haunting him with their inaudible and thundering denunciations, dazzling, more than naked underneath the seven veils of modesty. Those who, with a single word of the body, have inscribed the vertiginous immensity of a history which is sprung like an arrow from the whole history of men and from biblico-capitalist society, are the women, the supplicants of yesterday, who come as forebears of the new women, after whom no intersubjective relation will ever be the same. You, Dora, you the indomitable, the poetic body, you are the true "mistress" of the Signifier. Before long your efficacity will be seen at work when your speech is no longer suppressed, its point turned in against your breast, but written out over against the other.

In body.—More so than men who are coaxed toward social success, toward sublimation, women are body. More body, hence more writing. For a long time it has been in body that women have responded to persecution, to the familial-conjugal enterprise of domestication, to the repeated attempts at castrating them. Those who have turned their tongues 10,000 times seven times before not speaking are either dead from it or more familiar with their tongues and their mouths than anyone else. Now, I-woman am going to blow up the Law: an explosion henceforth possible and ineluctable; let it be done, right now, *in* language.

Let us not be trapped by an analysis still encumbered with the old automatisms. It's not to be feared that language conceals an invincible adversary, because it's the language of men and their grammar. We mustn't leave them a single place that's any more theirs alone than we are.

If woman has always functioned "within" the discourse of man, a signifier that has always referred back to the opposite signifier which annihilates its specific energy and diminishes or stifles its very different sounds, it is time for her to dislocate this "within," to explode it, turn it around, and seize it; to make it hers, containing it, taking it in her own mouth, biting that tongue with her very own teeth to invent for herself a language to get inside of. And you'll see with what ease she will spring forth from that "within"—the "within" where once she so drowsily crouched—to overflow at the lips she will cover the foam.

Nor is the point to appropriate their instruments, their concepts, their places, or to begrudge them their position of mastery. Just because there's a risk of identification doesn't mean that we'll succumb. Let's leave it to the worriers, to masculine anxiety and its obsession with how to dominate the way things work—knowing "how it works" in order to "make it work." For us the point is not to take possession in order to internalize or manipulate, but rather to dash through and to "fly."[7]

Flying is woman's gesture—flying in language and making it fly. We have all learned the art of flying and its numerous techniques; for centuries we've been able to process anything only by flying; we've lived in flight, stealing away, finding, when desired, narrow passageways, hidden crossovers. It's no accident that *voler* has a double meaning, that it plays on each of them and thus throws off the agents of sense. It's no accident: women take after birds and robbers just as robbers take after women and birds. They (*illes*)[8] go by, fly the coop, take pleasure in jumbling the order of space, in disorienting it, in changing around the furniture, dislocating things and values, breaking them all up, emptying structures, and turning propriety upside down.

What woman hasn't flown/stolen? Who hasn't felt, dreamt, performed the gesture that jams sociality? Who hasn't crumbled, held up to ridicule, the bar of separation? Who hasn't inscribed with her body the differential, punctured the system of couples and opposition? Who, by some act of transgression, hasn't overthrown successiveness, connection, the wall of circumfusion?

A feminine text cannot fail to be more than subversive. It is volcanic; as it is written it brings about an upheaval of the old property crust, carrier of masculine investments; there's no other way. There's no room for her if she's not a he. If she's a her-she, it's in order to smash everything, to shatter the framework of institutions, to blow up the law, to break up the "truth" with laughter.

For once she blazes *her* trail in the symbolic, she cannot fail to make of it the chaosmos of the "personal"—in her pronouns, her nouns, and her clique of referents. And for good reason. There will have been the long history of gynocide. This is known by the colonized peoples of yesterday, the workers, the nations, the species off whose backs the history of men has made its gold; those who have known the ignominy of persecution derive from it an obstinate future desire for grandeur; those who are locked up know better than their jailers the taste of free air. Thanks to their history, women today know (how to do and want) what men will be able to conceive of only much later. I say woman overturns the "personal," for if, by means of laws, lies, blackmail, and marriage, her right to herself has been extorted at the same time as her name, she has been able, through the very movement of mortal alienation, to see more closely the inanity of "propriety," the reductive stinginess of the masculine-conjugal subjective economy, which she doubly resists. On the one hand she has constituted herself necessarily as that "person" capable of losing a part of herself without losing her integrity. But secretly, silently, deep down inside, she grows and multiplies, for, on the other hand, she knows far more about living and about the relation between the economy of the drives and the management of the ego than any man. Unlike man, who holds so dearly to his title and his titles, his pouches of value, his cap, crown, and everything connected with his head, woman couldn't care less about the fear of decapitation (or castration), adventuring, without the masculine temerity, into anonymity, which she can merge with, without annihilating herself: because she's a giver.

I shall have a great deal to say about the whole deceptive problematic of the gift. Woman is obviously not that woman Nietzsche dreamed of who gives only in order to.[9] Who could ever think of the gift as a gift-that-takes? Who else but man, precisely the one who would like to take everything?

If there is a "propriety of woman," it is paradoxically her capacity to depropriate unselfishly, body without end, without appendage, without principal "parts." If she is a whole, it's a whole composed of parts that are wholes, not simple partial objects but a moving, limitlessly changing ensemble, a cosmos tirelessly traversed by Eros, an immense astral space not organized around any one sun that's any more of a star than the others.

This doesn't mean that she's an undifferentiated magma, but that she doesn't lord it over her body or her desire. Though masculine sexuality gravitates around the penis, engendering that centralized body (in political anatomy) under the dictatorship of its parts, woman does not bring about the same regionalization which serves the couple head/genitals and which is inscribed only within boundaries. Her libido is cosmic, just as her unconscious is worldwide. Her writing can only keep going, without ever inscribing or discerning contours, daring to make these vertiginous crossings of the other(s) ephemeral and passionate sojourns in him, her, them, whom she inhabits long enough to look at from the point closest to their unconscious from the moment they awaken, to love them at the point closest to their drives; and then further, impregnated through and through with these brief, identificatory embraces, she goes and passes into infinity. She alone dares and wishes to know from within, where she, the outcast, has never ceased to hear the resonance of fore-language. She lets the other language speak—the language of 1,000 tongues which knows neither enclosure nor death. To life she refuses nothing. Her language does not contain, it carries; it does not hold back, it makes possible. When id is ambiguously uttered—the wonder of being several—she doesn't defend herself against these unknown women whom she's surprised at becoming, but derives pleasure from this gift of alterability. I am spacious, singing flesh, on which is grafted no one knows which I, more or less human, but alive because of transformation.

Write! and your self-seeking text will know itself better than flesh and blood, rising, insurrectionary dough kneading itself, with sonorous, perfumed ingredients, a lively combination of flying colors, leaves, and rivers plunging into the sea we feed. "Ah, there's her sea," he will say as he holds out to me a basin full of water from the little phallic mother from whom he's inseparable. But look, our seas are what we make of them, full of fish or not, opaque or transparent, red or black, high or smooth, narrow or bankless; and we are ourselves sea, sand, coral, seaweed, beaches, tides, swimmers, children, waves . . . More or less wavily sea, earth, sky—what matter would rebuff us? We know how to speak them all.

Heterogeneous, yes. For her joyous benefits she is erogenous; she is the erotogeneity of the heterogeneous: airborne swimmer, in flight, she does not cling to herself; she is dispersible, prodigious, stunning, desirous and capable of others, of the other woman that she will be, of the other woman she isn't, of him, of you.

Woman be unafraid of any other place, of any same, or any other. My eyes, my tongue, my ears, my nose, my skin, my mouth, my body-for-(the)-other—not that I long for it in order to fill up a hole, to provide against some defect of mine, or because, as fate would have it, I'm spurred on by feminine "jealousy"; not because I've been dragged into the whole chain of substitutions that brings that which is substituted back to its ultimate object. That sort of thing you would expect to come straight out of "Tom Thumb," out of the *Penisneid* whispered to us by old grandmother ogresses, servants to their father-sons. If they believe, in order to muster up some self-importance, if they really need to believe that we're dying of desire, that we are this hole fringed with desire for their penis—that's their immemorial business. Undeniably (we verify it at our own expense—but also to our amusement), it's their business to let us know they're getting a hard-on, so that we'll assure them (we the maternal mistresses of their little pocket signifiers) that they still can, that it's still there—that men structure themselves only by being fitted with a feather. In the child it's not the penis that the woman desires, it's not that famous bit of skin around which every man gravitates. Pregnancy cannot be traced back, except within the historical limits of the ancients, to some form of fate, to those mechanical substitutions brought about by the unconscious of some eternal "jealous woman"; not to penis envies; and not to narcissism or to some sort of homosexuality linked to the ever-present mother! Begetting a child doesn't mean that the woman or the man must fall ineluctably into patterns or must recharge the circuit of reproduction. If there's a risk there's not an inevitable trap: may women be spared the pressure, under the guise of consciousness-raising, of a supplement of interdictions. Either you want a kid or you don't—*that's your business*. Let nobody threaten you; in satisfying your desire, let not the fear of becoming the accomplice to a sociality succeed the old-time fear of being "taken." And man, are you still going to bank on everyone's blindness and passivity, afraid lest the child make a father and, consequently, that in having a kid the woman land herself more than one bad deal by engendering all at once child—mother—father—family? No; it's up to you to break the old circuits. It will be up to man and woman to render obsolete the former relationship and all its consequences, to consider the launching of a brand-new subject, alive, with defamilialization. Let us dematerpaternalize rather than deny woman, in an effort to avoid the cooptation of procreation, a thrilling era of the body. Let us defetishize. Let's get away from the dialectic which has it that the only good father is a dead one, or that the child is the death of his parents. The child is the other, but the other without violence, bypassing loss, struggle. We're fed up with the reuniting of bonds forever to be severed, with the litany of castration that's handed down and genealogized. We won't advance backward anymore; we're not going to repress something so simple as the desire for life. Oral drive, anal drive, vocal drive—all these drives are our strengths, and among them is the gestation drive—just like the desire to write: a desire to live self from within, a desire for the swollen belly, for language, for blood. We are not going to refuse, if it should happen to strike our fancy, the unsurpassed pleasures of pregnancy which have actually been always exaggerated or conjured away—or cursed—in the classic texts. For if there's one thing that's been repressed, here's just the place to find it: in the taboo of the pregnant woman. This says a lot about the power she seems invested with at the time, because it has always been suspected, that, when pregnant, the woman not only doubles her market value, but—what's more important—takes on intrinsic value as a woman in her own eyes and, undeniably, acquires body and sex.

There are thousands of ways of living one's pregnancy; to have or not to have with that still invisible other a relationship of another intensity. And if you don't have that particular yearning, it doesn't mean that you're in any way lacking. Each body distributes in its own special way, without model or norm, the non-finite and changing totality of its desires. Decide for yourself on your position in the arena of contradictions, where pleasure and reality embrace. Bring the other to life. Women know how to live detachment; giving birth is neither losing nor increasing. It's adding to life an other. Am I dreaming? Am I misrecognizing? You, the defenders of "theory," the sacrosanct yes-men of Concept, enthroners of the phallus (but not of the penis):

Once more you'll say that all this smacks of "idealism," or what's worse, you'll splutter that I'm a "mystic."

And what about the libido? Haven't I read the "Signification of the Phallus"? And what about separation, what about that bit of self for which, to be born, you undergo an ablation—an ablation, so they say, to be forever commemorated by your desire?

Besides, isn't it evident that the penis gets around in my texts, that I give it a place and appeal? Of course I do. I want all. I want all of me with all of him. Why should I deprive myself of a part of us? I want all of us. Woman of course has a desire for a "loving desire" and not a jealous one. But not because she is gelded; not because she's deprived and needs to be filled out, like some wounded person who wants to console herself or seek vengeance. I don't want a penis to decorate my body with. But I do desire the other for the other, whole and entire, male or female; because living means wanting everything that is, everything that lives, and wanting it alive. Castration? Let others toy with it. What's a desire originating from a lack? A pretty meager desire.

The woman who still allows herself to be threatened by the big dick, who's still impressed by the commotion of the phallic stance, who still leads a loyal master to the beat of the drum: that's the woman of yesterday. They still exist, easy and numerous victims of the oldest of farces: either they're cast in the original silent versions in which, as titanesses lying under the mountains they make with their quivering, they never see erected that theoretic monument to the golden phallus looming, in the old manner, over their bodies. Or, coming today out of their *infans* period and into the second, "enlightened" version of their virtuous debasement, they see themselves suddenly assaulted by the builders of the analytic empire and, as soon as they've begun to formulate the new desire, naked, nameless, so happy at making an appearance, they're taken in their bath by the new old men, and then, whoops! Luring them with flashy signifiers, the demon of interpretation—oblique, decked out in modernity—sells them the same old handcuffs, baubles, and chains. Which castration do you prefer? Whose degrading do you like better, the father's or the mother's? Oh, what pwetty eyes, you pwetty little girl. Here, buy my glasses and you'll see the Truth-Me-Myself tell you everything you should know. Put them on your nose and take a fetishist's look (you are me, the other analyst—that's what I'm telling you) at your body and the body of the other. You see? No? Wait, you'll have everything explained to you, and you'll know at last which sort of neurosis you're related to. Hold still, we're going to do your portrait, so that you can begin looking like it right away.

Yes, the naives to the first and second degree are still legion. If the New Women, arriving now, dare to create outside the theoretical, they're called in by the cops of the signifier, fingerprinted, remonstrated, and brought into the line of order that they are supposed to know; assigned by force of trickery to a precise place in the chain that's always formed for the benefit of a privileged signifier. We are pieced back to the string which leads back, if not to the Name-of-the-Father, then, for a new twist, to the place of the phallic-mother.

Beware, my friend, of the signifier that would take you back to the authority of a signified! Beware of diagnoses that would reduce your generative powers. "Common" nouns are also proper nouns that disparage your singularity by classifying it into species. Break out of the circles; don't remain within the psychoanalytic closure. Take a look around, then cut through!

And if we are legion, it's because the war of liberation has only made as yet a tiny breakthrough. But women are thronging to it. I've seen them, those who will be neither dupe nor domestic, those who will not fear the risk of being a woman; will not fear any risk, any desire, any space still unexplored in themselves, among themselves and others or anywhere else. They do not fetishize, they do not deny, they do not hate. They observe, they approach, they try to see the other woman, the child, the lover—not to strengthen their own narcissism or verify the solidity or weakness of the master, but to make love better, to invent.

Other love.—In the beginning are our differences. The new love dares for the other, wants the other, makes dizzying, precipitous flights between knowledge and invention. The woman arriving over and over again does not stand still; she's everywhere, she exchanges, she is the desire-that-gives. (Not enclosed in the paradox of the gift that takes nor under the illusion of unitary fusion. We're past that.) She comes in, comes-in-between herself me and you, between the other me where one is always infinitely more than one and more than me, without the fear of ever reaching a limit; she thrills in our becoming. And we'll keep on becoming! She cuts through defensive loves, motherages, and devourations: beyond selfish narcissism, in the moving, open, transitional space, she runs her risks. Beyond the struggle-to-the-death that's been removed to the bed, beyond the love-battle that claims to represent exchange, she scorns at an Eros dynamic that would be fed by hatred. Hatred: a heritage, again, a reminder, a duping subservience to the phallus. To love, to watch-think-seek the other in the other, to despecularize, to unhoard. Does this seem difficult? It's not impossible, and this is what nourishes life—a love that has no commerce with the apprehensive desire that provides against the lack and stultifies the strange; a love that rejoices in the exchange that multiplies. Wherever history still unfolds as the history of death, she does not tread. Opposition, hierarchizing exchange, the struggle for mastery which can end only in at least one death (one master—one slave, or two nonmasters ≠ two dead)—all that comes from a period in time governed by phallocentric values. The fact that this period extends into the present doesn't prevent woman from starting the history of life somewhere else. Elsewhere, she gives. She doesn't "know" what she's giving, she doesn't measure it; she gives, though, neither a counterfeit impression nor something she hasn't got. She gives more, with no assurance that she'll get back even some unexpected profit from what she puts out. She gives that there may be life, thought, transformation. This is an "economy" that can no longer be put in economic terms. Wherever she loves, all the old concepts of management are left behind. At the end of a more or less conscious computation, she finds not her sum but her differences. I am for you what you want me to be at the moment you look at me in a way you've never seen me before: at every instant. When I write, it's everything that we don't know we can be that is written out of me, without exclusions, without stipulation, and everything we will be calls us to the unflagging, intoxicating, unappeasable search for love. In one another we will never be lacking.

NOTES

1. Men still have everything to say about their sexuality, and everything to write. For what they have said so far, for the most part, stems from the opposition activity/passivity from the power relation between a fantasized obligatory virility meant to invade, to colonize, and the consequential phantasm of woman as a "dark continent" to penetrate and to "pacify." (We know what "pacify" means in terms of scotomizing the other and misrecognizing the self.) Conquering her, they've made haste to depart from her borders, to get out of sight, out of body. The way man has of getting out of himself and into her whom he takes not for the other but for his own, deprives him, he knows, of his own bodily territory. One can understand how man, confusing himself with his penis and rushing in for the attack, might feel resentment and fear of being "taken" by the woman, of being lost in her, absorbed or alone.
2. I am speaking here only of the place "reserved" for women by the Western world.
3. Which works, then, might be called feminine? I'll just point out some examples: one would have to give them full readings to bring out what is pervasively feminine in their significance. Which I shall do elsewhere. In France (have you noted our infinite poverty in this field?—the Anglo-Saxon countries have shown resources of distinctly greater consequence), leafing through what's come out of the twentieth century—and it's not much—the only inscriptions of femininity that I have seen were by Colette, Marguerite Duras, . . . and Jean Genet.
4. *Dé-pense*, a neologism formed on the verb *penser*, hence "unthinks," but also "spends" (from *dépenser*).—Tr.
5. Standard English term for the Hegelian *Aufhebung*, the French *la relève*.
6. Jean Genet, *Pompes funèbres* (Paris, 1948), p. 185 [privately published].
7. Also, "to steal." Both meanings of the verb *voler* are played on, as the text itself explains in the following paragraph.—Tr.
8. *Illes* is a fusion of the masculine pronoun *ils*, which refers back to birds and robbers, with the feminine pronoun *elles*, which refers to women.—Tr.
9. Reread Derrida's text, "Le style de la femme," in *Nietzsche aujourd'hui* (Union Générale d'Editions, Coll. 10/18), where the philosopher can be seen operating an *Aufhebung* of all philosophy in its systematic reducing of woman to the place of seduction: she appears as the one who is taken for; the bait in person, all veils unfurled, the one who doesn't give but who gives only in order to (take).

CASTRATION OR DECAPITATION?

On sexual difference: Let's start with these small points. One day Zeus and Hera, the ultimate couple, in the course of one of their intermittent and thoroughgoing disagreements—which today would be of the greatest interest to psychoanalysts—called on Tiresias to arbitrate. Tiresias, the blind seer who had enjoyed the uncommon fortune of having lived seven years as a woman and seven years as a man.

He was gifted with second sight. Second sight in a sense other than we might usually understand it: it isn't simply that as a prophet he could see into the future. He could also see it from both sides: from the side of the male and from the side of the female.

The subject of the disagreement was the question of sexual pleasure: "Of man and woman, who enjoys the greater pleasure?" Obviously neither Zeus nor Hera could answer this without giving their *own* answer, which they saw would be inadequate, since the ancients made fewer assumptions than we do about the possibility of making such identifications. So it came about that Tiresias was sought, as the only person who could know "which of the two." And Tiresias answered: "If sexual pleasure could be divided up into ten parts, nine of them would be the woman's." Nine. It's no coincidence that Tiresias makes another appearance in none other than the oedipal scene. It was Tiresias who, at Oedipus's command, reminded Oedipus that blindness was his master, and Tiresias who, so they say, "made the scales fall from his eyes" and showed Oedipus who he really was. We should note that these things are all linked together and bear some relation to the question "What is woman for man?"

It reminds me of a little Chinese story. Every detail of this story counts. I've borrowed it from a very serious text, Sun Tse's manual of strategy, which is a kind of handbook for the warrior. This is the anecdote. The king commanded General Sun Tse: "You who are a great strategist and claim to be able to train anybody in the arts of war. . . . take my wives (all one hundred and eighty of them!) and make soldiers out of them." We don't know why the king conceived this desire—it's the one thing we don't know. . . . it remains precisely "un(re)countable" or unaccountable in the story. But it is a king's wish, after all.

So Sun Tse had the women arranged in two rows, each headed by one of the two favorite wives, and then taught them the language of the drumbeat. It was very simple: two beats—right, three beats—left, four beats—about turn or backward march. But instead of learning the code very quickly, the ladies started laughing and chattering and paying no attention to the lesson, and Sun Tse, the master, repeated the lesson several times over. But the more he spoke, the more the women fell about laughing, upon which Sun Tse put his code to the test. It is said in this code that should women fall about laughing instead of becoming soldiers, their actions might be deemed mutinous, and the code has ordained that cases of mutiny call for the death penalty. So the women were condemned to death. This bothered the king somewhat: a hundred and eighty wives are a lot to lose! He didn't want his wives put to death. But Sun Tse replied that since he was put in charge of making soldiers out of the women, he would carry out the order: Sun Tse was a man of absolute principle. And in any case there's an order even more "royal" than that of the king himself: the Absolute Law. . . . One does not go back on an order. He therefore acted according to the code and with his saber beheaded the two women commanders. They were replaced and the exercise started again, and as if they had never done anything except practice the art of war, the women turned right, left, and about in silence and with never a single mistake.

It's hard to imagine a more perfect example of a particular relationship between two economies: a masculine economy and a feminine economy, in which the masculine is governed by a rule that keeps time with two beats, three beats, four beats, with pipe and drum, exactly as it should be. An order that works by inculcation, by education: it's always a question of education. An education that consists of trying to make a soldier of the feminine by force, the force history keeps reserved for women, the "capital" force that is effectively decapitation. Women have no choice other than to be decapitated, and in any case the moral is that if they don't actually lose their heads by the sword, *they only keep them on condition that they lose them*—lose them, that is, to complete silence, turned into automatons.

It's a question of submitting feminine disorder, its laughter, its inability to take the drumbeats seriously, to the threat of decapitation. If man operates under the threat of castration, if masculinity is culturally ordered by the castration complex, it might be said that the backlash, the return, on women of this castration anxiety is its displacement as decapitation, execution, of woman, as loss of her head.

We are led to pose the woman question to history in quite elementary forms like, "Where is she? Is there any such thing as woman?" At worst, many women wonder whether they even exist. They feel they don't exist and wonder if there has ever been a place for them. I am speaking of woman's place, *from* woman's place, if she takes (a) place.

In *La Jeune Née*[1] I made use of a story that seemed to me particularly expressive of woman's place: the story of Sleeping Beauty. Woman, if you look for her, has a strong chance of always being found in one position: in bed. In bed and asleep—"laid (out)." She is always to be found on or in a bed. Sleeping Beauty is lifted from her bed by a man because, as we all know, women don't wake up by themselves: man has to intervene, you understand. She is lifted up by the man who will lay her in her next bed so that she may be confined to bed ever after, just as the fairy tales say.

And so her trajectory is from bed to bed: one bed to another, where she can dream all the more. There are some extraordinary analyses by Kierkegaard on women's "existence"—or that part of it set aside for her by culture—in which he says he sees her as sleeper. She sleeps, he says, and first love dreams her and then she dreams of love. From dream to dream, and always in second position. In some stories, though, she can be found standing up, but not for long. Take Little Red Riding Hood as an example: it will not, I imagine, be lost on you that the "red riding hood" in question is a little clitoris. Little Red Riding Hood basically gets up to some mischief: she's the little female sex that tries to play a bit and sets out with her little pot of butter and her little jar of honey. What is interesting is that it's her mother who gives them to her and sends her on an excursion that's tempting precisely because it's forbidden: Little Red Riding Hood leaves one house, mommy's house, not to go out into the big wide world but to go from one house to another by the shortest route possible: to make haste, in other words, from the mother to the other. The other in this case is grandmother, whom we might imagine as taking the place of the "Great Mother," because there are great men but no great women: there are Grand-Mothers instead. And grandmothers are always wicked: she is the bad mother who always shuts the daughter in whenever the daughter might by chance want to live or take pleasure. So she'll always be carrying her little pot of butter and her little jar of honey to grandmother, who is there as jealousy . . . the jealousy of the woman who can't let her daughter go.

But in spite of all this Little Red Riding Hood makes her little detour, does what women should never do, travels through her own forest. She allows herself the forbidden . . . and pays dearly for it: she goes back to bed, in grandmother's stomach. The Wolf is grandmother, and all women recognize the Big Bad Wolf! We know that always lying in wait for us somewhere in some big bed is a Big Bad Wolf. The Big Bad Wolf represents, with his big teeth, his big eyes, and his grandmother's looks, the great Superego that threatens all the little female red riding hoods who try to go out and explore their forest without the psychoanalyst's permission. So, between two houses, between two beds, she is laid, ever caught in her chain of metaphors, metaphors that organize culture . . . ever her moon to the masculine sun, nature to culture, concavity to masculine convexity, matter to form, immobility/inertia to the march of progress, terrain trod by the masculine footstep, vessel. . . . While man is obviously the active, the upright, the productive . . . and besides, that's how it happens in History.

This opposition to woman cuts endlessly across all the oppositions that order

culture. It's the classic opposition, dualist and hierarchical. Man/Woman automatically means great/small, superior/inferior . . . means high or low, means Na-
ture/History, means transformation/inertia. In fact, every theory of culture,
every theory of society, the whole conglomeration of symbolic systems—everything, that is, that's spoken, everything that's organized as discourse, art, religion, the family, language, everything that seizes us, everything that acts on us—
it is all ordered around hierarchical oppositions that come back to the
man/woman opposition, an opposition that can only be sustained by means of a
difference posed by cultural discourse as "natural," the difference between activity and passivity. It always works this way, and the opposition is founded in the
couple. A couple posed in opposition, in tension, in conflict . . . a couple engaged
in a kind of war in which death is always at work—and I keep emphasizing the
importance of the opposition as *couple*, because all this isn't just about one word;
rather everything turns on the Word: everything is the Word and only the Word.
To be aware of the couple, that it's the couple that makes it all work, is also to
point to the fact that it's on the couple that we have to work if we are to decon-
struct and transform culture. The couple as terrain, as space of cultural struggle,
but also as terrain, as space demanding, insisting on, a complete transformation
in the relation of one to the other. And so work still has to be done on the couple . . . on the question, for example, of what a completely different couple relationship would be like, what a love that was more than merely a cover for, a
veil of, war would be like.

I said it turns on the Word: we must take culture at its word, as it takes us into
its Word, into its tongue. You'll understand why I think that no political reflection can dispense with reflection on language, with work on language. For as
soon as we exist, we are born into language and language speaks (to) us, dictates
its law, a law of death: it lays down its familial model, lays down its conjugal
model, and even at the moment of uttering a sentence, admitting a motion of
"being," a question of being, an ontology, we are already seized by a certain kind
of masculine desire, the desire that mobilizes philosophical discourse. As soon
as the question "What is it?" is posed, from the moment a question is put, as soon
as a reply is sought, *we are already caught up in masculine interrogation*. I say
"masculine interrogation": as we say so-and-so was interrogated by the police.
And this interrogation precisely involves the work of signification: "What is it?
Where is it?" A work of meaning, "This mean that," the predicative distribution
that always at the same time orders the constitution of meaning. And while
meaning is being constituted, it only gets constituted in a movement in which
one of the terms of the couple is destroyed in favor of the other.

"Look for the lady," as they say in the stories. . . . "Cherchez la femme"—we
always know that means: you'll find her in bed. Another question that's posed in

History, rather a strange question, a typical male question, is: "What do women want?" The Freudian question, of course. In his work on desire, Freud asks somewhere, or rather doesn't ask, leaves hanging in the air, the question "What do women want?" Let's talk a bit about this desire and about why/how the question "What do women want?" gets put, how it's both posed and left hanging in the air by philosophical discourse, by analytic discourse (analytic discourse being only one province of philosophical discourse), and how it is posed, let us say, by the Big Bad Wolf and the Grand-Mother.

"What does she want?" Little Red Riding Hood knew quite well what she wanted, but Freud's question is not what it seems: it's a rhetorical question. To pose the question "What do women want?" is to pose it already as answer, as from a man who isn't expecting any answer, because the answer is "She wants nothing." . . . "What does she want? . . . Nothing!" Nothing because she is passive. The only thing man can do is offer the question "What could she want, she who wants nothing?" Or in other words: "Without me, what could she want?"

Old Lacan takes up the slogan "What does she want?" when he says, "A woman cannot speak of her pleasure." Most interesting! It's all there, a woman *cannot*, is unable, hasn't the power. Not to mention "speaking": it's exactly this that she's forever deprived of. Unable to speak of pleasure = no pleasure, no desire: power, desire, speaking, pleasure, none of these is for woman. And as a quick reminder of how this works in theoretical discourse, one question: you are aware, of course, that for Freud/Lacan, woman is said to be "outside the Symbolic": outside the Symbolic, that is outside language, the place of the Law, excluded from any possible relationship with culture and the cultural order. And she is outside the Symbolic because she lacks any relation to the phallus, because she does not enjoy what orders masculinity—the castration complex. Woman does not have the advantage of the castration complex—it's reserved solely for the little boy. The phallus, in Lacanian parlance also called the "transcendental signifier," transcendental precisely as primary organizer of the structure of subjectivity, is what, for psychoanalysis, inscribes its effects, its effects of castration and resistance to castration and hence the very organization of language, as unconscious relations, and so it is the phallus that is said to constitute the a priori condition of all symbolic functioning. This has important implications as far as the body is concerned: the body is not sexed, does not recognize itself as, say, female or male without having gone through the castration complex.

What psychoanalysis points to as defining woman is that she lacks lack. She lacks lack? Curious to put it in so contradictory, so extremely paradoxical, a manner: she lacks lack. To say she lacks lack is also, after all, to say she doesn't miss lack . . . since she doesn't miss the lack of lack. Yes, they say, but the point is "she lacks The Lack," The Lack, lack of the Phallus. And so, supposedly, she misses the great lack, so that without man she would be indefinite, indefinable, non-sexed, unable to recognize herself: outside the Symbolic. But fortunately there is man: he who comes . . . Prince Charming. And it's man who teaches woman (because man is always the Master as well), who teaches her to be aware of lack, to be aware of absence, aware of death. It's man who will finally order woman, "set her to rights," by teaching her that without man she could "misrecognize." He will teach her the Law of the Father. Something of the order of: "Without me, without me—the Absolute—Father (the father is always that much more absolute the more he is improbable, dubious)—without me you wouldn't exist, I'll show you." Without him she'd remain in a state of distressing and distressed undifferentiation, unbordered, unorganized, "unpoliced" by the phallus . . . incoherent, chaotic, and embedded in the Imaginary in her ignorance of the Law of the Signifier. Without him she would in all probability not be contained by the threat of death, might even, perhaps, believe herself eternal, immortal. Without him she would be deprived of sexuality. And it might be said that man works very actively to produce "his woman." Take for example *Le Ravissement de Lol V. Stein*,[2] and you will witness the moment when man can finally say "his" woman, "my" woman. It is that moment when he has taught her to be aware of Death. So man *makes*, he makes (up) his woman, not without being himself seized up and drawn into the dialectical movement that this sort of thing sets in play. We might say that the Absolute Women, in culture, the woman who really represents femininity most effectively . . . who is closest to femininity as *prey* to masculinity, is actually the hysteric. . . . he makes her image for her!

The hysteric is a divine spirit that is always at the edge, the turning point, of making. She is one who does not make herself . . . she does not make herself but she does make the other. It is said that the hysteric "makes-believe" the father, plays the father, "makes-believe" the master. Plays, makes up, makes-believe: she makes-believe she is a woman, unmakes-believe too . . . plays at desire, plays the father . . . turns herself into him, makes him at the same time. Anyway, without the hysteric, there's no father . . . without the hysteric, no master, no analyst, no analysis! She's the *unorganizable* feminine construct, whose power of producing the other is a power that never returns to her. She is really a wellspring nourishing the other for eternity, yet not drawing back from the other . . . not recognizing herself in the images the other may or may not give her. She is given images that don't belong to her, and she forces herself, as we've all done, to resemble them.

And so in the face of this person who lacks lack, who does not miss lack of lack, we have the construct that is infinitely easier to analyze, to put in place—manhood, flaunting its metaphors like banners through history. You know those metaphors: they are most effective. It's always clearly a question of war, of battle. If there is no battle, it's replaced by the stake of battle: strategy. Man is strategy, is reckoning . . . "how to win" with the least possible loss, at the lowest possible cost. Throughout literature masculine figures all say the same thing: "I'm reckoning" what to do to win. Take Don Juan and you have the whole masculine economy getting together to "give women just what it takes to keep them in bed" then swiftly taking back the investment, then reinvesting, etc., so that nothing ever gets given, everything gets taken back, while in the process the greatest possible dividend of pleasure is taken. Consumption without payment, of course.

Let's take an example other than Don Juan, one clearly pushed to the point of paroxysm . . . Kafka. It was Kafka who said there was one struggle that terrified him beyond all others (he was an embattled man, but his battle was with death—in this sense he was a man greater than the rest): but in matters concerning women his was a struggle that terrified him (death did not). He said the struggle with women ended up in bed: this was his greatest fear. If you know a little about Kafka's life you should know that in his complete integrity, his absolute honesty, he attempted to live through this awful anguish in his relationships with women, in the struggle whose only outcome is bed, by working . . . finally to produce a neurosis of quite extraordinary beauty and terror consisting of a life-and-death relationship with a woman, but at the greatest possible distance. As close as possible and as distanced as possible. He would be betrothed, passionately desire a marriage which he feared above all else, and keep putting off the wedding day by endless unconscious maneuvers . . . by a pattern of repeated breakups that took him right to his deathbed, the very deathbed he's always wanted—a bed, that is, in which he could finally be alone with death. This work of keeping women at a distance while at the same time drawing them to him shows up strikingly in his diary, again because Kafka was honest enough to reveal everything, to say everything. He wrote in little columns, putting debits on the left and credits on the right . . . all the reasons I absolutely must marry, all the reasons I absolutely must not. This tension points to the spirit of male/female relationships in a way it isn't normally revealed, because what is normally revealed is actually a decoy . . . all those words about love, etc. All that is always just a cover for hatred nourished by the fear of death: woman, for man, is death. This is actually the castration complex at its most effective: giving is really dicing with death.

Giving: there you have a basic problem, which is that masculinity is always associated—in the unconscious, which is after all what makes the whole economy function—with debt. Freud, in deciphering the latent antagonisms between parents and children, shows very well the extent to which the family is founded, as far as the little boy is concerned, on a fearful debt. The child *owes* his parents his life and his problem is exactly to *repay* them: nothing is more dangerous than obligation. Obligation is submission to the enormous weight of the other's generosity, is being threatened by a blessing . . . and a blessing is always an evil when it comes from someone else. For the moment you receive something you are effectively "open" to the other, and if you are a man you have only one wish, and that is hastily to return the gift, to break the circuit of an exchange that could have no end . . . to be nobody's child, to owe no one a thing.

And so debt, what is always expressed in religions by laws like "a tooth for a tooth," "a gift for a gift," "an eye for an eye," is a system of absolute equivalence . . . of no inequality, for inequality is always interpreted by the masculine as a difference of strength, and thus as a threat. This economy is ruled by price: there's a price to pay, life is dear, the price of life has to be paid. And here lies a difficulty in connection with love, in that, at coming, love starts escaping the system of equivalence in all sorts of ways. It's very hard to give back something you can't pin down. What's so frightening in relations between male and female at the moment of coming (*au niveau de la jouissance*) is the possibility that there might be more on one side than on the other and the Symbolic finds it really tough to know who wins and who loses, who gives more in a relationship of this sort. The memory of debt and the fear of having to recognize one's debt rise up straightaway. But the refusal to know is nonetheless ambivalent in its implications, for not knowing is threatening while at the same time (and this is where the castration complex comes in) it reinforces the desire to know. So in the end woman, in man's desire, stands in the place of not knowing, the place of mystery. In this sense she is no good, but at the same time she is good because it's this mystery that leads man to keep overcoming, dominating, subduing, putting his manhood to the test, against the mystery he has to keep forcing back.

And so they want to keep woman in the place of mystery, consign her to mystery, as they say "keep her in her place," keep her at a distance: she's always not quite there . . . but no one knows exactly where she is. She is kept in place in a quite characteristic way—coming back to Oedipus, the place of one who is too often forgotten,[3] the place of the sphinx . . . she's kept in the place of what we might call the "watch-bitch" (*chienne chanteuse*). That is to say, she is outside the city, at the edge of the city—the city is man, ruled by masculine law—and there she is. In what way is she there? She is there not recognizing: the sphinx doesn't recognize herself, she it is who poses questions, just as it's man who holds the answer and furthermore, as you know, his answer is completely worthy of him: "Man," simple answer . . . but it says everything. "Watch-bitch," the sphinx was called: she's an animal and she sings out. She sings out because women do . . . they do utter a little, but they don't speak. Always keep in mind the distinction between speaking and talking. It is said, in philosophical texts, that women's weapon is the word, because they talk, talk endlessly, chatter, overflow with sound, mouthsound: but they don't actually *speak*, they have nothing to say. They always inhabit the place of silence, or at most make it echo with their singing. And neither is to their benefit, for they remain outside knowledge.

Silence: silence is the mark of hysteria. The great hysterics have lost speech, they are aphonic, and at times have lost more than speech: they are pushed to the point of choking, nothing gets through. They are decapitated, their tongues are cut off and what talks isn't heard because it's the body that talks, and man doesn't hear the body. In the end, the woman pushed to hysteria is the woman who disturbs and is nothing but disturbance. The master dotes on disturbance right from the moment he can subdue it and call it up at his command. Conversely the hysteric is the woman who cannot ask the master what he wants her to want: she wants nothing, truly she wants nothing. She wants . . . she wants to want. But what is it she wants to want? So she goes to school: she asks the master: "What should I want?" and "What do you want me to want, so that I might want it?" Which is what happens in analysis.

Let's imagine that all this functioned otherwise, that it could function otherwise. We'd first have to imagine resistance to masculine desire conducted by woman as hysteric, as distracted. We'd first have to imagine her ceasing to support with her body what I call the realm of the proper. The realm of the proper in the sense of the general cultural heterosocial establishment in which man's reign is held to be proper: proper may be the opposite of improper, and also of unfitting, just as black and white are opposites. Etymologically, the "proper" is "property," that which is not separable from me. Property is proximity, nearness: we must love our neighbors, those close to us, as ourselves: we must draw close to the other so that we may love him/her, because we love ourselves most of all. The realm of the proper, culture, functions by the appropriation articulated, set into play, by man's classic fear of seeing himself expropriated, seeing himself deprived . . . by his refusal to be deprived, in a state of separation, by his fear of losing the prerogative, fear whose response is all of History. Everything must return to the masculine. "Return": the economy is founded on a system of returns. If a man spends and is spent, it's on condition that his power returns. If a man should go out, if he should go out to the other, it's always done according to the Hegelian model, the model of the master-slave dialectic.

Woman would then have to start by resisting the movement of reappropriation that rules the whole economy, by being party no longer to the masculine return, but by proposing instead a desire no longer caught up in the death struggle, no longer implicated in the reservation and reckoning of the masculine economy, but breaking with the reckoning that "I never lose anything except to win a bit more" . . . so as to put aside all negativeness and bring out a positiveness which might be called the living other, the rescued other, the other unthreatened by destruction. Women have it in them to organize this regeneration, this vitalization of the other, of otherness in its entirety. They have it in them to affirm the difference, *their* difference, such that nothing can destroy that difference, rather that it might be affirmed, affirmed to the point of strangeness. So much so that when sexual difference, when the preservation or dissolution of sexual difference, is touched on, the whole problem of destroying the strange, destroying all the forms of racism, all through History, is also touched on. If women were to set themselves to transform History, it can safely be said that every aspect of History would be completely altered. Instead of being made by man, History's task would be to make women, to produce her. And it's at this point that work by women themselves on women might be brought into play, which would benefit not only women but all humanity.

But first she would have to *speak*, start speaking, stop saying that she has nothing to say! Stop learning in school that women are created to listen, to believe, to make no discoveries. Dare to speak her piece about giving, the possibility of a giving that doesn't take away, but *gives*. Speak of her pleasure and, God knows, she has something to say about that, so that she gets to unblock a sexuality that's just as much feminine as masculine, "de-phallocentralize" the body, relieve man of his phallus, return him to an erogenous field and a libido that isn't stupidly organized round that monument, but appears shifting, diffused, taking on all the others to oneself. Very difficult: first we have to get rid of the systems of censorship that bear down on every attempt to speak in the feminine. We have to get rid of and also explain what all knowledge brings with it as its burden of power: to show in what ways, culturally, knowledge is the accomplice of power: that whoever stands in the place of knowledge is always getting a dividend of power: show that all thinking until now has been ruled by this dividend, this surplus value of power that comes back to him who knows. Take the philosophers, take their position of mastery, and you'll see that there is not a soul who dares to make an advance in thought, into the as-yet unthought, without shuddering at the idea that he is under the surveillance of the ancestors, the grandfathers, the tyrants of the concept, without thinking that there behind your back is always the famous Name-of-the-Father, who knows whether or not you're writing whatever it is you have to write without any spelling mistakes.

Now, I think that what women will have to do and what they will do, right from the moment they venture to speak what they have to say, will of necessity bring about a shift in metalanguage. And I think we're completely crushed, especially in places like universities, by the highly repressive operations of metalanguage, the operations, that is, of the commentary on the commentary, the code, the operation that sees to it that the moment women open their mouths—women more often than men—they are immediately asked in whose name and from what theoretical standpoint they are speaking, who is their master and where they are coming from: they have, in short, to salute . . . and show their identity papers. There's work to be done against *class*, against categorization, against classification—classes. "Doing classes" in France means doing military service. There's work to be done against military service, against all schools, against the pervasive masculine urge to judge, diagnose, digest, name . . . not so much in the sense of the loving precision of poetic naming as in that of the repressive censorship of philosophical nomination/conceptualization.

Women who write have for the most part until now considered themselves to be writing not as women but as writers. Such women may declare that sexual difference means nothing, that there's no attributable difference between masculine and feminine writing. . . . What does it mean to "take no position"? When someone says "I'm not political" we all know what that means! It's just another way of saying: "My politics are someone else's!" And it's exactly the case with writing! Most women are like this: they do someone else's—man's—writing, and in their innocence sustain it and give it voice, and end up producing writing that's in effect masculine. Great care must be taken in working on feminine writing not to get trapped by names: to be signed with a woman's name doesn't necessarily make a piece of writing feminine. It could quite well be masculine writing, and conversely, the fact that a piece of writing is signed with a man's name does not in itself exclude femininity. It's rare but you can sometimes find femininity in writings signed by men: it does happen.

Which texts appear to be woman-texts and are recognized as such today, what can this mean, how might they be read?[4] In my opinion, the writing being done now that I see emerging around me won't only be of the kinds that exist in print today, though they will always be with us, but will be something else as well. In particular we ought to be prepared for what I call the "affirmation of the difference," not a kind of wake about the corpse of the mummified woman, nor a fantasy of woman's decapitation, but something different: a step forward, an adventure, an exploration of woman's powers: of her power, her potency, her everdreaded strength, of the regions of femininity. Things are starting to be written, things that will constitute a feminine Imaginary, the site, that is, of identifications of an ego no longer given over to an image defined by the masculine ("like the woman I love, I mean a dead woman"), but rather inventing forms for women on the march, or as I prefer to fantasize, "in flight," so that instead of lying down, women will go forward by leaps in search of themselves.

There is work to be done on female sexual pleasure and on the production of an unconscious that would no longer be the classic unconscious. The unconscious is always cultural and when it talks it tells you your old stories, it tells you the old stories you've heard before because it consists of the repressed of culture. But it's also always shaped by the forceful return of a libido that doesn't give up that easily, and also by what is strange, what is outside culture, by a language which is a savage tongue that can make itself understood quite well. This is why, I think, *political* and not just literary work is started as soon as writing gets done by women that goes beyond the bounds of censorship, reading, the gaze, the masculine command, in that cheeky risk taking women can get into when they set out into the unknown to look for themselves.

This is how I would define a feminine textual body: as a *female libidinal economy*, a regime, energies, a system of spending not necessarily carved out by culture. A feminine textual body is recognized by the fact that it is always endless, without ending: there's no closure, it doesn't stop, and it's this that very often makes the feminine text difficult to read. For we've learned to read books that basically pose the word "end." But this one doesn't finish, a feminine text goes on and on and at a certain amount the volume comes to an end but the writing continues and for the reader this means being thrust into the void. These are texts that work on the beginning but not on the origin. The origin is a masculine myth: I always want to know where I come from. The question "Where do children come from?" is basically a masculine, much more than a feminine, question. The quest for origins, illustrated by Oedipus, doesn't haunt a feminine unconscious. Rather it's the beginning, or beginnings, the manner of beginning, not promptly with the phallus in order to close with the phallus, but starting on all sides at once, that makes a feminine writing. A feminine text starts on all sides at once, starts twenty times, thirty times, over.

The question a woman's text asks is the question of giving—"What does this writing give?" "How does it give?" And talking about nonorigin and beginnings, you might say it "gives a send-off" (*donne le départ*). Let's take the expression "giving a send-off" in a metaphysical sense: giving a send-off is generally giving the *signal* to depart. I think it's more than giving the departure signal, it's really giving, making a *gift* of, departure, allowing departure, allowing breaks, "parts," partings, separations . . . from this we break with the return-to-self, with the specular relations ruling the coherence, the identification, of the individual. When a woman writes in nonrepression she passes on her others, her abundance of non-ego/s in a way that destroys the form of the family structure, so that it is defamilialized, can no longer be thought in terms of the attributions of roles within a social cell: what takes place is an endless circulation of desire from one body to another, above and across sexual difference, outside those relations of power and regeneration constituted by the family. I believe regeneration leaps, age leaps, time leaps. . . . A woman-text gets across a detachment, a kind of disengagement, not the detachment that is immediately taken back, but a real capacity to lose hold and let go. This takes the metaphorical form of wandering, excess, risk of the unreckonable: no reckoning, a feminine text can't be pre-dicted, isn't predictable, isn't knowable and is therefore very disturbing. It can't be anticipated, and I believe femininity is written outside anticipation: it really is the text of the unforeseeable.

Let's look not at syntax but at fantasy, at the unconscious: all the feminine texts I've read are very close to the voice, very close to the flesh of language, much more so than masculine texts . . . perhaps because there's something in them that's freely given, perhaps because they don't rush into meaning, but are straightway at the threshold of feeling. There's *tactility* in the feminine text, there's touch, and this touch passes through the ear. Writing in the feminine is passing on what is cut out by the Symbolic, the voice of the mother, passing on what is most archaic. The most archaic force that touches a body is one that en-ters by the ear and reaches the most intimate point. This innermost touch always echoes in a woman-text. So the movement, the movement of the text, doesn't trace a straight line. I see it as an outpouring . . . which can appear in primitive or elementary texts as a fantasy of blood, of menstrual flow, etc., but which I pre-fer to see as vomiting, as "throwing up," "disgorging." And I'd link this with a ba-sic structure of property relations defined by mourning.

Man cannot live without resigning himself to loss. He has to mourn. It's his way of withstanding castration. He goes through castration, but is, and by subli-mation incorporates the lost object. Mourning, resigning oneself to loss, means not losing. When you've lost something and the loss is a dangerous one, you refuse to admit that something of your self might be lost in the lost object. So you "mourn," you make haste to recover the investment made in the lost object. But I believe women *do not mourn*, and this is where their pain lies! When you've mourned, it's all over after a year, there's no more suffering. Woman, though, does not mourn, does not resign herself to loss. She basically *takes up the challenge of loss* in order to go on living: she lives it, gives it life, is capable of unsparing loss. She does not hold onto loss, she loses without holding onto loss. This makes her writing a body that overflows, disgorges, vomiting as op-posed to masculine incorporation. . . . She loses, and doubtless it would be to the death were it not for the intervention of those basic movements of a feminine unconscious (this is how I would define *feminine sublimation*) which provide the capacity of passing above it all by means of a form of oblivion which is not the oblivion of burial or interment but the oblivion of *acceptance*. This is taking loss, seizing it, living it. Leaping. This goes with not withholding: she does not with-hold. She does not withhold, hence the impression of constant return evoked by this lack of withholding. It's like a kind of open memory that ceaselessly makes way. And in the end, she will write this not-withholding, this not-writing: she writes of not-writing, not-happening. . . . She crosses limits: she is neither outside nor in, whereas the masculine would try to "bring the outside in, if possible."[5]

And finally this open and bewildering prospect goes hand in hand with a certain kind of laughter. Culturally speaking, women have wept a great deal, but once the tears are shed, there will be endless laughter instead. Laughter that breaks out, overflows, a humor no one would expect to find in women—which is nonetheless surely their greatest strength because it's a humor that sees man much further away than he has ever been seen. Laughter that shakes the last chapter of my text *LA*,[6] "she who laughs last." And her first laugh is at herself.

NOTES

This article first appeared as "Le Sexe ou la tête?" in *Les Cahiers du GRIF*, no. 13 (1976), pp. 5–15. The text was transcribed from a conversation between Hélène Cixous and the editors of *Les Cahiers du GRIF* which took place in Brussels during 1975. The present translation follows the published transcript with two exceptions (signaled in nn. 4 and 5) and is published with the permission of Hélène Cixous. The approach and arguments are developed in Cixous's more recent work. See, e.g., *Vivre l'orange* (Paris: Editions des femmes, 1979), written in French and English, and *Illa* (Paris: Editions des femmes, 1980). Thanks are due to to Elaine Marks for suggesting this translation of the title, to Keith Cohen for advice on specific points of translation, and to Chris Holmlund for bibliographical assistance.

1. Hélène Cixous and Catherine Clément, *La Jeune Née* (Paris: 10/18, 1975) (translator's note).

2. Marguerite Duras, *Le Ravissement de Lol V. Stein* (Paris: Gallimard, 1964). There are two English translations of this work: *The Ravishing of Lol V. Stein*, trans. Richard Seaver (New York: Grove Press, 1966), and *The Rapture of Lol V. Stein*, trans. Eileen Ellenbogen (London: Hamish Hamilton, 1967) (translator's note).

3. "La place de celle qu'on oublie en française trop souvent parce qu'on dit 'sphinx' au lieu de 'sphinge' ": That is, the French form of the word would suggest that the sphinx is male, whereas the sphinx of the oedipal myth is in fact female (translator's note).

4. There follows in the original a passage in which several categories of women's writing existing at the time (1975) are listed and discussed. These include: " 'the little girl's story,' where the little girl is getting even for a bad childhood," "texts of a return to a woman's own body," and texts which were a critical success, "ones about madwomen, deranged, sick women." The passage is omitted here, at the author's request, on the grounds that such a categorization is outdated, and that the situation with regard to women's writing is very much different now than it was five or six years ago (translator's note).

5. The following passage, deleted from the main body of the text, is regarded by the author as expressing a position tangential to the central interest of her work, which has to do with homosexuality: "And it's this being 'neither out nor in,' being 'beyond the outside/inside opposition' that permits the play of 'bisexuality.' Female sexuality is always at some point bisexual. Bisexual doesn't mean, as many people think, that she

can make love with both a man and a woman, it doesn't mean she has two partners, even if it can at times mean this. Bisexuality on an unconscious level is the possibility of extending into the other, of being in such a relation with the other that *I* move into the other without destroying the other: that I will look for the other where s/he is without trying to bring everything back to myself" (translator's note).
6. Hélène Cixous, *LA* (Paris: Gallimard, 1976) (translator's note).

ROOTPRINTS

THE HEART IS THE HUMAN SEX

When I speak of the human, it is perhaps also my way of being always traversed by the mystery of sexual difference. By the sort of double listening that I have. I am always trying to perceive, to receive, excitations, vibrations, signs coming from sexed, marked, different places; and then, in a certain place—barely a point, a full stop or a semicolon—the difference gives way to (but it is rather that the two great currents mix, flow into each other, so as only to be) what awaits us all: the human. This is how I have come to distinguish 'the sex' and 'the heart', saying that what the sexes have in common is the heart. There is a common speech, there is a common discourse, there is a universe of emotion that is totally interchangeable and that goes through the organ of the heart. The heart, the most mysterious organ there is, indeed because it is the same for the two sexes. As if the heart were the sex common to the two sexes. The human sex. . . .

COPYING REALITY

H.C.: By copying reality: living, non-repressed reality. If one could x-ray-photo-eco-graph a time, an encounter between two people of whatever sex they might be, by some extraordinary means; and if one could conserve the radiation of this encounter in a transparent sphere, and then listen to what is produced in addition to the exchange identifiable in the dialogue—this is what writing tries to do: to keep the record of these invisible events—one would hear the rumour of a great number of messages that are expressed in other ways. The glances, the tension of the body, the continuities, the discontinuities, this vast material which at times carries signs that contradict the message contained in the dialogue properly speaking. It is the art of writing or rather the art of theatre to know how to make this appear, at sentence-corners, with silences, with mute words; all that will not have been pronounced but will have been expressed with means other than speech—and that can then be taken up in the web of writing.

> *Ancient voice, voice come from elsewhere (very rare voices).*
> *Enemies of the voice: the false voices, borrowed voices, topical voices.*

Telephone, for example: we will never again be able to imagine love without the telephone. What did we do 'before' to make the most exquisite, the most intimate, the most delicate love, the most delicately loving? Love always needs telephones: this passage of the most naked voice, the most real and sublime voice directly to the ear of the heart, without transition, the voice never dares to be so naked as on the telephone. What I cannot say to you in the full light of presence I can say to you in the common night of the telephone.

What do I say to you on the telephone? I give you the music, I make you hear the originary song. Love loves to return, to bring back to the origin, to begin loving from the first instant, love wants to love everything, wants to love the other from the maternal womb.

Telephone | is the far near
*   it's the outsideinside*
= relationship that a | pregnant (mother) woman has
*   with her child*
* | mother has with the uterine child*
Cannot be closer, cannot be farther.
*   In a certain sense this is the definition of the mother–child relationship, above all mother–daughter: one cannot imagine closer to farther (more similar to more strange).*

In the person, the voice is what finds its source at the most ancient layer.

On the telephone—of love, it is the root itself that speaks.

On the telephone I hear your breath,—all your breaths that sigh between the words and around the words. Without the telephone, no breath.

On the telephone, you breathe me. Friends speak to each other on the telephone. The far in the near. The outside in the inside. The telephone is the imitation of the loving aspiration to be the one in the other. This is why we love the telephone cord so much: it is our umbilical cord. It is our windpipe.

Souls make love by the narrow interior canals, by throats, by arteries.

The voices that touch us most strongly are the voices that come still naked, voices from before the door of Paradise, from the time when we knew neither shame nor fear. The telephone undresses. Thanks to the Telephone—we call ourselves, we call each other, without violence. From very far, we launch the most restrained, the most murmured call. . . .

. . . [T]he word 'bisexual' does not belong to my universe of writing, I believe, but it comes from a language of the time. It was a time when there were reactions to the existence of a women's movement or of feminist demonstrations in practically all places of discourse. There was for example a special issue of the journal *Psychanalyse* on bisexuality. Women questioned themselves or women questioned others about the existence or the value of what is called bisexuality. There was also the concept of androgyny which was in circulation. So these words come up in a text that belongs to this field of theoretical density rather than to writing. If this term, which is so dated thus so obsolete, had appeared in the field of writing, I would have made fun of it I would have played it: I would have turned it in all directions, I would have shown its connotation, its topical weight, thus its already outdated side. But nonetheless, if it came up, it is indeed that at the time—because it is really the past, for me at least—I had to deal with very violent manifestations and effects of sexual opposition, to which, by the way, all of Derrida's texts were responding, in undoing the opposition.

> *Bi: two—only??*
> *Why not all the twos* [**tous** les deux]
> *and the between/s*

As for *Neutre*, as for the question of the neuter that is to say *neuter*: neither the one nor the other, you did well to suggest that obviously I do not want to keep it in a usage that would be marked by the negative and thus the exclusion of reality—neither this nor that, then what? In a certain sense, I do not like this word. It is rich in meaning possibilities, that is why I made use of it but I could not content myself with it. In the text, which I have very largely forgotten, I remember that one of the themes I tried to treat was the difficulty of defining human 'nature'. In our uneven life of human beings, one of the first questions that comes into conflict with our destiny is: to what extent can one call human nature human? What is legitimately to be called 'human' in the fields of ethics, biology, law, etc. . . . . In *Neutre*, the questioning was engendered by anomaly. Take the example of chromosomal mutations. What is a being who has an extra chromosome? Or who is not precisely adequate with respect to the genetic code? Is it still human? In this way the question is constantly moving, it's that one cannot define, finish, close human definition—no more than sexual definition. On all sides there are vanishing points, points of communication, points of more and of less. It is we, with our language, who operate the closure. I remember having heard the following sentence: a Down's syndrome patient is a vegetable, at best an animal. One can ask oneself what that means. That sentence was the expression of a doctor. It is we, with our language, who make the law. Who draw the borders and produce the exclusion. Who grant admittance. Who are the customs officers of communication: we admit or we reject. One of the roots of *Neutre* was a reflection on the destiny of the 'human' mystery—a mystery that is settled violently most of the time. Because ordinary human beings do not like mystery since you cannot put a bridle on it, and therefore, in general they exclude it, they repress it, they eliminate it—and it's *settled*. But if on the contrary one remains open and susceptible to all the phenomena of overflowing, beginning with natural phenomena, one discovers the immense landscape of the *trans-*, of the passage. Which does not mean that everything will be adrift: our thinking, our choices, etc. But it means that the factor of instability, the factor of uncertainty, or what Derrida calls the *undecidable*, is indissociable from human life. This ought to oblige us to have an attitude that is at once rigorous and tolerant and doubly so on each side: all the more rigorous than open, all the more demanding since it must lead to openness, leave passage; all the more mobile and rapid as the ground will always give way, always. A thought which leads to what is the element of writing: the necessity of only being the citizen of an extremely inappropriable, unmasterable country or ground.

> *It is not the movement of throwing off track [*dépistage*]—(it's a question of losing the reader).*
> It is the movement 'towards the far East'
> cf.: Ingeborg. Grosse Landschaft bei Wien
> *'Asiens Atem ist jenseits'*
> *The breath of Asia* | *is over there*
> | *beyond*

THERE IS NO *JOUISSANCE* WITHOUT DIFFERENCE

So at that time the accent was placed on the question of sexuality in so far as it was disputed. To say that I believe in sexual difference is a statement that, with the decades that have past, has taken on a sort of political value, a sort of authority that is all the more insistent since it is denied by a huge number of people. But to believe in sexual difference is to know that difference is the differential. It is precisely—and this is wonderful—that there can only be difference if there are at least two sources. And that difference is a movement. It always passes, always comes to pass, between the two. And when there is opposition, an awful thing but one that exists, there is only one: which is to say nothing. So to believe in sexual difference comes down to what we were saying just now in a sense. But this time, it is not the exterior edge that is in question. In the case of chromosomal anomalies we are at the edge, at the limit of human nature; when the question comes up: how far? Sexual difference is 'the middle'. It develops, lives, breathes between two people. What is intoxicating, what can be disturbing, difficult—is that it is not the third term, it is not a block between two blocks: it is exchange itself. And since it gives from the one to the other, it is ungraspable, even if one can try to follow it. It cannot be seen. What we *see* is only appearance, not difference. The visible does not make the difference.

We make the difference, between us. Between ourselves also. It is our reading. And like all readings, it varies, between us, between me, inside of me, to me(s), according to whether it is more or less lively, sleepy, irritated, according to the place, the circumstances, whether it is evoked or repressed. And at times we experience it as a suavity in the mouth, at times as a bite. It is innumerable, obviously never reducible to a sex or gender or a familial or social role. It is a wonderful myriad of differential qualities. It passes. It surpasses us. It is our incalculable interior richness. But if we cannot know it, define it, design it, can we enjoy it, can we feel it? Yes, in love's book of hours, in those extreme moments where separation is extinguished in the tightest embrace. It is there, it is then, in the infinitesimal and infinite space of proximity (the word approximation!!!), in the instant we approximate ourself in the embracing, it is there at the point of contact, that we feel it, that we touch it, we touch difference and it touches us, in what form? It is the ultimate, voluptuous and cruel point of temptation: if only I could pass to the other side, if only I could one time slide myself in you, and get to now that thing of yours—by which you belong to a world I cannot enter—refused to me from the beginning and for eternity, that *jouissance* of yours to which I am and I remain an enchanted and unknowing witness. But I cannot, because we were created to desire (to enter) and not to enter. And to be protected and to protect ourselves. And to safeguard the double secret of *jouissance*. Moreover, it is all well made: we cannot 'betray' ourselves, we cannot communicate ourselves mutually in translation. We cannot 'give' ourselves. If not the inexhaustible resource of a desire: I would like to kno-masculine *jouissance*; I will never know it; I would like to know the *jouir* of the other sex. What I know is the point of contact between two impossibilities: I will never know, you will never know. Both at the same time we know that we will never know. In that instant I touch at what remains your secret. I touch your secret, with my body. I touch your secret with my secret and that is not exchanged. But smiling, we share the bitter and sweet taste (regret and desire mixed) of that impossibility.

> Scenes of love = scenes of origin
> Love brings back to the origin. Return
>   Rising
> Love: its effect or its proof is to bring back to the origin,
> You love the loved starting from his or her origins, from the belly.
> Love reestablishes the totality of existence.
> It is only in love that we want to know the origin, the genealogy of
>   someone.

IN THE EXCHANGE: THE INEXCHANGEABLE

M.C-G.: So there is always the inexchangeable in the exchange. And that inexchangeable perpetuates the desire for exchange. Perpetuates the desire.

H.C.: In that instant where we hold together, in this point where we would give anything to exchange ourselves and the exchange does not happen, the inexchageable makes its strange and invisible presence felt. How we want to 'explain' ourselves: to say: to translate: to show: to paint: to add the one to the other, the one in the other, there, precisely, in that unparalleled experience, precisely that experience where desire and impossibility have never been so acute. So acute that a sort of paradoxical miracle is produced: right where the exchange is impossible, an exchange happens, right where we are unable to share, we share this non-sharing, this desire, this impossibility. Never before has what separates us united us with such tender ties. We stand separaunited, tasting separately-together the inexpressible taste of sexual difference, as it gives itself (without giving itself)—to enjoy in the *jouissances* of the one and the other sex. Sexual difference [*La d.s.*] is truly the goddess of desire. If she does not give 'herself,' she gives us the most of us possible. She gives us to me by you, from you. She gives us the *jouissance* of our own body, of our own sex and our own *jouissance plus* the other one. *Plus* the mixture.

> We hear without eyes, we scratch the night with our eyelashes.

At the same time, yes, this inexchangeable is again at the source of desire. The fact that, for example, there is something that I, as a woman, will never know: what masculine *jouissance* is, intimate, organic, carnal masculine *jouissance* properly speaking, and what accompanies it. Because it is accompanied by a sort of interior discourse, a thought—if I can put it that way. Not a philosophical thought, but a *self-thinking* that is undoubtedly serious, that is in relation with the image one has of oneself—a self-imagination. I am speaking here of a man, but I could turn it around to the side of a woman. The way a man lives his body: I imagine it for that other powerful powerless animal self. And also how he has a history with his body; how what is at once himself and his house, his interior and his exterior, is subject to thousands of events—either simply on the order of its functions, or on the order of dysfunctions, sicknesses, accidents. This forms an immense weaving, it is an interior destiny that runs through a whole life and out of which behaviours appear, either in the present, or in the future, in terms of future projects, in relation to the story one tells oneself: concerning one's own vitality, one's own mortality. For me this is totally fascinating and remains mysterious. I see, I guess, but I do not know. There are so many little secrets and big secrets that remain forever inaccessible to me. And that I would love to know, because of a sublime superior necessity: as a painter of intimacies, if I could know, I would be extraordinarily happy. But there is also the curiosity of love: if I could be in a man's body, I would be able to love *better* because I would also be better able to locate the needs, the worries, the threats and the joys. If I loved a man. And in the same way there is what is inaccessible in every woman, to every man.

> *The always singular body of the other: every time a history, a memory, sensations, scars, ways of perceiving—in sum of reading the book of the world with one's body.*

I ought to sing of curiosity, this first state of desire: this drive to know what you feel on your side, when you *jouis*, this craving to know how what is good for you is good, without which there is neither desire, nor love, nor *jouissance*. Because the secret of *jouissance* is that even while being not-exactly communicable, it is nourished by the unknowable-*jouissance*-of-the-other. That is the mystery: this *jouissance* which escapes me (mine, yours, escaping me differently, mine escapes my attempt to transmit, but not my flesh), I want to give it to you, I want to give it to me, it is indeed the only one, it is indeed the only pleasure that is structurally indissociable from this dream of sharing. Double and divided joy. (We do not feel the same painful need to share other experiences of the senses it seems to me, at least not in the same mode of decisive necessity. This is what gives the act of love its venerable character as it is absolutely without equivalent.)

This urgency, this need to decipher what cannot be said, what is expressed otherwise than in verbal speech which nonetheless arouses the desire for words, this is our human drama. We are always in fine messes. . . .

INDEX

Linné, Carl von, 98n9
lips, threshold of the, 235
Lispector, Clarice, 253, 256
literature, 35, 36, 47, 153, 155, 162, 164, 196, 227, 260; French, 13, 153; male, 196
Little Marguerites, the, 120
logic, 36, 41
logos, 37, 40, 178
love, ix, 23, 24, 27–29, 32–34, 108, 118n7, 195, 236, 238, 240, 249, 261, 275, 278, 283, 295, 296; between mother and daughter, 238; between the sexes, 234; genuine, 33; idolatrous, 34; man's, 30, 33; maternal, 23, 26, 184; of the mother, 250; mystique of, 106; other, 274; and telephones, 291, 292; voice of, 263
Lysistra, 11

madness, 242, 244, 246, 248, 249; collective, 241; masochistic, 29; women's, 241, 242, 244
magazines, women's, 26, 44
The Main Enemy, 60
*Maldoror,*163
Mallarmé, Stephane, 158, 163, 168
Malraux, André, 33
man, 7, 8, 10, 150, 202, 231; category of, 120–22, 131, 132, 140, 141; ideal, 156; and society, 222; and the woman in love, 29, 30; work of, 229
The Mandarins, 2
Manifeste des 343, ix, 2
Man's Fate, 33
Mansfield, Katherine, 47
Mao Zedong, 146
mark(ing), 89, 129; of the body, 86–88, 90; class, 89; by clothing, 88; conventional, 93, 99n16; morphological, 88, 89; natural, 90, 93, 99n16; schema of, 89; somatic, 99n12

marriage, ix, 2, 4, 16, 23–25, 46, 94, 97, 99, 121, 126, 233, 237
Marx, Karl, 15, 48, 133, 146–48, 213, 214, 216, 218, 219, 226n3; and Engels, 125, 144, 145, 149
Marxism, 133
masculine, 8, 62, 65, 124, 234; arrogance, 17; attitude, 15, 34n3; experienced as time, 228; privilege, 20n3
masculine, the, 72, 286, 289
masculinity, ix, 72, 277, 280–82
masochism, 28, 29
master and slave, 2, 11, 12, 123, 147, 148, 234, 284
materialism, 134; historical, 19
maternal, the, 154, 173; authority, 154, 155; function, 156; repressed, 155; sado-masochism, 24
maternity, 20–22, 25, 26, 85, 177, 195, 196; discourse of, 155, 156; fatherless, 195
Mathieu, Nicole-Claude, 67, 69, 117, 143n8
matriarchy, 129; myth of, 121
Mauriac, Claude, 15
Mauss, Marcel, 172
May 1968, viii, 120, 157, 186, 188, 253
Mead, Margaret, 61, 63–65, 71–73
meaning, 3, 51, 140, 142, 148, 158, 159, 162, 164, 165, 181, 188, 189; communal, 179; entrance into, 161; and poetic language, 158, 160; semiotic, 159
Medea, 11
Medusa, 255, 266, 267
melancholia, and pregnancy, 22
melancholy, 178
Memoirs of a Dutiful Daughter, 54
memory, 186, 235, 288; archaic, 187; collective, 182; cultural and religious, 182; instinctual, 178; prelinguistic, 178
menopause, 100
Merleau-Ponty, Maurice, 2
metaphor, 36, 161

Védrine, Hélène, 51
Venus and Adonis, 35, 57n8
Virgil, 49
virgin(ity), 43, 45, 222, 223
Virgin Mary, 103, 155, 181n1
voice, female, 38
Voltaire, 150

wage(s), 96; equality of, 104; hierarchy
    of, 112, 118n8; level, 93, 97; women's,
    40
War and Peace, 26
waste, corporeal, 171–73
The Waves, 47
What Is To Be Done?, 43
wife, 16, 23, 26, 27, 43, 106; the philoso-
    pher's, 208; as property, 85, 100
wife-mother, 42
Wittig, Monique, ix, 2, 59, 70, 119–22
woman, 6, 7, 10–13, 17–19, 20n10, 26,
    27, 46, 54, 106, 156, 184, 197, 202,
    203, 206, 231, 258, 262, 270, 271, 277;
    becoming, 229; category of, 78,
    120–22, 131, 132, 140, 141; drama of,
    19; as extinguished subject, 42; ideal,
    156; inferiority of, 25; in love, 27,
    29–34; and maternity/childbearing, 20,
    23, 24; modern Western, 27; Mon-
    tesquieu on, 24; myth of, 16, 121, 127,
    129, 131, 132, 134; New, 260; phallic,

52; pregnant, 21; rights of, 13, 14, 113;
    universal, 186; unsatisfied, 29; virginal,
    222
womb, 6, 247
women, ix, 3, 6, 7, 10, 12–15, 38, 43, 44,
    91, 107; American, 7; battered, 127;
    bodies of, 84; as defined social group,
    100; differences between, 53; eco-
    nomic subordination of, 60; exchange
    of, 211, 221; fate of, 125; Marxist, 134;
    oppression of, 40 (*see also* oppression,
    women's); natural group, 128; nature
    of, 90; New, 273; and philosophy, 36;
    position of, 50, 65; proletarian, 11;
    scholars, 132; Western European, 188;
    work of, 126
wonder, 231, 232
Woolf, Virginia, 47, 132
Word, the, 279
work, 94, 106, 125, 126, 127, 223; ab-
    stract, 217; concrete, 217; of death,
    265; domestic, 42, 43, 91, 93, 97,
    106, 114, 127; man's, 231; procre-
    ative, 115; productive, 212; scientific,
    74
World War II, 2, 182
writing, 35, 168, 265; history of, 261;
    male, 260; women's, 61, 196, 197, 257,
    262, 264, 265, 287. See also *ecriture
    féminine*

ABOUT THE EDITOR

Kelly Oliver is Associate Professor of Philosophy and Women's Studies at SUNY Stony Brook. She is the author of *Witnessing: Beyond Recognition* (University of Minnesota 2000); *Subjectivity without Subjects: From Abject Fathers to Desiring Mothers* (Rowman & Littlefield 1998); *Family Values: Subjects between Nature and Culture* (Routledge 1997); *Womanizing Nietzsche: Philosophy's Relation to "the Feminine"* (Routledge 1995); and *Reading Kristeva: Unraveling the Double-Bind* (University of Indiana 1993). She has edited several books, including *Ethics, Politics and Difference in Kristeva's Writings* (Routledge 1993); *Feminist Interpretations of Neitzsche* (with Marilyn Pearsall, Pennsylvania State University Press 1998); and *The Portable Kristeva* (Columbia 1998).

Notes on mothers

From Beauvoir:

Poor teen mom: the ultimate antifeminist? Gives herself up to her body,
to being "ensnared by nature"? (21)
Become "life's passive instrument"?
→ Why does she assume that pregnancy
is passivity? Why automatically equate
the two?